Yeats Studies Series

GENERAL EDITORS

Robert O'Driscoll and Lorna Reynolds

This series is devoted to the critical assessment and publication of unpublished works of W. B. Yeats and the Yeats family: unpublished poems, plays, and prose works; drafts of poems, plays, prose works, diaries, memoirs, letters, and other manuscript materials that deepen our understanding of the creative process and the finished work.

Yeats and The Theatre, edited by Robert O'Driscoll and Lorna Reynolds

Yeats and The Occult, edited by George Mills Harper

In preparation

The Speckled Bird by William Butler Yeats,
edited by William H. O'Donnell

Unpublished Memoir of John Butler Yeats,
edited by William M. Murphy

Yeats and The Irish Tradition,
edited by Robert O'Driscoll and Lorna Reynolds

Yeats and The Occult

Engraving from Knorr von Rosenroth's *Kabbala Denudata*, 1677. As far as can be read, the difficult Latin inscriptions on parts of the picture are: Metaphysicagentibus (sky), Mare Concupiscentia (sea), lucet (candle), Intrum male (cave mouth), Iterat (left foot), Domat (right foot), and the symbols near the cave mouth read ♍♈♄♉♌♃.

Yeats Studies Series
GENERAL EDITORS
Robert O'Driscoll and Lorna Reynolds

Yeats and The Occult

EDITED BY

George Mills Harper

MACMILLAN OF CANADA
MACLEAN-HUNTER PRESS

ISBN 0-7705-1308-5

This book has been published with the help of a grant from the Humanities Research Council of Canada, using funds provided by the Canada Council.

Printed in Canada for
The Macmillan Company of Canada Limited

Contents

List of Illustrations

ix

Note to the Reader

The following abbreviations have been used throughout the volume:

CP   *The Collected Poems of W. B. Yeats* (London: Macmillan, 1967).

CPL *The Collected Plays of W. B. Yeats* (London: Macmillan, 1972).

VP   *The Variorum Edition of the Poems of W. B. Yeats*, edited by Peter Allt and R. K. Alspach (London: Macmillan, 1957).

VPL *The Variorum Edition of the Plays of W. B. Yeats*, edited by R. K. Alspach and Catherine C. Alspach (London: Macmillan, 1965).

M   *Mythologies* (London: Macmillan, 1959).

F.   *Explorations* (London: Macmillan, 1962).

E&I *Essays and Introductions* (London: Macmillan, 1961).

A   *Autobiographies* (London: Macmillan, 1955).

V   *A Vision* (1937) (London: Macmillan, 1962).

Bracketed page references are to these editions.

Acknowledgements

As a group, we are indebted to many other scholars and their work, and we have sought to recognize our debt at appropriate places in our individual essays. As editor of the volume, I am also indebted, in particular, to Mr. Michael Horniman of A. P. Watt and Son and Senator Michael B. Yeats, without whose co-operation and encouragement this collection would have been impossible.

G.M.H.

The General Editors of the series acknowledge the assistance of the following distinguished advisors:
Russell K. Alspach
Suheil Bushrui
David R. Clark
Eric Domville
Denis Donoghue
Richard Ellmann
Ian Fletcher
René Fréchet
George M. Harper
A. Norman Jeffares
John Kelly
Brendan Kennelly
F. S. L. Lyons
Norman H. MacKenzie

Desmond Maxwell
Georgio Melchiori
William M. Murphy
William H. O'Donnell
Shotaro Oshima
Kathleen Raine
Balachandra Rajan
Ann Saddlemyer
Michael Sidnell
Francis Warner

The General Editors also acknowledge the assistance of St. Michael's College, University of Toronto, and University College, Galway.

Introduction

This volume of the *Yeats Studies Series* is devoted to the study of Yeats and the occult. The time has passed when it was necessary, in order to preserve intellectual respectability, to express either astonishment or dismay at the nature of Yeats's intellectual pursuits. The "occult" means literally the covered, the hidden, the veiled; and during his life Yeats was concerned with the hidden significance underlying the appearances of the universe and of human life. He was, as he said himself, a religious man, and deprived of a comfortable belief in orthodox Christianity by the lively scepticism of his father, he sought in many quarters and opened up many veins in his quest for the jewel of enlightenment which would make intelligible "the burthen of the mystery . . . Of all this unintelligible world".

In this volume, which makes use of primary materials as well as the insights of modern scholars but still only scratches the surface of the subject, we can trace something of Yeats's spiritual Odyssey. He began by attaching himself to the Theosophical Society and then to the rituals and investigations of the Hermetic Order of the Golden Dawn, founded by MacGregor Mathers, W. R. Woodman, and William Wynn Westcott in 1888. Yeats was initiated into the Golden Dawn in March 1890, and remained a member of the Order, and its successor, the Stella Matutina, for thirty-two years, from the age of twenty-four to fifty-six. He hoped, by means of the techniques transmitted in such bodies, to become an Adept, a Mage, capable of supernatural experiences and of creating a channel of supernatural power. In this phase Yeats came to see the world as a symbol, and he learned from Mathers the practical use of symbols to induce visions. He uses age-old metaphors to describe his activities: he must "tread this path, open this gate, seek this light". MacGregor Mathers, it is clear, made an indelible impression on Yeats, and he appears as Maclagan in *The Speckled Bird* and as the "fiction", or "mask", or "persona" of Michael Robartes, with far-reaching implications for Yeats's poetry and prose.

Yeats had been familiar, of course, with the ghost and fairy lore of the Irish countryside from his boyhood days in Sligo, and later, with Lady Gregory, he turned his attention more seriously to this tradition, finding in Irish folk stories of the fairies, the race of "good people", apparitions, and mysterious manifestations of all kinds, further evidence of the existence of an invisible world, of the continuance of life after death, and of the immortality of the soul. What has not yet been pointed out is the important part which certain doctrines of the Catholic Church played in this general belief of the Irish people in ghosts and visions. In the Ireland of Yeats's time, the doctrines of the existence of Purgatory and of the "communion of souls" were, of course, firmly held. The poor souls in Purgatory might appear, it was believed among the people, to ask the help of the living; and the "communion of souls" meant that the living and the dead, as long as they were in a state of grace, might help one another by prayer. The power of prayer was seen as able to influence the bestowal of God's grace; Heaven might be taken by assault from earth. The world of the country people, therefore, was open to the influx of the supernatural from two sides: that of their Christian religion, and that of the ancient fairy faith which they shared with other branches of the Celtic race. What Chesterton called the "small arrogant oligarchy" of the living fell into perspective against this continual pressure of the swarming dead, out of sight, but not out of mind.

Yeats, however, was never content with belief in another world: he had always wanted access to it. After the death of Synge, he turned once again to techniques through which this access might be gained, this time to the techniques of spiritualism, to the use of mediums, and of automatic writing. We can see from the hitherto unpublished essay, "Preliminary Investigation of the Script of ER", how seriously, though at the same time how cautiously, he approached the phenomena of spiritualism, and how he sought help in the world beyond for the problems of this life. His experience with automatic writing culminated after his marriage in 1917, and resulted in the writing, with his wife as medium, of *A Vision*: a triumphant vindication of his belief in the spirit world.

Yeats had always been interested in writers whose minds were attuned to the Neo-platonic tradition. In his early twenties he also studied Swedenborg and Boehme, and found in them, as well as in other occult sources, a key to the work of William Blake. From these writers he was led, naturally enough, to Plato and his followers, especially Plotinus, who had incorporated in their philosophical expositions an age-old view of the universe. In the Platonic tradition, as Jung points out, individual human life is seen as the ephemeral flower blooming from the perennial rhizome, in death returning to the great ocean of being, withering and descending into the rhizome, to bloom again in another spring, in another incarnation. The universe is not dead matter, but a living creature. Mankind is not complete, the initiator of action, but merely the foam upon the deep, merely the momentary blossom of some spiritual impulse. Through him the invisible moods of the universe work their will; the great unchanging myths are constantly being enacted and re-enacted. As Henry Vaughan puts it, the soul "... though here born yet is acquainted/Elsewhere". Or as Yeats wrote:

> From our birthday, until we die,
> Is but the winking of an eye.

It is no small part of the measure of Yeats's genius that he persisted, against the intellectual current of his day, in exploration and experiment within a great tradition that, for three centuries, had had only a subterranean life.

Parke Cottage LORNA REYNOLDS
Eyrecourt
County Galway
Ireland

St. Michael's College ROBERT O'DRISCOLL
University of Toronto
Toronto

Errata
page 36 line 25: for ζωου read ζῶον
page 49 line 25: for σφαιος read σφαῖρος
page 49 line 26: for φιδια read φιλία
page 49 line 27: for ευδαιμουεστατος Θεσς
read εὐδαιμονέστατος Θεός

In Memory of
T. R. Henn

Yeats and The Occult

Yeats's Occult Papers

George Mills Harper

In August 1969, at the invitation of Senator Michael B. Yeats, Kathleen Raine and I met in Dublin to examine the extensive mass of largely unexplored and unpublished papers of W. B. Yeats classified by Senator Yeats as "occult" and separated from other papers in his library. After independent examinations and numerous consultations, Miss Raine and I concluded that if properly digested and explained these papers would make clear much that students and critics of Yeats have either distorted or completely misunderstood, and we agreed that we would consider a collaborative effort to organize the material and write a critical book on Yeats's religion including brief historical sketches of the Golden Dawn and related societies which Yeats belonged to. With the assistance of Senator Yeats I reproduced some of the materials, and Miss Raine prepared a partially descriptive catalogue which enabled us to evaluate at leisure the kind and extent of occult papers. Miss Raine had already examined the extensive materials in the Aleister Crowley collection belonging to Gerald Yorke[1] and had discovered that Ellic Howe was preparing a history of the Golden Dawn.[2] Upon her return to London Miss Raine discussed our

1. Most of these papers are now deposited in the Library of the Warburg Institute. Mr. Yorke, who was one of Crowley's trustees, very graciously permitted me to examine the papers and books remaining in his personal library.

2. *The Magicians of the Golden Dawn: A Documentary History of a Magical Order 1887-1923* (London: Routledge and Kegan Paul, 1972).

project with Mr. Howe, who outlined his own work; and we decided that the brief history we had planned would be unnecessary. Nevertheless, Miss Raine concluded that our proposed project was still enormous, and she finally decided not to participate. Despite her decision I am greatly indebted to her for reading and criticizing what I have written to date,[3] for introductions to numerous scholars working on related projects, and for continued encouragement. Even the brief survey of materials in this essay would have been far more difficult without her advice and assistance.

Since both the extent and significance of Yeats's commitment to occult studies, Rosicrucianism in particular, have generally been underestimated, denigrated, or deliberately undervalued, it seems useful to describe for this volume of *Yeats Studies Series* the papers concerned with occult studies and experiments which Yeats preserved. Conscious of his role as prophet and seer, he was careful not to destroy anything—of friends and associates as well as his own— which might illuminate his life and art. This brief survey will, I hope, convince the sceptical of the value Yeats placed upon preserving the record.[4] Again and again, through notes, comments, recorded dates, etc., he emphasized the surety of his convictions and his hopes for the future. One significant act will illustrate this. In the back of a large notebook devoted to facts about and studies in the literature and lore of the Golden Dawn, Yeats pasted the copy of his invitation to initiation in the Order of the Golden Dawn on March 7, 1890.[5] Almost thirty years later, in recording the date for posterity, he suggests how important the date was to him: "my admission, W B Yeats, Dec. 28, 1919".

One of several notebooks kept by Yeats to describe exercises and record details of his studies in the Golden Dawn, this manuscript has a special interest for most students of Yeats because it was a present from Maud Gonne. It opens with an account of a series of spiritual experiences with Maud in 1908, and closes with questions (dated March 23, 1917) to himself about Maud and Iseult Gonne. An early note suggests the link between Maud and the Golden Dawn in Yeats's mind: "think meditation should be representative

3. I am especially indebted to her for assistance with my book on *Yeats's Golden Dawn* (London: Macmillan, 1974).
4. See my review article " 'Passion and Precision': Some Observations on Editing Yeats," *The Southern Review*, xi, No. 2 (1975): 452-63.
5. For details see *Yeats's Golden Dawn*, p. 159.

of initiation in the coffin of Father Rosy Cross. Must work out relation between this and mystic marriage."[6] This reminder is written beside a letter from Maud pasted in the notebook at the appropriate place.

Of the several other notebooks devoted partially or wholly to Rosicrucian studies, one is far more important than the remainder. It is marked PRIVATE and signed "DEDI, June 28, 1893". Because it contains restricted information about the Order, there is a printed form signed by Yeats on the back of the front cover with instructions that "in case of my death or incapacity" it should be returned, "unread and unopened, to Sapere Aude", which is the Order motto of William Wynn Westcott.[7] Containing approximately 280 pages of text and diagrams, this book consists chiefly of Yeats's study notes for various progress examinations to be passed in the attainment of the Degree of 5-6[8] in the Second Order.

Although no other notebook in Yeats's hand is devoted wholly to primary materials about the Golden Dawn, several exercise books are concerned with such related matters as the Enochian Tablet, the Celtic Mysteries, horoscopes, Talismanic experiments, and Tarot exercises.

There are three Tarot packs in the library: one belonged to Yeats and is marked with card symbols and attributions in his hand; another belonged to George Pollexfen and has some signs added in his hand; a third, cleaner and newer, probably belonged to Mrs. Yeats. There are also two sets of Tattwa cards, one signed inside the flap: "W. B. Yeats, 18 Woburn Buildings". Other materials for work in the Golden Dawn include a dagger, a wand, a pentacle, and a broken lotus, all presumably made and constructed by Yeats according to instructions. His Order motto, Demon Est Deus Inversus, is written on the pentacle. Also preserved are a cardboard rose cross, a black silk sash of the 4-7 Degree, a white silk sash of the 5-6 Degree, several cardboard seals or sigils, and numerous

6. For further details about this notebook and the spiritual marriage, see *Yeats's Golden Dawn*, p. 168.
7. *Yeats's Golden Dawn*, Appendix x (pp. 314-16), identifies more than 100 of Yeats's friends and associates in the Outer and Inner Orders.
8. Howe, p. 16, explains the Degree structure of the Golden Dawn. See also Virginia Moore, *The Unicorn* (New York: Macmillan, 1954), p. 134, and *Yeats's Golden Dawn*, p. 160. Yeats achieved the Degree of 6-5 on October 16, 1914. See *Yeats's Golden Dawn*, pp. 306-7, for the record of the ceremony.

cardboard stars (both pentagram and hexagram are important in the rituals).

Of the other materials directly concerned with the Golden Dawn, the most important are the notebooks containing rituals and instructional matter: (1) flying rolls on such subjects as "Alchemy" by N.O.M., "Know Thyself" by V.N.R., "Suggestions on Will Power" by S.S.D.D., with additional notes by D.D.C.F.,[9] and many others (there were at least 36 different flying rolls in the library of the Second Order); (2) numerous rituals for advancement from one Degree to another in both Outer and Inner Orders; (3) miscellaneous "manuscripts" on such subjects as "History for Neophytes", "General Orders", "Microcosm", and "Hodos Cameolonis"; (4) clairvoyant investigations and visions. Yeats had almost a complete study library for both Orders, including numerous duplicates of rituals and flying rolls. Many of the manuals came from the library of George Pollexfen,[10] who had copied them out with elaborate care, often in several colours. Yeats must have brought these away with him after Pollexfen's funeral in September 1910. A typed set of the rituals in uniform blue folders belongs to a later date, probably after 1916. Among the most exciting of the duplicates is "the Jewish Schemahamphorasch with its seventy-two Names of God in Hebrew characters" which Yeats was to recall having read and copied out with Moina Bergson (later Mrs. Mathers).[11]

Another important body of materials records the details of two quarrels among members of the Second Order (Rosae Rubeae et Aureae Crucis): (1) the first quarrel, resulting in the expulsion of MacGregor Mathers from the Order in April 1900, is outlined

9. That is, Non Omnis Moriar (William Wynn Westcott), Vestigia Nulla Retrorsum (Mrs. MacGregor Mathers), Sapientia Sapienti Dono Data (Mrs. Florence Farr Emery), and Deo Duce Comite Ferro (MacGregor Mathers).

10. According to a letter from Lily Yeats to John Butler Yeats dated September 20, 1910, Pollexfen kept the "books on astrology, symbolism and such" in an upstairs room. They were "all in perfect order" when he died. See William M. Murphy, *The Yeats Family and the Pollexfens* (Dublin: Dolmen Press, 1971), pp. 43-4. The best account of the Yeats-Pollexfen interrelations may be found in this excellent monograph.

11. *A Vision* (London, 1925), p. ix. In an earlier draft of the Dedication "To Vestigia" (i.e., Moina Mathers), Yeats wrote: "... we copied out everything we could borrow, or find in some library that bore upon our subject including the Jewish Schemahamphorasch...."

in detail on a printed "List of Documents" prepared by Yeats and Florence Farr Emery[12]; (2) the second quarrel, resulting finally in a division of the Second Order, is more important to students of Yeats because he wrote and preserved the essays and open letters to the Order which support his side of the argument. He also preserved the manuscript of Annie Horniman's summary of "The Scribe's Account of the Executive Difficulty" which summarizes the issues of the debate and identifies (by Order mottoes) the opposing factions. This quarrel culminated in Yeats's splendid defense of ritual magic, "Is the Order of R.R. & A.C. to remain a Magical Order?" This privately printed monograph (written in March 1901) and the "Postcript" (written on May 4, 1901) are among the rarest of Yeats items.[13]

In addition to the rituals and study materials necessary to progress through the Degrees of the Order, Yeats preserved a considerable body of related but peripheral matter: for example, a typescript headed "Impression of 6-5 Ceremony, describing astral appearance of Postulant, Frater D.E.D.I. Oct. 16, 1914[14]; "Formula for Personal Spiritual Development"; "Remembrances of F.E.R." (a series of astral explorations of past lives by Miss Horniman); copies of Bye-laws [sic] of the Second Order (1900, revised 1902); a printed pamphlet "Concerning the Revisal of the Constitution and Rules of the Order R.R. et A.C."; a folding file containing Mrs. Yeats's notes and lectures with such headings as "Elementary Notes on Astrology", "Meditation Subjects", "On Recruiting for the Order", "The Twelve Tribes", etc.; extracts from Thomas Taylor's Chaldean Oracles; a series of "Clairvoyant Investigations and Visions" by several members of the Second Order; "Visions on the Paths" (by Per Mare Ad Astra, Mary Briggs), a typed account (dated October 1, 1910) of a spiritual visitation of F.L. (Festina Lente, George Pollexfen), five days after his death, to assembled members of the Second Order; a huge diagram (perhaps three feet

12. For details see my article " 'Meditations upon Unknown Thought': Yeats's Break with MacGregor Mathers," Yeats Studies, 1 (1971): 175-202; also Yeats's Golden Dawn, pp. 14-26 and 201-20.
13. For a detailed account of this quarrel including the relevant documents, see Yeats's Golden Dawn, passim.
14. See ibid., pp. 306-7, for a reproduction of this "impression" of Yeats's advancement to what is perhaps the highest Degree he achieved in the Order. However, his papers include a copy of the ritual for the Degree of 7-4 ,which he may have attained.

square) of the Sephirotic Tree of Life; an equally large and carefully drawn coloured diagram of the Phases of the Moon on oiled silk material; and much more.

Most important of the remaining primary materials is the enormous and bewildering mass concerned with the gestation, development, and composition of both versions of *A Vision*, which is a direct outgrowth of Yeats's experiences in the Golden Dawn. Although the ultimate study of *A Vision* must begin with the Dublin Hermetic Society, which Yeats helped to organize in 1885, he apparently began serious and careful planning of *A Vision* only after his marriage on October 20, 1917. Four days later, according to Yeats, his wife attempted automatic writing, and he proposed "to spend what remained of life explaining and piecing together those scattered sentences".[15] If indeed he is right about the date, as he usually was, the record of the first few days of the writing is lost, misplaced, or destroyed. The first recorded writing preserved in the papers is dated November 5, 1917. Since this writing is in answer to written questions he posed to Mrs. Yeats, it may be that he preserved the record only after it responded to his direction, that is, after it fitted his plans for *A Vision*. At any rate, he apparently preserved all the record, including some stray scraps of paper, from this date until March 29, 1920, when Mrs. Yeats wrote: "I prefer to use other methods." Her "New Method" is designated "sleeps". Although Yeats speaks of "some fifty copy-books of automatic script, and of a much smaller number of books recording what had come in sleep",[16] according to my count there are only thirty-six notebooks or envelopes containing lists of questions by him and responses from Mrs. Yeats. It may be, however, that Yeats's count was different because several of the envelopes contain two or more sections or parts of the script fastened together by paper clips. Dates, hours, places, and names of the communicators are carefully recorded for the script and the sleeps. As a result of his own study of these automatic experiences, while they were still in progress, I think, Yeats began organizing his material in a large notebook which contains many diagrams, sketches of gyres, Phases of the Moon, etc. The next and much fuller stage of development is represented by a card-file index of some 750 cards arranged alphabetically.[17] Frequently the cards contain digests of, or reflections

15. *A Vision* (London: Macmillan, 1937), p. 8.   16. *Ibid.*, pp. 17-18.
17. *Ibid.*, p. 18. "I had already a small concordance in a large manuscript book, but now made a much larger, arranged like a card index."

upon, the automatic script and sleeps. These are working notes, and the handwriting is very difficult.

The remainder of the matter directly concerned with *A Vision* consists largely of many hundred pages for both versions (1925 and 1937) of generally disorganized materials (manuscript and typescript) in brown folders which usually have notes by Yeats on the flaps and attached notes by Curtis Bradford, who examined but did not transcribe these materials. Of most interest are the rejected sections and the elaborately revised manuscripts, much of which seems to defy complete and exact transcription. There is considerable duplication in the typescripts.

Several essays among the occult papers record experiments and experiences which Yeats thought should be preserved. Not the best essay but perhaps the most important is entitled "Preliminary Examination of the Script of E R". Since it exists in a clean manuscript (signed W B Yeats and dated October 8, 1913) and a typescript of thirty-three pages (dated June 7, 1914) with numerous revisions and notes in Yeats's hand, he obviously considered both the subject matter and his observations important. The experiences examined in this essay, including Yeats's reflections and explanations, were clearly influential in his directing and evaluating Mrs. Yeats's automatic script four years later.[18] Yeats also preserved records of many experiments upon which the essay is based as well as letters from E R (Elizabeth Radcliffe) and her sister Margaret.[19] Unfortunately, the letters are not very exciting.

Related to the essay on the "Script of E R" is an extensive typescript by the Rev. W. Stainton Moses, a member of the Societas Rosicruciana in Anglia and first editor of the spiritualist periodical *Light*.[20] How his long, rambling, often tedious account of medi-

18. There is some evidence that Miss Hyde-Lees had observed directly the automatic writing of Miss Radcliffe. Among the Yeats papers is an undated sheet of paper signed "G. Hyde-Lees" which contains notes "Concerning Anna Luise Karschin [*sic*]," Anna Louise Karsch, an occult friend of Goethe who had appeared several times during the experiments. Apparently, Yeats had asked Miss Hyde-Lees to search for the information.
19. See Harper and Kelly, "Preliminary Examination of the Script of E R," herein, for the text of the essay and details about Yeats's experiments. We are indebted to Mrs. Margaret Radcliffe van Straubenzee, the younger of the sisters, for information about Yeats's acquaintance with them.
20. A close friend of Anna Kingsford, Edward Maitland, Madame Blavatsky, and others, Moses was prominent in occult circles. He joined the Societas Rosicruciana in Anglia on December 17, 1877, the same day as Robert Palmer Thomas, who later became a close associate of Yeats in

ums, controls, and automatic experiences came to be in Yeats's possession I cannot say. Since Moses was a member of the Theosophical Society, he probably met Yeats there and asked him to read, perhaps with a view to publication, the astonishing account of his experiences. Its primary value to us is the light it sheds on Yeats's interests and experiments at the beginning of his occult life.

A more interesting manuscript is Henri Bergson's "Presidential Address to the S.P.R." Since he was President in 1913, it was probably translated and copied in that year by some friend of Yeats in the SPR. As a reasoned defense of "psychic research", it surely was convincing to Yeats.

Two other essays have a greater attraction for students of Yeats: a typescript of thirteen pages titled "Clairvoyant Search for Will" and an untitled manuscript about a bleeding oleograph at Mirebeau, France. The "Clairvoyant Search" is concerned with an account of a series of seances in which Yeats attempted to communicate with the spirit of Hugh Lane about a legal codicil to his will leaving a collection of pictures to the city of Dublin. Yeats also preserved in typescript the record of one of these seances (dated December 27, 1916) and a radio broadcast about the unwitnessed codicil and the likelihood of the pictures' being returned to Ireland.

The essay on the bleeding oleograph is in the handwriting of Maud Gonne, who wrote at Yeats's dictation. It begins with the arrival at Mirebeau of Yeats, Maud, and Everard Feilding, who had been sent "to investigate a miracle", and ends with their leaving impressed but uncertain. Two months later Feilding informed Yeats that it was not human blood.[21] Always willing, even eager, to experiment, Yeats was never credulous.

Senator Yeats's library also contains numerous odd notebooks: several in the hand of Yeats with notes on the Enochian Tablet, Tarot cards, trial horoscopes, etc.; one in the hand of Georgie Hyde-Lees with notes from her reading in the Book of Enoch, Pico

---

the Golden Dawn. For further information, see Howe, p. 32; Edward Maitland, *Anna Kingsford: Her Life, Letters, Diary, and Work*, 3rd ed. (London, 1913), II: 16-19; Arthur Edward Waite, *Shadows of Life and Thought* (London, 1938), p. 60.

21. See Harper, "A Subject of Investigation," herein, for the text of the essay and details about the analysis of the blood made by the Lister Institute.

della Mirandola, the Zohar, etc.; a half-dozen or more devoted wholly or in part to horoscopes (chiefly by George Pollexfen)— of the family, of friends, of famous literary and political figures. Related to these horoscopic materials is a considerable body of correspondence from such well-known professional astrologers as Claude Dumas, Kymry, J. R. Wallace, and Ely Starr.

A somewhat larger body of correspondence is concerned with psychic experiments, seances, business matters and internal squabbles of the Golden Dawn. Yeats was clearly the centre of balance in these affairs: his opinion was sought by an unusual variety of people, from crackpots and aspiring but uninspired writers to such well-known friends and occultists as Annie Horniman, Florence Farr Emery, Moina and MacGregor Mathers, William Force Stead, and William Thomas Horton—to mention only the best known.[22]

Finally, there is a considerable body of material recording seances and visionary experiences. Yeats wrote or dictated many of the accounts of seances soon after the events, and he was usually careful to record times, places, and names of people present, including the presiding medium. Also preserved are numerous accounts of visionary explorations. These are records of experiences by various members of the Second Order of the Golden Dawn. In one series, headed Celtic Visions, Yeats was the conductor; and he was apparently a member of the groups at most of the recorded experiments with one notable exception, an extended series of visionary flights by Annie Horniman and Frederick Leigh Gardner. The rather sizeable body of materials which belonged to and are often in the handwriting of Miss Horniman suggests an intimate friendship with Yeats over an extended period of time. Since she was frequently at odds with fellow members of the Second Order, Yeats was her advocate and remained her defender until she withdrew her support of the Abbey Theatre in 1910. She was already out of the Golden Dawn, having been forced to resign (for the second time) in February 1903.[23]

In this brief account I have not intended to catalogue but rather to suggest the extent of the occult materials Yeats chose to preserve, and I have no doubt omitted reference to numerous miscel-

22. Richard J. Finneran, William M. Murphy, and I are editing a selection of letters to Yeats to be published by Macmillan (London).

23. See Yeats's Golden Dawn, passim, for details of her numerous quarrels and forced resignations, first in December 1896, again in February 1903.

laneous items of interest to many students and scholars. An itemized catalogue might reach several hundred pages, depending on the amount of descriptive detail in the accounting of letters, seances, *A Vision*, Golden Dawn manuals, etc. That great task remains to be done. My primary object is to convey some idea of the massive amount of materials and to make clear to the sceptics that the religious experiments and experiences preserved in these materials were not lightly regarded by Yeats. Recording them alone must have taken an immense amount of his time. Although many students and scholars will deplore the time he spent, wishing that it might have been devoted to poetry or drama or criticism, it ought to be recognized that Yeats's life and creative art would have been greatly different, and most certainly poorer, without the occult religious experiences partially recorded and described in these papers. Yeats himself suggested that he might not have been a poet at all if he had not made magic his "constant study". "The mystical life," he wrote to John O'Leary, "is the centre of all that I do and all that I think and all that I write." Considering himself "a voice of what I believe to be a greater renaissance", Yeats was leading "the revolt of the soul against the intellect".[24] This observation was made in 1892; forty-five years later he published a second and radically modified version of *A Vision* which, like the 1925 version, was written for and addressed to his "old fellow students" and surely represents the essence of his "mystical philosophy". Although Yeats realized that he was not a traditional visionary, he wished that he were: in 1891, he referred to himself as a "Churchless mystic", and he assured Ethel Mannin only a month before his death that he had "seen the raising of Lazarus and the loaves and fishes".[25] The man who wrote that had not been playing esoteric games, peripheral to his art, throughout a long and fruitful career. Surely, there can no longer be any doubt that Yeats was equally at home in "two living countries, the one visible and the one invisible".[26]

24. Allan Wade, ed., *The Letters of W. B. Yeats* (New York: Macmillan, 1955), p. 211.
25. *Ibid.*, pp. 173, 921.
26. From *The Hour-Glass*, in *The Variorum Edition of the Plays of W. B. Yeats* (New York: Macmillan, 1966), p. 578.

Psychic Daughter, Mystic Son, Sceptic Father

William M. Murphy

John Butler Yeats's aversion to his son's dabblings with the occult began early and never ended. He boasted to his brother Isaac Butt Yeats in 1918 that he had helped Willie grow: "I abolished religion and insincerity," he declared.[1] But, as he knew only too well, he had merely abolished Christianity and other conventional forms of belief in which vast groups of people find comfort in the face of the insoluble mysteries of human existence. He had not abolished William Butler Yeats's hunger for religion, which the son sought to feed through magic and mysticism. As early as 1892 the evidence of his father's dislike of mysticism is clear. John O'Leary had apparently suggested that his protégé sprinkle cold water upon the heat and flame of his occultism. WBY's reply is eloquent:

> Now as to Magic. It is surely absurd to hold me "weak" or otherwise because I chose to persist in a study which I decided deliberately four or five years ago to make, next to my poetry, the most important pursuit of my life. Whether it be, or be not, bad for my health can only be decided by one who knows what magic is and not at all by any amateur. The probable explanation however of your somewhat testy postcard is that you were out at Bedford Park and heard my father discoursing about my magical pursuits out of the immense depths of his ignorance as to everything that I am doing and thinking.[2]

1. JBY to Isaac Yeats Jan. 28, 1918 (Coll.: Anne Yeats).
2. WBY to John O'Leary, week of July 23, 1892, in *The Letters of W. B. Yeats*, ed. Allan Wade (London: Rupert Hart-Davis, 1954), p. 210.

Father described his son's attitude toward the occult as "hot and credulous",[3] and his opinion of George Russell and Willie acting in concert is hinted indirectly in his letter to Sarah Purser of July 7, 1897: "I don't know where Willie is or what he is doing. The last I heard was that he and Russell had gone west (Sligo or thereabouts) to find a new God."[4]

A quarter of a century later his attitude had not changed. When Lady Gregory sent him newspaper clippings about WBY's *Per Amica Silentia Lunae* he wrote his son sadly:

> I am sorry you are returning to mysticism. Mysticism means a relaxed intellect. It [is] of course very different from the sentimentalism of the affections and the senses which is the common sort, but it is sentimentalism all the same, a sentimentalism of the intellect. *"I will make the unknown known, for I will present it under such symmetrical forms that everyone will be convinced—and what is more important I shall convince myself."* So speaks the mystic, according to my idea. AE is a man of genius marred by mysticism, at least forced down into a lower grade. I must respect my poet, I must feel to my core that he has a vigorous character and an intellect clear as crystal. Otherwise I am soon tired of his melodious verses.[5]

John Butler Yeats recognized and acknowledged the importance to a poet of an imagined world out of which he could generate the surface substance of his poetry. His apprehension about his son's occultism arose from a quite different source, from a fear that it might mean a disorder of the poet's intellect or personality. Even Ezra Pound, not recognized as a model of psychic stability, made an interesting observation on his behaviour when WBY was working out his theories on lunar phases to explain human character. "Bit queer in the head about 'moon'," Pound wrote John Quinn, "whole new metaphysics about 'moon', very very very bughouse."[6] The subject of the occult was such a touchy one

3. JBY to Lily Aug. 1, 1894 (*Letters from Bedford Park*, ed. William M. Murphy [Dublin: Cuala Press, 1973], p. 12).

4. JBY to Sarah Purser July 7, 1897 (*Letters from Bedford Park*, p. 36).

5. JBY to WBY Apr. 27, 1918 (Coll.: Michael B. Yeats, hereafter cited as MBY).

6. B. L. Reid, *The Man from New York* (Oxford: 1968), p. 389 (Pound to Quinn Dec. 13, 1919). Reid also quotes George Russell on WBY: "His mind is subtle but never very clear in its thought" (Russell to Quinn July 10, 1919, pp. 386-7).

between father and son that it was seldom alluded to in correspondence, though the shards of evidence scattered over a period of thirty-five years form a clear pattern.[7]

It is tempting to believe that JBY's objections to WBY's mysticism arose naturally out of his own deconversion from Christianity, which he regarded as "myth and fable". He had adopted the methods and conclusions of Mill, Comte, and Darwin long before they had become fashionable among the intellectual community, and he stuck to them in great measure throughout his life. One might easily conclude, therefore, that his distaste for his son's metaphysical extravagances was a simple outgrowth of his own agnosticism, a mere disagreement with a prejudice that didn't coincide with his own.

But such a conclusion falls apart when one consider's JBY's attitude toward the parasensory experiences of his eldest daughter, who was christened "Susan Mary" in 1866 but was always known as "Lily". In her family she was closest to her elder brother both in age and sympathy.[8] Because of what happened to her, John Butler Yeats in the last few decades of his life—which lasted from 1839 to 1922—listened with respect to those who asserted ties with another world or another dimension, though never deserting his disbelief in the metaphysical and insisting that the claims be somehow associated with rational process. He took to palm reading and fortune-telling by tea leaves, if never very seriously. But even in the early 1870s a palmist had foretold that he would become a success only late in life, and he remembered the prophecy to the end of his days.[9]

Lily Yeats was a forthright observant lady of unusual common sense, straightforward in nature, but gifted with a nice sense of irony. She wrote magnificently readable letters which were, as her

---

7. See JBY to WBY Sept. 6, 1915 (second letter of this date beginning "I hope I am not ..."): "A mystic is a man who believes what he likes to believe and makes a system of it and plumes himself on doing so" (Coll.: MBY).
  See also JBY to Mrs. Edward Caughey Sept. 21, 1915: "I hate mysticism, which to me is muddled thinking. Either we know or we don't know. But a mystic neither knows or not knows—he just wishes that things be so and then according to him they are so" (Coll.: Princeton).
8. William Butler Yeats, 1865-1939; Susan Mary ("Lily"), 1866-1949; Elizabeth Corbet ("Lollie"), 1868-1940; Robert Corbet, 1870-1873; John Butler, Jr. ("Jack"), 1871-1957; Jane Grace, 1875-1876.
9. The seer was the sister of Edwin Ellis, with whom WBY collaborated on an edition of Blake.

brother put it, "full of observation". Born prematurely, she suffered
all her life from an enlarged thyroid gland which caused symptoms
misdiagnosed at different times in her life as pneumonia and tuber-
culosis. In middle age she was, in Leonard Elton's words, a "large
comfortable lady" and a "fine woman in her own right".[10] She
was her father's favourite child and everyone else's favourite too.
John Quinn, the New York lawyer who watched over her father
in his declining years in New York, wrote by choice to her rather
than to her sister Lollie (Elizabeth Corbet Yeats, the publisher of
the Cuala Press). Lollie was utterly dependent on her sister during
a life that often encountered severe emotional distress. Lily's
brother Jack felt closer to her than to anyone else in the family.
She was one of the few people inside the family or out that William
Butler Yeats felt easy with. Utterly without pretension as intellectual, writer, or metaphysician, she took life pretty much as it
came and exhibited remarkable courage and forbearance in circumstances that might have shattered others.[11] When a person
of her humour and rationalism had "visions" that proved either
accurate replays of past events of which she had no knowledge or
remarkable predictions of future ones, yet made no special claims
about them or her own powers, those about her would naturally
pay attention, as her father did.

Lily Yeats did not leave behind a detailed body of written description of her experiences, though she and her father alluded to
them often. Nevertheless, we have several letters and notes which
shed light on their nature, and for a couple at least we have cor-
roborative evidence of their retrospective or predictive accuracy.
Lily's experiences can be divided into three broad categories.
The first can be subdivided into two groups: the simple dream

10. Leonard Elton to WMM in conversation. I am indebted to Mr. Elton, son
of Professor Oliver Elton, for giving me access to the Yeats material in
his possession.
11. Because of her father's improvidence Lily never received a formal education, lacked a dowry to attract men of her class and station—the only men
who ever attracted her "in that way", as her sister Lollie put it, were in
any event J. M. Synge and John Quinn, who were both otherwise spoken
for—and had to run a household which included her father (until his
departure for New York in late 1907) and Lollie, an excitable, talkative,
frustrated spinster who suffered emotional problems which were never
serious enough to require hospitalization but which were devastating in
their effect at home.

fantasy, the kind of thing common to us all, a jumble of irrational and sometimes frightening events, often rising to the intensity of nightmare;[12] and the vision (defined as a visual sensation of something not objectively present, the sensation occurring either in a waking state or in the state of half-waking just before sleep) in which the experiences are not easily referable to external people or events. For our purposes this category can be disregarded.[13]

12. Lily described three such dreams to Oliver Elton:

You ask if I have had any dreams lately. Last year I had three curious dreams in which I saw an evil spirit. I did not note the dates, but the dreams were weeks apart. My room at home is outside Lolly's. To get to hers you would have to go through mine. In the first dream I dreamed I was in bed and that a powerful evil spirit came and tried to get Lolly. I fought it and had a very hard struggle, the bed clothes being twisted in every direction. I felt great fear, saw nothing, but felt a great evil power against me. I kept making the sign of the cross on myself, and made it in a way that would have been impossible unless I was out of my body, because I made it right from my head to my toes and across from shoulder to shoulder tip. The evil one faded away and I woke up to find all in perfect order.

The second dream was some weeks later. Again I was in bed and a spirit came in the form of a strong and very cold wind which blew on my face and head. I made no physical struggle this time, but made over and over again the sign of the cross, saying 'In the name of the Father,' etc. I was even more frightened than in the other dream. It faded and I awoke.

The third dream came on a night Lolly was sleeping in town for the night. In this dream I felt no fear at all because of her absence. My fear in the dreams was never for myself but for her.

This time I saw the spirit, a goblin-like form about 3 feet high, covered with black skin like a bat, which felt like uncooked plucked chicken. I caught it by the arm, which was very long, and I flung it up and over my bed, banged it down between the wall and the bed, flung it over again, and onto the floor. I scored with my thumb the sign of the cross in its horrible little sunken chest, saying each time, 'Never come near me again.' It vanished and I looked up and have had no more visits from evil spirits   (Lily to Oliver Elton Dec. 22, 1923).

13. Two of these visions involved "The Red Rose" and "The White Rose", and Lily wrote a detailed account of each. She begins the first:

In the late summer of 1895—I think—I was sitting in the dining room of Blenheim Road, Bedford Park, London, with my father and three friends of his (Professor York Powell, Mr. Nash and John O'Leary). They were all smoking and talking politics.

I gave up listening to them and I sat and looked at a match box which was on the table; it had a blue oblong end which was towards me. I thought that this opened and that I saw a flight of steps of very old

The second category is that of the dream or vision in which an object seems to be a significant symbol of an event. Lily had a "sort of dream" just before the death of her mother Susan Pollexfen Yeats in 1900, in which a white sea-bird was "flapping its wings" in her face. A few weeks later the bird appeared again, and a day or so later her Uncle John Pollexfen died, suddenly and unexpectedly, in Liverpool.[14] In 1910 she dreamed again of the strange bird, and Uncle George Pollexfen kept the symbolism consistent by obligingly dying.[15]

Then, in February 1913, her sister Lollie was visited by the bird, which she had never seen before. She "woke with a scream and said there was a great wingless bird in her room, a penguin, she thought." The following night Lily woke up "feeling sure there was a sea-swallow on the table by my bed." Because of her three previous experiences she confidently waited to hear of the death of another Pollexfen. More than four months passed and she had almost forgotten the vision when she got word from the family lawyers that Uncle William Middleton Pollexfen, incurably mad

---

worn stones; I thought that they led up from the sea and they were between two walls of houses, and it was bright sunshine.

I walked up these steps and I could see into the house, the windows were open. I thought that they were full of people and life and movement but all invisible to me.

At length a "Messenger" gave her from the altar of a church a red rose, "perfectly flawless", out of which came "two tiny blue moths". Ultimately everything vanished.

Sixteen years later, in January 1911, she had just gone to bed one night and found herself "standing again on the steps of the little church holding the red rose". The "messenger" of the first vision reappeared, she at length was given a white rose, and after further details the vision ended as the first one had. But we are given no external events to which either vision is connected. (The accounts of both the red rose and the white rose are in typewritten form in the collection of MBY.)

14. See my " 'In Memory of Alfred Pollexfen': W. B. Yeats and the Theme of Family," *Irish University Review*, i, No. 1 (Autumn 1970): 30-47. The last lines of Yeats's ode are:

> *At all these death-beds women heard*
> *A visionary white sea-bird*
> *Lamenting that a man should die;*
> *And with that cry I have raised my cry.* [CP, 177]

15. He died September 26, 1910. Lily also thought she heard the banshee wail a day earlier.

for almost forty years in a hospital in Nottingham, had died in February.[16]

The third class of vision, and by far the most interesting, is that in which events and people fairly easy to identify—or to find parallels for—are clearly seen in either vision or dream. This class can be subdivided into three groups: the first the vision or dream of events in the distant past; the second of events in the near future; the third of events in the distant future. Fortunately, we have at least one full and precise account of each kind.

Lily described one of the first kind to Oliver Elton in 1916. The vision itself took place two years earlier. She wrote:

One Sunday in July 1914 Lolly and I got an outside car and drove to Glencullen to see the Joseph Campbells, who had not long [since] moved into the house there. It was a most beautiful hot calm day. We went about four miles up into the hills and found the house, very lonely and buried away, a big old house with a view of the Sugarloaf mountains. It was partly furnished by the Campbells and partly by furniture belonging to the landlord. We only looked into the house, and then went into the garden, where we stayed for our whole visit. . . .

The moment I got there I felt in touch with some other world— a most pleasant feeling, almost an exalted feeling; but I could get no quiet, and so saw nothing. This feeling remained with me all the time, and all the time of the drive home, and till I went to bed.

The moment I was in darkness, I saw I was back again at the house. The house was closed, but (I thought) furnished—only closed up for a time. Then round the side of the house came a lady, a tall woman in the dress of (I judged) the forties or early fifties. She was not handsome, not a girl; elegant, full of charm, and, I thought, something of a personage. With her was a man younger than she. —Then I seemed to get out of my own mind and into hers. I saw with her mind and felt with it. She was very unhappy, and full of thoughts of an old love-story of her youth, and at the same time trying to talk cleverly to the man—I think he was more or less a stranger—all the time her mind full of sorrow. France and Ireland were woven in and out of each other, one moment France then Glencullen. I saw her lover—young man, thick set, very sallow, fine head, rather big; I thought he was a Pole or a Frenchman, and a musician or artist, and I felt she knew George Sand. I saw him ill on a sofa—a lingering illness, slow consumption perhaps. I knew they had lived together, and knew no one knew. Then I saw his funeral. It seemed to leave the steps of the Glencullen house, and yet it was France—a very country place, but I

16. Lily to JBY July 9, 1913 (Coll.: MBY).

thought not far from Paris. I saw the coffin and on it a tossed laurel wreath tied with the tricolour. A priest and two acolytes in red followed, that was all. The priest and the boys looked rough peasants, as if they had come from working on the land, freckled and sunburnt, not very well washed. There it ended.

Next day Lily went to work to learn what she could about Glencullen and its history. Without letting the Campbells know the contents of her dream—merely telling them she had had one—she asked them whether the house had had connections with France in the forties or fifties. They knew nothing but referred her question to the owner, Mr. O'Connell FitzSimon. "He said his grandmother had lived there and was a daughter of Dan O'Connell and had been in France in her youth, been very happy there and knew many literary people."

Lily thereupon described her dream to the Campbells. They searched through the books in the house and found a volume of poems by Mrs. FitzSimon. One of them was "addressed to a friend who had died alone in France." A friend from Dundrum, G. E. Hamilton, provided Lily with further information about O'Connell's family. A daughter Ellen, he reported, married Christopher FitzSimon of Glencullen; she died on June 27, 1883. William Butler Yeats helped to confirm some of the details of the vision:

> I have been looking into a life of O'Connell. A daughter of his 'a few' years after his wife's death (1835) became melancholy because of some 'sin'. There are two very moving letters by O'Connell to her urging her to submit to the directions of her confessor, and speaking of salvation and repentance. She was married and had a child or children.

The coincidences are startling. Some people Lily spoke to about her dream ascribed it to indigestion or fright, but she disagreed. "I can't explain it," she told Elton. "Lobster suppers and rats—both fail. What has the sceptic left? He better believe. It is the easiest."[17]

Under questioning by Elton, Lily expanded on the dream and her discoveries after it:

17. Lily to Oliver Elton Aug. 28, 1916. With this letter is also "Account of A Vision Seen by Me, Lily Yeats, in July 1914", dated at Dundrum Aug. 28, 1916. I have referred to a copy of her account typed by Oliver Elton Aug. 29, 1916. The references to WBY's undated letter to Lily, and to the letter of G. E. Hamilton to Lily Oct. 22, 1915, are taken from the same copy (Coll.: Leonard Elton).

No, I had no knowledge of the history of the house. I did not even know the [word omitted] of the house. I knew of the O'Connell FitzSimons, and knew Mr. FitzSimon but did not know their relationship to the great Dan. I never even saw Dr. FitzSimon till the rebellion [of 1916]. ... He has the same nose that the lady of my vision had, but he is short and she was tall. ... Her nose had a rather unexpected sort of sharp end, which her grandson has.

No, I thought she had not seen the funeral. That seemed to be my own bit of vision, but of that I can't be sure. ...

Sorrow and regret and misery of mind were what I felt the vision lady had in acute form, and also the feeling that it was her great secret known to no one. This feeling was very strong. The whole story was her sad secret I think.

She wore a gray dress, loose straightjacket, and a bonnet rather of the wide poke shape. She was graceful. Elegant is, I am sure, the word of her day with the meaning of her day that would describe her best.[18]

Equally startling was a vision of 1906 which was followed within a fortnight by a chillingly suggestive set of events. While Lollie was visiting in New York in the fall of that year Lily wrote her of a vision—not a dream—in which she had seen "a funeral come out of the Dun Emer gate", with a "light-coloured coffin" in evidence. Dun Emer was the building in Dundrum occupied by Miss Evelyn Gleeson and used by her and the Yeats sisters as the workshop of the Dun Emer Industries, which produced books, embroideries, and rugs. About a week after Lily's vision Miss Gleeson learned that her only brother had been taken ill. The next day he died suddenly. Lily was "relieved", she told Lollie, as "now my vision is out." It was easier to absorb the death of someone she didn't know well than of one of the employees at Dun Emer whom she saw every day. But it developed that the vision was not "out". Less than a week after Mr. Gleeson's death, a 17-year-old nephew of Miss Gleeson arrived at Dun Emer to be taken care of. He had been sent down from Clongowes School with a letter from the school doctor containing "an alarming account of his health". The boy was large and slow and had been behaving strangely. Miss Gleeson promptly took him into Dublin, where three physicians looked him over. All pronounced him healthy, telling Miss Gleeson he was merely "hysterical".

18. Lily to Oliver Elton Aug. 30, 1916. As a postscript she wrote: "Show my vision to anyone interested, of course" (Coll.: Leonard Elton).

The next morning at Dun Emer the boy died, the victim of a brain tumour. When Lily reached Dun Emer that morning after the walk from her home, she knew immediately what had happened when she saw three doctors standing together at the Dun Emer gate. At the time she had the vision she was hardly aware of the nephew's existence and did not know he was ill.[19]

Two other visions of which we have specific record are equally interesting, perhaps more so, as they involve predictions of the future, one of a quite distant future. Both Lily and her father had for years been desolate at the possibility that the Yeats family line, at least the branch descended from him, would die out. Willie shared their concern and suffered in addition a twinge of guilt. The first poem in *Responsibilities*, "Pardon, old fathers", was his *apologia* for having failed to produce offspring to carry on the family name. It ended with the passage:

> Pardon that for a barren passion's sake,
> Although I have come close on forty-nine,
> I have no child, I have nothing but a book,
> Nothing but that to prove your blood and mine. [CP, 113]

At forty-nine he was still unmarried, as were Lily and Lollie. Jack had been married for twenty years (to Mary Cottenham White) but was childless. Certainly, prospects for a line descending from John Butler Yeats were, in those days, poor.

Then, in the fall of 1917, William Butler Yeats married Bertha Georgie Hyde-Lees, twenty-seven years his junior. A few months later Lily had a dream in which she saw "a high stone tower, on the top of it a Herald blowing a trumpet. Out of the trumpet came not notes but the words, 'The Yeatses are not dead'." She sent the account to her father. "Wasn't that good?" she asked.[20] Not long afterward Mrs. William Butler Yeats announced to those in the family that there was to be a child born to her and the poet. The following February Anne Butler Yeats was born. Lily thought the dream must have been a forecast of her birth.

But it was the long paragraph that followed which is by far the most impressive of Lily's visions, one that came to her in October

---

19. Lollie to John Quinn Nov. 25, 1906 (Coll.: New York Public Library, Berg Collection).
20. Lily to JBY Sept. 22, 1918 (Coll.: MBY).

1911, when Willie was 46 years old and viewed by friends and family as a perpetual bachelor. Here are her words, written to her father on September 22, 1918:

> Then I'll tell you another story that will please you. Seven years ago next month, I was in London at an exhibition of women's work. I lodged near Victoria and used to walk up every day into Bond St. One morning I was going up to Hyde Park Corner when I thought it was a sad pity you had no grandchildren, when in a flash I saw a grandson of yours. He was like Willy, only taller, bigger features and more colour, blue eyes. I thought he was a brilliant man, perhaps a statesman, and that he was in and out of the Embassies that are all about Hyde Park there. He was almost 40 in my glimpse, a man of great vitality. In another flash I saw he had my portrait on his wall, a dark wall, panelled I think, and thought a great deal of it.[21]

Students of the Yeats family may well be astonished by this vision. Almost exactly ten years after Lily experienced it, and three years after she recorded it, Michael Butler Yeats, the poet's first (and only) son and second child, was born.[22] Lily died in January 1949, when her nephew was 28. Her letters, kept neatly in manila envelopes, remained in the home of Mrs. William Butler Yeats in Palmerston Road, Dublin, until her death in August 1968. To the best of my knowledge they were never consulted by anybody during that period, and certainly not by Michael Yeats. There is no question whatever about the authenticity of Lily's letters or the unplanned nature of the parallels I now relate.

The facts are that Michael Yeats, in his forties, was (as he still is) tall and dark, strongly resembling his father. He is a member of the Senate of the Republic of Ireland, once served (1969-73) as Chairman of the Irish Senate, and is currently a member of the European Parliament—in other words, a "statesman". In the music room of his home in Dalkey, which because of the topography of the area receives virtually no sunlight, John Butler Yeats's oil portrait of Lily hangs on the wall. Senator Yeats is in fact a great admirer of his grandfather's works generally, and portraits by JBY

21. *Ibid.*
22. After Michael's birth Lily wrote WBY promptly about her vision. He replied that he thought "the boy's horoscope ... quite compatible with a diplomatic career" (WBY to Lily Sept. 1 [1921], Coll.: MBY).

are generously distributed through the house. Lily's vision has proved eerily accurate.[23]

John Butler Yeats was impressed by his daughter's gift. He wrote to his cousin Frank Yeats in 1920: "My daughter Lily is psychic, extraordinarily psychic and can foresee the future of which I could give you many instances. But she is too intelligent and too well taught to believe in the supernatural. Her words are, 'It is something which the Marconis of the future will make use of.'"[24] The emanations she received, like radio waves, were physical phenomena, he believed, and Lily never accepted them as anything else. Indeed, she shared her father's feelings about people who thought they had contact with the spirit world. Writing to her father about a friend of hers who had been "sent away" for a time, she was vehement. "That spiritualism of hers is most dangerous for her, I think, and fearful nonsense in any case." The woman and her friends frequently "called up" Parnell and Gladstone. One day the woman looked at Lily and said, "You will marry a man with kind eyes and a taste for agriculture." Lily replied, "Must be Horace Plunkett. I'll start in pursuit tomorrow."[25] Van Wyck

23. For those interested in combinations, permutations, and probabilities, a further note might be added here. In July of 1969 at my summer home in Nova Scotia I was deciphering the letter cited above and dictating its contents into a recording machine. In the middle of the transcription, just after Lily's account of the dream and before that of the vision, the tape ended, and I decided it was as good a time as any to walk to the foot of the hill and pick up the day's mail. In it was a letter from Michael Yeats. Immediately after reading it I came to the account of the vision of the "statesman". I offer this footnote without commentary to occultists and mathematicians who might find food for thought in it.

24. JBY to Frank Yeats Sept. 8, 1920 (Coll.: Harry Yeats). In an interview with Marguerite Wilkinson JBY attributed Lily's words to Willie: "He expects a Marconi some day in the future to explain the occult to us." Or could Miss Wilkinson have misunderstood JBY's identifications? When she asked him if WBY belonged to "any cult or society devoted to occultism", he gave her a look of benign surprise. Then he shook his head. 'No indeed,' he said, 'he keeps himself free'." The impression one gains from the interview is that WBY's interest in the occult was minor (Marguerite Wilkinson, "A Talk with John Butler Yeats," *The Touchstone*, [Oct. 1919]: 10-17).

25. Lily to JBY Nov. 14, 1910 (Coll.: MBY). JBY suggested that the Pollexfens made use of the gift of second sight more than other families, including his own, but wasn't sure whether environmental influences modified or suppressed it. In his unpublished Memoirs he writes:

Brooks, the American literary historian who knew John Butler Yeats intimately during the last years of the painter's life in New York, observed that despite his occasional involvement in palm-reading and fortune telling he never fell over the cliff. He had a combination of interests, Brooks wrote, "that made for an infinite, if a somewhat bewildering wit—a wit, however, that, where spirits were concerned, drew the line just the other side of the banshee."[26]

> *When my son Jack, at the time a young schoolboy, went to Liverpool on his way from London to Sligo with the intention of spending a night at his aunt's house in Liverpool, my wife remained restlessly awake till long past midnight, being convinced that he had lost himself. Afterward we found it was true and that when he found his aunt's house it was precisely at the time when she consented to fall asleep. I think perhaps that we have at birth the gift of second sight, but that we become immersed in the multitudinous details of everyday life and so neglect it—but that my wife's family being not much interested in these distractions retain and exercise the gift. Yet this doesn't fully explain it, for my daughters have the liveliest sense of everything that passes and yet have the gift—of which I could give you many instances from my daughter Lily's experiences. I am certain that we all have this gift but that we are carefully taught to abandon it and forget it.*

JBY's early recognition of the Pollexfen tendency to place great faith in dreams and his own scepticism about their powers is revealed in a letter he wrote to his wife, Feb. 15, 1873, in reply to one of hers that has disappeared:

> *You must not dream dreams, although, whether from your mother or from some old-fashioned aunt or from some servant like Nellie, you have all learned to have a kind of half belief in dreams and to worry yourself and others with narratives of your dreams. You are all great dreamers, and yet they have never helped any of you to divine correctly anything.*

It is unfortunate that we do not know the content of Susan Pollexfen's dream, for just sixteen days later, on March 3, Robert Corbet Yeats, their second son, died suddenly of croup at the age of three.

26. Van Wyck Brooks, "A Reviewer's Notebook," *The Freeman*, Mar. 1, 1922, p. 599. Lily and her father liked each other so much that they never quarreled about the differences in their own views. She believed in immortality and in reincarnation. When "Papa" wrote her that he believed that death was merely a change in a universe where change is the law of life, she gave her own view: "I think like you that life goes on. I am sure I have lived many times, and will live many times more, and I am sure I have been the mother of a great many children" (Lily to JBY Apr. 6, 1919, Coll.: Princeton). With Lollie she attended services at the Church of Ireland (or England) regularly (quietly going to Roman Catholic mass instead during the Boer War as a protest against English policy and pulpitry). Three weeks after her father's death she wrote Willie: "I feel

In John Butler Yeats's mind there was clearly a sharp distinction between Lily's activities and Willie's. He did not object to "psychics", only to "mystics". A "psychic" was one who, like Lily, received visions effortlessly, one to whom things happened unsought and unforced. A "mystic", on the other hand, was one who, like Willie, deliberately looked for signs from the other world, stared into crystal balls (as WBY did for years with his Uncle George Pollexfen), consulted astrological charts, waved "magic" wands about, joined eccentric societies like the Order of the Golden Dawn, and regarded with awe and reverence Indian swamis who brought in their train the inscrutable wisdom of the mysterious East. The first was a normal person who simply recorded what happened; the second was one to whom little happened but who went "bughouse" in trying to induce supernatural experiences. Like an earlier Celtic poet who took his magical powers with equal seriousness, W. B. Yeats thought he could "call spirits from the vasty deep"; in the family drama John Butler Yeats was content to play the role of Hotspur, with about as much success as his Shakespearean counterpart.

Readers of *The Speckled Bird*—that intense, astonishingly personal autobiographical novel[27]—will understand and appreciate the

he has found his two children that died so long ago and is delighting in the likenesses he finds in them to his children here on earth" (Lily to WBY Feb. 23, 1922, Coll.: MBY).

JBY remained sceptical to the end. In complaining to John Sloan that he had never had his fling he came as close as he ever would to expressing a hope for an afterlife. "It is not one man *in a thousand who gets his fling* —and it is because none of us gets his fling that I have a hope that there may be a hereafter—a very faint hope" (JBY to John Sloan Aug. 14, 1917). He once wrote to a friend: "There are things for which I would thank God if I knew where to find him" (JBY to Martha Fletcher Bellinger Aug. 26, 1916).

As he entered "on the last stretch before that harbour which sooner or later will receive us all" (JBY to Isaac Yeats July 29, 1921) he became somewhat less pessimistic, but there was no doubt about his basic feeling. "I have never thought about my soul," he wrote eight months before his death. "I am neither an early Christian nor a modern. I am as little interested in my soul as if I were a vegetable—just to live and go on clinging to my environment is all I want" (JBY to Martha Fletcher Bellinger June 10, 1921).

27. I am indebted to Professor William H. O'Donnell for sharing with me his findings on Yeats's novel, which he transcribed and edited for publication by the Cuala Press in 1974.

depth, earnestness, and sincerity of the poet's devotion to the occult. But they will understand also the fears of his father, who after 1890 was virtually cut off from any knowledge of his son's mystical pursuits. Yet it was not only his father—and Ezra Pound—who saw WBY as he never saw himself. Father would have been vexed, if also partly amused, by Joseph Holloway's account in his diary of George Russell's commentary on WBY's talk before the Theosophical Society in Dublin in January 1918. Russell, according to Holloway, "told many strange and droll incidents of Yeats's adventures in search of 'spookish' experiences. . . . AE has the saving grace of humour to keep him sane and cool on such subjects. He thinks they [*i.e.*, mystics] must be very ill-informed if they can't give a clearer message from the unknown than those."[28]

Chiefly John Butler Yeats, the perpetual artist, feared that his son's mysticism might weaken his poetry by making it "vague" and "insincere". In a long letter to WBY critical of the Syrian painter and poet Kahlil Gibran he spoke indirectly to his son:

> Vagueness is always insincerity, and of it are two kinds. When a man does not take the trouble to think or to know precisely, he is vague—and if this come from human weakness or laziness or because it is so soothing in itself to a disturbed mind, then it is so human as to be likeable or even lovable, and great poets have shown themselves not averse—only with this condition, that as honest men they must not pretend that it is a conviction, or, as some of your second-class mystics, that it is a religion. There is another kind of vagueness which no poet or artist should touch with his delicate and sensitive fingers: that is where there is calculation that vagueness may be of popular advantage to the writer. . . . Cleverness itself is an insincerity (it was the bane of Edwin Ellis) since its aim is not the essential truth but success. Of course the Poet rules over a wide Kingdom and may at will and according to his artistic judgment practice all the insincerities; only he must never be their dupe.[29]

Whether William Butler Yeats was their dupe or not is a judgment perhaps best left to the dispassionate reader. One can only suggest, however, that it was fortunate that John Butler Yeats died

28. *Joseph Holloway's Abbey Theatre: A Selection from His Unpublished Journal*, ed. Robert Hogan and Michael J. O'Neill (Carbondale: Southern Illinois University Press, 1967), p. 202.
29. JBY to WBY Feb. 12, 1919 (Coll.: MBY).

three years before the publication of *A Vision*, for that book would certainly have killed him.[30]

30. Cp. Padraic Colum, "John Butler Yeats," *Atlantic Monthly*, 172 (July 1943): 82.

W.B. had to create for himself an imaginative belief that included, not only his own version of God, Freedom, and Immortality, but esoteric doctrines and magical practices: nothing could be further from J.B.'s serene and uncritical rationalism than is his son's summa, A Vision.

The Esoteric Flower:
Yeats and Jung

James Olney

Of the parallels between the historical cycles given to him by the instructors for *A Vision* and the cycles of history in Spengler's *Decline of the West*, Yeats says, "I knew of no common source, no link between him and me, unless through

> The elemental things that go
> About my table to and fro." [v, 19]

Yeats could have said the same thing about his thought and that of C. G. Jung. For Yeats, had he been aware (as apparently he was not) of the manifold similarities between his own work and Jung's, would no doubt have accounted for them by the operation of "the elemental things"—"things", as Yeats tells us in "To Ireland in the Coming Times", that he had

> discovered in the deep,
> Where only body's laid asleep.
> For the elemental creatures go
> About my table to and fro,
> That hurry from unmeasured mind
> To rant and rage in flood and wind.

Moreover, the operations of those elemental things provided one of the major studies that the two men, though largely ignorant of one another, were pursuing at the same time. Both of them gazed long and steadily into the deep and there found what became a principal subject for each: those elemental spiritual and psychic forces or beings, whatever we shall call them, that inhabit the realm of the great unconscious and of "unmeasured mind" but that also appear occasionally to startle the unwary individual consciousness and that can be called up and put to use by the adepti—whether magicians or alchemists, poets or psychotherapists—who know the fitting words and who understand the proper rituals. Jung too, like his Irish counterpart, had, as Yeats says of himself, "come to believe so many strange things because of experience" [E&I, 51], and having come to the beliefs by way of irrefutable experience, the two men produced works in poetry and psychology which were determined by the strange experiences they had known. Yeats, it would be fair to say, eagerly sought the experience while Jung, sometimes willingly, sometimes hesitantly, merely acknowledged that it had come to him. Though assured of the reality of these "parapsychological phenomena" (as the scientist in Jung sometimes urged him to phrase it), both Yeats and Jung also sought—and found—confirmation for their ideas in written sources: in alchemical and Gnostic texts, in Plotinus and the Neoplatonists, eventually in Plato himself and in his pre-Socratic predecessors. Jung "amplified" his clinical experience from the writings of antiquity; Yeats sought confirmation in Plato, Plotinus, Empedocles, and Heraclitus of the elemental things revealed by his instructors. In fact, both found confirmation in the same sources.

"Were I not ignorant," Yeats lamented in "Swedenborg, Mediums, and the Desolate Places" [E, 60], reflecting on those tales he had gathered with Lady Gregory in which he seemed to find an "ancient system of belief"—"Were I not ignorant, my Greek gone and my meagre Latin all but gone, I do not doubt that I could find much to the point in Greek, perhaps in old writers on medicine,[1]

1. Unless he had in mind someone like Paracelsus, it is doubtful that Yeats would really have found what he wanted in old writers on medicine; for they, almost alone among ancient writers who had anything to do with philosophy, as F. M. Cornford has pointed out, were empiricists inclined to inductive science rather than metaphysicians given to deductive systematizing. "The physician approached the question of the nature of man as it were from below, advancing towards it from what seemed to him the certain facts observed in particular cases. . . . Philosophy . . . reached its theories of man's nature from the opposite quarter, descending to it from above. The philosophers began with cosmogony, inheriting the traditional problems implied in cosmogonical myths" (*Principium Sapientiae* [New York: Harper Torchbooks, 1965], p. 38). Yeats, I think, was by nature predisposed to the approach "from above" and this, in fact, is one

much in Renaissance or Mediaeval Latin." It may be that Yeats's small Latin and less Greek prevented his getting right back to the earliest spokesmen for the "ancient system", but if Yeats could not read, in the original languages, those springtime flowerings of the human spirit, he nevertheless found the same ideas blossoming in other languages and in other writers, as well as in the translations of those ancient writers from whom he was linguistically debarred. Jung, on the other hand, knew Greek and Latin, in addition to three or four modern languages, so he could be confident when he wrote to Erich Neumann on December 22, 1935: "Analytical psychology ... has its roots deep in Europe, in the Christian Middle Ages, and ultimately in Greek philosophy. The connecting-link I was missing for so long has now been found, and it is alchemy. ..."[2] One might not care to say of Yeats or of Jung (as St. Augustine said of Plotinus) that either was "a man in whom Plato lived again"; but one could say, and demonstrate, that the tradition which we call Platonism or Neoplatonism—and to which St. Augustine as well as Plotinus contributed richly—lived again in Yeats and Jung; and further, that this tradition had, as an essential aspect of its make-up, or as a sort of mirror-image of itself, an occult component or an esoteric parallel. Going back to Plato himself, and even earlier to Pythagoras and Empedocles, the exoteric philosophic tradition had its counterpart in a parallel esoteric tradition; and point by point along their parallel paths the philosophy offered justification for that other darker brother.

One could suggest that Yeats and Jung came to the same esoteric conclusions because they were both prone to the hearing of voices and the seeing of visions; but this does not explain why their voices should have said the same things in Ireland and in Switzerland, or why the schematic representations of *A Vision* and of the "Red Book" should have looked so much alike. When we understand, however, that the same voice had spoken before to Heraclitus and Pythagoras, to Plato and Plotinus, then we begin to see the pro-

---

way in which he differs from the physician Jung who claimed an empirical origin for all his theories. That they came to the same conclusions about the nature of man from opposite directions would seem to intensify the significance of the many parallels in thought, imagery, and expression between Yeats and Jung.

2. *C. G. Jung: Letters*, ed. Gerhard Adler with Aniela Jaffé, tr. R. F. C. Hull (Princeton: Princeton Univ. Press, 1973), 1: 206.

found implications of the Yeats-Jung parallels, and we begin to realize why Yeats heard what Jung heard and why the vast design conjured up in the poet's mind, explaining all things both in the world above and in the world below, was the same as that which the psychologist discovered empirically in the tens of thousands of dreams, fantasies, visions, and hallucinations that he met with in the clinic and in the dark areas of his own psyche. In poetry and in psychology, Yeats and Jung continued, and in their different creations momentarily completed, a work that had been begun centuries before and that would, they both believed, continue for centuries to come. Their works, to borrow a favourite image from Jung, are like flowers blossoming in the twentieth-century moment from a perennial rhizome so ancient that, though we call it Platonism, we know it is older than Plato, and indeed we cannot find any first and original source for it. "It is strange," Jung wrote in a letter of November 7, 1932, "that the broad, shining surface of things always interests me much less than those dark, labyrinthine, subterranean passages they come out of. Civilizations seem to me like those plants whose real and continuous life is found in the rhizome and not in the quickly fading flowers and withering leaves which appear on the surface and which we regard as the essential manifestation of life. . . . I almost believe that the real history of the human mind is a rhizome phenomenon" [*Letters*, 1: 102]. It is hardly surprising that Jung should "almost believe" this since he was well aware that all his work had been nourished by the same mother root as sustained the work of such spiritual ancestors as Paracelsus, Meister Eckhart, the alchemists, Plotinus, the Gnostics, Plato, and the pre-Socratics. And, though Jung was not aware of this, Yeats too was drawing nourishment from that same root at the same time; he realized that his predecessors in the tradition, forming a line nicely parallel to Jung's, were Blake, Swedenborg, the astrologers, Plotinus, Thrice-Greatest Hermes, Plato, and the pre-Socratics. In the work of Yeats and Jung we have a flowering of the perennial rhizome of the Platonic tradition, with its dual aspects.

Of the occult sciences,[3] Jung had a particular interest in al-

---

3. I use "sciences" in the Jungian sense: "astrology represents the sum of all the psychological knowledge of antiquity." ("Richard Wilhelm: In Memoriam," *The Collected Works of C. G. Jung* [Princeton: Princeton Univ. Press], xv: 56. Subsequent references to the *Collected Works* will be given as cw in the text.)

chemy. Yeats, though he did not restrict himself to one study, nor
go into any one as thoroughly as Jung did into alchemy, was most
interested in the theory and practice of magic. Jungian alchemy
and Yeatsian magic were grounded and justified in ancient philosophy (especially in the central document of Platonism and Neoplatonism, i.e., the *Timaeus*); they therefore had an unbroken
history stretching from pre-Platonic sources to the twentieth century. There is a third occult science, a Jungian innovation with
distinctly Yeatsian reverberations, that will reveal much about
the relationship of the ideas of Yeats and Jung and about their
joint relationship to the philosophic tradition. Throughout Yeats
and Jung, as throughout the philosophic tradition, there recurs an
image or symbol (as a plane figure, the circle; as a solid figure, the
sphere) the understanding of which is necessary not only to an
understanding of the esoteric in Yeats and Jung but also of the
esoteric in general—what its essential nature is and why it has en-
dured for so long.

"The alchemist, in his small way, competes with the Creator, and
therefore he likens his microcosmic opus to the work of the world
creator" [cw, xiii: 197]. It is easy to turn this observation of Jung's
around and to recognize why it is that Plato, when in the *Timaeus*
he describes the Demiurgos' cosmic creation, could almost as well
be describing the alchemist at work in his laboratory with his four
elements, his retorts and vessels, his formulas and invocations. The
Timaeus not only describes an alchemical operation of cosmic proportions but simultaneously provides a philosophic rationale for
the literal practice of alchemy and an apology for the philosopher's
descent from the world of being to the world of becoming, or
from the level of spirit and psyche to the level of matter and
physics. In the beginning, according to Timaeus and all subsequent alchemists, Gnostics, Hermetists, and Neoplatonists, the
Demiurgos created the physical universe of becoming and motion
out of four elements, the Empedoclean *rhizōmata*: fire and earth,
air and water. Timaeus' fine, harmonic explanation of why the
Demiurgos used four rather than two or three elements in the
construction of the universe must have pleased Jung who could
scarcely analyse a dream, read a Gnostic or alchemical text, or
study the products of his own lively and active unconscious without discovering the seemingly ubiquitous quaternity.[4] From com-

4. See *Timaeus*, 31b-32c. In Jung's magnificent library, which is still intact

binations of fire and earth, air and water comes the entire physical universe that, as Timaeus says with notably Heraclitean emphasis, is in perpetual process and unceasing transformation.

The elements as described in the *Timaeus* are Empedoclean, but they are Empedoclean with a difference, and it is precisely this difference that makes the transmutations of alchemy theoretically possible. Plato's four elements are like Empedocles' in that they combine and recombine in different proportions to form different compounds, different living forms; they differ from his, however, in that they are not themselves ultimate or immutable. (It has been well said that Empedocles was a Parmenidean monist but that, in order to make cosmogony possible, as it was not in Parmenides' system, he began with four "ones" instead of a single "One". Hence his elements are as ultimate, and separately as indivisible, as Parmenides' One.) W. K. C. Guthrie remarks that "It should be noted . . . , in case anyone should be tempted to see Empedocles as an ancestor of the alchemists, that if Aristotle had not over-thrown his doctrine that the elements are indestructible and immutable, the basic theory of alchemy would have been impossible."[5] Before Aristotle did his work, however, Plato—or Timaeus, as one likes—had circumvented the irreducibility of Empedocles' four roots by introducing both Heraclitean and Pythagorean concepts; and he thereby laid the ground for both a physical and a philosophic alchemy. At *Timaeus* 49c-50c, Plato declares, with Heraclitean intent, that it is wrong to refer to an element as if it *were* itself consistently and always; rather, we should say that it is always *becoming* itself, or becoming one of the other elements, for they are in constant process of changing and interchanging qualities. (Heraclitus, as reported by Maximus of Tyre: "Fire lives the death of earth and *aer* lives the death of fire, water lives the death of *aer*, earth that of water.") Later [53c-61c], developing

in Küsnacht, there are at least five different editions of the *Timaeus*. In two German translations, Jung has marked the passage cited and others around it with heavy underlining and occasional marginalia as if in an ecstasy of agreement.

5. *The History of Greek Philosophy* (Cambridge: Cambridge Univ. Press, 1964), II: 149, n. 1 carried over from p. 148. Jung did precisely what Guthrie warns against and saw Empedocles "as an ancestor of the alchemists"—transformed, however, as I suggest in the text is necessary, by Plato's doctrine in the *Timaeus*: see, for example, "The Spirit Mercurius," cw, XIII: 195.

a Pythagorean concept, Plato gives a mathematical and geometric structure to the elements and expressly states that these forms (his elements are ultimately determined formally rather than materially, and are to be spoken of as qualities rather than things) can interpenetrate and intertransform.[6] The heavens, likewise, according to the *Timaeus*, are ordered on formal and Pythagorean principles, and so, going in whichever direction we prefer—from the physical realm of the elements to the spiritual realm of the World Soul or vice versa—we encounter an ultimate reality that is formalistic and that displays a series of perfect, formal correspondences throughout.

The premise of all esoteric studies, as of Pythagorean and Platonic cosmology, is formalist rather than materialist: ultimate reality inheres in form—in ritual and in style, as Yeats might put it—rather than in matter, and in changing a form one changes the reality. When Timaeus describes the creation of the World Soul (which will become the orbits or the tracks of the heavenly bodies, those gods who, in their movement, realize the soul of the universe and determine the destiny of the world), he divides the soul substance into concordant musical intervals and he states everything in mathematical terminology; that is to say, his Demiurgos proceeds on Pythagorean assumptions, as he does also in the conceptual modification of Empedocles' four elements, and proves to be Pythagorean in both psychic and physical creation. And those created gods, who in "perfect" (i.e., circular) motion trace out the World Soul and make a beginning of time itself—the planets, the sun and the moon, the fixed stars—are given the task by the Demiurgos, who has created them, of fashioning in their

---

6. Cf. A. E. Taylor, *A Commentary on Plato's "Timaeus"* (Oxford: Clarendon Press, 1928), p. 472: "It is just the great Pythagorean thought on which mathematical physics is based, the thought that the properties of particles depend on their geometrical structure, which makes it possible for Timaeus to get rid of the 'irreducibility' of the 'roots'." F. M. Cornford later made the point more explicit in reference to alchemy in *Plato's Cosmology* (London: Routledge & Kegan Paul, 1937), p. 252: "From this account of the metals, it does not appear that there is any bar to the transmutation of any metal into any other.... All metals consist solely of water icosahedra, and free transmutation between grades of icosahedra should make any one convertible into any other. It would be interesting to know whether the alchemists were encouraged by this theory to attempt the transmutation of metals."

turn all the living creatures of the world; hence man's destiny in the "likely" story of the *Timaeus* is directly determined by the heavenly bodies, and those heavenly bodies, as the *Timaeus*, the *Laws*, and the *Epinomis* all make clear, should be worshipped as divinities. This is astrology intensified and accounted for mythically, and it points up the way in which Plato fuses alchemy and astrology—the physical elements and the psyche of man on the one hand, the bands of the World Soul and the universal psyche on the other—into a single philosophic science uniting things above with things below. As Frances Yates has said, "The Hermetic science *par excellence* is alchemy; the famous *Emerald Tablet* [cited, incidentally, very frequently by both Yeats and Jung], the bible of the alchemists, is attributed to Hermes Trismegistus and gives in a mysteriously compact form the philosophy of the All and the One."[7] In spite of the chronological confusion of the Renaissance, Hermes Trismegistus did not come before Plato, nor the *Emerald Tablet* before the *Timaeus*, and in the *Timaeus*, as in Pythagorean doctrine even earlier, we can see a pre-Hermetic source for the idea of microcosmic and macrocosmic correspondences whereby "That which is above is like that which is below" [*ibid.*, n. 2]. In arguing for an essential correspondence between the psyche of the universe and man's psyche and between physical nature and human physique, Plato confers his precedent authority on Jung's psychological reading of alchemical literature: as base metals, with their ultimately formal structure, can be transmuted into gold, so unconscious components, presenting themselves as archetypal images (as Jung always insisted, "archetypes" are determined in form, not in content), can be transformed into individuated self. The analogy was implicit in Plato before becoming esoteric doctrine in the alchemists and explicit psychology in Jung. In his great devotion to psyche, Jung was of course, as he very well knew, dealing with nothing other than the Platonic ψυχη : the soul or the spirit, the mysterious breath that "bloweth where it listeth" and that is equally of man and of the cosmos.

If alchemical literature presents the reader with certain difficulties of interpretation because of its double significance—often being both literal chemistry and symbolic psychology—it is, nevertheless,

7. *Giordano Bruno and the Hermetic Tradition* (London: Routledge & Kegan Paul, 1964), p. 150.

nothing like so complicated an affair as magic. Partly this is because alchemy is removed from us in time, and is thus a matter of history, in a way that magic is not: few alchemists nowadays go into a laboratory, but there are unquestionably people engaged in magical practices of one sort or another. Moreover, the difficulty is compounded by the fact that it is not at all easy to say what magic is, what its intentions are, where its boundaries lie, or how it relates to other occult practices. Is alchemy a variety of magic? Is a medium possessed of magical powers? How does magic stand in relation to the miracles of religion? "The theory of universal animation," Frances Yates says in *Giordano Bruno and the Hermetic Tradition* [p. 381], "is the basis of magic." Whatever any individual variety of magic may turn out to be in performance, this, as a theoretic explanation of how it comes to be what it is, is a convenient approach to the essential nature of magic in itself. Here again, as with the doctrine of correspondences, the Renaissance mistakenly attributed philosophic originality to ancient Egypt and supposed Hermes Trismegistus to have been "the one who first taught that the world is an animal"[8] and that the universe is a single vast organism, a living and breathing creature. But Plato had taught this in the *Timaeus* centuries before it was appropriated and passed on as esoteric Hermetic doctrine. As his model for universal creation, Plato's Demiurgos looks to "that Living Creature of which all other living creatures, severally and in their families, are parts" [*Timaeus*, 30c, tr. Cornford]. In the Living Creature which serves as model there are all the Forms or Ideas that will be realized in creation as genres and species, but the Living Creature, like its created image, is a unique and single being: there is only one Living Creature and consequently only one universe which is its likeness. "For that [Living Creature] embraces and contains within itself all the intelligible living creatures, just as this world contains ourselves and all other creatures that have been formed as things visible. For the god, wishing to make this world most nearly like that intelligible thing which is best and in every way complete, fashioned it as a single visible living

8. The remarks quoted from *Giordano Bruno* are a commentary on a passage from the first book of Campanella's *Theologia*: "...docet Virgilius, Lucanus et poetae omnes, et Platonici mundum esse animal, quod Trismegistus apprime docet....Propterea contendit Trismegistus non esse mortem, sed transmutationem, quam vocat transmutationem" (p. 380).

creature, containing within itself all living things whose nature is of the same order" [30c-d]. To the Living Creature other names are given by other people, and Plato himself calls it by other names in other places, for what Timaeus describes as the Demiurgos' model is clearly the same as the intelligible realm of Forms or Ideas that we find in the *Meno*, the *Republic*, the *Symposium*, the *Phaedo*, and the *Phaedrus*. It is also the "Pleroma" about which Jung, in the guise of Basilides, preaches in the first of his *VII Sermones ad Mortuos*[9]; and—except that the collective unconscious and Anima Mundi are most often conceived as being subsequent to human experience rather than prior to it—the Living Creature is the equivalent of the Jungian collective unconscious and of the Yeatsian Anima Mundi, that "general cistern of form" [M, 351] from which come all the images, symbols, and archetypes of poetry and psychology through which we endeavour to trace our way back to the source and model of our being. "Here at last," Timaeus says as he concludes his cosmogonical myth, "let us say that our discourse concerning the universe has come to its end. For having received in full its complement of living creatures, mortal and immortal, this world has thus become a visible living creature embracing all that are visible and an image of the intelligible, a perceptible god, supreme in greatness and excellence, in beauty and perfection, this Heaven single in its kind and one" [92c]. So much for the priority of Hermes Trismegistus as advocate of the doctrine that the world is an animal (Plato's word is ζῶου, i.e., an animal, or living creature): like Yeats and Jung, Hermes, whoever he may have been, was undoubtedly aware that the *Timaeus* taught universal animation.

When Yeats addressed his fellow adepti in the Order of the Red Rose and the Cross of Gold on a matter of obviously great importance to him ("Is the Order of R. R. & A. C. to remain a Magical Order?"), he may not have been consciously echoing the *Timaeus* in what he said and in the way he said it—for the students of the Golden Dawn did, after all, think of themselves as Hermetists

9. Jung, in an attempt not to compromise his scientific standing, had the book—the occult origins of which he describes in *Memories, Dreams, Reflections* (New York: Pantheon, 1963), pp. 189-93—privately and anonymously published by John Watkins in 1925; a public edition, acknowledging Jung's authorship, was published by Stuart & Watkins (London) in 1967.

rather than Platonists—but both his vision of what a magical order should be and the language he chose to describe it are remarkably close in spirit to Timaeus' account of cosmic creation. Against those who wanted to establish separate groups within the Second Order (i.e., within the "Ordo Rosae Rubeae et Aureae Crucis" itself), Yeats argued that the Order was a living creature reflecting in its organic form the Third—and invisible—Order from which the Second Order derived its shape, its life, and its power. "A Magical Order," he told his companions in magic, "differs from a society for experiment and research in that it is an Actual Being, an organic life holding within itself the highest life of its members now and in past times. . . . "[10] As the Demiurgos created the heavenly bodies in the image of the Living Creature and those divinities in their turn fashioned all living creatures after their own being, so there is a regular progression—or rather a devolution— as Yeats imagines, from the Supreme Life to the Third Order to the Second Order. Maintaining the traditional rituals and examinations, and thus "passing . . . from one Degree to another," he argued, "is an evocation of the Supreme Life, a treading of a symbolic path, a passage through a symbolic gate, a climbing towards the light which it is the essence of our system to believe, flows continually from the lowest of the invisible Degrees to the highest of the Degrees that are known to us" [p. 7]. It is precisely this belief that makes magic theoretically possible at all, but this belief was Platonic and Neoplatonic (not to say Orphic and Pythagorean) before it was Hermetic.

Yeats, however, at least for a certain period, professed a great interest in practical as well as in philosophical magic, and for the conjuration of spirits (which I take to be the common element in the different varieties of magic) one might imagine that no great philosophic system would be requisite. Yet even here abstruse philosophical matters entered in. Given their belief in the two Platonic realms or modes of being and their corollary doctrine of a hierarchical universe, Neoplatonic theurgists and Hermetic magicians necessarily found the question of immanence or transcend-

10. *Is the Order of R. R. & A. C. to remain a Magical Order?*, a pamphlet, according to the title-page, "written in March 1901, and given to the Adepti of the Order of *R. R. & A. C.* in April, 1901" (privately printed), pp. 10-11. Reprinted in Harper, *Yeats's Golden Dawn* (London: Macmillan, 1974) pp. 259-68.

ence of crucial importance rather than of mere academic interest. If one goes about calling spirits from the vasty deep, the success of the venture depends a good deal on being sure just what that deep is and where. I or any man can call them up, but will they come? The practising magician, however—at least in the theurgic tradition of Neoplatonism and Hermetism—would say that they come not by chance nor by some Glendower-like gift of nativity but because he understands the nature of their being—he participates in it and it in him—and knows the appropriate rites, received through esoteric tradition, that will make their powers palpable, manifest, and effective in the human realm. Containing in himself, in small, that same vital, organic, and hierarchic cosmos created by the Demiurgos in the *Timaeus*, the theurgist can invoke spiritual powers and make them operative in the physical (and, of course, the psychic) realm. For not only is the physical universe of the *Timaeus* a vast and vital organic animal, but it is moreover seamlessly interwoven throughout its being with a corresponding psychic entity, the two everywhere interpenetrating so as to compose a single, inner-outer, spiritual-physical entity. "When the whole fabric of the soul had been finished to its maker's mind," Timaeus tells his companions, "he next began to fashion within the soul all that is bodily, and brought the two together, fitting them centre to centre. And the soul, being everywhere interwoven from the centre to the outermost heaven and enveloping the heaven all round on the outside, revolving within its own limit, made a divine beginning of ceaseless and intelligent life for all time" [36d-e]. It was an inner awareness of this coherent physical/psychic being, endlessly contained and reflected in all its microcosmic parts, and a sympathetic participation in that essential being, that gave theurgic powers to those men who took up Plato's system after him and developed the implications of his cosmology in occult directions. For those followers in the Platonic tradition, according to R. T. Wallis, "It had always been a problem to distinguish theurgy from vulgar magic."[11] No doubt. Not every eye would be capable of discerning the fine and wavering line separating the two when in fact they shared the same explanation and justification, the same end and intention, and often the same techniques. Plotinus, who did not practise magic but who "believed in" it, provided the philo-

11. *Neoplatonism* (London: Duckworth, 1972), p. 153.

sophic bridge between Plato and the Neoplatonic theurgists in his explanation of how magic works: "But magic spells; how can their efficacy be explained? By the reigning sympathy and by the fact in Nature that there is an agreement of like forces and an opposition of unlike, and by the diversity of those multitudinous powers which converge in the one living universe. . . . The magician, too, draws on these patterns of power, and by ranging himself also into the pattern is able tranquilly to possess himself of these forces with whose nature and purpose he has become identified. Supposing the mage to stand outside the All, his evocations and invocations would no longer avail to draw up or to call down; but as things are he operates from no outside standground, he pulls, knowing the pull of everything towards any other thing in the living system."[12] Any ritual knowledgeably performed by any component of this coherent, homgeneous, microcosmic-macrocosmic, living creature will have reverberations and effects throughout the organism and up and down the implicated hierarchies. "Every symbol," Yeats remarked in his 'Journal', "is an invocation which produces its equivalent expression in all worlds."[13] It was according to this principle that Yeats would have had magic performed by the magi of the Golden Dawn—Hermetists or Rosicrucians in their costumes but Platonists in their philosophy.

"Shortly before this experience I had written down a fantasy of my soul having flown away from me. This was a significant event: the soul, the anima, establishes the relationship to the unconscious. In a certain sense this is also a relationship to the collectivity of the dead; for the unconscious corresponds to the mythic land of the

12. Fourth *Ennead*, tractate 4, no. 40; tr. Stephen MacKenna, 4th ed. (London: Faber & Faber, 1969). Cf. Proclus' *De Sacrificiis et Magia* in the paraphrase by Thomas Taylor (with whom Yeats was familiar): "so the ancient priest, when they considered that there was a certain alliance and sympathy in natural things to each other, and of things manifest to occult powers, and by this means discovered that all things subsist in all, they fabricated a sacred science from this mutual sympathy and similarity. Thus they recognized things supreme, in such as are subordinate, and the subordinate in the supreme: in the celestial region terrene properties subsisting in a causal and celestial manner; and in earth celestial properties, but according to a terrene condition" (in *Thomas Taylor, the Platonist: Selected Writings*, ed. Kathleen Raine and George Mills Harper [London: Routledge & Kegan Paul, 1969], p. 194).
13. *Memoirs*, ed. Denis Donoghue (London: Macmillan, 1972), p. 166.

dead, the land of the ancestors. If, therefore, one has a fantasy of the soul vanishing, this means that it has withdrawn into the unconscious or into the land of the dead. There it produces a mysterious animation and gives visible form to the ancestral traces, the collective contents. Like a medium, it gives the dead a chance to manifest themselves." This is not, as it happens, the "mystical" poet but the "empirical" psychologist speaking [*Memories*, p. 191]; however, were it not for the occasional "scientific" terminology ("anima", "collective contents", etc.) one could easily be forgiven a certain confusion. And when Jung proceeds to the lines that follow, after having told us that "the unconscious corresponds to the mythic land of the dead, the land of the ancestors", he speaks a language that Yeats would have understood very well indeed: "From that time on [i.e., 1916, when he was compelled by the unsatisfied voices of the dead to write *Septem Sermones ad Mortuos*], the dead have become ever more distinct for me as the voices of the Unanswered, Unresolved, and Unredeemed; for since the questions and demands which my destiny required me to answer did not come from outside, they must have come from the inner world" [pp. 191-2]. It was to satisfy the ancestral voices, thus completing their being, and to fulfill the demands of the unconscious—one and the same thing, according to Jung's vision—that he wrote his *Collected Works* and, for the same reason, constructed his Tower in Bollingen. "The historical form" of the Tower, Jung told a correspondent in 1934, "had to be there in order to give the ancestral souls an abode pleasing to them. I can tell you that the doyen of that corps chuckled when he found himself again in the accustomed frugal rooms ['Where all's accustomed, ceremonious,' as Yeats has it], smelling of smoke and grits, and occasionally of wine and smoked bacon. As you know, in olden times the ancestral souls lived in pots in the kitchen. *Lares* and *penates* are important psychological personages who should not be frightened away by too much modernity" [*Letters*, 1: 168]. The "unconscious", the "mythic land of the dead", the "land of the ancestors", the "abode" of "the ancestral souls"—these are all names, psychological, literary, and metaphoric, for the same thing, and it is that same thing for which the Tower itself stands as a symbolic image. Yeats called it Anima Mundi and Plato called it the Living Creature; nor does it matter that the Living Creature should be paradoxically composed mostly of spirits not living but dead, for Yeats and Jung are taking a human view, from after ages of human experience, of that which in the *Timaeus* is described from a divine view, before either experience or time had a start. For the poet and the psychologist, all lives and all psyches have gone to compose the life of the Living Creature and the collective unconscious of the Universal Psyche—which, for the philosopher, is the creative model for individual lives and individual psyches. In any case, whether we choose to look on it as poet, as psychologist, or as philosopher, the world—like Yeats's poetry and his Tower, like Jung's *Collected Works* and his Tower—is through and through a symbolic artifact, a temporal living image of the eternal Living Creature.

In "The Philosophy of Shelley's Poetry", Yeats speaks of "the sudden conviction"—a conviction that he no doubt often felt, and so did Jung—"that our little memories are but a part of some great Memory that renews the world and men's thoughts age after age, and that our thoughts are not, as we suppose, the deep, but a little foam upon the deep" [E&I, 79]. It was in the deep, we may recall, "where only body's laid asleep", that Yeats discovered the "elemental things"; and it was from the deep that the fantasies and voices and visions came to startle Jung into elaborating his theory of a collective unconscious with its archetypal figures and its "synchronistic" freedom from time and space. "The collective unconscious", according to the man who brought it to the attention of the modern world and who claimed that its reality was denied only by the ignorant and the naive, "seems to be . . . something like an unceasing stream or perhaps ocean of images and figures which drift into consciousness in our dreams or in abnormal states of mind" [CW, VIII: 350]. This collective deep, which provides the material of dreams, visions, and hallucinations, contains "the accumulated deposits from the lives of our ancestors", and, if we were to personify it, Jung says, "we might think of it as a collective human being combining the characteristics of both sexes, transcending youth and age, birth and death, and, from having at its command a human experience of one or two million years, practically immortal. If such a being existed, it would be exalted above all temporal change; the present would mean neither more nor less to it than any year in the hundredth millennium before Christ; it would be a dreamer of age-old dreams and, owing to its limitless experience, an incomparable prognosticator. It would have lived countless times over again the life of the individual, the family, the tribe, and the nation, and it would possess a living sense of the rhythm of growth, flowering, and decay" [cw, viii: 349-50]. This, very simply, is the Living Creature after it has lived: having descended into the fragmented world of time, it gathers itself back into the wholeness of eternity. In it, because there time and space have no force, causality is thrown off in favour of significance (things happen not because of a precedent event but because they add to a pattern and establish a meaning) and synchronicity obtains without temporal or spatial hindrance.

Yeats was being a good, if unconscious, Jungian when he decided that "all our mental images no less than apparitions (and I see no reason to distinguish) are forms existing in the general vehicle of *Anima Mundi*, and mirrored in our particular vehicle" [M, 352]. Or perhaps one should say that Jung was perfectly Yeatsian when he wrote to Albert Oeri, "So far as I can grasp the nature of the collective unconscious, it seems to me like an omnipresent continuum, an extended Everywhere. That is to say, when something happens here at point A which touches upon or affects the collective unconscious, it has happened everywhere . . ." [*Letters*, 1: 58]. Whether Yeats was Jungian or Jung Yeatsian—actually, of course, in philosophic terms they were both Platonic: contemporary flowers nourished by a perennial rhizome (which, they would both have agreed, might be taken as an historical working out of the intention of a collective Great Mind)—there can be no doubt that, though starting from very different points, they came to the same conclusion about an indefinable and mysterious, immensely powerful and all-embracing collective spirit which is the ultimate psychic (i.e., human) reality, and that as a result of this shared concept they developed much the same thoughts about the phenomenon that Jung called "synchronicity". In his essay on "Magic", Yeats speaks of experiences that proved to him "that there is a memory of Nature that reveals events and symbols of distant centuries" [E&I, 46], and in *The Trembling of the Veil* he refers to "certain studies and experiences, that were to convince me that images well up before the mind's eye from a deeper source than conscious or subconscious memory" [A, 183]. While Yeats could be casual about the "experiences" and could leave his terminology imprecise, Jung, as a psychologist, felt constrained to offer copious evidence (experiences both of his own and of others), give a definition to the phenomenon ("a coincidence in time of two or more causally unrelated events which have the same or a similar meaning" [cw, viii: 441]), find historic precedents for it (synchronicity "is basically nothing other than *correspondentia* more specifically and precisely understood, and was ... one of the elements in the medieval explanation of the world" [*Letters*, i: 547]), and try to fit synchronicity into his general theory of the psychic structure of mankind. It was a cardinal principle of Jung's psychology and his psychotherapy that we ought to consider the individual psyche not only in relation to its past and how it comes to be as it is but in relation also to its future and what it "wants" to become as it differentiates itself in consciousness from the collective psyche. Psychic phenomena, according to Jung, "whether historical or individual, cannot be explained by causality alone, but must also be considered from the point of view of what happened afterwards. Everything psychic is pregnant with the future" [cw, xiv: 58]. If personal consciousness, as Jung said often enough in one metaphor or another, is like a tiny point of light risen out of the shadowy personal unconscious and finally out of the illimitable darkness of the collective unconscious, where neither time nor space has any meaning, then it is scarcely wonderful that psyche, which is deeply implicated in that collective being, should be able to communicate and to make itself felt without regard to the limitations that would be imposed by the absolute rules of temporal and spatial causality. "The soul cannot have much knowledge till it has shaken off the habit of time and of place," Yeats says in "Anima Mundi"; and that it was capable of so freeing itself into the eternal moment he never doubted. "Yet even now we seem at moments to escape from time in what we call prevision, and from place when we see distant things in a dream and in concurrent dreams" [m, 358]. It was the simultaneity of causally unrelated psychic events that persuaded both Yeats and Jung to believe in the real existence of a collective psyche that produced the correspondences and concurrences in and across time and space. Indeed, a consideration of the parallels between Yeats and Jung might persuade many readers to adopt the same belief. "It seems as though time," Jung remarked, "far from being an abstraction, is a concrete continuum which possesses qualities or basic conditions capable of manifesting themselves simultaneously in different places by means of an acausal parallelism, such as we find, for instance, in the simultaneous occurrence of identical thoughts, symbols, or psychic states ..." [cw, xv:

56]. If the similarities in Yeats and Jung might be accounted for by the operation of the "elemental things", then the proper designation for the manifest parallels throughout their works would have to be "synchronicity", for the elementals went about their business of producing the same images and ideas simultaneously in the *Collected Works*, the *Sermones*, the *Memories*, and the *Letters* of the Swiss psychologist and in the *Poems*, the *Vision*, the *Autobiographies*, the *Essays*, and the *Letters* of the Irish poet.

"No symbol tells all its meaning to any generation," Yeats believed [E&I, 148], and Jung would doubtless have concurred. There is one symbol, however, or a unified complex of symbols figured in a variety of related images, which tantalizes and frustrates (and has done for twenty-five centuries) more than any other, yielding many meanings to the seeker yet seeming at the same time to withhold at least as many meanings as it gives up. That image or symbol —and it occurs as the central symbol of all esoteric studies from Pythagoras, Heraclitus, Parmenides, Empedocles, and Plato down to W. B. Yeats and C. G. Jung—is the gyre, the cycle, the circle, the sphere. There are hundreds of ways it can appear (a winding staircase, a snake eating its own tail, a round tower, a cycle of history, the philosopher's stone of the alchemists, the flight of a falcon, an Unidentified Flying Object—to mention but a few); however it may be figured in a particular instance, it contrives to reveal to us some mysteries but to suggest at the same time that it holds other mysteries that we can never hope to comprehend—at least not during the mere moment that we are incarnate in this world. This is why both Yeats and Jung in the end urge that we *experience* that state symbolized by the sphere rather than—which is fruitless anyway—merely trying to grasp it with the conscious mind. For both of them, the symbol—and this is why it is impossible to encompass it with conscious mind—mediates between the fragmented existence that we know in time and space and the unified existence of eternity, between consciousness and the unconscious, between the physical realm of objects and the intelligible realm of Forms. With this last contrast it becomes clear that what is in question is the Platonic distinction between two different modes of being—or, rather, the distinction between that which is always coming into being but never *is*, and that which always *is* but has never come into being. To figure the one there are Yeats's cones and antinomies or Jung's *enantiodromia* and opposites, for the other there is the Sphere whose centre is everywhere and circumference nowhere; or, in the wonderful description of the *Timaeus*, there is on the one hand the "moving image of eternity" which is time, and there is on the other hand eternity itself. "The nature of the Living Being was eternal, and it was not possible to bestow this attribute fully on the created universe; but he determined to make a moving image of eternity, and so when he ordered the heavens he made in that which we call time an eternal moving image of the eternity which remains for ever at one. For before the heavens came into being there were no days or nights or months or years, but he devised and brought them into being at the same time that the heavens were put together . . . ; for they are all forms of time which in its measurable cycles imitates eternity" [37d-38a, tr. H. D. P. Lee]. Thus time itself is the primordial, the quintessential, the first and the last symbol, and Jung could say with truth of the many symbols he elaborated that "my works . . . are fundamentally nothing but attempts, ever renewed, to give an answer to the question of the interplay between the 'here' and the 'hereafter' " [*Letters*, 1: 299].

"I recall what Plato said of memory," the fictitious John Aherne writes to Yeats in one of the several prologues to *A Vision*, "and suggest that your automatic script, or whatever it was, may well have been but a process of remembering. I think that Plato symbolised by the word 'memory' a relation to the timeless . . ." [p. 54]. Aherne may well be right, for memory in Plato (which we find, along with the corollary doctrine of reincarnation, in the *Meno*, the *Phaedo*, the *Republic*, and the *Phaedrus*) is a function of time that nevertheless draws on knowledge acquired outside of time. When someone pointed out to Jung that he seemed to have anticipated, in an early work, all the discoveries he was to publish twenty and thirty years later in his books on alchemy, Jung responded with this same Platonic concept of anamnesis that turns on the distinction and the relationship between time and eternity. "As a matter of fact we have actually known everything all along; for all these things are always there, only we are not there for them. . . . What we call development or progress is going round and round a central point in order to get gradually closer to it. In reality we always remain on the same spot, just a little nearer to or further from the centre. . . . Originally we were all born out of a world of wholeness and in the first years of life are still completely contained in it. There we have all knowledge without knowing it. Later we lose it, and call it progress when we remember it again" [*Letters*, 1: 274-5]. When Jung decided that this same "circumambulation of the self", as he calls it in his autobiography [p. 196], is the real goal of all psychic development, he was of course aware that the image of circular motion had had a long history as a symbol for a timeless state and that one of its earliest occurrences in that role was in the *Timaeus*.

Yeats acknowledges having read only a very few volumes of philosophy before he received the material that became *A Vision*, but among those few volumes he mentions "two or three of the principal Platonic dialogues" [p. 12]. It seems very likely either that the *Timaeus* was one of those dialogues or that Plato himself, communicating from another world, was one of the ghostly instructors, for there are a number of significant correspondences between the system of the *Timaeus* and the system of *A Vision*. In discussing that system Yeats specifically refers to Heraclitus (on the incessant warring opposites of DK Fr. 53 and on the two modes of being of DK Fr. 62, which Yeats liked so much that he quoted it half a dozen or more times: "Immortal mortals, mortal immortals, living each other's death and dying each other's life") and to Empedocles (with his gyre-like cycles of expanding and contracting "Concord" and "Discord" and his Sphere of perfect "Concord"); but the system into which Yeats incorporates the insights of Heraclitus and Empedocles in *A Vision* is very much the system of the *Timaeus*. And one of the things that he most emphasizes is that the Sphere can never be more than a symbol for us while we live because where there is no opposition and conflict—i.e., in the Sphere—there is no life. The Heraclitean-Empedoclean gyres and cycles and cones go on reversing one another and interchanging incessantly, and as long as we are ourselves a part of that unceasing flow we can do no more than imagine the Parmenidean Sphere symbolically and ideally. It was precisely the Heraclitean and Empedoclean vision of life as ceaseless process and the Parmenidean vision of real being as a stable sphere that Plato first put together in a complete metaphysical system—and left for such later Platonists as Yeats to draw upon in their visions. "The whole system is founded upon the belief that the ultimate reality, symbolised as the Sphere, falls in human consciousness, as Nicholas of Cusa was the first to demonstrate, into a series of antinomies" [v, 187]. Nicholas was the first to demonstrate it if he lived before the communal efforts of Heraclitus, Parmenides, Empedocles, and Plato which issued finally in the system of the *Timaeus*—but otherwise he was not. "My instructors," Yeats tells us, "keeping as far as possible to the phenomenal world, have spent little time upon the sphere, which can be symbolised but cannot be known" [p. 193]; in their perception the instructors were good Platonists, for it was Plato who first contended that the created world in process is but a symbol of the reality of stable being, and time a moving image of eternity. Again Yeats warns that "even the [Empedoclean] sphere formed by Concord is not the changeless eternity, for Concord or Love but offers us the image of that which is changeless" [pp. 67-8]. Though time, according to the *Timaeus*, shall have no end, yet it is not the same as eternity which, in contrast to time, is by definition unmeasured and unmeasurable. Just so, Jung repeated almost *ad nauseam* that mandalas or other archetypal images, while they are products of the unconscious and symbols expressing it, are not themselves the unconscious which has no shape, no form, no visual or audible properties; "for I think," Yeats declared, and he could have been speaking for Jung when the latter had divested himself of his scientist's garb, "as did Swedenborg in his mystical writings, that the forms of geometry [e.g., mandalas and their circular first-cousins in Greek philosophy] can have but a symbolic relation to spaceless reality, *Mundus Intelligibilis*" [v, 69-70]. The geometric form and the reality, the mandala and the archetype *per se*, man and the Idea of Man—these are of different modes of existence as Plato was the first to find the appropriate philosophic language to say. He was not the last, however, as Yeats demonstrates in his poetry and his *Vision* and Jung in his psychology and his *Sermones*.

Even before Plato, but very darkly and imperfectly, Parmenides had hinted at two modes of existence in his "Way of Truth" and his "Way of Seeming", but in flatly denying any kind of reality to the latter he left out a half of all that must be accommodated in any complete physics and metaphysics; nevertheless, in his description of what is really real, Parmenides did give symbolic form to the intelligible world, and both Empedocles and Plato followed him in their figurative conception of the supreme reality. The "One Being," according to Parmenides, "is complete on every side, like the mass of a well-rounded Sphere, everywhere equally poised from the midst. . . . For it is every way equal to itself and meets with its limits uniformly."[14] Empedocles, too, hinted at two different worlds—the state of the Sphere when Love or Concord completely dominates and everything is at rest, and the state of the twin cycles as first Strife or Discord and then Love increases—but he conceived of them as alternating, rather than simultaneous, states of motion and stability. Thus he took one step from Parmenides towards Plato without, however, going the whole way; and doing so, he retained as his image for the superior reality, when Love dominates entirely, that image which Parmenides had used for the only reality and which Plato would later assume as the perfect form of cosmic creation: "Thus everything," in the state of perfect Concord, "is held fast in the close obscurity of Harmonia, a rounded Sphere rejoicing in its circular stillness."[15] Finally with Plato we arrive at the system fully concatenated and discover that all circular movements, all cycles, and all gyres here are merely imperfect reflections of the changeless Sphere which exists, not in some other time as with Empedocles, nor as the only reality as with Parmenides, but in a different mode from this world yet always related to it as a model to an image. As a shape, according to Timaeus, the Demiurgos gave to the cosmos "that which is fitting and akin to its nature. For the living creature that was to embrace all living creatures within itself, the fitting shape would be the figure that comprehends in itself all the figures there are; accordingly, he turned its shape rounded and spherical, equidistant every way from centre to extremity—a figure the most perfect and uniform of all" [33b, tr. Cornford]. Likewise, when the created gods of the *Timaeus* in turn created human bodies and human souls [69c] they naturally imparted to them the same spherical shape and circular motion that was given in the beginning to the planetary gods themselves. That human souls now stagger drunkenly rather than describing perfect, smooth circles is due not to the nature or the intention of the creative power but to the recalcitrance of Anankē ("Necessity") which has great force in this world. It is the task of philosophy, by contemplating the heavenly motions, to restore to the human soul, beyond the power of Necessity, that circular motion which is its appropriate and primordial motion.

14. DK Fr. 8, ll. 42-44 and 49, tr. Cornford, *Plato and Parmenides* (London: Kegan Paul, Trench, Trubner, & Co., 1939), p. 44.
15. Empedocles, DK Fr. 27, tr. Guthrie, *History of Greek Philosophy*, II: 169.

"In Neoplatonic philosophy," Jung remarks, "the soul has definite affinities with the sphere. The soul substance is laid round the concentric spheres of the four elements above the fiery heaven" [cw, xii: 83-4]. Elsewhere, commenting on the tremendous paradox implied in the point and the circle—figures which contain in themselves all other figures and all opposites and so symbolize the *coniunctio oppositorum*—Jung says, "The most perfect form is round, because it is modelled on the point. The sun is round and so is fire.... God fashioned the sphere of light round himself. 'God is an intelligible sphere whose centre is everywhere and whose circumference is nowhere' " [cw, xiv: 47]. Not the least of the paradoxes implied by the circle, nor the least of the opposites joined therein, is that it symbolizes in psychic terms not only God but also the self. The circle represents the unknown, the ineffable, the indefinable both at the ubiquitous centre and at the non-existent circumference. And those two psyches—or that Psyche and that psyche—are merely the objective and the subjective faces of one and the same thing: "The collective unconscious stands for the objective psyche, the personal unconscious for the subjective psyche" [cw, vii: 66, n. 4]. The circle is thus the figure that encompasses both God and man, both the "transpersonal" unconscious and the private unconscious, and that in itself connects, as all varieties of the occult would agree, the above with the below. Discussing the *prima materia* of the alchemists, Jung refers to Empedocles' cosmogony where "the σφαιος (spherical being) springs from the union of dissimilars, owing to the influence of φιδια. The definition of this spherical being as ευδαιμουεστατος θεος, 'the most serene God', sheds a special light on the perfect, 'round' nature of the *lapis*, which arises from, and constitutes, the primal sphere" [cw, xii: 325]. The intended result of Hermetic magic and of the alchemical transitus[16], as of Yeatsian poetic symbolism, Jungian individuation, and Platonic philosophy, is a return to that "most blessed", prelapsarian or precarnate state of wholeness which was "the primal sphere" of our beginning and which remains the longed-for "primal sphere" of our end. For as Heraclitus (who was the favourite pre-Socratic of both Yeats and Jung) said: "In a

---

16. "One aspect of the transitus...is the ascent and descent through the planetary spheres....As the 'Tabula Smaragdina' shows, the purpose of the ascent and descent is to unite the powers of Above and Below" (cw, xiv: 218).

circle the beginning and the end are common"; and, more generally, "The way up and the way down are one and the same."

Yeats poetically and philosophically, Jung psychologically and
philosophically, and Plato philosophically, poetically, and psychologically, all tried to speak, in human language, of that which
is much more than human, and so, in the end, they all had recourse
to symbolic and mythic expression. In his *Memories* Jung says
he can "only 'tell stories' ", or "tell my personal myth" [p. 3], just
as Timaeus warns Socrates and his other listeners that the most
he can do is to recount a "likely story" [29d]. But in telling their
symbolic stories and myths, Jung and Timaeus were exercising
what Yeats, in his essay on "Magic", claims to be the greatest of
magical powers: "I cannot now think symbols less than the greatest
of all powers whether they are used consciously by the masters of
magic, or half unconsciously by their successors, the poet, the
musician and the artist" [E&I, 50]. Yeats, of course, had little use for
science in any form, and from time to time he said some particularly hard things about psychology; hence he did not include
psychiatrists among the successors to the masters of magic. But it
is sufficiently clear from what Jung himself said about his own
practice of psychotherapy that it had very basic ties, in its principle and its technique, with magic. Jung did not, as did Paracelsus
or Gerard Dorn or their fellow alchemists, carry his investigations
into a chemical laboratory; yet there is no doubt but that he
thought of himself, in the *Mysterium Coniunctionis*, in *Psychology
and Alchemy*, and in the essays of *Alchemical Studies*, as completing the work of his predecessors and as bringing back into
consideration a great tradition of experimentation, of learning, and
of understanding that had dropped out of sight (or virtually so)
for three centuries. What Jung intended, of course, was to transfer
the site of experimentation from the chemical laboratory to the
human psyche and to understand the process in question as primarily a psychological or spiritual one and only secondarily as a
chemical or physical one. (It should be pointed out, nevertheless,
that Jung, like Yeats, posited a very close connection between
psychological and physical processes, reversing, however, the order
of events as conceived by the medicine of his time: Jung was mainly
interested, again like Yeats, in how psyche influences the physical
universe rather than vice versa.) "The production of the *caelum*,"

Jung says of a central process of alchemy, "is a symbolic rite performed in the laboratory. Its purpose was to create, in the form of a substance, that 'truth', the celestial balsam or life principle, which is identical with the God-image. Psychologically, it was a representation of the individuation process by means of chemical substances and procedures, or what we call active imagination. This is a method which is used spontaneously by nature herself or can be taught to the patient by the analyst" [cw, xiv: 494]. This is a very striking admission—the sort of thing that several times over caused Jung to be burned at the stake for occult heresy by his scientific colleagues. For if the "active imagination" of analytical psychology is nothing other than an alchemical procedure, and if the analyst, like his occult brother, is able to exercise his power because he is in full possession of this secret of nature whereby the elements are transmuted, then he is very simply—or very grandly—an alchemist, not to say a magician and astrologer, in modern clinical dress. With an understanding of the regular hierarchical correlation between World Soul, individual soul, and the mathematical structure of matter—that correlation and cosmic sympathy on which all magic depends—the alchemist, whether physical or psychological, would, like the poet, be able to "call down among us certain disembodied powers," as Yeats says, "whose footsteps over our hearts we call emotions" [E&I, 157]. I don't suppose that Jung would have approved Yeats's terminology, but in certain unguarded moments—in his letters and in his autobiography—Jung revealed that as a psychotherapist he was really practising a very Yeatsian art. "I would like to draw a radical distinction between psychology as a science and psychology as a technique," Jung wrote to a psychotherapist in Southern California [Letters, i: 433]; and the distinction he had in mind to draw was as sharp as the difference between scientific method and magical procedure. Psychology as a science may be, as Jung always claimed, empirical; but psychology as a technique is, not to put too fine a point upon it, an occult art. When it came to psychotherapy, Jung was evidently prepared to abandon his scientific terminology—archetypes, libido, transference, the whole lot—and get right down to esoteric bases: "In practice I have no compunction, if the case seems to me sufficiently clear, in speaking simply of spirits."[17] Jung was un-

17. *Ibid.* Elsewhere in the *Letters*, Jung says of astrology, "I've been interested in this particular activity of the human mind for more than 30 years."

questionably more cautious than Yeats, who gladly spoke of spirits in season and out, but in the full heat of the performance of psychology he was willing enough to recognize spiritualist claims and to admit the possibility that the powers affecting his patients—powers which he, as an alchemist-analyst, presumably knew how to invoke—might be more than "only" psychological or "merely" subjective.

I have already remarked that in the *Timaeus* Plato provides [at 59b-d] a rationale for the alchemical art. What Timaeus says immediately after this apologia for the alchemist, however, reveals that Plato's own interest (and this may be true for some medieval alchemists also as it is undoubtedly true for Jung—and for Yeats) is not so much in change within this physical world as it is in transformation of temporal human components to an eternal transcendent condition; in other words, though he sets up alchemy as a respectable enough pastime, his ultimate concern is with the spiritual transformation effected by philosophy rather than with the relatively vulgar desire to change lead, by chemical means, into gold. "And if, for relaxation," Timaeus says, "one gives up discussing eternal things, it is reasonable and sensible to occupy one's leisure in a way that brings pleasure and no regrets, by considering likely accounts of the world of change" [59c-d, tr. Lee]. But the significant change, for which this physical one only serves as a metaphor, is the change between modes of existence that philosophy alone can bring about and that raises the adept out of the toils of endless reincarnations to the perfected and precarnate state of Platonic Man: "For we are creatures not of earth but of heaven, where the soul was first born, and our divine part attaches us by the head to heaven. . . . But a man who has given his heart to learning and true wisdom and exercised that part of himself is surely bound if he attains to truth, to have immortal and divine thoughts, and cannot fail to achieve immortality. . . . And the motions in us that are akin to the divine are the thoughts and revolutions of the universe. We should each therefore attend to these motions and by

---

As I am a psychologist I'm chiefly interested in the particular light the horoscope sheds on certain complications in the character. In cases of difficult psychological diagnosis I usually get a horoscope in order to have a further point of view from an entirely different angle. I must say that I often found that the astrological data elucidated certain points which I otherwise would have been unable to understand" (1: 475).

learning about the harmonious circuits of the universe repair the damage done at birth to the circuits in our head, and so restore understanding and what is understood to their original likeness to each other. When that is done we shall have achieved the goal set us by the gods, the life that is best for this present time and for all time to come."[18] If the earlier passage provided justification for physical alchemy, the present passage not only justifies but exalts philosophical alchemy, philosophical astrology, and indeed all varieties of the philosophical occult. It also provides a reasonable gloss on what Jung meant when he said, in apparent contradiction to all his claims to be no more than an empiricist and a natural scientist with no philosophy and no system of his own, "The psychotherapist must be a philosopher in the old sense of the word. Classical philosophy was a certain view of the world as well as of conduct. . . . There were philosophical systems for a satisfying or happy way of living. Psychotherapy means something of the sort too. It must always deal with the whole man and not merely with organs. So it must also proceed from the whole of the doctor" [*Letters*, I: 456]. As a psychotherapist, as a whole man, as something more than rational intellect and empirical observation, Jung did not deny the necessity of philosophy and "philosophical systems" in finding the meaningful life and in achieving what he, like Yeats and Plato and the Neoplatonists and the Hermetists, felt was the goal of all their activities: psychic transformation and simultaneous transcendence. As Yeats puts it, "When all sequence comes to an end, time comes to an end, and the soul puts on the rhythmic or spiritual body or luminous body and contemplates all the events of its memory and every possible impulse in an eternal possession of itself in one single moment" [M, 357]. This is not very remote from what Jung said in a letter a short time after he had himself nearly died and had experienced the remarkable visions of transcendence recounted in *Memories, Dreams, Reflections*: "What happens after death is so unspeakably glorious that our imagination and our feelings do not suffice to form even an approximate conception of it. . . . What shall we still know of this earth after death? The dissolution of our time-bound form in eternity brings no loss of meaning. Rather does the little finger know itself a member of the hand" [*Letters*, I:

18. *Timaeus*, 90a-d, tr. Lee. In both his German translations of the *Timaeus*, Jung had marked these lines and, in one volume, had inserted a placemarker at this passage.

343]. Jung too thought—though it happens to have been Yeats who said it (and some twenty years before Jung himself took a serious interest in alchemy)—"that alchemy was the gradual distillation of the contents of the soul, until they were ready to put off the mortal and put on the immortal" [M, 283-4]. It should not dismay us that in this same piece ("Rosa Alchemica") Yeats refers to alchemy as "no merely chemical fantasy, but a philosophy they applied to the world, to the elements and to man himself" (p. 267), while Jung ordinarily thinks of it as a *"projected psychology of the collective unconscious"*[19]; for ψυχη is both the soul (individual and universal), and thus the concern of philosophy, and it is also the psyche of psychology. The aim of either Yeatsian philosophy or Jungian psychology, as also of philosophical alchemy, astrology, and magic, was to fulfill the same injunction that Pythagoras imposed on his followers and that Plato emphasized throughout the dialogues: to so purify the soul through love of wisdom and search for it that individual soul reattains a perfect harmony with divine Soul and thus becomes immortal. Yeats's philosophy, then, is in the end the same flower as Jung's psychology, and both have their roots deep in the philosophical psychology and the psychological philosophy of the Platonic system, a rhizome formed from the elements of Plato's predecessors and which, moreover, between the fourth century BC and the twentieth century AD, nourished a long succession of other, but similar, individual esoteric blossoms.

19. Printed as a preface to *Alchemy and the Occult* (Yale University Library, 1968), I: vii; italics are Jung's.

Yeats as Adept and Artist:
The Speckled Bird, The Secret Rose,
and
The Wind among the Reeds

William H. O'Donnell

Today, most readers are willing to admit the existence of Yeats's interest in ritual magic, even though they only vaguely understand the implications of that admission. This necessary first step is conveniently exemplified in Curtis Bradford's recounting of a conversation he had with Mrs. Yeats in 1954: "I said next that my work [on Yeats's manuscripts] had forced me to discard as untenable the widely accepted notion that Yeats's esoteric interests were, so to speak, the price we had to pay for his poetry; that though I could not yet define the relationship between the poetry and the esoteric studies, I was now convinced that the two were utterly involved together and could not be separated." Mrs. Yeats nodded in agreement.[1]

The bare chronology of Yeats's esoteric activities is readily available and demonstrates the persistence of his interests, but the significance of those events is much less accessible. For example, it does us little good to know that Yeats joined the Golden Dawn in 1890 if we do not know what it meant to be a member of that Order. Our difficulties become more evident if we pay heed to Kathleen Raine's knowledgeable opinion that we, the uninitiated, may never be able to comprehend the Golden Dawn. She cautions us that "the kind of knowledge to which members of that Order aspired cannot in its nature be understood in academic terms.

1. Curtis B. Bradford, "George Yeats: Poet's Wife", *Sewanee Review*, 77 (1969): 403.

The merely academic study of magical symbolism may be likened to the analysis of musical scores by a student who does not know that the documents he meticulously annotates are merely indications for the evocation of music from instruments of whose very existence he is ignorant."[2] Certainly it requires considerable imaginative effort for an academic (or even a non-academic) to recognize that the seemingly interminable rituals, the often dreary texts full of pentacles, some of which were to be drawn with bat's blood,[3] and all the other magical paraphernalia are tools for gaining the breath-taking excitement that comes with even a momentary glimpse into a supernal world of spirits who possess incredible powers and wisdom. Yeats not only believed that he had been given several such glimpses, but that it was possible for a mortal to become one of those supernal creatures; most readers will not share his convictions.

Quite apart from those imaginative difficulties, any attempt at comprehending the role of magic in Yeats's art and life is confronted by some severe methodological problems. The Theosophical Society and the Golden Dawn were very elaborate, eclectic systems which drew on a huge variety of sources and which were never reducible to simple summaries of purpose. In the Golden Dawn's Neophyte initiation, the candidate was asked, "Why seekest thou admission to our Order?" That, of course, is precisely the question to which we would like to have Yeats's response. The Golden Dawn's ritual answer, while far too vague to be of much help to us, was perhaps as specific as so inclusive a system could support: "My soul wanders in Darkness and seeks the Light of Hidden Knowledge, and I believe that in this Order Knowledge of that Light may be obtained."[4]

If we restrict our study to the occult lore which Yeats chose to incorporate in his art, we have a much smaller and more manageable body of evidence. But exegesis of those selected details, although often essential for clarifying the local implication of particular works, offers surprisingly little help in understanding the

2. Kathleen Raine, "Yeats, the Tarot, and the Golden Dawn", *Sewanee Review*, 77 (1969): 412.

3. S. L. MacGregor Mathers, trans., *The Greater Key of Solomon*, 2nd ed. (Chicago: DeLaurence, Scott, 1917), p. 54; first published 1889.

4. Israel Regardie, *The Golden Dawn*, 4th ed. (River Falls, Wisc.: Hazel Hills, 1971), II: 21.

general issues. In comparison with the vast array of symbols that Yeats encountered in occult texts and rituals, he made public use of very few, and many of those he did use are confined to incidental details that are either self-explanatory or easily accessible in non-occult traditions. The process of selection was so random that the individual items cannot be combined into a significant, comprehensible aggregate.

In seeking to understand occultism and its specific impact on Yeats, I have found it useful to focus on some common denominators which appear in most occult systems, especially belief in the possibility of a mortal transforming himself into a magus. Solomon the Mage, Simon Magus, Christian Rosencreuz, Comte de Saint-Germain, and the title character of Bulwer-Lytton's novel *Zanoni* are some of the many models available for Yeats's Michael Robartes of "Rosa Alchemica" (1896), a man who has gained access to immortal realms while still a mortal. Both Madame Blavatsky and MacGregor Mathers believed in the existence of magi and claimed to have been personally instructed by "masters" or magi; Mathers announced to his followers in 1896: "For my part I believe them to be human and living upon this earth; but possessing terrible super-human powers."[5] This belief that mortals could be turned into magi was the central organizing principle for the Golden Dawn's ritual initiations, which chart the progression from Neophyte, through four ranks of the Outer Order, to the Inner Order with its three "Adeptus" grades. Beyond this lay the mysterious Third Order, consisting of Magister Templi, Magus, and Ipsissimus. Yeats's ambition to reach the higher levels of the Adeptship is implicit in his long membership in the Golden Dawn and can be explicitly supported by his statement in the autobiography's first draft that, during the early 1890s, he "always cherished the secret hope of some mysterious initiation".[6] The attraction of becoming a magus was so powerful that Yeats did not allow himself to be dissuaded by the possibility, or even probability, that the three highest degrees were beyond the reach of mortals. He told his fellow members of the Golden Dawn in 1901: "It matters nothing whether the Degrees above us are in the body or out of the body, for none the

5. Quoted in Ellic Howe, *The Magicians of the Golden Dawn* (London: Routledge, 1972), p. 129.
6. *Memoirs*, ed. Denis Donoghue (London: Macmillan, 1972), p. 36.

less we must tread this path and open this gate, and seek this light."[7]

This acknowledgement that supreme Adeptship is antithetical to material existence can be seen as the pivotal issue in Yeats's debate with himself about whether to "tread this path" to Adeptship. Antimaterialism is a fundamental tenet in all the occult systems Yeats knew: one aim of Madame Blavatsky's Theosophical Society was "to oppose the materialism of science";[8] in Gnostic redemption the soul is freed from the devils of material existence; and, according to tradition, the alchemical transmutation of base metals into gold can only be accomplished when the alchemist's soul has been similarly purified of material or earthly dross. Yeats, who often voiced his dislike of the materialistic modern world of science, commerce, and tea-tables, could enthusiastically support the Golden Dawn's instruction to "QUIT THE MATERIAL AND SEEK THE SPIRITUAL".[9] The proffered rewards were unquestionably magnificent. Yeats says in a Golden Dawn pamphlet of 1901: "We receive power from those who are above us by permitting the Lightning of the Supreme to descend through our souls and our bodies. The power is forever seeking the world, and it comes to a soul and consumes its mortality." To become an agent of the supernal world and have one's mortality consumed is a great spiritual victory, but the completion of that spiritual triumph requires physical death, as Yeats hints later in the same pamphlet: "When [a mortal] goes his way to supreme Adeptship, he will go absolutely alone, for men attain to the supreme wisdom in a loneliness that is like the loneliness of death."[10] A person who loves material life might decide that death is too high a price to pay even for immortality and supernal wisdom. Yeats found it to be a difficult decision.

His magical ambitions were also inhibited by the sometimes painfully apparent shortcomings of his fellow occultists. Maud Gonne, who resigned from the Golden Dawn after quickly advancing through four initiations, recalls being "oppressed by the drab appearance and mediocrity of my fellow-mystics," who were, she continues, "the very essence of British middle-class dullness. They looked so incongruous in their cloaks and badges at initiation cere-

7. *Is the Order of R. R. & A. C. to remain a Magical Order?* (Privately printed, 1901), pp. 7-8.
8. Quoted in C. J. Ryan, *Madame Blavatsky and the Theosophical Movement* (Point Loma, Calif.: Theosophical Press, 1937), p. 61.
9. Regardie, *Golden Dawn*, II: 73.
10. *Is the Order of R. R. & A. C. to remain a Magical Order?*, pp. 26-7.

monies."[11] The eccentricities of contemporary occultists, their petty jealousies and willingness to compromise idealistic goals with hastily conceived and occasionally shoddy means, are satirized in Yeats's unfinished autobiographical novel, *The Speckled Bird*, on which he worked from 1896 until circa 1902.

The novel's hero is further disappointed with London occultists because of the irreconcilable rift between his own artistic taste and their inability to recognize, let alone esteem, beauty. In a preliminary draft of the novel, a character modeled on MacGregor Mathers discards all of the Yeats-figure's careful plans for beautiful decorations and then announces scornfully, "I have come to recognize that you are not a magician, but some kind of an artist, and that the *summum bonum* itself, the potable gold of our masters, were less to you than some charm of colour, or some charm of words." [National Library of Ireland microfilm P6072, frames 287 left half and 287 right half, hereafter abbreviated FR 287L/R] This was telling criticism. Despite a continuing admiration of Adeptship, Yeats was always an artist and, as such, could not renounce the physical universe which provides the materials for communicable artistic expression. He even went so far as to regret that Blake and Shelley, two of his favourite poets, had not made fuller use of a recognizable physical world.

Yeats's long debate over the contradictory demands of art and Adeptship provides an important perspective for interpreting *The Speckled Bird*, several stories of *The Secret Rose* (1897), and poems of *The Wind among the Reeds* (1899), as well as some of his later work. If it is necessary to remind ourselves of the complexity of his reactions to the issues in his debate and that there is never a straightforward relation between actual events or attitudes and their fictional representation in art, we need only turn to *The Speckled Bird*. The novel chronicles the autobiographical hero's unsuccessful efforts to establish a mystical brotherhood which would combine artistic idealism with ritual magic. The hero's conflicting loyalties to art and Adeptship are apparent when he describes his plans:

> I do not hope very much at first, but I am certain that a delight in making the rites of the myths beautiful with designs and tapestries and perhaps with musical songs for harps and zythers, and the

11. Maud Gonne MacBride, *A Servant of the Queen: Reminiscences*, 2nd ed. (Dublin: Golden Eagle Books, 1950), pp. 247-8.

desire to express the innumerable mystical or passionate stories and images that come to us in trances and dreams, will soon begin to make poems and pictures, and so soon as anybody with a little genius comes among us, trances and dreams will give him a strange intensity. Men will see in his pictures or in his poems, besides the charm that his genius gives him, the fanaticism of the saints or of those that fling themselves upon spears. It will be as though one was to live in Eden with his eyes burning with the fanaticism of the desert. Gradually the myths will begin to live again everywhere ... and religion will have made its peace with the arts and with all the passions that seek beauty. All the powers of the world shall have become one power, and all the classes shall have one common impulse again, so that when the wise thinker or the great artist sits by the roadside among the country people, he shall be understood as Homer was understood. [FR 244 L/R]

The eventual failure of this project is implicit even in the version of the novel which was written in the summer of 1900, while Yeats was still actively pursuing his real-life ambition of founding an order of Celtic mysteries. Yeats-the-artist is thus using the novel to lament, if not mock, the contemporaneous activity of Yeats-the-Adept, as described in the first draft of his autobiography:

I ... had long been dreaming of making it [i.e., Castle Rock in Lough Key, which he saw in 1896] an Irish Eleusis or Samothrace. An obsession more constant than anything but my love itself was the need of mystical rites—a ritual system of evocation and mediation—to reunite the perception of the spirit, of the divine, with natural beauty. . . . I meant to initiate young men and women in this worship, which would unite the radical truths of Christianity to those of a more ancient world. . . . I wished by my writings and those of the school I hoped to found to have a secret symbolical relation to these mysteries, for in that way, I thought, there will be a great richness, a greater claim upon the love of the soul, doctrine without exhortation and rhetoric. Should not religion hide within the work of art as God is within His world?[12]

Soon after the turn of the century, his work shows a strong endorsement of physicality and a concomitant recognition of the artistic limits of spirituality, but he remained strongly attracted to the wisdom and power of Adeptship. By 1906 he had firmly established what was to remain his permanent "solution" to the problem of having to choose between the mutually exclusive requirements of

12. *Memoirs,* pp. 123-4.

art and Adeptship. Instead of attempting to impose a false synthesis, he accepted the validity both of art and of Adeptship. His decision, later given philosophical respectability by his discovery of Kant's antinomies, was simply that no decision was possible, that he had no choice but to recognize the merits of materialistic art and anti-materialistic Adeptship.

The remainder of this essay, which will trace the course of the art-versus-Adeptship debate and its impact on Yeats's work, might prudently be prefaced by a renewed appeal for the reader to admire Adeptship. If we permit ourselves to recognize its extraordinary attractions, or at least are willing to admire a safely fictional magus such as Zanoni, who "had powers beyond the race of worldly sages",[13] we will be able to participate imaginatively in Yeats's painful recognition of the contradictions between spiritual magus and material artist. The extreme emphasis placed on Adeptship in this essay can be justified by noting that although we all presumably stand in awe of artistic masterwork, few of us aspire to Adeptship. If the Adept's side of the argument is left tacit, then the debate which Yeats felt so strongly will lose much of its force, and the reader will find himself either skipping some of Yeats's serious works altogether or superficially condemning them as mere examples of an otherwise talented poet somehow gone philosophically "wrong".

In the early 1890s Yeats's success with the Golden Dawn's methods of evocation and his continuing progress to higher ranks allowed him to begin regarding himself as at least a partial Adept. In 1889 he had stated a hope that some day an occultist might be able to explain the cause of peasant visions of fairies, and in 1892 he himself provided those occult explanations in the *Irish Theosophist*, asserting that he was "trained in the correspondence of sensuous form and supersensuous meaning".[14] Adeptship's emerging influence and the accompanying decrease in his artistic loyalty to the material world may be seen by comparing the famous "small cabin ... of clay and wattles made" from "The Lake Isle of Innisfree", published in 1890, with a poem written and published in 1898, "He hears the Cry of the Sedge", in which the familiar lake-

---

13. Edward Bulwer-Lytton, *Zanoni* (London: Saunder & Otley, 1842), 1: 174.
14. "Irish Fairies, Ghosts, Witches, etc." (1889) and "Invoking the Irish Fairies" (1892), rpt. *Uncollected Prose by W. B. Yeats*, ed. John P. Frayne (New York: Columbia University Press, 1970), 1: 130-1, 247.

edge setting seems "desolate" because the speaker realizes that his desire cannot be fulfilled until after the material world ends. It is hardly coincidental that this latter poem uses Golden Dawn paraphernalia in an apocalyptic image [VP, 117, 165].[15]

In 1893, just before his advancement to the Golden Dawn's prestigious Inner Order, Yeats published "The Heart of Spring", a short story which gives a uniquely straightforward account of an Adept's triumph over mortality. The hero is a nearly fleshless old man dressed, appropriately enough for an anti-materialist, in threadbare clothes. His "search for the Great Secret" took him to a Spanish monastery where, in accordance with the occult tradition of discovering secret books of wisdom, he found a Hebrew manuscript containing a magical procedure that will enable him to "become like the Immortal Powers themselves". After a lifetime of fasting and magical labours, he metamorphoses himself into an immortal, joining "the brave and the beautiful" in "the eternal kingdom" of his youth [M, 173-4].

This fictional celebration of the search for Adeptship was reprinted in *The Secret Rose* (1897), a collection of seventeen stories which are extravagantly described in a preface as having "but one subject, the war of spiritual with natural order".[16] Many of the stories do contribute to a debate about the merits of Adeptship, but the range of subjects covered in the volume is far too broad to permit calling *The Secret Rose* a grimoire or magician's manual. Nonetheless, it might qualify as a talisman or physical symbol of magical wisdom because its ornately decorated covers are nearly identical with those of a magical order's textbook described in "Rosa Alchemica" (1896), one of the stories included in the collection. The cover of the "Rosa Alchemica" magical order's book has, "in very delicate colours, and in gold, the Alchemical Rose with many spears thrusting against it, but in vain, as shown by the shattered points of those nearest to the petals" [M, 283]. On the back cover of the 1897 London edition of *The Secret Rose*, in gold

---

15. "And hands hurl in the deep/The banners of East and West." (ll. 6-7) Interestingly enough, this apocalyptic prophecy may have been fulfilled in 1967, when some Golden Dawn materials, including the banners of East and West, were found on a Sussex beach. (Francis King, *Ritual Magic in England: 1887 to the Present Day* [London: Spearman, 1970], photograph facing p. 160.)

16. "Preface", *The Secret Rose* (London: Lawrence & Bullen, 1897), p. vii.

stamping, is an opened rose mounted on a cross and surrounded by broken spears which have vainly attempted to attack it. This explicit parallel can be reinforced by observing that the front cover of *The Secret Rose*, which shows two lovers kissing in a rose tree that is rooted in an armed knight's skeleton, matches the front cover of the "Rosa Alchemica" book as described in a cancelled portion of the page proofs for *The Secret Rose*: ". . . a book bound in velum, and having a rose-tree growing from an armed anatomy, and inclosing the faces of two lovers painted upon the one side, to symbolize certainly the coming of beauty out of corruption, and probably much else."[17] And these art nouveau decorations are far from meaningless. The broken spears which fruitlessly attack the rose-cross on the back cover are identical with the front cover's disused spear, which rests alongside the "armed anatomy", and with Lug's blood-thirsty spear, quieted by having its point immersed in a potion of pounded poppy leaves, as illustrated on the book's spine. In all three cases, the spear, a representative of worldly deeds, has been rendered ineffective. This triumph for the spiritual world is further supported by the front cover's man and woman kissing in a rose tree that grows from a skeleton. Here, the alchemical goal of distilling spiritual perfection from the corrupt dross of the material world is incorporate with the Cabalistic notion of progressing upwards in the Tree of Life. As Richard Ellmann has noted, the three highest and superhuman sephiroth are represented by the three roses at the top of the tree, above the kissing lovers.[18] And as MacGregor Mathers tells us in a footnote to his *Kabbalah Unveiled*, the lovers' kiss can symbolize "the union of the soul with the substance from which it emanated".[19]

Probably Yeats's best-known declaration of at least a partial allegiance to Adeptship is "To Ireland in the Coming Times". This poetic apologia of 1892, even though seeking to defend his position as an Irish national writer, proclaims that his work includes wisdom gleaned from mystical vision:

17. Quoted in Curtis B. Bradford, *Yeats at Work* (Carbondale: Southern Illinois University Press, 1965), p. 324. Warwick Gould has pointed out to me that Bradford has transcribed incorrectly two words in this passage, and that "vellum" and "enclosing" are in the original.
18. Richard Ellmann, *The Identity of Yeats*, 2nd ed. (London: Faber, 1964), p. 65.
19. MacGregor Mathers, *The Kabbalah Unveiled* (1887; rpt. London: Routledge, 1968), p. 253.

> Nor may I less be counted one
> With Davis, Mangan, Ferguson,
> Because to him who ponders well
> My rhymes more than their rhyming tell
> Of the dim visions old and deep,
> That God gives unto man in sleep.
> For round about my table go
> The magical powers to and fro.   [VP, 138; 1892 version]

There is ample evidence that he is not just referring to Irish fairy lore. The Golden Dawn's evocation techniques substantially increased his visionary powers and he did not hesitate to make artistic use of these visions. The idea for "The Cap and Bells" (1894), a poem which by Yeats's own admission meant a great deal to him, came in a "beautiful and coherent" vision that gave "the sense of illumination and exultation that one gets from visions" [VP, 808]. He told a fellow occultist that the *Secret Rose* stories were not "mere phastasies but the signatures ... of things invisible and ideas".[20] And one of those stories, "Out of the Rose" (1893), could have had its origins in a vision he had circa 1890: "It arose in three minds ... without confusion, and without labor ... and more swiftly than any pen could have written it out. It may be, as Blake said of one of his poems, that the author was in eternity. In coming years I was to see and hear of many such visions" [E&I, 35-6]. The narrator of "Rosa Alchemica" is profoundly affected by brief access to "the certainty of vision" in which he glimpses "that Death which is Beauty herself" and the "Loneliness which all the multitudes desire without ceasing" [M, 277]. The autobiographical hero of *The Speckled Bird* has several visions and, in some early drafts of the novel, so does his father.

Our interest in "To Ireland in the Coming Times" goes beyond its important mention of visionary access to "dim wisdom old and deep". In the midst of the third stanza's description of the coveted supernal goal, we are told that material existence is too brief to be important: "From our birthday, until we die,/Is but the winking of an eye." Forgael says much the same thing in an early draft of *The Shadowy Waters:* "The life of man is ... a/Mere days flight from his own [?]/Spirit." He goes on to apply this not only to man, but to all material things and even the gods themselves.[21] This

20. 1895 letter to Olivia Shakespear, *The Letters of W. B. Yeats*, ed. Allan Wade (London: Macmillan, 1954), p. 255.
21. *Druid Craft*, ed. Michael J. Sidnell, George P. Mayhew, David R. Clark (Amherst: University of Massachusetts Press, 1971), p. 70.

denial of the importance of material existence is an occult common-place which figures prominently in much of Yeats's work during the late 1890s. The title of a rigorously anti-materialistic short story, "Where There is Nothing, There is God" (1896), uses the Ptolemaic cosmology of astrologers to communicate a truth accepted by all Adepts.[22] In "The Valley of the Black Pig", also published in 1896, a "dream-awakened" visionary who is "weary of the world's empires" announces that the material world is transitory and that the supernal world is all that finally matters [VP, 161]. An Adept would agree with Paul Ruttledge in the play *Where There is Nothing* (1902) that death is to be welcomed as "the last adventure, the first perfect joy" [VPL, 1160], that "we must get rid of everything that is not measureless eternal life" [VPL, 1139], and that fasting is a legitimate way to demonstrate one's scorn of material life. Like the old knight in "Out of the Rose" (1893), Paul Ruttledge had to be watched at "meal times for fear he should starve himself [VPL, 1127]. The autobiographical hero of *The Speckled Bird* fasts to induce visions, one time extending the fast for more than ten days until he is awarded a spectacular vision, only to faint from hunger a few hours later. His strong preference for the spiritual world is exhibited with startling clarity, elsewhere in the novel, when he says that the fabled Elixir of Life holds little appeal for him because he "would not like to go on living in the world" [FR209R].

The willingness of an Adept to regard death as "the beginning of wisdom and power and beauty" [M, 115] and therefore to scorn any prolongation of his material existence emphasizes the complete incompatibility of the supernal world with the material world. The feathered king in "Wisdom" (1895) makes this very clear: "[Worldly] Law was made by man for the welfare of man, but wisdom the gods have made, and no man shall live by its light, for it ... follow[s] a way that is deadly to mortal things" [M, 170]. Thus, if we take a supernal viewpoint, mortal actions are inconsequential. On the other hand, supernal creatures are incapable of effective physical action within the material world. Finivaragh, an immortal king of the fairies, can "understand many things that even

22. The story explains: " 'There are nine crystalline spheres, and on the first the moon is fastened ... on the eighth are fastened the fixed stars; but the ninth sphere is a sphere of the substance on which the breath of God moved in the beginning.' 'What is beyond that sphere?' said the child. 'There is nothing beyond that; there is God' " (*The Sketch*, 21 October 1896, p. 548).

the archangels do not understand", but he is unable to overcome the physical strength of a mortal.[23] Yeats must have been keenly aware of the limitations which dreamy supernal wisdom could impose on mortal action. The hero of "Out of the Rose", a story published in 1893, is a fourteenth-century knight who, by combining physical prowess with spiritual idealism, represents one of Yeats's fondest ambitions: "He seemed to be that strange being who appears but seldom in the world, and, when he does, binds the hearts of men with his look of mystery—doer and dreamer in one."[24] But just as in "The Tables of the Law", *The Speckled Bird*, and *The Unicorn from the Stars*, every attempt to implement spiritual idealism in a material world must fail dismally. The knight is on a valid spiritual quest, but the world has already become so materialistic and alien to spiritual ideals that his purposeful courage earns him Quixotic humiliation. The knight's address to the Divine Rose of Intellectual Flame is interrupted by the squealing of two stolen pigs. Later, when he lies dying of wounds incurred in a battle fought to recover the pigs, he is deserted by everyone except an uncomprehending idiot. Then, at a cock's crow, the idiot runs away and leaves the corpse unburied. Because Yeats thought that materialism was more pervasive in the modern world than in the fourteenth-century setting of this story, any modern attempt to duplicate the knight's active spiritual idealism would likely be even more ludicrous than the knight's. Thus, this story, in addition to being a complaint against the overly materialistic condition of the world, stands as a powerful argument against embarking on a spiritual quest.

Even had Yeats been willing to content himself with "dreams" and to abandon all allegiance to the material world, he would not have been free of doubts. It still would have been necessary to assure himself that the particular occult path he chose to follow would actually lead to the supreme Adeptship. Presumably even the most ridiculous of the occult movements which he satirized so amusingly in *The Speckled Bird* had at least a few devoted disciples. How could Yeats be absolutely certain that the Golden Dawn's Cabalism was a better choice than building a private chapel with an altar to Shelley, or investigating the Odic light, or joining a Sweden-borgian utopian community in America, or even joining an anti-

23. "The Cradles of Gold," *The Senate*, 3 (1896): 408.
24. *The National Observer*, 27 May 1893, p. 41.

Swedenborgian utopian community in America? The novel's autobiographical hero is fully aware that his occult labours may prove fruitless. He says of himself: "I am going on this way that must either be uttermost wisdom or uttermost foolishness" [FR2 19R]. Similarly, when the hero is reluctant to accept material alchemy as a literal fact rather than a spiritual metaphor, the Mathers-figure rebukes him: "To say that is to insult the traditions of our knowledge. . . . It is to deny the truth for fear of ridicule." The Yeats-figure replies: "You are perhaps right. I am often afraid I am too timid, too much afraid of ridicule. I often envy you your perfect faith. It gives you great strength. You are not afraid to face the whole world" [FR 214 L/R]. The phrases "perfect faith" and "great strength" are attractive, but the novel makes it clear that in this instance they are near relations of "blindness" and "egomania". The hero's lingering doubts are not helped by a visit to the country home of a highly respected occultist, in whose herb garden "three generations of mystics of the Hermetic school had discussed their visions". This supposedly venerable figure is discovered "lying on his back and quite naked" inside "a long box slightly tipped on one end with a lid of orange glass". The old man, whose bizarre situation is, as George M. Harper points out, a parody of the Christian Rosencreuz myth used in the Golden Dawn's Adeptus Minor initiation, explains himself with comic seriousness: "I am getting old, very old, and the orange light does me a world of good. I always like a sun-bath; when I am ill I vary the colours of the glass according to the illness, but orange is the only colour that increases the vitality" [FR 236 L/R].

Yeats's enthusiasm for visions and Adeptship had to confront not only these doubts about particular occult movements, but also his self-admitted "dread of all loss of consciousness", which dated from his very first seance.[25] Given all this, it is hardly surprising that even a poem written directly out of his role as Adept-manqué, "To his Heart, bidding it have no Fear" (1896), should acknowledge the liabilities as well as the merits of magic. Probably even the most stalwart candidates for Adeptship are susceptible to an occasional moment of doubt, but it would be highly unlikely that they would

25. See the records of this first seance, circa 1886, in *The Autobiography of William Butler Yeats* (New York: Collier Books, 1967), pp. 69-70, and of an encounter in 1892 or 1893 with "a magician of an exceedingly medieval sort", quoted in Bradford, *Yeats at Work*, pp. 862-4.

want to call public attention to this faltering by writing a poem
about it unless that poem, unlike Yeats's, left no question about
eventually having quieted the trembling heart. The speaker of
"To his Heart, bidding it have no Fear" desires to become an
immortal Adept and has acquired at least some of the doctrinal
wisdom necessary for attaining that goal. But the poem does not
reveal whether the speaker accepts the "wisdom out of the old
days" and becomes an Adept or if he denies this wisdom and thus
deserves to be covered and hid. The inference is possible that he is
afraid to implement it [vp, 158].[26] Despite the continuing attractions of Adeptship, Yeats remained fully capable of writing such
completely non-occult poems as "The Lover speaks to the Hearers
of his Songs in Coming Days" (1895), which is a Hanrahan poem
which could easily win the imprimatur of an Irish bishop or Dante,
and "The Lover pleads with his Friend for Old Friends" (1897).
Of the three songs published in 1898 under the collective title
"Aodh to Dectora/Three Songs", we have already seen one of
them, "He hears the Cry of the Sedge", to be a doctrinaire Adept's
version of "The Lake Isle of Innisfree". But one of the poems is
anti-occult. In "He thinks of those who have Spoken Evil of his
Beloved", the speaker is very proud of his ability to write a poem
that will enjoy the permanence of art, and he offers this to a mortal
woman as consolation from the material world's attacks. An Adept
would not heed the material world's opinion, much less invoke
artistic immortality in lieu of spiritual immortality.

Here then was a poet who sought Adeptship, but refused to abandon poetry. And because of his opinion that the spiritual loyalties
of an Adept conflicted with a poet's necessary ties to the material
world, the prospect of discovering a tertium quid or synthesis between art and Adeptship became enormously attractive to Yeats.
His long search was already under way in 1892 with "To the Rose
upon the Rood of Time". The poet-speaker asks the mystical Rose
to come near him, not because he wants to become part of the
supernal world or, like Forgael in The Shadowy Waters, fall into
a rapturous swoon in the presence of overpowering mystical wisdom, but rather so that he can discover, within the material world,
instances of eternal beauty: "In all poor foolish things that live a

26. The poem's association of the three highest elements (fire, air, and water)
    with the "lonely, proud, winged multitude" (1896 version) adequately
    differentiates that multitude from earthly mortals.

day,/Eternal beauty wandering on her way." He announces that he is a poet and that he does not wish to renounce the materialistic world, despite all its shortcomings:

> Come near, come near, come near—Ah, leave me still
> A little space. . . .
> Lest I no more hear common things . . .
> . . . .
> And Heavy mortal hopes that toil and pass;
> But seek alone to hear the strange things said
> By God to the bright hearts of those long dead,
> And learn to chaunt a tongue men do not know.   [VP, 101][27]

The persistence of his search for a *tertium quid* between Adept and artist can be inferred from the long printing history of "The Binding of the Hair", one of his weakest stories. Its hero, Aodh, is capable of being, according to his whim, either a courageous warrior or a "dream-distraught" lover with Adept-like powers that enable him to sing a love song to a beautiful young queen after he has been decapitated. This supernatural feat does not, however, win union for Aodh with his completely mortal queen. Yeats was aware of the story's lack of artistic merit, and his remark in 1896 about "a wretched story which has in the end refused to achieve itself" almost certainly refers to "The Binding of the Hair".[28] Nonetheless, he allowed it to appear in the premier issue of *The Savoy* and, after extensive verbal revision, made it the lead story in *The Secret Rose* (1897). Even after 1908, when the story was dropped from his canon, Aodh's song from the story continued to appear, without substantial revision, in collections of his poetry. Further testimony to the story's psychological attraction for Yeats is supplied by his re-use of the story's plot in 1933 and 1934 for *The King of the Great Clock Tower* and *A Full Moon in March*.

Aodh is but one of a large cast of Yeatsian characters who cannot find a *tertium quid*. "The Tables of the Law" (1896) dramatizes another unsuccessful attempt at compromise, this time with a historical precedent. Aherne tries to duplicate Joachim de Flora's twelfth-century combination of an orthodox loyalty to the Catholic

---

27. Similarly, an essay of 1895, "The Moods", tells artists to "discover immortal moods in mortal desires, and undecaying hope in our trivial ambitions, [and] a divine love in sexual passion" [E&I, 195].
28. *Letters*, p. 258.

Church and a heretical insistence on his freedom to break any law which might interfere with a life of contemplation directed towards spiritual ecstasy. Aherne's desire to remain within the jurisdiction of Christian salvation proves inimical to Adeptship. His lack of an Adept's necessarily total renunciation of the ordinary world is signalled by the story's description of him as a doer and dreamer; success in the spiritual quest requires abdication of all desire to "do": "He had the nature, which is half alchemist, half soldier of fortune, and must needs turn action into dreaming, and dreaming into action."[29] Aherne's attempts at implementing his spiritual ideals in the service of "the beautiful arts" [M, 294] are as unsuccessful as the quite similar plans for a mystical brotherhood in *The Speckled Bird* and Yeats's real-life scheme for an order of Celtic mysteries. In "The Tables of the Law", both Aherne and the narrator profess a hatred of materialism, but neither of them is willing to extend that hatred to the material world's official religion, Christianity.

One of the most significant barriers to establishing a harmonious compromise between Adept and artist was sexual lust. Yeats's fictional candidates for Adeptship are troubled by a habit of seeing mortal and spiritual beauty coexistent in the person of a beloved woman. When, as is invariably the case, they attempt to satisfy physical desire simultaneously with an ascetic pursuit of the symbolical aspects of the woman's beauty, the result is failure on both levels. The woman in "He remembers Forgotten Beauty" (1896) exactly parallels *The Speckled Bird*'s heroine, whom the hero erroneously considers to be unusually sensitive to ideal beauty and well-suited for Adeptship and whom he regards as a modern representative of the mythic past to which he has visionary access. The poem makes this multiple perspective explicit:

> When my arms wrap you round I press
> My heart upon the loveliness
> That has long faded from the world;
> ....
> And when you sigh from kiss to kiss
> I hear white Beauty sighing, too.   [VP, 155-6]

The speaker is obviously dissatisfied with the present condition of the material world, and the poem's final section demonstrates positive awareness of the supernal world, even though such harsh

29. *The Savoy*, November 1896, p. 79.

terms as "iron knees" and "lonely" preclude any more than a hesitant endorsement of the apocalypse's fiery destruction of the material world. He values his beloved's physical beauty for its own sake and for its inescapable analogy with supernal beauty, but because he is incapable of spiritualizing away his lust he addresses this love poem to the mortal woman rather than to ideal Beauty.

Red Hanrahan, who in the short stories has contact with both mortal and immortal women, expresses his preference for physicality far more clearly than does the speaker of "He remembers Forgotten Beauty", perhaps offering a partial explanation for the change of that poem's titular speaker in 1899 to Michael Robartes from O'Sullivan Rua, the Red Hanrahan precursor. Red Hanrahan uses magical sigils from a secret book by Cornelius Agrippa to evoke supernal spirits in the earliest of his stories, "The Devil's Book" (1892),[30] and he attains union with an immortal woman after his earthly death in "The Death of Hanrahan" (1896; revised 1905). But despite all this, he is no Adept. In "The Twisting of the Rope" (1892) he proclaims himself a poet descended from Oisin, whose allegiance to the material world was so immense that his "heart knew unappeased three hundred years of daemonic love". When courting a young maiden, Hanrahan outrages the traditional asceticism of Adepts by describing immortality as "one long sweet dance of love"; the innocent girl's reply speaks volumes: "They say you have been very wicked."[31] Hanrahan wants to find some way of escaping mortality, but only if he can bring along a wench. Hanrahan's lust is so extravagant that it excludes him from Adeptship and even from being a viable tertium quid. In "The Death of Hanrahan" he does attain eternal union with a perpetually beautiful woman, a reward which corresponds with that of an Adept, assuming, of course, that the woman is sufficiently spiritual. But this reward comes without his ever making a clear choice between material and spiritual values, and thus the story begs the question upon which any tertium quid must centre.

Hanrahan is no more an Adept than Forgael, who in the 1911 version of *The Shadowy Waters* hopes to gain access to the spiritual world without sacrificing his material existence. Specifically, he

---

30. In 1903 this story was purified, with Lady Gregory's assistance, into a traditional fairy "touch" story and was retitled "Red Hanrahan".
31. *The National Observer*, 24 December 1892, p. 132; the first passage was deleted in the 1905 version.

refuses to accept death: "I only of all living men shall find it" [VPL, 322]. Forgael, like Yeats, vacillates between transitory visionary faith and lingering doubts, between allegiance to spiritual ecstasy and to physical beauty. When Aibric proposes that Forgael decide either to seek bliss "in the habitable world,/Or leap into that sea and end a journey/That has no other end" than death, Forgael's reply is an important summation of Yeats's position during the 1890s:

> I cannot answer.
> I can see nothing plain; all's mystery.
> Yet sometimes there's a torch inside my head
> That makes all clear, but when the light is gone
> I have but images, analogies,
> . . . .
> Old stories about mystic marriages,
> Impossible truths? But when the torch is lit
> All that is impossible is certain,
> I plunge in the abyss.   [VPL, 323]

In a late-1890s typescript of the play, Forgael the warrior tells the beautiful Dectora about his supposedly spiritual aspirations, but he uses an extraordinarily voracious image that is obviously anti-thetical to Adeptship: "My dreams would drink your beauty as wolf-hounds/Hot with the chase, drink up a wayside pool."[32]

This self-defeating mixture of physical desire and spiritual ambition provides one of the most important motifs in Yeats's work during the 1890s. Yeats, who many years later spoke of his youthful asceticism having to coexist with "an adoration of physical beauty that made it meaningless",[33] could have found a striking parallel between his own doubts over Adeptship and Dante's famous hesitation at the uppermost ring of purgatory, especially as depicted in Blake's water-colour illustrations for that twenty-seventh canto of the *Purgatorio*.[34] Dante shrinks back in terror

32. *Druid Craft*, p. 217.
33. "Preface", *Letters to the New Island*, ed. Horace Reynolds (Cambridge, Mass.: Harvard University Press, 1934), p. xii.
34. This scene is the subject of illustrations numbers 84 and 85. The former, to which Yeats refers in a letter of 1927, is a preliminary study for the latter. Yeats saw these then unpublished water-colours at the Linnell house when preparing the Blake edition. He praises the series in a three-part essay, "William Blake and his Illustrations to the *Divine Comedy*," *The Savoy*, July, August, September 1896, pp. 41-57, 25-41, 31-36, revised and rpt. in *Essays and Introductions*, pp. 116-45. The eight reproductions

from entering the flames which will purge him of lust. Only after Virgil tells him that Beatrice is waiting on the other side does Dante enter these final flames. In the illustration, Dante's simultaneously sexual and spiritual motives are reinforced visually by the Blakean addition of four graceful females, clad in nearly transparent robes, who dance within the wall of flame. In a letter to Olivia Shakespear in 1927, Yeats mentions this illustration and observes that "spiritual excitement" and "sexual torture" are "somehow inseparable": "It is the eyes of the Earthly Beatrice—she has not yet put on her divinity—that makes Dante risk the fire 'like a child that is offered an apple'."[35]

Those purgative flames, populated by dancing women and symbolizing the conjunction of "spiritual excitement" and "sexual torture", probably contributed to the mystical dance ritual of "Rosa Alchemica" (1896), in which the story's narrator, unlike Dante, cannot overcome his doubts and flees in terror from the necessary flames of his spiritual initiation. This story, Yeats's best achievement in prose fiction, offers yet another proof of the impossibility of discovering a viable *tertium quid*. The narrator initially attempts to have access to mutually exclusive beliefs, to "everything which has moved men's hearts in any age" [M, 267], but he refuses to commit himself to any of them: "I had gathered about me all gods because I believed in none, and experienced every pleasure because I gave myself to none, but held myself apart, individual, indissoluble, a mirror of polished steel" [M, 268]. He sees visions of "eternal things" and has written a book on alchemy, but he is afraid to follow Michael Robartes' example of absolute dedication to the spiritual world. The narrator tells Robartes: "Your philosophy is charming as a phantasy, but, carried to the point of belief, it is a supreme delusion, and, enforced by mesmeric glamour, a supreme crime. You would sweep me away into an indefinite

which accompany the article are the first published selection from the drawings, except for seven engraved *Inferno* plates. Numbers 84 and 85 were not chosen for the *Savoy*, but number 86, which shows Dante asleep just after having passed through the fires, appears in the August 1896 issue, p. 39. Number 85 was exhibited in the Royal Academy's Winter Exhibition, London, 1893. The entire series is available in Albert S. Roe, *Blake's Illustrations to the Divine Comedy* (Princeton: Princeton University Press, 1953).

35. *Letters*, p. 731.

world which fills me with terror."[36] This attempted retreat into a limbo of noncommittal has already been cut off by Robartes' insistence that everyone must make an exclusive and irrevocable choice between materialism and spiritualism: "I have been with many and many dreamers at the same crossways. You have shut away the world and gathered the gods about you, and if you do not throw yourself at their feet, you will be always full of lassitude, and of wavering purpose, for a man must forget he is miserable in the bustle and noise of the multitude in this world and in time; or seek a mystical union with the multitude who govern this world and time" [M, 273]. Despite lingering doubts, the narrator begins a spiritual initiation, during which supernatural voices command him to enter their fiery dance. Characteristically, he does not make a deliberate decision, but instead is "swept, neither consenting nor refusing, into the midst" [M, 289]. He dances with "an immortal august woman, who ... seemed laden with a wisdom more profound than the darkness that is between star and star" [M, 289-90], but even this emblem of the supernal kingdom's magnificent beauty and wisdom is not enough to convince him to abandon the material world, and he drops away from the initiatory dance. His earlier, Paterian ideal of mirror-like detachment has already been discredited, and now that he has refused to commit himself to the spiritual world, the only remaining alternative is to embrace materialism and its orthodox religion, Christianity. This outcome does not undermine the story's pro-spiritual and anti-Christian bias; orthodox Christianity is represented in the story by a mob of murderous, bigoted peasants. Nonetheless, "Rosa Alchemica", rather than being a paean to Adeptship, is an expression of reluctance to subscribe to an ecstatic spiritual path and an agonized recognition that no compromise is available. The narrator's timidity, so roundly condemned both here and in "The Tables of the Law", is the central issue. Even after ten years in the refuge of orthodoxy, the narrator has still not made a final choice. He wears a crucifix around his neck so that, as he admits, "whenever the indefinite world, which has but half lost its empire over my heart and my intellect ... is about to claim a new mastery, I press the cross to my heart. ... And then the war that wages within me at all other times is still and I am at peace."[37]

36. *The Savoy*, April 1896, p. 61.   37. *Ibid.*, p. 70.

Yeats's attitude towards Adeptship was as complex and mixed in real life as it was in fiction such as "Rosa Alchemica". There was much to disillusion him from ritual magic at the turn of the century. His confidence in the Golden Dawn could hardly have avoided being disturbed by the unpleasantries attending the expulsion of Mathers in 1900 and the ensuing internal disputes; his work on a ritual for the order of Celtic mysteries was proving unsuccessful. In the fictional portrayal of these troubling events, the hero of *The Speckled Bird* becomes increasingly disgusted with contemporary occultists and finally abandons his plan of founding a mystical order. Despite all this, the novel's ending, which was written circa 1902, shows the hero embarking on the traditional Adept's journey to the East in search of mysterious wisdom [FR 300L].[38] Similarly, Yeats's essay "Magic", first published in 1901, makes it impossible to say that he had renounced the spiritual world: "I believe in magic, in what I must call the evocation of the spirits, though I do not know what they are, in the power of creating magical illusions, in the visions of truth in the depths of the mind when the eyes are closed" [E&I, 28]. Fifteen years later, just after passing a Golden Dawn initiation, Yeats mentions "an Order of Christian kabalists" in the first draft of his autobiography: "I am still a member and, though I attend but little, value a ritual full of the symbolism of the Middle Ages and the Renaissance, with many later additions. One passes from degree to degree, and if the wisdom one had once hoped for is still far off there [is] no exhortation to alarm one's dignity, no abstraction to deaden the nerves of the soul."[39]

Those pronouncements, however, are a far cry from an Adept's complete commitment to the spiritual world. Yeats is becoming satisfied with a dual allegiance, in which his primary loyalty to art need not obliterate his attraction to Adeptship. For example, in the

38. Owen Aherne in "The Tables of the Law" and Michael Robartes in *Stories of Michael Robartes* also subscribe to this tradition. Christian Rosencreuz was taught by Arabs. Morien, a twelfth-century Roman alchemist, went on a pilgrimage to Jerusalem and then turned hermit, finally settling in Egypt. Cagliostro spent several years in Egypt as an Adept during the eighteenth century and, according to A. E. Waite's *Lives of the Alchemystical Philosophers* (London: Redway, 1888), an Irish gentleman named Butler acquired the philosopher's stone in Arabia and brought "a large portion of the red powder" back to Ireland (Waite, pp. 53-4, 168, 236).

39. *Memoirs*, pp. 26-7.

Discoveries essays of 1906-1907, where he is speaking very much as an artist, he sees no paradox in marshalling occult imagery into some very striking illustrations of the absolute difference between artist and Adept. In Cabalistic systems of symbolism, such as used by the Golden Dawn, the candidate for supreme Adeptship seeks to rise from Malkuth (Kingdom), the lowest of the ten sephiroth in the Cabalistic Tree of Life, up to Kether (Crown) at the apex. But Yeats's essay "The Tree of Life" says that "we artists" should "ascend out of common interests, the thoughts of the newspapers, of the marketplace, of men of science, but only so far as we can carry the normal, passionate, reasoning self, the personality as a whole. We must find some place upon the Tree of Life . . . set high that the forked branches may keep it safe, yet low enough to be out of the little wind-tossed boughs, the quivering of the twigs" [E&I, 270, 272]. Kether, the supreme goal, is variously symbolized as being located at the still centre of a turning wheel or out beyond the wheel's rim, which is described either as a serpent or rainbow.[40] The Adept's escape from mortal reality can be represented either by a descent into this still centre or by the radial path of an arrow, whose straight flight is antithetical to the circling forms of active life. A *Discoveries* essay entitled "In the Serpent's Mouth" tells us that because saints and, we might add, Adepts devote themselves to spiritual things, they are assigned to the quiet hub of this symbolic wheel, but artists, because of their loyalty to material existence, remain at the active circumference:

> If it be true that God is a circle whose centre is everywhere, the saint goes to the centre, the poet and artist to the ring where everything comes round again. The poet must not seek for what is still and fixed, for that has no life for him; and if he did, his style would become cold and monotonous, and his sense of beauty faint and sickly . . . but he must be content to find his pleasure in all that is for ever passing away that it may come again, in the beauty of woman, in the fragile flowers of spring, in momentary

40. Regardie, *Golden Dawn*, ii: 185, quoting the Portal Ritual's Rite of the Five Paths: "While the Wheel revolves, the hub is still. Seek ever then the centre, look from without to within. . . . From the many coloured Bow, is loosed in Yesod [the next to the lowest of the sephiroth], the Arrow of Sagittarius—Samekh, soaring upward to cleave open the Veil unto the Sun in Tiphareth [the sixth highest of the sephiroth]. Thus it is a fit symbol for hope and aspiration." See also iv: 89: "The Point within the Circle = Kether".

heroic passion, in whatever is most fleeting, most impassioned [E&I, 287-8].

The image reappears eleven years later in *Per Amica Silentia Lunae*, this time with the saintly renunciation of active life being symbolized by the arrow's flight rather than by a descent into the still centre: "I think that we who are poets and artists, not being permitted to shoot beyond the tangible, must go from desire to weariness and so to desire again ... in the humility of the brutes. ... Only when we are saint or sage, and renounce experience itself, can we, in imagery of the Christian Cabbala, leave ... the path of the serpent and become the bowman who aims his arrow at the centre of the sun"[41] [M, 340].

Yeats remains capable of affirming in 1908 that "what is most mystical still seems to me the most true" [VP, 800], but his lingering admiration for Adeptship is no longer a direct threat to his mandatory allegiance as an artist to the mortal world. Many poems in *The Green Helmet and Other Poems* (1910) extol the strength and courage of active, eagle-like men, who are seen to be the true nobility of the temporal world. His increasing endorsement of active life, together with his refusal to abandon magical ambitions, is dramatized by the two characters in "Running to Paradise", a poem written in 1913. The drunken sleeper speaks anti-materialistic dogmas that would be fully appropriate for an Adept or the old man in "The Heart of Spring":

> For all life longs for the Last Day
> And there's no man but cocks his ear
> To know when Michael's trumpet cries
> That flesh and bone may disappear,
> And souls as if they were but sighs,
> And there be nothing but God left. [VP, 306-07]

The peg-legged beggar, whose optimism and allegiance to life are indefatigable, is outraged by the sleeper's ennui and promptly begins to beat him. But he "might have pummelled at a stone/For all the sleeper knew or cared" [VP, 307]. From a supernal perspective, the beggar's otherwise delightful loyalty to material existence is worthless.

41. This eloquent affirmation of the separateness of poet from Adept or saint endorses Schopenhauer's postulate that the negation and calmness which are characteristic of a saint or sage are not available to an active artist.

We can detect Yeats's strengthening commitment to art rather than Adeptship by comparing two of his attempts at compromise. The ideal member of *The Speckled Bird*'s mystical brotherhood would be someone who was completely dedicated to Adeptship but who also happened to have a secondary interest in art. Those priorities are reversed in "A Tower on the Apennines", a *Discoveries* essay of 1907. The underlying dream is still to merge art with sanctity's higher wisdom, but now Yeats is content with a vague hope that absolute loyalty to art might eventually produce some Adept-like wisdom:

> I was alone amid a visionary, fantastic, impossible scenery.... Away south upon another mountain a mediaeval tower, with no building near nor any sign of life, rose into the clouds. I saw suddenly in the mind's eye an old man, erect and a little gaunt, standing in the door of the tower.... He was the poet who had at last, because he had done so much for the word's sake, come to share in the dignity of the saint.... And though he had but sought it for the word's sake, or for a woman's praise, it had come at last into his body and his mind   [E&I, 291].

Despite what might seem a bewildering variety of personae and poses, Yeats never really altered his position in the debate over the relative attractions of art and Adeptship. As we have seen, "To the Rose upon the Rood of Time" in 1892 called for the artist to find "in all poor foolish things that live a day,/Eternal beauty wandering on her way", which is precisely equivalent to his dicta in the *Discoveries* essays of 1906-1907 and *Per Amica Silentia Lunae* in 1918. He preferred art, but refused to condemn Adeptship. The debate, which could only be ended by an exclusive choice between the mutually contradictory duties of art and Adeptship, continued for so long that Yeats accepted his unwillingness ever to settle it. We may easily imagine his glee when, late in life, he discovered a philosophically respectable precedent for his otherwise illogical insistence that both sides of the antinomy comprised of art and Adeptship are equally valid. Kant's antinomies, by recognizing the imperfections of human knowledge and reason, allow preserving opposites without combining them into a Hegelian synthesis. In *Stories of Michael Robartes*, first published in 1931, the title character states his belief in Kant's antinomies and, in fact, goes Kant one better by saying that an antinomy is not merely an "appearance imposed upon us by the form of thought but [is] life itself which burns, now here, now there, a whirling and a bitterness" [v, 52; see also 40].

For a final reminder that Yeats's consistent preference for the artist's materialistic world did not entail renunciation of the spiritual realms of Adeptship, we have his fully justifiable assertion in 1934: "I am Blake's disciple, not Hegel's: 'contraries are positive. A negation is not a contrary' " [vp, 835]. If we are to read his work with understanding, it is necessary to study both halves of his debate between materialism and spirituality, between art and Adeptship.

Hades Wrapped in Cloud

Kathleen Raine

Yeats wrote in 1914, to accompany the second volume of Lady Gregory's *Visions and Beliefs in the West of Ireland*, an essay which anticipates much that he was later to include in *A Vision*. His title, "Swedenborg, Mediums, and the Desolate Places," relates seemingly unrelated topics which are no part of what most of us know, nor of what we have been taught to regard as knowledge. Knowledge, for any society, is, after all, no more than an agreed area of experience from which other areas of experience are excluded as irrelevant or worse; as alchemy and other primitive scientific studies were excluded from scholasticism, and as now scholasticism, indeed theology as such, is excluded from the positivist scientific definition of knowledge. The three topics Yeats has here brought together cover a very wide field of the excluded knowledge of his time; a doctrine of the soul and the nature of the post-mortem state is no part of what modern humanism sees as the study of man.

At a time when few believed in the soul and still fewer in its survival after death, Yeats's "so-called system" (the phrase is George Orwell's) was not taken seriously. It was known that he "dabbled" in spiritualism and astrology and other "hocus-pocus"—I am still quoting Orwell—who conceded only that "One has not, perhaps, *the right to laugh* [my italics] at Yeats for his mystical beliefs—for I believe it could be shown that *some* degree of belief in magic is almost universal—but neither ought one to write such things off as mere unimportant eccentricities."[1] But many critics, including some whose motive is to "protect" Yeats's reputation, have continued to scoff. The "almost universal" belief in magic and mysticism was, for Orwell—one of the most intelligent of the left-wing critics, a man with an appreciation not only of poetry but of Yeats's poetry—excluded knowledge; or rather, was not knowledge at all. R. P. Blackmur, in 1957, in a considered essay on "The Later Poetry of W. B. Yeats" said that "fatalism, Christianity, and magic are none of them disciplines to which many minds can consciously appeal today . . . for emotional strength and moral authority. The supernatural is simply not part of our mental furniture."[2] In the same year John Wain, writing about Yeats's reference to a passage in Porphyry's *The Cave of the Nymphs* and the doctrine of rebirth, proposed "simply to brush aside his reading of his own words" as a "personal fandango of mysticism and superstition".[3] I. A. Richards, more wary than these dismissive critics, wrote, as early as 1927, that "the resort to trance, and the effort to discover a new world-picture to replace that given by science, are the two most signifi-cant points for our purpose in Mr. Yeats's work".[4] Dr. Richards knows his Plato too well to treat Yeats's world-picture, albeit not his own, with contempt. W. H. Auden was typical of his generation in blaming Yeats for not being sufficiently aware of the leading ideas of his time (he presumably meant left-wing political ideologies). But is it not already becoming clear that Yeats's thought *was* the leading thought of his time?

To Yeats himself the current materialist philosophies seemed mere ignorance. He made no attempt to answer the criticism of positivists, for we can discuss only with those who share our knowledge, and he knew them ignorant of his knowledge. In one of his series of letters to Sturge Moore (for whom Bertrand Russell was the supreme philosopher, an admiration not shared by Yeats) he put his finger on the implicit dishonesty of those who want not to know evidence which could cause them to change their minds:

1. George Orwell, "W. B. Yeats", in *W. B. Yeats: A Critical Anthology*, ed. William H. Pritchard (Harmondsworth, Middlesex: Penguin Books, 1972), p. 189.
2. *Ibid.*, pp. 113-14.
3. *Ibid.*, p. 238. Yeats's note refers to a symbol in "Among School Children": "honey of generation".
4. *Ibid.*, p. 90. The essay is entitled "Some Contemporary Poets".

I read a book of Catholic apologetics a few years ago which contended with much proof that the Church had not condemned Galileo's doctrine but merely Galileo for teaching it before he could fully prove it. It is a subconscious trick which must tempt every creed which is incompatible with some fact to perpetually demand to have that fact proved over and over again. There need be no end to this process, especially if the ecclesiastics, scientific or theological, do not look at the proofs.[5]

Setting aside the great mass of experimental evidence available, how many of Yeats's critics had read even Porphyry and the other Neoplatonists, the Indian and Far Eastern scriptures, and philosophical writings of the kind the Theosophists were studying at the turn of the century? Or even William Law's Boehme, or Thomas Taylor the Platonist, to whom Blake and Coleridge and other Romantic poets and painters are so indebted? Had these critics any inkling of the scope, the consistency, the articulation, and coherence of (to quote Thomas Taylor) "that sublime theology... which, however it may be involved in oblivion in *barbarous,* and derided in *impious* ages, will again flourish for very extended periods, through all the infinite revolutions of time".[6]

Many at the time felt that Eliot was on surer ground than Yeats; for the language, if not always the beliefs, of the Christian religion was still widely shared. I remember an occasion when the Chilean poet Gabriela Mistral (herself a student of Vedanta) asked Eliot why he had not pursued his early studies in Indian philosophy.[7] He answered that in order to do so he would have had to learn to use an alien language; as a man of the Western civilization his terms must be found within the Christian tradition.

Between the two great contemporary poets, we now see, lies a watershed of civilization. Yet in so many ways they thought alike. For both, spiritual reality was paramount; both saw with bitter regret the old European civilization drawing to its term; both were

5. Ursula Bridge, ed. *W. B. Yeats and T. Sturge Moore: Their Correspondence 1901-1937* (London: Routledge and Kegan Paul, 1953), p. 86.
6. Thomas Taylor, *Miscellanies in Prose and Verse,* 2nd ed. (London, 1820), p. v.
7. Stephen Spender, who was also present, has given a rather different account of this occasion, saying that "Buddhism" was under discussion. The detail may seem unimportant to those not themselves interested in these matters, but to the best of my own recollection it was Vedanta, not Buddhism.

deeply concerned with history. Eliot as a young man had studied Vedanta, to whose wisdom Yeats turned in his last years, and had considered the possibility of making Indian metaphysics rather than Christian faith his philosophic ground. Yeats, on the other hand, was more nearly Christian than is sometimes thought. The higher grades of the Order of the Golden Dawn (the Rosae Rubeae et Aureae Crucis) were Rosicrucian, and an explicit dedication to "Magister Ihesus Christus Deus et Homo" was inscribed by every initiate—by Yeats himself—upon the rose-cross worn at all meetings of the Order.

But if Eliot was the last great poet of European Christendom, Yeats looked towards the uncharted New Age of which his two earliest masters, Swedenborg and Blake, had declared themselves prophets. Yeats, also looking towards the immediate future as the new dark age Eliot had foreseen, chose, or was chosen by, the new forms of knowledge which, as the "Age of Aquarius" begins to emerge, seem to belong to the new configuration. A metaphysical eclecticism based upon the universal tradition of the Perennial Philosophy seems already not more but less obscure than the language of Christian theology. Christian civilization was to become, sooner even than Eliot had guessed, a dead past. Believing the world to be in essence what Christians have also believed, Yeats understood that Blake's proclamation that "All Religions are One" is the inevitable form of the future. Like Eliot, Yeats believed also in spiritual revelation, but a revelation accessible at all times because reality is omnipresent; the Christian appeal to history was no part of his "system":

> Where got I that truth?
> Out of a medium's mouth,
> Out of nothing it came,
> Out of the forest loam,
> Out of dark night where lay
> The crowns of Nineveh.

By his use of the past tense—"lay" rather than "lie"—Yeats condenses into the image of Nineveh his whole doctrine of civilization. Nineveh came out of that darkness, that forest loam, and into that darkness has passed; but the force of the poem is energized towards the future, not the past. If the nature of things spiritual be such as the Church has taught, it will remain so when Christendom with its great cathedral structure of sublime theology is laid in the dark with Nineveh and Tyre. Yeats could with great bitterness lament that "Many ingenious lovely things are gone", but he could also write of "Magnus Annus at the spring". As the great tree of European Christendom dies, its seed is already germinating.

What seemed to many at the time (comparing Yeats with Eliot) his weakness, his willful obscurantism, we can now see as a source of his strength and of his lucidity in the New Age we are entering. Cultural frontiers are dissolving, and to many the language of Indian metaphysics seems closer to spiritual experience and psychological knowledge than the over-rational theology of the Christian Church. "Those that Rocky Face holds dear", Yeats wrote in "The Gyres",

> . . . shall,
> From marble of a broken sepulchre,
> Or dark betwixt the polecat and the owl,
> Or any rich, dark nothing disinter
> The workman, noble and saint, and all things run
> On that unfashionable gyre again.

A new age is determined by new premises, and a change of premises brings a mutation of history. The excluded knowledge of one culture becomes the ground of another. Michael Robartes, figure of the "mysterious wisdom won by toil" which is the structure of Yeats's thought, was to be found in Watkins' bookshop, the famous bookshop founded at the wish of Madame Blavatsky herself, where the texts of the excluded knowledge were to be found. Scientific knowledge, valid within its own terms, excludes mind—spirit—from its premises; and when Blake declared that "Mental Things are alone Real",[8] he was proclaiming the premises of the New Age. When the history of that reversal comes to be written, historians will see the first wave of the new flow in the Platonic revival of the end of the eighteenth century to which, at the end of the nineteenth, was added the impact of those Indian and Far Eastern philosophies for which mind, not matter, is primary. These studies the Theosophical Society lifted out of the region of mere scholarship as Thomas Taylor, a hundred years before, had outraged the scholars of his day when he proclaimed the Platonic theology as the true religion.

The turn of the nineteenth century saw also the beginnings of

8. Geoffrey Keynes, ed. *Blake: Complete Writings* (London: Oxford University Press, 1969), p. 617.

psychical research, of the psychology of the unconscious, of Egyptology, of the foundation on the Continent of such movements as Rudolf Steiner's Anthroposophy, and in England the Order of the Golden Dawn where Yeats himself studied the Western esoteric tradition. This was also the time of the great collections of folk-lore and primitive beliefs. Not all who read Frazer's *Golden Bough*, that mine of information about the "almost universal" magical beliefs of primitive peoples, accepted its author's rational interpretations of the material he assembled. With gathering momentum, all this excluded knowledge has now become a current of change which makes us ask who, ten years from now, will be claiming Orwell's "right to laugh".

In his essay on "Swedenborg, Mediums, and the Desolate Places", Yeats refers to a period some fifteen years earlier, when he had accompanied Lady Gregory on some of her expeditions in search of folk beliefs:

> I had noticed many analogies in modern spiritism and began a more careful comparison, going a good deal to séances for the first time and reading all writers of any reputation I could find in English or French. . . . I did not go there for evidence of the kind the Society for Psychical Research would value, any more than I would seek it in Galway or in Aran. I was comparing one form of belief with another, and like Paracelsus, who claimed to have collected his knowledge from midwife and hangman, I was discovering a philosophy.[9]

Yeats was not looking for so-called "proofs" of survival, in terms of the prevailing materialist philosophy; for him the soul's immortality was not in question. What Yeats was seeking to discover was the nature of the discarnate world or state, the relation of the discarnate and incarnate worlds to one another. If Yeats did not stop to argue with his positivist critics, who dismissed as "superstition" an interest in little-regarded facts (which in their own culture-heroes they would have praised as scientific curiosity), it was because he knew that whoever cared to follow him could verify his discoveries. He knew the evidence was open to more

9. "Swedenborg, Mediums, and the Desolate Places", in *Visions and Beliefs in the West of Ireland Collected and Arranged by Lady Gregory* (Gerrard's Cross: Colin Smythe, 1970), p. 311. Hereafter cited in the text as VB, and followed by page numbers. Yeats's essay was dated 14 October 1914, but *Visions and Beliefs* was not published until 1920.

than one possible explanation; but he also knew that the facts were too numerous, consistent, and widely reported to be explained away.

Yeats's own collection of *Fairy and Folk Tales of the Irish Peasantry* had been published in 1888 and *The Celtic Twilight* in 1893, both before he met Lady Gregory. Any theory about the nature of the fairy-faith shared with her came from Yeats, and he claims originality: he had "pieced together stray thoughts written out after questioning the familiar of a trance medium or automatic writer . . . till I believed myself the discoverer of a vast generalization. I lived in excitement, amused to make Holloway interpret Aran, and constantly comparing my discoveries with what I have learned of mediaeval tradition among fellow students [a reference to the Western esoteric tradition of the Golden Dawn], with the reveries of a Neoplatonist, a seventeenth-century Platonist, of Paracelsus or a Japanese poet" [VB, 312]. Yeats had perceived that the phenomena of the seance are similar to the visions "seen" by country people: the "other world" of faery is the same as the "other world" of the dead.

This is the thesis of W. Y. Evans Wentz (later to become famous as the translator of the Tibetan *Book of the Dead*) in his first book, *The Fairy-Faith in Celtic Countries* (1911), dedicated to Yeats and to AE. The young American, fresh from Oxford where he had studied under Sir John Rhys and Andrew Lang, evidently considered Yeats to be an authority on Irish folk-lore. Possibly Yeats imparted his "vast generalization" to Evans Wentz, who writes that most of the evidence "points so much in one direction that the only verdict which seems reasonable is that the Fairy-Faith belongs to a doctrine of souls; that is to say, that Fairyland is a state or condition, realm or place, very much like, if not the same as, that wherein civilized and uncivilized men alike place the souls of the dead, in company with other invisible beings."[10] *The Fairy-Faith* contains contributions by Andrew Lang, Douglas Hyde, Alexander Carmichael, Sir John Rhys, and other eminent folklorists, who on the whole supported this view.

Yeats's "vast generalization" cannot have been as original as he claimed; for Andrew Lang in his contribution to Evans Wentz's book summarized his own conclusion, that the fairy-folk "tend to

10. Evans Wentz, W. Y., *The Fairy-Faith in Celtic Countries* (London: Oxford University Press, 1911), p. 18.

shade away, on one side, into the denizens of the House of Hades—phantasms of the dead. The belief in such phantasms may be partially based on experience.... As far as psychical research studies report of these phantasms, it approaches the realm of 'the Fairy Queen Proserpine'. As far as such research examines the historical or contemporary stories of the *Poltergeist*, it touches on fairies: because the Irish, for example, attribute to the agency of fairies the modern *Poltergeist* phenomena."[11] Stripped of their colouring of the social life or environment of some peculiar culture, Andrew Lang goes on to say, the fairies "become ghosts of the dead or other spiritual beings". The phantasms of the dead, the dying or the absent, frequently reported in the annals of psychical research, would have been in Ireland, or Brittany, or Scotland attributed to the fairy-world.

In his commentary on that classic of fairy-lore in Scotland, the Rev. Robert Kirk of Aberfoyle's *Secret Commonwealth of Elves, Fauns, and Fairies*, reprinted in 1893 from a tract dated 1691, Lang commended Kirk for having regarded "the land of faery as a mere fact in nature", the laws of which he attempts to investigate. Lang regarded Kirk as "an early student in folk-lore and in psychical research—topics which run into each other".[12] There is a copy of this work in Yeats's library; with his interest in the subject and his friendship with Evans Wentz, Yeats must have known Lang's views, which are also stated in other writings. If this be so, whatever Yeats's theory loses in originality is more than made up by what it gains in learned support.

Douglas Hyde (also in a contribution to Evans Wentz's book) commits himself to an acceptance of "the belief in ghosts or revenants, which make up the greatest part of the fairy-lore of Ireland". Even those "who may be most sceptical about the Sidhe-folk and the leprechauns are likely to be convinced (on the mere evidence) that the existence of 'astral bodies' or 'doubles' or whatever we may call them, and the appearances of people, especially in the hour of their death, to other people who were perhaps hundreds of miles away at the time, is amply proven."[13] The materialist premises of Anglo-American academic culture were not

11. *Ibid.*, pp. 475-6.
12. *The Secret Commonwealth of Elves, Fauns, and Fairies*, with commentary by Andrew Lang (1893), p. xv.
13. Evans Wentz, *Fairy-Faith*, p. 29.

shared by Ireland's first President, nor her Church, nor her people; in his own country Yeats had no need to justify a view of the nature of things shared, in essence, by all.

Yeats's early poems directly based on Irish folk-beliefs are authentic. "The Ballad of Father Gilligan" describes the gift of "bilocation" held by the Church to be a mark of sanctity, though there have been, and doubtless are, many "astral projectors" who are not saints. "The Host of the Air" is based on a story told to this day with many variants both in Scotland and Ireland. A mortal finds himself among a dancing throng, among them his recently dead wife, who warns him to refuse fairy food, as Persephone had long ago been warned to refuse the food of Hades. "The Stolen Child" and the play made from the same theme, *The Land of Heart's Desire*, describe the alluring aspect of the astral world. The "summerland" of the spiritualists, a recreation of this world but in a clearer light and incorruptible perfection, has the same character as Yeats's "Happy Townland" or land of heart's desire.

But more interesting than these direct transcriptions are the cross-parallels, these being based on the universal and essential truth of the beliefs; for example, in "All Souls' Night", it is the poet himself who sets two glasses of wine, one for himself, the other for the spirits of the dead friends he summons, just as in many cottages, as Lady Gregory was told, the country-people leave an offering of food—spring-water and potatoes will suffice—for the "fairies". Yeats finds a parallel also in modern spiritualism: "Certain London Spiritualists for some years past have decked out a Christmas tree with presents that have each the names of some dead child upon them, and sitting in the dark on Christmas night they hear . . . the clamorous voices of the children as they are distributed. Yet the presents still hang there and are given next day to an hospital" [v, 221].

The compulsive power of fairy music to draw some mortal into the dance is a common theme. Like Yeats, John M. Synge believed that certain places have their memories, and on Inishmaan believed that he had heard the fairy music in a dream. The account was published in the second number of *The Green Sheaf* in 1903:

> The music increased continually, sounding like the strings of harps, tuned to a forgotten scale, and having a resonance as searching as the strings of the 'cello.

Then the luring excitement became more powerful than my will, and my limbs moved in spite of me.

In a moment I was swept away in a whirlwind of notes. My breath and my thoughts and every impulse of my body, became a form of the dance, till I could not distinguish between the instruments and the rhythm and my own person or consciousness.

For a while it seemed an excitement that was filled with joy, then it grew into an ecstasy where all existence was lost in a vortex of movement. I could not think there had ever been a life beyond the whirling of the dance.

Then with a shock the ecstasy turned to an agony and rage. I struggled to free myself, but seemed only to increase the passion of the steps I moved to.

When Synge dragged himself, trembling, to the window of the cottage and looked out, "the moon was glittering across the bay, and there was no sound anywhere on the island."[14]

Is there some recollection of Synge's strange and terrible mystical experience in the lines in "Byzantium"?

> Where blood-begotten spirits come
> And all complexities of fury leave,
> Dying into a dance,
> An agony of trance,
> An agony of flame that cannot singe a sleeve.

It may be so. Both dance and music belong to many descriptions of faery, and also to "communications" through mediums. We remember too Plotinus's "choiring" of the souls that look "upon the wellspring of Life".[15]

Such beliefs and experiences are only the insular summits of a great submerged continent, joined, in its rocky substratum, into an underlying coherence. Neither country people nor most spiritualists have any knowledge of the philosophic tradition of Neoplatonism, Gnosticism, the Cabbala, Vedantism—which supports their own isolated experiences. Evans Wentz indeed believed the Celtic fairy-faith to be a lingering memory of the teaching of the Druids; Lady Gregory gives several examples of the belief in reincarnation which is no part of the Christian faith. But that

14. J. M. Synge, *Collected Works*, 4 vols. (London: Oxford University Press, 1966), II: 99-100.
15. Stephen MacKenna, trans. *Plotinus: The Ethical Treatises*, Ennead VI. 9. 9 (Boston: Branford, [1948]), II: 249.

memory would not have lingered had not repeated experience of
the discarnate world kept it alive. The stories told to Lady Gregory
and other collectors were seldom hearsay—most were first-hand
and concerned the recently dead.

It was to Swedenborg that Yeats turned for some ordering principle to bring coherence to all this material. Writing in 1914 of
"some fifteen years ago", Yeats tells that one day he opened "*The
Spiritual Diary of Swedenborg*, which I had not taken down for
twenty years". Swedenborg "I had read with some care before the
fascination of Blake and Boehme had led me away" [VB, 312], he
goes on—that would have been 1880 or earlier, when Yeats was in
his 'teens. It is noteworthy that he did not come to Swedenborg
through his Blake studies. The first two or three volumes of the
Spiritual Diary are among the works by Swedenborg in Yeats's
library, and must be regarded as an essential source of his doctrine
of souls.

"It was indeed Swedenborg who affirmed for the modern world,
as against the abstract reasoning of the learned, the doctrine and
practice of the desolate places, of shepherds and of midwives, and
discovered a world of spirits where there was scenery like that of
earth, human forms, grotesque or beautiful, senses that knew
pleasure and pain, marriage and war" [VB, 312]. Indeed although
Swedenborg has entitled his most famous book *Heaven and Hell*,
he describes an endless and ever-changing variety of those intermediate states traditionally called Purgatory. Protestant Swedenborg does not use the word, but speaks of "vastation", a form of
purgatorial suffering through which the spirits of the dead are,
through self-chosen, self-created fantasies of punishment, purified.
The time of vastation may be brief, or infinitely long, by which the
spirits are fitted to progress, by degrees, towards some angelic
community.

All angels, according to Swedenborg, were once men, being
those celestial spirits who have been purified through "vastation".
Other spirits make their way, through the attraction of like to like
which is the law of the discarnate world, to the various hells, where
their punishment is to live in the realization of their own fantasies
of cruelty, lust, greed, and the rest, and in the company of their
kind. Because, out of the body, no dissimulation is possible, they
make their way by the necessity of their choice, to their own place.
Blake criticized Swedenborg for perpetuating "all the old false-

hoods" of conventional religion, and especially for teaching that there is an eternal hell for the wicked. But in the *Spiritual Diary*, in which Swedenborg recorded his day-to-day visions of the spirit world, there is little to suggest that the hells of "vastation" are eternally binding upon the spirits who are in these "states", and much to indicate that these are only places of more painful and profound purgation. These spirits—as in Dante's Purgatory also—are free to leave some mind-created place, built up in "correspondence" with their own interior condition.

The spirit, Yeats writes, paraphrasing Swedenborg,

> will slip from state to state until he finds himself after a few days "with those who are in accord with his life in the world; with them he finds his life, and, wonderful to relate, he then leads a life similar to that he led in the world." . . . Then follows a period which may last but a short time or many years, while the soul lives a life so like that of the world that it may not even believe that it has died, for "when what is spiritual touches and sees what is spiritual the effect is the same as when what is natural touches what is natural." It is the other world of the early races, of those whose dead are in the rath or the faery hill, of all who see no place of reward and punishment but a continuance of this life, with cattle and sheep, markets and war [VB, 313-14].

In Yeats's "happy townland" the "strong farmer" may fight and drink beer, as in Valhalla the Viking warriors fight and drink mead at Hela's board, and as Ireland's country fairies play hurley, while their women milk fairy cattle. Robert Kirk wrote of the "subterranean people" that they are "seen to wear Plaids and variegated Garments in the Highlands of Scotland", and "ther Women are said to Spine very fine, to Dy, to Tossue and Embroyder", while the men have "many disastorous Doings of their own, as Convocations, Fighting, Gashes, Wounds and Burialls, both in the Earth and Air."[16]

To return to Yeats's account of Swedenborg: "This earth-resembling life is the creation of the image-making power of the mind, plucked naked from the body, and mainly of the images in the memory. All our work has gone with us, the books we have written can be opened and read or put away for later use, even though their print and paper have been sold to the buttermen" [VB, 314].

16. *Secret Commonwealth*, pp. 14-15.

Many of her informants told Lady Gregory that "they" can build up houses at their pleasure, and Swedenborg describes how the discarnate can in a moment build up scenes and surroundings that are related by "correspondence" to their passing thoughts. Yeats was amused by Swedenborg's formal eighteenth-century paradises, his equation of rocky solitudes and desolate places with the hells. But it was from Swedenborg that he learned that "heaven and hell are built always anew and in hell or heaven all do what they please and all are surrounded by scenes and circumstances which are the expression of their natures and the creation of their thought" [VB, 315]. So the fairy-child in *The Land of Heart's Desire* tells Mary Bruin:

> ... we are but obedient to the thoughts
> That drift into the mind at a wink of the eye.   [CPL, 70]

And in "The Phases of the Moon",

> ... they speak what's blown into the mind;
> Deformed beyond deformity, unformed,
> Insipid as the dough before it is baked,
> They change their bodies at a word.

The faith that Yeats declared as his own is Blake's belief that "mental things are alone real",

> Death and life were not
> Till man made up the whole,
> Made lock, stock and barrel
> Out of his bitter soul,
> Aye, sun and moon and star, all,
> And further add to that
> That, being dead, we rise,
> Dream and so create
> Translunar Paradise.   [CP, 223]

If it was from Berkeley that Yeats learned to call sun and moon and stars mental images, the nature of his "translunar Paradise" he learned from Swedenborg, mediums, and the people of Ireland's desolate places.

Both in the earlier essay and in *A Vision* Yeats compares the Celtic fairy-faith to the Japanese Nō theatre. The power of the Nō drama lies in its power of uniting, so long as the dramatic exaltation lasts, the worlds of the living and the dead into a single whole, whose intensity exceeds anything possible in either half alone. The "names and words of the drama it [the spirit] must obtain ... from some incarnate Mind, and this it is able to do because all spirits inhabit our unconsciousness or, as Swedenborg said, are the Dramatis Personae of our dreams. One thinks of those apparitions haunting the places where they have lived that fill the literature of all countries and are the theme of the Japanese Nō drama" [v, 226-7]. In the early essay Yeats tells the plot of Motome Zuka, *The Maiden's Tomb*, the story of a ghost unable to escape the flames of her own hell, even though a travelling Buddhist priest tells her that could she only understand that these fires are illusion, she could be free. In *A Vision* he finds an even closer parallel: "I think of two ghost lovers in a Japanese play [*Nishi Kigi*] asking a wandering Buddhist priest to marry them, of two that appeared to a Catholic priest in Aran, according to an Aran tale, with a like object" [v, 222].[17] The essence of the Nō drama is the interplay of the two worlds, those meetings of the dead and the living in which it may be—as in *Sumida Gawa* for the mother who finds the grave of her son—the living person whose doubts and anguish are resolved. At other times the living may release some ghost from its hell. The travelling priest brings peace to the ghosts of the weaving girl and her lover by bringing them together after their death. It is no wonder that Yeats should have attempted an Irish Nō drama; for Lady Gregory gives many examples of the belief, indistinguishable from the Japanese Shinto faith, that "those that die are left in the place where they lived to do their penance" [vB, 214]. In *The Dreaming of the Bones* the Young Man says:

> My Grandam
> Would have it they did penance everywhere;
> Some lived through their old lives again.

Here the ghost character takes up the theme:

> In a dream;
> And some for an old scruple must hang spitted
> Upon the swaying tops of lofty trees;
> Some are consumed in fire, some withered up
> By hail and sleet out of the wintry North,
> And some but live through their old lives again.
> [CPL, 436-7]

17. This story is told in vB, 334-5.

Yeats was told by an old Mayo woman of two ghosts doing their penance just as described by the Stranger: "There is a bush up at my own place, and the people do be saying that there are two souls doing their penance under it. When the wind blows one way the one has shelter, and when it blows from the north the other has shelter" [M, 98]. In *Purgatory*, the last of Yeats's ghost plays, the Old Man states, unadorned by imagery, the same doctrine; he speaks of

> The souls in Purgatory that come back
> To habitations and familiar spots ...
> Re-live
> Their transgressions, and that not once
> But many times; they know at last
> The consequence of those transgressions
> Whether upon others or upon themselves;
> Upon others, others may bring help,
> For when the consequence is at an end
> The dream must end; if upon themselves,
> There is no help but in themselves
> And in the mercy of God.   [CPL, 682]

In both *The Dreaming of the Bones* and *Purgatory* the ghost characters are earthbound through passionate and guilty love; both have betrayed their country through passion, in the earlier play Diarmuid and Dervorgilla because they called the Normans in against the King of Ireland.

The betrayal by the heiress in *Purgatory* is of inherited tradition, the learning of

> ... old books and books made fine
> By eighteenth-century French binding, books
> Modern and ancient ....

And earlier the Old Man says:

> ... to kill a house
> Where great men grew up, married, died,
> I here declare a capital offence.   [CPL, 683]

When she mated with "a groom in a training stable", she betrayed an inherited culture no less than did Dervorgilla. The later play is incomparably the more dramatic; for the story, with all its symbolic and political overtones, remains at the same time the drama of the ghost-mother and the Old Man who attempts to free his mother from her hell. In *A Vision* Yeats writes of the *Dreaming Back*: "the

Spirit is compelled to live over and over again the events that had most moved it; there can be nothing new, but the old events stand forth in a light which is dim or bright according to the intensity of the passion that accompanied them" [v, 226]. They repeat themselves again and again. In *The Dreaming of the Bones* the ghost-characters hope that, after seven centuries of penance, the young man who has taken part in the Easter Rising may forgive them; but he does not do so: the consequences of their act are not exhausted in Irish history. In *Purgatory* the Old Man hopes when he has killed his son—"My father and my son on the same jack-knife"—that his mother's ghost will be freed, the consequences being at an end; but the hoof-beats of her dream return:

> Twice a murderer and all for nothing,
> And she must animate that dead night
> Not once but many times!
> > O God,
> Release my mother's soul from its dream!
> Mankind can do no more. Appease
> The misery of the living and the remorse of the dead.
> > [CPL, 689]

One might find many answers to the question of why the hoof-beats return. Was the mother, who had begotten a son to make him twice a murderer, unable to rest because of him? Or is the implication of the play, like *The Dreaming of the Bones*, political also? That great house with its library burned to a ruin must also be accounted the consequence of her loss of caste, a national as well as a personal tragedy.

Like the ghosts of the earlier and the later plays, the spirits of Swift, Stella, and Vanessa re-enact in *The Words upon the Window-Pane* their passionate torment. Yeats's only experiment in realistic drama takes, paradoxically, the other world for its theme, and the ghost-characters speak through the medium, Mrs. Henderson. The seance is a reconstruction of many Yeats must have attended, with the triviality of motive of sitters like Mrs. Mallet who is "thinking of starting a tea-shop in Folkestone. I followed Mrs. Henderson to Dublin to get my husband's advice.... He advises me about everything I do, and I am utterly lost if I cannot question him" [CPL, 602-3]. Like the ghosts of the earlier and later plays, the spirits go through the same drama again and again, "just as if they were characters in some kind of horrible play".

Of the three, *The Dreaming of the Bones* is the closest to the Nō structure it imitates; but the bringing of ghost characters on to a Western stage has (apart from Shakespeare) no tradition to support it; and doubtless *Purgatory*, in which the ghost is seen by the Old Man and the Boy but not by the audience, is dramatically the most successful, as it also is as poetry and in the dramatic passion of its representation of Yeats's doctrine of souls.

In his earliest poems the other world is the escapist land of heart's desire, drawing the spirit away from its earthly life. Later, Yeats exploited the tragic situations of the earth-bound; he was never to write a ghost-play of the blessed spirits, but the poem "Ribh at the Tomb of Baile and Aillinn", where the passion that draws the ghosts is memory of their love, might have provided a theme of ghostly beatitude:

> Here in the pitch-dark atmosphere above
> The trembling of the apple and the yew,
> Here on the anniversary of their death,
> The anniversary of their first embrace,
> Those lovers, purified by tragedy,
> Hurry into each other's arms; these eyes,
> By water, herb and solitary prayer
> Made aquiline, are open to that light.
> Though somewhat broken by the leaves, that light
> Lies in a circle on the grass; therein
> I turn the pages of my holy book.   [CP, 328]

These words, which might have been spoken by the wandering Buddhist or Shinto priest who is often the *Waki* character in a Nō play, are spoken by the poet wearing the mask of the Irish hermit he chose for the expression of his spiritual wisdom. It was truly in "that light" Yeats himself turned the pages of his holy book, a Bible containing many strange chapters.

As to mediums, Yeats wasted no time in proving or justifying what he had to impart. "I shall write as if what I describe were everywhere established, everywhere accepted, and I had only to remind my reader of what he already knows" [VB, 324]. He does give, in a footnote, a dozen or so names of reputable authors on the subject but adds, "I have myself been a somewhat active investigator."[18]

18. VB, 324. The footnote is as follows: "Besides the well-known books of Atsikof, Myers, Lodge, Flammarion, Flournoy, Maxwell, Albert De Rochas, Lombroso, Madame Bisson, Delanne, etc., I have made consider-

He is his own authority, and knows (a point also made in *The Words upon the Window-Pane*) that the only way to conviction is experience of these things. But if Yeats (having no disbelief to vindicate) wasted no time in the exposure of "frauds", just how critical he was of the material thus obtained any reader of his early essays, or of *A Vision*, will discover. He took nothing at its face value; the spirits were not necessarily the persons they claimed to be, nor their communications true: "They have a passion for inventing; and do not always know that they invent"—so he quotes from Swedenborg:

> It has been shown me many times that the spirits speaking with me did not know but that they were the men and women I was thinking of; neither did other spirits know the contrary. Thus yesterday and today one known of me in life was personated. The personation was so like him in all respects, so far as known to me, that nothing could be more like. For there are genera and species of spirits of similar faculty (? as the dead whom we seek), and when like things are called up in the memory of men and so are represented to them they think they are the same persons. At other times they enter into the fantasy of other spirits and think that they are them [vb, 317-18].

There is in that world no such hard and fast separation between individuals as in ours. Yeats tells of a serial romance running in "some clerical newspaper no-one there has ever opened" communicated by a medium. In this he sees not an example of fraud but of the plastic, suggestible nature of spirits. "They have," he says, "bodies as plastic as their minds that flow so readily into the mould of ours" [vb, 318]. It is not those who know most of these subjects who are most inclined to treat spirit communications as infallible oracles.

Swedenborg himself, Yeats says, seems "to warn us against a movement whose philosophy he announced or created, when he tells us to seek no conscious intercourse with any that fall short

----

able use of the researches of D'Ochorowicz published during the last ten or twelve years in *Annales des Science* [*sic*] *Psychiques* and in the English *Annals of Psychical Science*, and of those of Professor Hyslop published during the last four years in the *Journal* and *Transactions of the American Society for Psychical Research*. I have myself been a somewhat active investigator." In Yeats's library there are also works by Hyslop, William James, Latoslavski, McTaggart, Osty, Schrenck-Notzing, Richet, etc.

of the celestial rank. At ordinary times they do not see us or know that we are near, but when we speak to them we are in danger of their deceits" [VB, 317]. And he himself writes from his own experience: "we never long escape the phantasmagoria nor can long forget that we are among the shape-changers. Sometimes our own minds shape that mysterious substance, which may be life itself, according to desire or constrained by memory, and the dead no longer remembering their own names become the characters in the drama we ourselves have invented" [VB, 327]. The "mysterious substance which may be life itself" of which Yeats speaks as plastic to our thoughts appears to be the "dough before it is baked" or "kneaded up" again of "The Phases of the Moon". Yeats quotes the Chaldean Oracle, "Stoop not down to the darkly splendid world wherein continually lieth a faithless depth and Hades wrapped in cloud, delighting in unintelligible images" [VB, 328].

"Materializations" were much discussed in the early days of psychical research, and Yeats was much interested in these most extreme manifestations of the power of imagination, in which "we are the spectators of a phantasmagoria that effects a photographic plate or leaves its moulded image in a preparation of paraffin. We have come to understand why the Platonists of the sixteenth and seventeenth centuries, and visionaries like Boehme and Paracelsus confused imagination with magic, and why Boehme will have it that it 'creates and substantiates as it goes' " [VB, 326]. In his letters to Sturge Moore he much bewildered his materialist friend by arguing that Ruskin's phantom cat had as good a claim to reality as the house cat. This "magical" view of reality as the work of imagination Yeats shared with Blake, and both poets with

> . . . God-appointed Berkeley that proved all things a dream,
> That this pragmatical, preposterous pig of a world, its farrow
>   that so solid seem,
> Must vanish on the instant if the mind but change its theme. . . .
>   [CP, 268]

Among the many books on the physical phenomena of psychical research in Yeats's library is Lombroso's *After Death—What?* in which are described sittings with the famous Italian materialization medium, Eusapia Paladino. At these seances limbs, draped figures, faces, even sometimes an apparent person would form, which it would be possible to touch, hands that would grasp the hands of the sitters even as fairy hands are said to be sometimes tangible.

Eusapia was said to be able to imprint wax (Yeats's "preparation of paraffin") with spirit portraits, of which "moulded images" many photographs are included in Lombroso's book.

One such materialization was of the mother of one of the learned sitters, and more than once she is alleged to have "held a regular conversation with him by gestures, pointing sorrowfully to his spectacles and his semi-baldness, as if she would make him understand how long a time had elapsed since she had left him a bold and beautiful youth."[19] In this sorrowful ghost a source of the "youthful mother" of "Among School Children", of whom the poet asks if she

> Would think her son, did she but see that shape
> With sixty or more winters on its head,
> A compensation for the pang of his birth,
> And the uncertainty of his setting forth?

The more tragic encounter of the ghost-mother and her son in *Purgatory* is a yet more powerful dramatization of this situation. Robert Kirk of Aberfoyle described the "subterranean" people of the seventeenth century as having "light changable Bodies, (like those called Astral,) somewhat in the Nature of a condensed Cloud, and best seen in Twilight. Thes Bodies be so plyable through the Subtilty of the Spirits that agitate them, that they can make them appear or disappear att Pleasure".[20] From the evidence of seances with such mediums as Eusapia, psychical researchers came to the conclusion (to quote Yeats again) that

> the images are made of a substance drawn from the medium who loses weight, and in a less degree from all present, and for this light must be extinguished or dimmed or shaded with red as in a photographer's room. The image will begin outside the medium's body as a luminous cloud, or in a sort of luminous mud forced from the body, out of the mouth it may be, from the side or from the lower parts of the body. One may see a vague cloud condense and diminish into a head or arm or a whole figure of a man, or to some animal shape. [VB, 325]

Yeats writes as one who has witnessed such things. He refers, in comparison, to a story told in full in *The Celtic Twilight* of a fairy

19. Cesare Lombroso, *After Death — What? Spiritistic phenomena and their interpretation*, trans. William Sloane Kennedy (Boston: Small, Maynard, [1909]), p. 196.
20. *Secret Commonwealth*, p. 5.

hurley match in which it seemed to the spectators that the players took their form from the presence of human beings, like materializations from a medium. His narrator told him that it is said that "the people of Faery cannot even play at hurley unless they have on either side some mortal . . . he 'would almost swear' they came back out of the bodies of the two men in dark clothes. These two men were of the size of living men, but the others were small" [M, 9-10].

There are spirit-photographs showing heads apparently emerging from Yeats himself. Under what conditions these were taken I do not know, but the faces certainly exhibit what he calls "a strange regularity of feature and we suspect the presence of an image that may never have lived, an artificial beauty that may have shown itself in the Greek mysteries. Has some cast in the Vatican, or at Bloomsbury been the model?" Certainly Yeats was far from accepting such forms at their face-value; for the passage goes on to tell how once in Paris "a rumour ran among the séance rooms to the bewilderment of simple believers, that a heavy middle-aged man who took snuff, and wore the costume of a past time, had appeared while a French medium was in his trance, and somebody had recognised the Tartuffe of the Comédie Française" [VB, 326].

The so-called ectoplasm of the seance was known in the ancient world. Porphyry, in his *De Antro Nympharum*, writes that "according to the opinions of some men aerial and celestial bodies are nourished by the vapours of fountains and rivers and other exhalations. . . . It is necessary therefore that souls, whether they are corporeal or incorporeal, while they attract bodies, must verge to humidity, and be incorporated with humid natures. . . . Hence the souls of the dead are evocated by the effusion of bile and blood: and souls ensnared by corporeal love, and attracting to their nature a humid spirit, condense this watery vehicle like a cloud." This cloud, "becomes the object of corporeal sight. And among the number of these we must reckon those apparitions of images, which from a spirit coloured by the influence of imagination, present themselves to mankind." It may possibly have been this passage which suggested to Yeats that materialized images might have been evoked in the Greek Mysteries.

Porphyry seems to see generation and the apparition of phantoms as similar in nature; in both cases the soul making for itself a body of moisture: "Hence Heraclitus observes 'that it appears delightful, and not mortal to souls, when they are born connected with

humidity'." Speaking of unembodied souls, Porphyry quotes Heraclitus' teaching that "we live their death, and we die their life" and
his other saying, incomprehensible unless this doctrine of moisture
be known, "A dry soul is the wisest".[21] The dry soul, like Mary
Bruin in *The Land of Heart's Desire*, chooses the discarnate world
or state.

Yeats makes frequent use of this water symbolism. In "The
Happy Townland", "Gabriel will come from the water" (the moist
element of generation over which Gabriel, as the angel of the
Annunciation, is held in esoteric terms to preside)

> . . . and talk
> Of wonders that have happened
> On wet roads where men walk.

The lines suggest that Yeats already doubted the greater wisdom
of the dry souls, for generated life provides all the good stories told
at the feasts of eternity. Later he was, without questioning the
doctrine, to choose generation:

> I am content to live it all again
> And yet again, if it be life to pitch
> Into the frogspawn of a blind man's ditch.   [CP, 267]

I have dwelt upon these materialization phenomena because
Yeats himself does so; they were crucial to his magical theory of
the Imagination. Probably he would have agreed with William
James's suggestion (quoted in Evans Wentz's *Fairy-Faith*) that if
"there were in the universe a lot of diffuse soul-stuff, unable of
itself to get into consistent personal form, or to take permanent
possession of an organism, yet always craving to do so, it might get
its head into the air, parasitically, so to speak, by profiting by weak
spots in the armour of human minds, and slipping in and stirring up
there the sleeping tendencies to personate."[22]

Yeats's critical discernment was no less when, in the writing of
A Vision, the medium was his own wife. Who were "they", the
communicators, the frustrators? It was clear to him all along that
Yeats and the spirits were engaged in a dialogue; the "unknown
writer" built up a classification in terms of Yeats's recently published *Per Amica Silentia Lunae* but, on the other hand, was "en-

21. *Thomas Taylor, the Platonist: Selected Writings*, ed. Kathleen Raine and
George M. Harper (Princeton: University Press, 1969), pp. 303-4.
22. Evans Wentz, *The Fairy-Faith*, p. 479.

raged" by his philosophic terminology. " 'I am always afraid', he said in apology, 'that when not at our best we may accept from you false reasoning' " [v, 21]. Often they spoke when Mrs. Yeats was asleep, and then sometimes her own dream would break in upon their communications. "They," on their side, were not clear about things in this world; once in a restaurant "because we had spoken of a garden they had thought we were in it" [v, 10]. They needed to draw upon Yeats's knowledge for terms in which to cast their thought, "and if my mind returned too soon to their unmixed abstraction they would say, 'We are starved' " [v, 12]. Other spirits "whom they named Frustrators attempted to confuse us or waste time. Who these Frustrators were or why they acted so was never adequately explained" [v, 12-13]. And Yeats asks whether communication itself may not be part of a drama, a conflict of forces of which we know nothing. "Was communication itself such a conflict? One said, as though it rested with me to decide what part I should play in their dream, 'Remember we will deceive you if we can' " [v, 13]. We are reminded of what Yeats had written in *Hodos Chameliontos*:

> I know now that revelation is from the self, but from that age-long memoried self, that shapes the elaborate shell of the mollusc and the child in the womb, that teaches the birds to make their nest; and that genius is a crisis that joins that buried self for certain moments to our trivial daily mind. There are, indeed, personifying spirits that we had best call but Gates and Gate-keepers, because through their dramatic power bring our souls to crisis. . . .
>
> [A, 272]

But then again the communicators would seem like living men, as when one asked Yeats to stop writing while he listened to an owl hooting in the poet's Oxford garden. We must not jump to the conclusion that because Yeats speaks of the spirits as inhabitants of the "buried self" or the "sleeping mind" that he did not believe his communicators to be ever, or in any sense, discarnate human spirits. On the contrary, he believed our dreams to be regions through which wander the dead and their memories and fantasies:

> In partly accepting and partly rejecting that explanation . . . , in affirming a Communion of the Living and the Dead, I remember that Swedenborg has described all those between the celestial state and death as plastic, fantastic and deceitful, the dramatis personae

of our dreams; that Cornelius Agrippa attributes to Orpheus these words: "The Gates of Pluto must not be unlocked, within is a people of dreams." [v, 23]

The matter of Yeats's thought is of so unknown a nature that we may easily fail to understand him. He himself is tentative in his conclusions. Only this perhaps can be discerned, that Yeats understood by the world of spirits the Anima Mundi of the Platonists, the Self of the Vedas, Jung's more recently named Collective Unconscious:

> ... again and again they have insisted that the whole system is the creation of my wife's Daimon and of mine, and that it is as startling to them as to us. Mere "spirits", my teachers say, are the "objective", a reflection and distortion; reality itself is found by the Daimon in what they call, in commemoration of the Third Person of the Trinity, the Ghostly Self. The blessed spirits must be sought within the self which is common to all.   [v, 22]

Although Yeats says that he read MacKenna's *Plotinus* with attention only after *A Vision* had been completed, a passage from *Ennead* IV (on the Problems of the Soul) may clarify his thought and ours at this point:

> But what place is left for the particular souls, yours and mine and another's?
> May we suppose the Soul to be appropriated on the lower ranges to some individual, but to belong on the higher to that other sphere?
> At this there would be a Socrates as long as Socrates' soul remained in body; but Socrates ceases to exist, precisely on attainment of the highest.
> Now nothing of Real Being is ever annulled.
> In the Supreme, the Intellectual-Principles are not annulled, for in their differentiation there is no bodily partition, no passing of each separate phase into a distinct unity; every such phase remains in full possession of that identical being. It is exactly so with the souls.
> By their succession they are linked to the several Intellectual-Principles, for they are the expression, the Logos, of the Intellectual-Principles, of which they are the unfolding; brevity has opened out to multiplicity; by that point of their being which least belongs to the partial order, they are attached each to its own Intellectual original: they have already chosen the way of division; but to the extreme they cannot go; thus they keep, at once, identification and difference; each soul is permanently a unity (a self) and yet all are, in their total, one being.

Thus the gist of the matter is established: one soul the source of all; those others, as a many founded in that one, are, on the analogy of the Intellectual-Principle, at once divided and undivided; that Soul which abides in the Supreme is the one expression or Logos of the Intellectual-Principle, and from it spring other Reason-Principles, partial but immaterial, exactly as in the differentiation of the Supreme.[23]

Are we to suppose that in the Plotinian Intellectual-Principle, the soul of the world, the Collective Unconscious, the Self, or whatever we may call it, that not only the memories of the dead but the dead themselves live on? If this be so, Yeats's contribution to the knowledge of our time must be (to all those who see it as an area of knowledge at all) highly significant. I was about to say "original"; but this is hardly so, unless by original we mean a return to the origins of knowledge which have been discovered and known again and again, and as often lost and forgotten; for all is in Plotinus, and in Swedenborg's unopened books. Swedenborg does not state his doctrine of souls in philosophic terms; he was not a philosopher. In his more anthropomorphic terms, he conceives the whole as the "Grand Man", in whose single life all individual lives are comprised; and within that cosmic body there are group-souls, multitudes of individuals in the same spiritual state who (as he often says, and Blake follows him) "from a distance" appear as a single individual. Since mind has no such frontiers as body has, all these interflowing, living multitudes comprise the living body of the Grand Man, the "Divine Humanity". Blake has summarized the Swedenborgian teaching of the many-in-one and one-in-many of the world of spirits:

> Then those in Great Eternity met in the Council of God
> As one Man, for contracting their Exalted Senses
> They behold Multitude, or Expanding they behold as one,
> As One Man all the Universal family.[24]

Swedenborg taught that individuals live not from themselves but from "the Lord"; whom Blake calls "Jesus, the Imagination"; whom both Jung and Yeats, taking the term from the supreme theology, the Indian, call the Self. Is that "Ghostly Self", Jung's Collective Unconscious, as Yeats's communicators seem to say, the habitation

23. MacKenna, Plotinus, Ennead IV.3.5, II: 13.   24. Keynes, Blake, p. 277.

of discarnate spirits and the sum of their knowledge and their memories? If Yeats persisted over so many years in his questioning of that faithless depth of Hades, it was because he sought to understand what Blake calls the Imagination, as it reveals itself in our dreams, as the poet divines it in the crisis of genius, in that situation known to every inspired poet when

> Like a long-legged fly upon the stream
> His mind moves upon silence. [CP, 381]

For Yeats this "crisis that joins that buried self for certain moments to our trivial daily mind" was the dramatic meeting-point of the human and the superhuman, of the individual and the Ghostly Self, of the living and the dead. He followed Blake's example, who also disregarded Swedenborg's warning when he boldly declared, to a timid Swedenborgian "angel", "if you please, we will commit ourselves to this void, and see whether providence is here also: if you will not, I will."[25] If Blake's protection in that void was spiritual, Yeats's was intellectual discernment.

Yeats and Mrs. Yeats gave up spirit communications some years before the poet's death. Yeats's friend and fellow-Vedantist Captain Dermott MacManus, who told me this, led me to understand that this was a deliberate decision. Had the Frustrators prevailed? Or had Yeats passed beyond this phase of his thought? Captain MacManus believed that Yeats "had cooled off Swedenborg in his later years. It was all quite incompatible with the Swami's teaching of Hinduism." Captain MacManus described Yeats's and his own teacher Shri Purohit Swami as the most impressive person he had ever met, Yeats not excepted, and "he certainly had the deepest effect on Yeats."[26] Rather than renouncing Swedenborg, it is possible that Yeats had simply no more to learn from him or from the spirits.

Too much has been made of the spirits' rejection of Yeats's offer to spend "what remained of life in explaining and piecing together these scattered sentences. 'No' was the answer, 'we have come to give you metaphors for poetry' " [v, 8]. For Yeats did nevertheless spend several years on the construction of that complete symbol of the Self he calls the Great Wheel. And the "symbols for poetry",

25. *Ibid.*, p. 155.   26. Letter to the author (May 1973).

if such they were, are on a scale comparable to Dante's mountain (also a system of spirals and inverted cones) and not such things as literary critics discuss. Such symbols belong to the order of the "sacred geometry" of the Pythagoreans, of Chartres Cathedral and its sacred maze; to the objective "ground" of the psyche; to an order of things not to be altered by the will of any artist; an order, rather to whose rigorous objective truth he must make his art conform.

AE (who was, it must be remembered, an accomplished astrologer and President of the Dublin Astrological Society), whose cast of mind was less diagrammatic than Yeats's, has many profound things to say on the Self as the habitation of spirits. AE was aware of the interflowing of minds, speaking, in *The Candle of Vision*, of the visions of dream and imagination which may come "reflected from spheres above us, from the lives of others and the visions of others".[27] The moment we close our eyes and are alone with our thoughts and the pictures of dream, we are alone with mystery and miracle. Or are we alone? Are we secure there from intrusion? Are we not nearer the thronged highways of existence where gods, demons, men and goblins all are psychical visitors?"[28] We have access, AE says, "to a memory greater than our own, the treasure-house of august memories in the innumerable being of Earth".[29] From this belief he develops his own view of the nature of genius:

> I have often thought the great masters, the Shakespeares and Balzacs, endowed more generously with a rich humanity, may, without knowing it, have made their hearts a place where the secrets of many hearts could be told; and they wove into drama or fiction, thinking all the while that it was imagination or art of their own, characters they had never met in life, but which were real and which revealed more of themselves in that profundity of being than if they had met and spoken day by day where the truth of life hides itself under many disguises.[30]

But while saying that "the fact that Earth holds such memories is itself important", AE too, like Yeats, like Swedenborg, like the Chaldean Oracle, like Orpheus himself, warns that "it is a world where we may easily get lost, and spend hours in futile vision."[31]

27. *The Candle of Vision* (London: Macmillan, 1918), p. 43.
28. *Ibid.*, p. 45.   29. *Ibid.*, p. 49.
30. *Song and its Fountains* (London: Macmillan, 1932), p. 42.
31. *The Candle of Vision*, p. 64.

Many academic readers of Yeats's poetry have chosen to disregard his answer to the question "what is man?" or dismissed that answer as irrelevant, a mere intrusion into certain poems and plays, but on the whole making no difference to our reading of his work. I believe, on the contrary, that Yeats at all times sees men and women—and how many of his poems celebrated his friends, his contemporaries—in the dignity, the wholeness, of their immortality. For him, as for Plotinus, a lifetime is a part enacted on a stage; we play the part for which past experience has fitted us, and we will play other parts, taking on the new roles for which we may prepare ourselves. And the meaning, the unity of the drama, belongs not to one part or another, but to the whole. Those he admired are those who play their predestined parts greatly; who

> should the last scene be there,
> The great stage curtain about to drop,
> If worthy their prominent part in the play,
> Do not break up their lines to weep.
> They know that Hamlet and Lear are gay .... [CP, 338]

And so with his politics. Neither the sentimental humanism nor the socialist egalitarianism of his time could ever have seemed to Yeats otherwise than as naïve palliatives of the injustices, the tragedies, the inequalities of the world. When he wrote "In Memory of Eva Gore-Booth and Con Markiewicz",

> Dear shadows, now you know it all,
> All the folly of a fight
> With a common wrong or right.
> The innocent and the beautiful
> Have no enemy but time;

he was passing upon the politics of time the judgment of the politics of eternity as he had come to understand it. The judgment is one those who make a religion of politics at all times resent, but is nonetheless the teaching of every religion which holds the soul to be immortal. For those who "dance on deathless feet" its injustices, tragedies, and inequalities are not only the infinitely various richness of life but also its justice. Yeats's "mysterious wisdom won by toil" has restored to our time the dignity of a self-knowledge whose wholeness includes both life and death, many lives and many deaths through whose course we may discover, express, create ourselves within the One; a knowledge of whose symbols he wrote: "they have helped me to hold in a single thought reality and justice."

Yeats, Spiritualism, and Psychical Research

Arnold Goldman

~~~

Of W. B. Yeats's interests in the esoteric and the occult, his attachment to spiritualism and to its investigation by means of so-called psychical research has attracted the least attention.[1] In part this neglect stems from Yeats himself, for once the intensity of his interest had waned, he could minimize its attraction and influence as compared to that of other, "harder" esoterica.[2] Thus, the spiritualist "interlude" has come to seem, when considered at all, a marking time between involvement in "magick" and in his own "system", as set out in *A Vision* and elsewhere. Even Virginia Moore, who gave Yeats's "spiritism" a chapter in her study of the poet's esotericisms, singled it out for a special disclaimer as "distasteful" [p. xv]. If the phase of spiritualist investigation was transitional, however, it has significant bearings upon the development of Yeats's thought and attitudes, and even upon the character and manner of his subsequent poetry.

Hone, Ellmann, and Virginia Moore agree in dating Yeats's interest in spiritualism from 1911, "encouraged greatly by an encoun-

---

1. See Joseph Hone, *W. B. Yeats, 1865-1939* (London: Macmillan, 1962), pp. 281-8; Richard Ellmann, *Yeats: The Man and The Masks* (London: Faber, 1961), pp. 196-205; Virginia Moore, *The Unicorn* (New York: Macmillan, 1954), pp. 218-55.
2. The "Introduction" to the 1937 revised edition of *A Vision*, dated "November 23, 1928, and later," is the most significant acknowledgment. It is discussed below.

ter, while he was in Boston in 1911, with a very remarkable American medium, the wife of a doctor named Crandon" [Hone, p. 281].[3] Very remarkable indeed that would have been in 1911, as Mrs. Crandon, the famous "Margery medium", did not begin to practise her mediumship until 1922. Hone, knowing that Yeats certainly became acquainted with Margery and Dr. Crandon in the latter twenties, had presumably seen references to a "Mrs. C." in Yeats's papers, and assumed it was Mrs. Crandon.

Yeats's "Mrs. C." of 1911 was undoubtedly "Mrs. Chenoweth", or "Mrs. C.", the name given to Mrs. Minnie Meserve Soule as a medium when under investigation by J. H. Hyslop, sometime Professor of Ethics at Columbia University and by 1911 in control of the American Society for Psychical Research (ASPR). While there is no reason to doubt that Yeats did indeed meet Mrs. Chenoweth in 1911, most likely by attending a seance, it is also possible that he knew about her before he left for America, for Hyslop had begun to make her his Exhibit A from 1909, in both the *Proceedings* and the *Journal* of the American SPR, which were subscribed to by the British SPR and by many individual British members of both societies. Any acquaintance with these journals or their readers would have alerted Yeats to the significance Hyslop was attributing to his "Mrs. C." In order to appreciate that significance, and to understand the precise point at which Yeats enters the history of spiritualism, a short résumé is necessary.

The mid-nineteenth century saw an explosion of mediumship in the United States, but it was usually of the "physical" variety—i.e., table-rapping, levitation, "transits", mysterious lights, etc. In England, Rev. W. Stainton Moses developed, around 1873, a form of "automatic writing" while in a trance state, and in 1882, he joined the Society for Psychical Research, founded by F. W. H. Myers and others for the objective and scientific investigation of such and similar psychic phenomena.[4] In 1886 Moses resigned from the SPR, claiming that it was impossible to convince his dogmatically scep-

3. Moore, who also says it was Mrs. Crandon (p. 222), cites Hone as her source. Ellmann names no names (p. 196).
4. See *William James on Psychical Research*, ed. Gardner Murphy and Robert O. Ballou (New York: Viking, 1960), pp. 29ff. The essay, "What Psychical Research Has Accomplished," was published in *The Will to Believe and Other Essays*, 1897, and was based on addresses and articles composed between 1890 and 1897.

tical colleagues of the legitimacy of the "controls" and other "manifesting spirits" who announced themselves through his script.

Moses' writing purported to come from deceased persons who offered instruction in philosophy and religion. These "Controls" claimed to form a cohesive group, which came to be called the Imperator Band. Under its "leader", "Imperator Servus Dei", and "Rector", another prominent Control, the Band purported to have assembled a collection of choice spirits who desired to warn (Western) man of the impending crisis of civilization. Subsequently, the script or trance-voices of other mediums, most prominently Mrs. Leonore Piper of Boston, Massachusetts, began to attest visits from the Imperator Band.[5]

In 1885, Mrs. Piper had come to the notice of William James, whose wife and mother were attending her seances. James, who was already interested in the phenomena of consciousness and the boundaries of scientific research, immediately saw certain possibilities for research and experiment in the tranced voice and automatic writing emanating from Mrs. Piper. He headed a committee which reported on her in the first *Proceedings* of the new American branch of the SPR[6], and when his work at Harvard precluded proper attention to the Piper phenomena, he asked the London SPR to send someone over to Boston to take charge of the investigation. The SPR appointed Richard Hodgson, who had earlier gained prominence and repute by exposing Madame Blavatsky's pretensions to mediumship (pretensions which she discouraged in her followers).

Mrs. Piper's mediumship went through a number of stages, marked by the predominance of different controls. In the first stage, her main control was "Phinuit", whom she appears to have taken over from the "psychic healer" she had consulted in 1884. Phinuit's pretensions to having been (in life) a French doctor of medicine were regarded as unproven by Mrs. Piper's investigators. From 1892 to 1897, Phinuit gave way to a new control, purporting to be George Pelham, a New Yorker who died in February 1892, and who had been known by Hodgson. Hodgson's sessions with Mrs. Piper during this period appear to have swung him away from

5. The Imperator Band deserves a separate study. It has a clear place in *fin de siècle* speculation with the "voices prophesying war" of decadent apocalyptism. Their warnings blended with other "prophecies" of the coming of world catastrophe.

6. James, pp. 196-200.

the scepticism of "secondary personality" theories towards theories of spirit survival and communication by the dead. In the next stage, a new control, purporting to be the late Stainton Moses, revealed that he had joined his Imperator Band and the Band itself became Mrs. Piper's principal (multiple) control, facilitated by the almost exclusive use of automatic (trance) writing. (In subsequent years many of the recently deceased founder psychic researchers would turn up as controls, not least among them Myers, Hodgson, and James.)

Hodgson and J. H. Hyslop, with James acting as advisor, laid out basic rules for investigating the veracity of mediums and began the task of categorizing the possible explanations of "non-fraudulent" mediumship. The poles of interpretation of the latter became, on the one hand, versions of multiple and suppressed/released personality, and on the other, the "spiritist" explanation, the conviction that the medium was the channel for communications between this world and "the other world", that the communicators were truly the deceased they purported to be, and therefore that individual spirit survived after physical death. Theses of "telepathy" ("thought-transferences", mind-reading) also entered into the possible explanations, more usually into the multiple-personality explanation. James himself considered the logical possibility that *all* the hypotheses might be true, even of the same medium.

In December 1905, Hodgson died unexpectedly. Reporting on Mrs. Piper to the SPR in 1909, James noted that "certain differences of opinions had been developing" [p. 142] among American SPR members in the wake of Hodgson's decease, particularly over such questions as the future of the American Branch and its "mass of records", especially the records of Mrs. Piper's sittings. James's diplomatic conclusion—"In the end, however, since we all had fair minds and good will"—does not disguise the nature of the rift. James in particular, and others, did not trust Hyslop, who had become a "convinced spiritist"—i.e., a believer that neither telepathy nor multiple personality explanations were valid but that the "voices" or "hands" were truly of the dead. James did not want Hyslop to inherit the Piper materials and the continuing Piper investigation, especially as Mrs. Piper had begun to develop a new control, who identified "himself" as Hodgson. The so-called "Hodgson-Control" was "introduced" in Piper communications by the Imperator Band. James, who kept Hyslop away from the new sessions, reported that the Hodgson-Control material was a poor case for evaluating the survival hypothesis.

The settlement of the James-Hyslop controversy was that Piper material would either be returned to the original sitters or to the London SPR and that Hyslop should not investigate Mrs. Piper further.[7] In return he would be allowed to re-charter the American SPR as an independent society, but not as a branch of the SPR in London. From 1907 Hyslop began publishing a new series, *Journal* and *Proceedings*, but it was obvious that he had no stellar attraction such as Mrs. Piper had been earlier, and however much he claimed that it was that lady who had convinced *him* of the survival hypothesis—and that she had convinced Richard Hodgson too (which others now disputed)—he would need to find a medium to investigate further, and one who would make his beliefs appear credible.

In his first *Journal* volume (1907), Hyslop had touched momentarily on a "Mrs. Smith" [pp. 133-5]. In 1909 he brought her back as "Mrs. Chenoweth", saying that he had to keep her identity a secret since publicity would be offensive to her. James had himself introduced Mrs. Soule/Chenoweth to Hyslop, in a letter of 1906 (James, p. 112), describing a seance he had attended in which "the Piper group" of controls (i.e., the Imperator Band), including "Hodgson", had appeared in Mrs. Soule's trance communication.

At first, Hyslop was only willing to hazard that Mrs. Chenoweth's trances threw light on "subliminal processes", but after interrogating her more and more for "cross-correspondences"[8], he claimed that far from needing to *argue* for survival, he could

7. James's long report on Mrs. Piper (James, pp. 115-210) was clearly a closing of the books in the wake of this controversy. It claims that in any case Mrs. Piper's use as a subject for serious study was over: "The content of [the Hodgson-control material] is no more veridical than is a lot of earlier Piper material. . . . And it is, as I began by saying, vastly more leaky and susceptible of naturalistic explanation than is any body of Piper material recorded before" (p. 210). James is conscious that his "tone" is giving "umbrage" to some of the "spiritistic friends" of the "Piper phenomenon", and apologises for the absence of "cordiality" in his report. "Naturalistic explanation" for him—as for Yeats later—includes much in the way of "telepathy" that others considered *un*scientific.

8. For an explanation of the method of "cross-correspondences", which Hyslop developed to allow the spirits to demonstrate their independent existence from the medium, see Gardner Murphy (with Laura A. Dale), *Challenge of Psychical Research* (New York: Harper & Row, 1961), Ch. VII, "Survival".

henceforth *assume* it. The parallels between the Piper and the Chenoweth materials are notable, even though they share common features with a number of other mediums of the time. As Mrs. Piper had a young Indian girl control, "Chlorine", so Mrs. C. developed "Starlight"[9]. From Mrs. Piper she took over Phinuit, George Pelham, and Hodgson. Myers, who died in 1901, was one of the first of the researchers to reappear as a "Control" voice or hand[10]; and in both Mrs. Piper's and Mrs. C.'s trances a Myers-control appeared, to claim immortality. (After his death in 1910, William James, sceptically open-minded to the end, began to appear to "Mrs. C."—a neat mode of co-option.) Among the most interesting of Mrs. C.'s controls is "Jennie P." (or "Whirlwind"), as rude and uninhibited as that lady was genteel and proper.[11]

Under Hyslop's attentions, Mrs. Chenoweth's "powers" flourished and she became to his new American society what Mrs. Piper had been to the old and to its British parent SPR. Voluminous reports of sittings with her and the conversations Hyslop had with her controls became the foundations upon which Hyslop placed his theory of survival. It was thus the "spiritistic", "convinced", and survival-oriented wing of spiritualism and psychical research which first attracted W. B. Yeats, and not the earlier more sceptical and open-minded school typified by James and, for a time at least, by Hodgson.

This is, of course, what one might have expected of Yeats, whose enthusiasm for new interests generally ran high. Katharine Tynan had attested to his early susceptibility to seance conditions:

> Willie Yeats was banging his head on the table as though he had a fit, muttering to himself.... He explained to me afterwards that the spirits were evil. To keep them off he had been saying the nearest approach to a prayer he could remember, which was the opening lines of *Paradise Lost*.[12]

9. Just as Hyslop "protected" Mrs. Soule with a pseudonym, so he said that even "Starlight" was pseudonymous! Starlight called Mrs. C. her "medie".
10. See Murphy, "The Lethe Case", pp. 214ff.
11. Reluctant as I am to point the parallel to Yeats's Crazy Jane, it is true that control-personnel vary between the innocent and pious and the mischievous and wayward. A genteel Boston medium could say things through an uninhibited control (sometimes a pirate or fish-wife) without losing her genteel status.
12. K. Tynan, *Twenty-five Years: Reminiscences* (New York: Devin Adair, 1913), p. 209. A. N. Jeffares, *W. B. Yeats: Man and Poet* (London: Faber & Faber, 1962) thinks 1886 may have been the date of this seance (p. 36).

This proclivity may have been held in check because of Madame Blavatsky's disapproval:

> When she [Countess W——] heard I had been to a spiritualistic séance she told me she had gone to many, till Madame Blavatsky told her it was wrong. So you need not fear spiritualistic influence coming to me from that quarter.
>
> [Yeats to K. Tynan, *Twenty-five Years*, p. 269]

Both Madame Blavatsky and the Order of the Golden Dawn discouraged mediumship and seance-attendance because the active will was surrendered for the passivity of trance, or, in the sitter's case, for dependence on the powers of another. It appears to have been precisely at the time that Lady Gregory set Yeats to gathering folk stories that he once again attended seances, apparently with Constance Gore-Booth in London,[13] but a more significant involvement was yet to come.

In any case, when Yeats returned from his American lecture tour of 1911, he seems almost immediately to have begun attending seances, and once again it was not the SPR-supervised mediums, but precisely the "convinced" opponents of the SPR whom he frequented.

The editor W. T. Stead had, in 1909, determined to open a "surgery" or bureau of mediums to comfort the bereaved with evidences of survival. Calling his endeavour the London Spiritualist Alliance, he set up "Julia's Bureau". Needing a reliable medium, and what is more one whose "controls" could be depended upon to contact (as "communicators") the dead relatives and friends of a wide variety of sitters, Stead accepted the recommendation of W. Usborne Moore, a retired British naval man who was touring America, and brought to England Mrs. Etta Wriedt of Detroit.[14] This first season of seances having proved to Stead's satisfaction, Mrs. Wriedt returned to Detroit in preparation for a prolonged removal to London, and she was in fact in New York when news

13. Jeffares, pp. 148-9. Yeats presumably alludes to this interlude in "Swedenborg, Mediums, and the Desolate Places," written in 1914 (*Explorations* p. 30). Virginia Moore (p. 221) cites the Introduction to *Resurrection*, where Yeats also connects folklore collection and spiritualism, and cites Lady Gregory's *Journals 1916-1930* (p. 261) for Constance Gore-Booth's involvement.

14. W. Usborne Moore wrote two books mostly about Mrs. Wriedt, *Glimpses of the Next State* (London, 1911) and *The Voices* (London, 1913).

came that the *Titanic* had foundered on her maiden voyage, taking Stead, who was travelling to collect Mrs. Wriedt, down with the ship.[15]

Mrs. Wriedt went to London anyway, Moore making the arrangements. Stead's former secretary, Miss E. K. Harper, recorded stenographically some two hundred sittings of Mrs. Wriedt at Cambridge House, Wimbledon, Stead's former home. These records have not yet come to light. Unlike most other mediums, Mrs. Wriedt did not go into a trance: voices began to be heard in the darkened room, either through a small metal telescopic "trumpet" or variously at a distance from the medium (who, naturally enough, came under suspicion as a ventriloquist). Mrs. Wriedt, unlike "trance" mediums, was able, as she was conscious, to question and converse with her own controls, of whom she had a large cast: Greyfeather, an Indian, who spoke a pidginized American English; Dr. Sharp, a supposed eighteenth-century emigrant from Glasgow to the U.S., whom Mrs. Wriedt had taken over from another U.S. medium; John King, who claimed he was also the Welsh pirate Henry Morgan, a control common to British mediums and who only began to appear to Mrs. Wriedt after her arrival in England; and Mimi and Blossom, two Amerindian girls. Much of the argument for the veracity of Mrs. Wriedt was based upon the multiplicity of languages in which her "voices" could speak to exotic sitters: Croatian, Arabic, Gaelic, Hindustani, Norwegian, and Welsh, among others, are claimed. Other controls, who appeared from time to time, were Stainton Moses, William James, and Andrew Jackson Davis, "the seer of Poughkeepsie", whom Yeats made much of in his essay "Swedenborg, Mediums, and the Desolate Places", and of whom he may first have heard through Mrs. Wriedt.

It was in a seance with Mrs. Wriedt, of which Yeats kept a record, that the Leo Africanus-control first appeared.[16] In his

15. Nandor Fodor, *Encyclopaedia of Psychic Science* (New York: University Books, 1966), relates that Mrs. Wriedt received details of Stead's death from her primary control two days after the sinking (p. 369). A Stead-control soon developed for Mrs. Wriedt and other mediums.

16. Virginia Moore, apparently following the text now published as Yeats's *Journal* (*Memoirs*, ed. D. Donoghue, London and New York: Macmillan, 1973, p. 264), dates Leo's appearance April 10, 1911. The text gives only the month and day, however. Yeats's "Report of Séance" gives May 9, 1912, as the date (MS. coll. Michael Yeats), which Donoghue, in a note, accepts.

"Report" on the seance, Yeats noted that "an exceedingly loud voice" came through the long tin trumpet, which was "standing on its broad end in the middle of the room". Yeats could not understand what the voice said, and Mrs. Wriedt said that it "claimed to come for 'Mr. Gates' ". Yeats then said "this was evidently me. It then said in a more distinct voice which I could follow and still very loud, that it had been with me from childhood."[17]

Yeats's willingness to identify himself as "Mr. Gates" may have sprung from his discoveries while attempting to establish a family coat of arms. In 1909, "for the purpose of a bookplate", Yeats had James Duncan searching on his behalf. Duncan came up with the coat of one Mary Yeats of Lifford, which Yeats described as "Per fess embattled argent and sable. Three gates counter-charged". And, he added, "Can my sister get back to 'Mary Yeats'?"[18]— meaning, in her genealogical researches. Though at this stage no relatives or ancestors appeared to Yeats in sittings (so far as is known), before long his late uncle and former collaborator in occult studies George Pollexfen, "the astrologer", would.[19] Thus Yeats's interest in "survival" trance-mediumship can be connected to his growing interest in his ancestry, a theme with which he is preoccupied in *Responsibilities* (1914) and *Reveries over Childhood and Youth* (written 1914, published 1916).

On the occasion of the appearance of "Leo", Yeats was at first "repelled by what I considered an appeal to my vanity", in that the spirit said "they [the spirit-world?] wanted to use my hand and brain." This, he wrote, made him somewhat inattentive. Then Leo identified himself as "the writer and explorer". Yeats "noticed that 'Leo' had a strong Irish accent, whereas the Medium had a strong American accent." The Irish accent he thought "not quite true",

> [t]he kind of accent an Irishman some years out of Ireland, or an Englishman who had a fair knowledge of Ireland, might assume in telling an Irish story.

17. This follows the wording in the "Report".
18. *Memoirs*, p. 196.
19. Virginia Moore suggests a relation between the death of George Pollexfen in September 1910 and Yeats's interest in spiritualism, though she misdates Yeats's sailing to America on his second lecture tour as in the same month (p. 222). Even if the Boston seances are further removed from Pollexfen's death, however, it might well have provided the necessary spur to Yeats's attendance at a "survival" medium's.

One of the sitters, however, told me that she considered the accent like my own, and not stronger than mine. I had thought it stronger.[20] I asked the Medium [who was conscious] the meaning of this Irish accent. She replied that the control had to get its means of expression from my mind.

Miss Harper, who was present, consulted Lemprière—Mrs. Wreidt having said that the control said "You will find me in the Encyclopedia"—but the Leo she found was no explorer. Yeats, writing his report, resolved "Not to look up the references till after next Seance as they might become a suggestion to the control."

Revealingly, Yeats concluded his "Report" with two paragraphs of astrological speculation. Leo, he thought, "may turn out to be a symbolic being." His being symbolic of the solar constellation "would account for the arrogance" of the control's impatience and the "appeal to my vanity". He recalls that he has "always supposed, that the influence under which I do my work and think my most profound thoughts, is what an Astrologer calls 'solar' ", and that a dozen years before another control "said to me very similar things". But, he worries, the voice of "the domineering jocular type of half-Irish, or English-Irish storyteller ... may be a lower solar form ... the perversion of the solar power, speaking astrologically", in which case he ought clearly to shun contact with Leo.

Despite his trepidation and his self-denying injunction, Yeats did apparently consult *Chambers' Biographical Dictionary* about Leo Africanus "before the next seance", suspicious that when Mrs. Wreidt didn't know a sitter's dead friends and relations she "looked up guides for her visitors in Chambers". There he found that Leo had been a "geographer and traveller", "for me no likely guide".[21] Then, however, consulting the 1896 Hakluyt Society edition of Leo Africanus's *The History and Description of Africa* (trans. John Pory, 1600), he "discovered that Leo Africanus was a distinguished poet among the Moores." This whetted his appetite for contact with the control. Further sessions with Mrs. Wreidt at which Leo "often" reappeared at times encouraged belief—as when Yeats brought with him an Italian-speaking woman and Leo conversed with her in what (he says) she said was "excellent" Italian.

20. In his "Leo Africanus" MS, Yeats conceded that the accent was "slight" though "a little more marked than my own" (MS. coll. Michael Yeats).
21. Ben Jonson refers to "Leo the *African*" in the introduction to his *Masque of Blackness* (1605).

This was, however, followed by reports of appearances of Leo when Yeats was not present, which made him "more and more sceptical". When Leo appeared one day, in Yeats's own rooms, to another medium ("who had heard my account of you"), matters took another turn. On this occasion, Leo "said if I would write a letter to you as if you were still living among your Moors or Sudanese, and put into it all my difficulties and [*sic*] you would answer it in your name you would overshadow me . . . and answer all my doubts."[22]

This Leo-control also announced he was Yeats's "opposite": "By association with one another we should become more complete. [Leo] had been unscrupulous and . . . [?] I was over cautious and conscientious."

Some months later, Yeats wrote out the "letter" which the Leo-control had told him to write. For twelve pages Yeats describes, as to Leo, the history of their relation, what he now knows of the historical Leo Africanus, and certain of his previous contacts with mediums. He expresses his recurring doubts whether "the shades who speak to me through mediums are the shades they profess to be. . . . How can I feel certain of your identity, when there has been so much to rouse my suspicion." In his "letter", Yeats notes "something artificial" in the control's voice. He wonders whether the control-voice may only be a "secondary" personality of the medium's, reflects on "Prof." Hyslop's dismissal of telepathic explanations and mentions the experiments on Mrs. Piper and her "Phinuit"–control. Yeats traverses the common ground of explanations, natural and supernormal, without coming to conclusions, though if one considers (as did many "scientific" minds then) certain telepathic phenomena to be within the realm of naturalistic explanation, Yeats could be said to incline towards the naturalistic. At least as far as his "doubts" and "difficulties" go, he is willing to distance himself from the Hyslop group of "convinced spiritists". Yeats's concluding speculation is that the "shade" who appears to him as Leo Africanus could be "becoming a second Leo Africanus . . . a strong echo", "made subtle [?] by powers" who have invested the control "with knowledge and faculties . . . from many minds", an untrustworthy simulacrum fashioned to lead him astray.

For twenty-six pages of manuscript, "Leo Africanus" then

22. MS. headed "Leo Africanus", coll. Michael Yeats.

"answers" Yeats's difficulties. There is in these pages no attempt by Yeats to alter his handwriting—he is not affecting "automatic writing"—nor does he imply he is reporting the words of a control-voice which he has heard. Writing in the first person as Leo, Yeats is writing fiction, though without attempting to endow his narrator with a distinctive literary style.

Leo replies that he "understand[s] enough of the thoughts of your age and understand[s] your difficulty, on philosophic grounds and because of certain experiences. . . ." He claims that Yeats, like "the majority of your contemporaries", believes only what "has been proved by deductive science". Leo cites "Professor Mr. Flournoy", whom Yeats had been reading, and begins to build a tradition of belief from "Henry More the Cambridge Platon" [*sic*], "Swendenborg [*sic*], Boem [*sic*], & Blake". Leo then moves to a comparison of Yeats and himself: Yeats is "cold", "whereas I am impetuous & hot. All living mind [*sic*] are surrounded by shades." He means dream images, and goes on to say that,

> To expound our nature & lay your doubts I shall began [*sic*] not from secondary personality, which are obscured, but with your d[r]eams. . . .

Again Henry More is brought in, before Leo shifts to a description of his own life after death: "After my death in battle I was for a time unconscious." On becoming conscious, he thought he was still fighting, then "I found myself in Fez where I had been as a young man." Eventually, "memory of my death returned." Then gradually he began "to meet faces I had known" and to "re-live . . . in a dream, a tragic event" of his student days. Leo describes his posthumous adventures at some length, rather bypassing the direct questions concerning the nature of "shades" that Yeats, writing as Yeats, had proposed, only to return once more to "Henry More who has gathered [?] up so much of the Platonism of the Renaissance" and More's consideration of immortality. Here, in the mouth of Leo, the phrase taken from More, "*spiritus mundi*" makes its appearance. Leo, after More, describes "when the animal spirits withdrew from the man in trance or in death, this [*spiritus mundi*] formed his airy body, and was . . . plastic." It is what in "error, your century has named the unconscious." Leo then proceeds to unfold an elaborate theory to account for the difficulty his original self has in getting through to Yeats and the existence of extraneous, sometimes "mischiefous" [sic], aspects. This argument constitutes, held at arm's length through the invention of a narrator though it is, Yeats's nearest approximation to a full-dress rehearsal of the possible ingredients and provenance of control-voices. Yeats's Leo is claiming that, however overlayered by extraneous elements (personality of the sitter, of the medium, of various present and absent intermediaries), "yet we are the same spirits"—not the "echo" of Yeats's "own" final speculation or the "lower solar form" of astrology, a deceptive fabrication. Here is the nub of the matter for Yeats:[23] did the voice of Leo, however intermixed and tainted, *originate* from the historical Leo, or did the control-voice originate elsewhere (not necessarily from the medium) and only accumulate notions of Leo as it went along? Yeats feared to be taken in by the latter, and he feared for his soul.

As the manuscript proceeds Leo insinuates himself closer to Yeats, claiming to "know all", to have read the same books, to "have shared in your joys and sorrow" by virtue of being Yeats's "opposite, your antithesis"; indeed "I alone am your Interlocutor." Leo shows his awareness of Yeats's fear of evil spirits, though, by concluding, "Yet do not doubt that I am also Leo African [sic] the traveller." Yeats's reply to Leo was short: where one might have imagined a lengthy examination of Leo's claims, Yeats says only that he is "not convinced that in this letter there is one sentence that has come from beyond my own imagination." As a way of cutting through the intricacies of the control-spirit the reply is practically Johnsonian, but it does perhaps betray a disappointment: Yeats might have hoped that resort to fictional technique (pretending to write as Leo), which was something of an approach to mediumship while stopping short of it, would result in his convincing himself of Leo's "truth". But, he notes, "I have been conscious of no sudden illumination": nothing that "Leo" has written "has surprised me". Concerned for some years that his *dramatis personae* might only be fragments of himself, that the conflicts he posited in drama and verse were only intra-psychic shadow-boxing—"rhetoric" not "reality" in another of his formulations—Yeats was perhaps hoping that spiritualism would put him in touch with something outside

23. Ellmann, p. 200: "The difficult but crucial question for Yeats to decide was whether Leo Africanus was an image or a phantom ... really the ghost of a dead poet from Fez or ... a creation of the living man's?"

himself, reduce the merely egocentric.[24] If Leo, hereafter abandoned, was not to provide that guarantee, he was a step in the invention of a larger systematization of masks, opposites and antitheses, of the anti-self, and of subjective and objective personalities, all meant in part to rescue the poet from mere subjectivity and from the mere romantic exploration of self.

"Leo" told Yeats nothing about "the Cambridge Platon Henry More" that Yeats did not by then know. Leo used More for precisely the purpose for which Yeats had earlier turned to him—to help construct an explanation of the imperfections of control-messages. If controls *were* who they claimed to be, why was their knowledge of their (former) selves often so imperfect, if at other times seemingly uncannily accurate? Whereas some researchers formulated explanations of telepathy, either supporting or doubting the authenticity of the control's claimed identity, and others, convinced spiritists, developed theories of the occlusion or hindrance of the messages due to seance-conditions (including the personality of the medium or of the sitters) or the mysterious nature of the "other world", Yeats turned to the Platonic philosophical tradition. In More he found discussions of what Virginia Moore terms the "hierarchy of intermediate spirits [which] ranges between God and man", and of the "mediated" borrowings which enable the spirit to return to earth to "greet friends and kindred".[25] In Emmanuel Swedenborg, too, Yeats found a doctrine of intermediate forms and of spirit-return which he could claim as a working hypothesis for the observed facts of trance mediumship. Each philosopher lent a sufficient authenticity to the spirits. Questing man was not being mocked.

Philosophical justification was accompanied by an attempt to prove the hypotheses in experiments. Yeats's discovery of the automatic writing talent of Elizabeth Radcliffe gave him a personal laboratory situation, and growing contact with the SPR—which, as we have seen, both the Hyslop society and the Stead establishment repelled or shunned—gave him a knowledge of the experimental tests proposed by the more scientific and sceptical wing of

24. The Leo Letter "shows his delight over the idea that his mask, instead of being his own deliberate mental creation, might be a full-blown personality ... it would prove his battle was not internal, but external ... " (Moore, p. 236). I find "delight" absent, desire and dubiety present.
25. Moore, p. 223.

psychical research. If the Radcliffe experiments, as he claimed, convinced him of the authenticity of the messages, they also taught him a respect for and use of "scientific" procedures which, in his hatred of "materialistic" science—as he understood it—he had never before had.[26]

In both of his major mediumistic encounters (before Elizabeth Radcliffe), Yeats began outside the aegis of the SPR, indeed with its particular American and English antagonists, but gradually he worked towards the more mainstream, less committed, more sceptical group. It could even be that his involvement as a "researcher"—however much he was simultaneously on the trail of "belief"—helped him to an augmented ability to pursue subjects with more rigorous tenacity and logic, and more organized questioning, and that his poetry of the middle 'teens and afterwards inherited this new legacy. Yeats himself later attributed his gain "in self-possession and mastery" in *The Tower* (1928) and *The Winding Stair* (1933) to the "incredible experience" of his wife's automatic writing and its revelation of a visionary system [v, 8]. Concluding his section on Yeats's spiritualist adventures, Richard Ellmann pointed to the "indecision" and "evasion" of the language of the *Responsibilities* poems and to the "reconciling" or "uniting" metaphors which "somersaulted over the question of literal belief" [pp. 203-5]. What Ellmann calls "indecision" is also a mode of *precision*, of not claiming more than is felt to be true, and Yeats's "psychical research" involved him heavily in such exact and careful formulations.

In his essay "Swedenborg, Mediums, and the Desolate Places" (1914), Yeats attempted to formalize what he had learned, and to join to the former two interests a third, the wisdom of the Irish folk. Indeed he claimed that it was precisely his inkling of an "ancient system of belief" in the stories and legends of the folk which Lady Gregory had been collecting—and for which his essay was to be an introduction—which had first sent him to seances [E, 30].[27] The three are linked in a sequence of expositions, and if no

26. William James, reviewing the achievements of psychical research, noted that it had been partly responsible for breaking a kind of scientific log-jam, and he hoped that the newer, less rigid ideas of science would win back to science numbers of fine minds who had earlier been repelled by it (James, pp. 44-7).

27. That Yeats should have chosen to link Swedenborg and spiritualism to the notional subject of the essay may not exactly have surprised Lady Gregory, but was probably not what she bargained for.

PLATE I: Spirit-photo of W. B. Yeats.

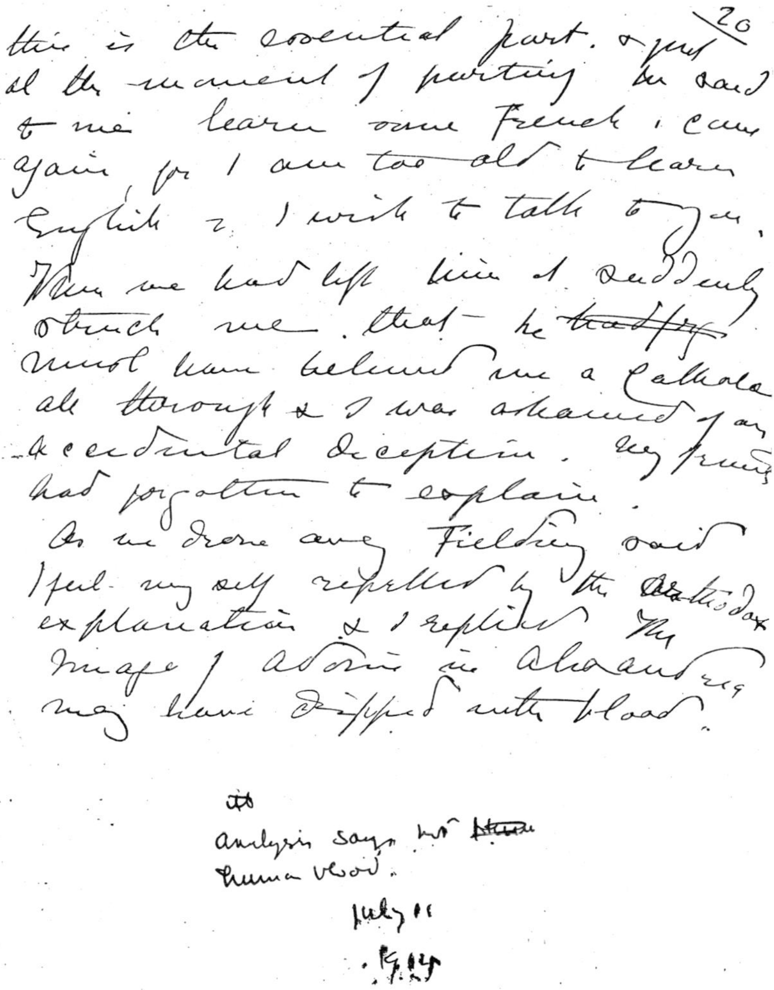
20

this is the essential part. & just at the moment of parting he said to me learn some French & come again for I am too old to learn English & I wish to talk to you.

When we had left him it suddenly struck me that he ~~had pro~~ must have believed me a Catholic all through & I was ashamed of an accidental deception. My friend had forgotten to explain.

As we drove away Fielding said I feel myself repelled by the ~~orth~~ orthodox explanation & I replied The image of Adonis in Alexandria may have dripped with blood.

it
Analysis says not ~~human~~ human blood.

July 11

1914

PLATE 2: (*opposite*) Photograph of bleeding oleograph.

PLATE 3: (*above*) Last manuscript page of Yeats's essay on the bleeding oleograph, in Maud Gonne's hand, with Yeats's note about the results of the blood test.

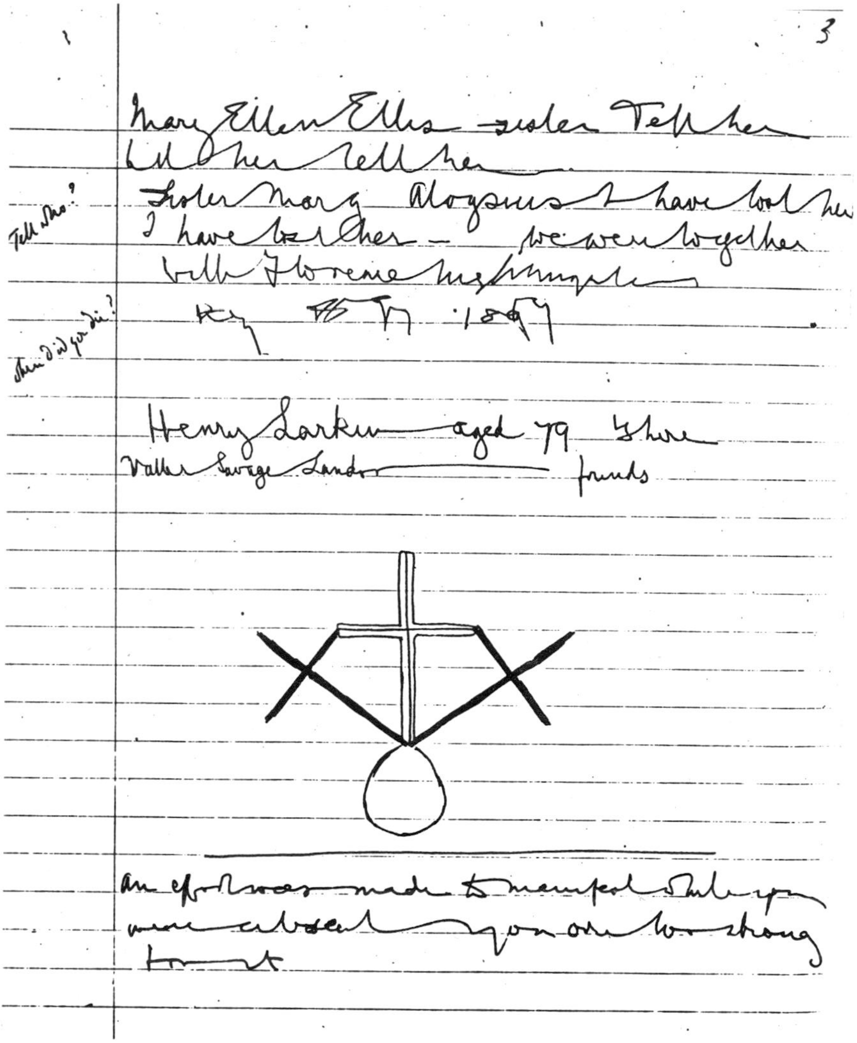

[Sheet of automatic script with handwritten text and marginal notes, largely illegible. Marginal notes include questions such as "Tell who?", "When did you die?". Legible fragments of the script read:]

Mary Ellen Ellis — sister Tell her
tell her — tell her
Sister Mary Aloysius — I have lost her
I have lost her — we went together
with Florence Nightingale
[symbols] 1867

Henry Larkin — aged 79 I have
Walter Savage Landor — friends

An effort was made to manifest while you
were absent — you are too strong
to resist

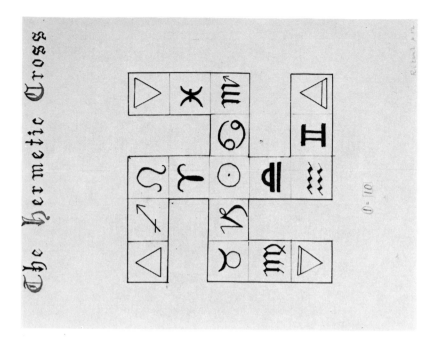

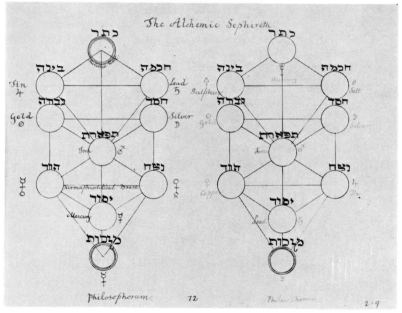

PLATES 6 & 7: "The Hermetic Cross" and "The Alchemic Sephiroth" from Georgie Hyde-Lees's Golden Dawn folder.

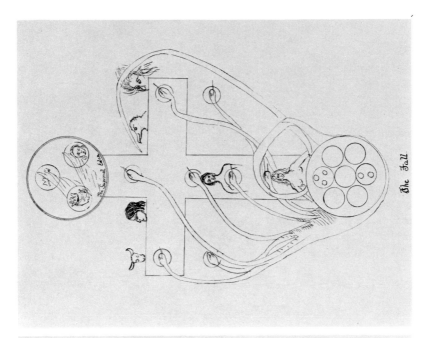

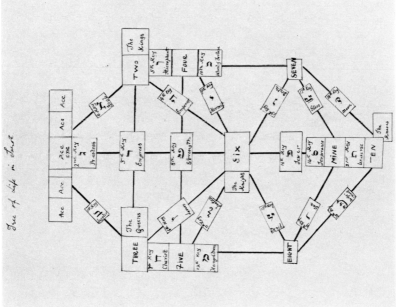

PLATES 8 & 9: "The Fall" and "Tree of Life in Tarot" from Georgie Hyde-Lees's Golden Dawn folder.

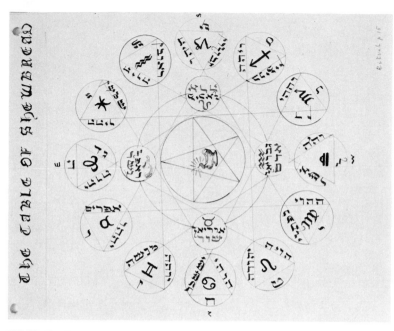

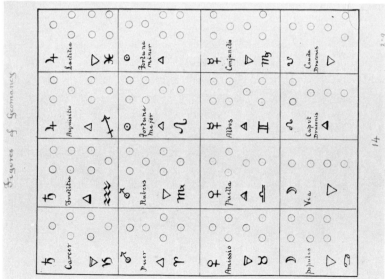

PLATES 10 & 11: "The Table of Shewbread" and "Figures of Geomancy" from Georgie Hyde-Lees's Golden Dawn folder.

direct transmission could be claimed to bind "the desolate places" with the other two, Yeats had by then read enough to assert that, "It was, I believe, the Frenchman Allen Cardoc and an American shoemaker's clerk called Jackson Davies [sic], who first adapted to the seance-room the philosophy of Swedenborg [E, 45].[28] Yeats attempts to account for the weakness and implausibility of many controls, not as "Leo" had, but in his own voice:

> If an image speak it will seldom seem very able or alert, for they come for recognition only, and their minds are strained and fragmentary.... All may seem histrionic or a hollow show....
> Most commonly, however, especially of recent years, no form will show itself, or but vaguely and faintly and in no way ponderable, and instead there will be voices flitting here and there in darkness, or in half-light, or it will be the medium himself fallen into trance who will speak, or without a trance write from knowledge and intelligence not his own [E, 54].

This is a neat, if unconvincing, reversal of the usual history of spirit phenomena. Whereas other observers were impressed by the increasing volume and greater articulateness of trance controls, Yeats is here claiming a degeneration or deterioration of activity from an earlier more complete physical presence. Somehow, modern disbelief has produced a counter-reaction in the spirit world, whose denizens, in Yeats's view, far from being spurred to greater activity to convert unbelievers, are themselves becoming paler and paler shades of their former more "physical" ghostly selves. The essay, which he might have hoped to be his *summa*, rather trails off, with ironic references to "my fat old woman in Soho". In the end, it was not in this kind of cognitive synthesis that Yeats was to invest his major energy but in his own "system", and *A Vision* has a consider-

28. Andrew Jackson Davis (1826-1910) became the "subject" for an itinerant mesmerist in 1843, and under the influence of other mesmerists dictated his *The Principles of Nature* (1847). His first psychic "flight through space" as described in *The Harmonial Philosophy, A Compendium and Digest of the Works of Andrew Jackson Davis*, ed. by "A Doctor of Hermetic Science" (London: William Rider & Son, 1917), pp. xxiii-xxiv, is closely followed by Yeats [E, 45-6]. Davis opened clairvoyant clinics, but from 1847 he dispensed with the assistance of mesmerists, claiming that he could autoinduce the trance state. Though he described his entranced experience thereafter, he did not speak while tranced. The Spiritualists did adopt him as a precursor (cf. *The Harmonial Philosophy*, p. viii), however, and compared him to Swedenborg (*Ibid.*, p. xxxi).

able claim to be considered the primary fruit of his years of involvement with spiritualism and psychical research.

Indeed, as he declared in the Introduction to the revised version of *A Vision*, the matter of the "vision" first came to him in his bride's automatic writing on October 24, 1917. The relationship between Yeats and Georgie Hyde-Lees had been cemented when she "started accompanying him to seances, and helping him check up on data."[29] Virginia Moore has described that extraordinary honeymoon, with Yeats abstracted and meditating a poem about his earlier loves:

> Mrs. Yeats knew a spade when she saw it. But, having accompanied this man to seances, she knew, also, an unfailing source of fascination. Four days after her marriage, and the very day he started his poem, she decided—she admits this very honestly—to "make an attempt to fake automatic writing."
>
> To her utter amazement, she says, her hand acted as if "seized by a superior power." The loosely held pencil scribbled out fragments of sentences on a subject of which she was ignorant. "Thomas of Odessa" claimed to be writing; then others. (p. 253)

Yeats eventually described the process in some detail [v, 8-25]:

> Except at the start of a new topic, when they would speak or write a dozen sentences unquestioned, I had always to question, and every question to rise out of a previous answer and to deal with their chosen topic. My questions must be accurately worded, and ... asked without delay or hesitation. [v, 10-11]

"Speak or write" because in 1919, "the communicator of the moment ... said they [*sic*] would soon change the method" and Mrs. Yeats began, less fatiguingly, to talk in her sleep.

It is significant that Yeats always spoke of Mrs. Yeats's "communicators", rather than "controls". Where for most mediums the controls transmit messages from unheard sources (the communicators), in some cases of multiple communications the figure of a control diminishes and "communicators" make their communications directly. The premier case of multiple communication was, of course, that of the Imperator Band as it appeared first to Stainton

29. Moore, p. 229; from conversation with Mrs. Yeats.

Moses and then to Mrs. Piper, in both of which cases Yeats was well versed.[30] Yeats's Communicators have a number of other features in common with the Imperator Band, though Yeats appears not to have claimed them for his (or Mrs. Yeats's) own: both groups were concerned with what Yeats called "years of crisis" (p. 11)—the gathering crisis of Western civilisation—and with the judgment of the soul; and the communications of each group were opposed by forces who impeded their work, and whom Yeats called "Frustrators". Mrs. Yeats and Yeats appear to have tapped significant aspects of the Moses-Piper communications for *A Vision*, the origins of which thus lay clearly within the development of trance mediumship phenomena in England and America. Hoax and mutual hoax explanations aside,[31] the multiple possibilities of subconscious recall, telepathic theories and convinced spiritist theories were less important to Yeats than the substance of the revelations: *A Vision* summarizes, formalizes, and codifies a number of esoteric traditions, spiritualism among them. The relationships between the parties in the trance situation also became available to Yeats as a poet, and aspects of the trance-mediumship scenario can be glimpsed in subsequent relationships between the poet, his narrators, and his characters.

Regret over the diminution of "visionary" powers punctuated the poems of these years: the second epigraph to *Responsibilities* (*"for a long time now/ I have not seen the Prince of Chang in my dreams"*), and "Lines Written in Dejection" ("When have I last looked on/ The round green eyes and the long wavering bodies/ of the dark leopards of the moon?") are characteristic of this Coleridgean depletion. The one specifically visionary poem of this period, "The Cold Heaven", revealingly turns, as did so much psychical research, speculation to the immediate life-after-death in its conclusion:

30. Yeats's manuscripts contain some 260 pages in an envelope marked "Note-Book of Stainton Moses". He refers to Mrs. Piper on a number of occasions, including his seance-set play, *The Words upon the Window-pane*.
31. Moore felt Mrs. Yeats "forthright and transparently honest" (p. 256) in claiming genuine mediumship powers, and doubted she "sustain[ed] years of deception": "deliberate hoax. On Mrs. Yeats's part, with Yeats as victim? No the eyes are too honest" (p. 257). But Moore then spends five pages discussing whether it might not have been a "joint" hoax, or dramatic fiction.

Ah! when the ghost begins to quicken,
Confusion of the death-bed over, is it sent
Out naked on the roads, as the books say, and stricken
By the injustice of the skies for punishment?

This seems to imply that "vision", should it return, would be chilling. A greater relish for this kind of bleak negative vision would come with the poetry written out of the *Vision* material itself, but in the intervening years Yeats did rely in part on the spiritualistic voice or visitation as he moved from absence to fulness of visionary power. The "Shade" of "To a Shade" is, for instance, a literal spirit-visitor. The poem's second paragraph has passion, but the use of the returned ghost of Parnell to open and close the poem is at once too purposeful and too facetious.

By "Ego Dominus Tuus", however, Yeats's "Ille" is calling for his own Leo Africanus, and with assurance he *summons* his "double", "opposite", and "anti-self", concepts which, as we know from their development in *Per Amica Silentia Lunae*, did not have to wait upon Mrs. Yeats's mediumship. "Hic", the poem's straight-man, is the romantic who wants only to "find myself": "Ille" wants to get beyond and outside of himself and he can prove to his own satisfaction that Dante and Keats did. While the sought-for control does not make an appearance in the poem, "Ille" does not fret over its absence: he confidently expects its coming.

Yeats in those years revived the figures of Owen Aherne and Michael Robartes, who had been rather expurgated in successive revisions of his poems (Joyce's Stephen Dedalus remembered a poem entitled "Michael Robartes Remembers Forgotten Beauty", but Yeats had by then altered it to "He Remembers . . ."). They enter a poem with no background, no biographies, and are inclined to vanish without explanation: here and in the "characters" of other Yeats poems, entrances and exits resemble somewhat those in the stenographic records of seances. Robartes in particular has the visionary faculty: "Although I saw it all in the mind's eye/ There can be nothing solider till I die" ("The Double Vision of Michael Robartes"): he seems both a character in a spirit-revelation and one *having* a revelation.

Other approaches to the mediumistic scene or the objects of psychical research appear. In "An Image from a Past Life" the new beloved fears the persistence of an old flame in her lover's psyche[32]

32. Yeats's intuition of his wife's state of mind at the time of their honeymoon?

as a kind of spirit-control's return to a medium or sitter. The "double" or "halved" dream of "Towards Break of Day" is just the kind of phenomenon the SPR documented over and over. But with a major poem like "The Second Coming" the narrator's voice comes to resemble the voice of a control in a trance-vision. The first stanza of the poem, or at the least the lines announcing "The Second Coming" are called "words out", i.e., words spoken, and the voice speaking them is superseded by another which announces "a vast image out of *Spiritus Mundi*": a control (or communicator) is speaking, and now telling us what he sees. As the "message" nears the end, "The darkness drops again", less the end of the desert day than of the control's vision. Yeats's use of the phenomena of trance mediumship is oblique: his voice plays on these contexts for tone and an assumption of power and control, a steadying framework for the dire vision.

Not only in "The Second Coming", but in "A Prayer for My Daughter" and the VIIth section of "Meditations in Time of Civil War" ("I See Phantoms of Hatred . . . "), the picture of "the future years", in its cataclysmic terribleness, appears to owe something to the notions of the Moses-Piper Imperator Band. As a metaphorical visionary in his later poetry, Yeats often evinces an *activity* of spirit removed from the passivity of certain mediums, an activity which comes in part from his assumption of an active sitter-researcher's role in relation to his own mediumistic imagination. In "The Tower" we see Yeats "pace upon the battlements"

> And send imagination forth . . .
> . . . and call
> Images and memories
> From ruin or from ancient trees,
> For I would ask a question of them all.

"All Souls' Night", which Yeats sub-titled "Epilogue to 'A Vision' ", describes a kind of seance, to which, on the appropriate night, Yeats will call three "ghosts"—deceased friends (W. T. Horton, Florence Emery, MacGregor Mathers) who themselves had spiritualistic/occult involvement. Acting as medium and sitter, Yeats invokes their presence, as presumed possessors of mysterious knowledge, to reinforce his own sense of being on the verge of

---

If his attention was being captured by such a spirit, Mrs. Yeats found more powerful attractions of the same sort.

revelatory wisdom.[33] Though the poet does not claim that his friends did return to him *as* spirits, his characterizations of them do make them present to us *in* spirit: the powers of the poet bear an analogy to those of the medium. His three friends "return", just as Myers, Hodgson, and James were purported to return as controls, to cheer and encourage the other researchers in their speculations at the frontier of secret knowledge. Despite the sad end of his friends, Yeats is comforted by his memory of them, by their presence in his poem.

Various aspects of the world of spiritualism and psychical research filtered into Yeats's poetry, and it should not surprise us that contrasting sides of Yeats were fed by them: credulity and scepticism; affirmation and dubiety. The passivity of the medium can be contrasted with the authority of the control-voice and the probing of the questioner. Yeats was always conscious of the ludicrous side of seances—he got it into *The Words upon the Window-pane*—and he was anxious to counter-balance his more vatic utterances with a humour sometimes bordering on scepticism.[34] He may also have appreciated the mischievous quality of control-utterances.

Yeats chanced upon the world of spiritualism at a moment when it seemed more pregnant of possibilities—including scientific ones—than subsequently[35], and when it was therefore more capable of providing both esoteric and exoteric satisfaction.

Far from being a closed episode which only the most devoted student of Yeats's esoteric interests should pursue—and then with "distaste"—Yeats's encounter with spiritualism and psychical research can bear sustained enquiry. It connects a number of his major interests and acts as a transforming agent or catalyst, unifying our picture of the man and the poet. Knowledge and analysis of the spiritualist episode is in fact only at the beginning: when more manuscripts and letters than have been hitherto available become

33. Cp. Yeats's apocalyptic expectations of the late 1890s, "the trembling of the veil".
34. If "Poet and sculptor, do the work" and "Irish poets learn your trade" have a certain element of humour, perhaps so does "Swear by what the sages spoke/ Round the Mareotic Lake" ("Under Ben Bulben").
35. After the outbreak of World War 1, bereaved parents of soldiers began to frequent mediums. It may be that the more sceptical investigators prudently withdrew their attentions, not wishing to upset the "comforted" relatives. In the 1920s, attention shifted to physical phenomena and to parapsychology experiments.

known, they will enable the picture to be further developed and clarified; and the analysis of Yeats's poetry and poetic procedures and strategies here presented by the use of the metaphor of mediumship will, I believe, prove suggestive and useful.

Preliminary Examination of the Script of E[lizabeth] R[adcliffe]

George Mills Harper &
John S. Kelly

INTRODUCTION

Critics generally recognize that the years immediately prior to the First World War were crucial to Yeats's development. This was the period, culminating in 1914 with *Responsibilities*, when his style changed, when he moved, as he himself variously described it, from a lunar to a solar influence,[1] from a feminine to a masculine mode, from poetry written for the eye to poetry written for the ear. This change was not a matter of caprice: it stemmed in large part from a conviction that had grown steadily throughout the first decade of the century, that his youthful optimism had been misplaced and that he was out of step with the world in which he found himself.

In the nineties he had proclaimed himself "a voice of what I believe to be a greater renaissance—the revolt of the soul against the intellect—now beginning in the world",[2] and he was confident that Ireland would play a leading part in such a renaissance. In a well-known passage in *Autobiographies* he tells how, deprived of ortho-

1. His mention of Plutarch's symposium "On the Apparent Face of the Moon's Orb" in the "Preliminary Investigation" (note 71) is of interest here, for in Plutarch the moon is equated with the soul and the sun with the mind—the distinction that Yeats himself uses. The latter part of Plutarch's essay may also have influenced his speculations about the different states of being experienced by the soul after death.

2. *The Letters of W. B. Yeats*, ed. Allan Wade (London: Rupert Hart-Davis, 1954), p. 211. Hereafter cited as *Letters*.

dox religious belief by the scepticism of his father, he had turned to imaginative literature to find or create there "the sacred book of the arts". Such a "book" was to provide modern man with powerful symbols, liberating images, which working through the collective mind would restore humanity to something of that unity of being and of culture that it had, so Yeats supposed, enjoyed before the rise of science and analytical, rather than imaginative, modes of thought. His views upon such matters evolved steadily throughout the decade as he moved from Swedenborg through Boehme to Blake and from the Dublin Hermetic Society through Theosophy to the Golden Dawn. Yet although he put forward his theories on magic, symbolism, and super-sensory perceptions with much confidence in these years he omits any detailed exposition. In seeking to explain terms or expressions taken from Platonic thought he tends to fall back on vague if picturesque archaisms. He was, as he confesses in *The Trembling of the Veil*, astray on the *hodos chameliontos*, lost amid an endless and unstructured procession of images.

He hoped for a long time that these images would, perhaps in combination with the rituals and thoughts he had noted down from his readings of the visionaries and mystics, bring him to the overwhelming revelation that he craved. Time after time one finds in his prose writings of these years the metaphor of gates swinging open to admit him (and contemporary civilization after him) into some new dispensation, some new golden age. "I had an unshakable conviction," he recalled, "that invisible gates would open as they opened for Blake, as they opened for Swedenborg, as they opened for Boehme" [A, 254], and to assist that opening he set out to establish a mystical Celtic Order and to find its "manuals of devotions" in all imaginative literature, but especially in Irish literature. Later, believing Ireland to be "the home of an ancient idealism", he founded the Irish Literary Theatre which was, in part, an attempt to widen the scope of the Celtic Mysteries.

However, the gates did not open with that world-shaking crash he had so confidently anticipated. By 1903 we find him admitting to AE that in the nineties he had mistaken "for a permanent phase of the world what was only a preparation",[3] and a little later he was to disparage the "region of shadows" he had inhabited in some of his earlier poetry as being "full of false images of the spirit and of the body".[4] There were many reasons why he should have revised and

3. *Letters*, p. 402.   4. *Ibid.*, p. 434.

reversed his former views after the turn of the century. Abroad the symbolist movement, by which he had set such predictive store, was dying, and Jarry had displaced Villiers de l'Isle Adam as the darling of the *avant garde*. At home the patrons of the Irish Literary Theatre and later the Abbey soon revealed that they preferred realistic plays to his own poetic and Synge's imaginative dramas, a token, as Yeats took it, that a new class, hostile to his opinions and inimical to his hopes, had arisen in Ireland. These gloomy signs seemed amply confirmed in the riots over *The Playboy of the Western World* and in the acrimonious controversy over the building of a gallery to house Sir Hugh Lane's collection of pictures. At a personal level, too, his life appeared to have taken a wrong turn. Maud Gonne was married, unhappily, to someone else, and he had attempted to console himself with a series of more-or-less unsatisfactory love affairs. Approaching his fiftieth year he saw himself with no wife and no heirs, nothing, as he put it in a celebrated poem, but a book. He had been wrong in his estimation of the mind and imagination of Ireland and wrong about the imminence of the "greater renaissance". It began to seem that his life had been no more than "a preparation for something that never happens" [A, 106], and he was beset by a nagging and radical fear that the transcendental beliefs upon which his whole philosophy of life was founded were based on erroneous or inadequate grounds.

In an attempt to prove otherwise he started to frequent mediums and to read widely, as the range of references in the following essay shows, in spiritualist writings. If the gates were not to crash open on the beyond in some magnificent illumination, then he must prise them open inch by inch and win what knowledge he could in the process. And the process was, as he soon discovered, laborious and uncertain. In his essay on Swedenborg he tells us that he did not go to seances in search of "evidence of the kind the Society for Psychical Research would value" [E, 31], but it was not long before he realized that if he was to find the proof he so eagerly wanted he must adopt a rigorous and discriminating attitude towards the phenomena he encountered. From reading Hyslop, Maxwell, and Flournoy, as well as from personal experience, he discovered that the human mind, being almost infinitely complex, is capable of the most extraordinary recollections and associations at a subconscious level and that, quite apart from the blatant frauds that a subject like spiritualism attracts, there were numerous examples of honest mediums who deceived their clients without knowing it, that the delicate and sensitive area of the psyche where mediumistic powers reside is susceptible to self-dramatization, telepathy, personation, and many other sublunary influences. Nor were apparently genuine messages easy to interpret and often there seemed to be contradiction and confusion. The very urgency of his desire for conviction obliged him to take up a more scientific posture, to collect evidence with care, to frame hypotheses, and then to test them with further experiments.

It was at this point in his career, shortly before the First World War, when, dispirited personally, in indifferent health, despondent about public life and confused in his search for proof of the soul's survival, he met Mrs. Wreidt, an American medium, and Elizabeth Radcliffe, a young English girl with a remarkable gift for automatic writing. Mrs. Wreidt put him in touch with Leo Africanus, who announced himself to be Yeats's anti-self and so started the poet on a series of speculations that were to result in, among other things, the closing dialogue poems of *The Wild Swans at Coole* and to influence the writing of *A Vision*. Elizabeth Radcliffe's scripts seemed to provide him with irrefutable proof that the messages she received were not the product of telepathy or unconscious memory but came from a supernatural source. They also helped him to evolve theories on the procedures of spirit recall and on the structure of the spirit world. It was in order to present these findings to the world that he wrote the "Preliminary Examination of the Script of E.R."

Since the essay is long and speaks for itself there is no need to do more here than outline its main conclusions and describe something of its genesis. Yeats met Elizabeth Radcliffe, as he tells us, in the spring of 1912, probably through Eva Fowler, an American friend of Olivia Shakespear's, married to a British army officer. His motive for consulting her in the first instance may well have been a personal one, for he recalled later that her spirits had saved him "from a serious error in a crisis of life".[5] Throughout 1912 and early 1913 consultations seem to have been intermittent, and most of the evidence upon which the "Preliminary Examination" is based appeared between May and August 1913. Once again, as his unpub-

5. Unpublished letter dated Monday, 29 December 1913. We are indebted to Senator Michael B. Yeats, A. P. Watt and Son, and Oxford University Press for permission to quote or cite unpublished letters in this essay.

lished letters to Miss Radcliffe reveal, there was an urgent private reason for his renewed interest. "The matter I asked about is of great importance,"[6] he writes in seeking guidance on the interpretation of an obscure sentence, and a few days later he describes it as having "tragic importance".[7] If he could interpret the message fully he would be able, he thinks, to "fit it to the problem of my life", for he explains that he is "living under much strain & anxiety" and that the words of her spirits "have been of much value".[8] A month later his appreciation is even more marked, "I can never make known to you my profound gratitude," he tells her, "you have changed most things for me & I know not how far that change will go . . . ."[9]

By this time, July 20, 1913, the scripts had taken on a more than personal significance. Writing had come in a number of languages, ancient and modern, and Yeats, who now hoped to prove a hypothesis about spirit communication, had resorted to experts—not always, it seems, without alarming consequences. He informed Lady Gregory that he seemed to be "deeply stirring the soul of the British Museum" since one of the authorities there "shortly after I had brought him some strange Assyrian information, saw a ghost in the Assyrian department".[10] In addition the throng of spirits who jostled to convey messages through Miss Radcliffe had grown in number. Yeats had been unimpressed with the earliest arrivals—they were easily traceable and offered nothing that could not have been gathered from readily available earthly sources. Now, however, three communications stood out as positively refuting the rationalist explanations of mediumistic phenomena. Thomas Emerson, who gave the time and place of his suicide and who could not be traced except with great difficulty and the reluctant help of Scotland Yard (for Yeats had not yet discovered that a register of births, marriages, and deaths had been kept at Somerset House since 1837), seemed to demolish the theory that apparently unknown spirits were in fact the product of unconscious memory. Sister Mary Ellis, who sought Yeats's help in locating her more recently dead friend, Sister Aloysius, seemed to disprove the same argument and also

6. Unpublished letter dated 8 June 1913.
7. Unpublished letter dated 12 June 1913.
8. Unpublished letter dated 17 June 1913.
9. Unpublished letter dated 20 July 1913.
10. *Letters*, p. 582.

gave him an insight into the different states of being that existed in the spirit world—a question that he was to return to both in this essay and in later works. Finally, Anna Louise Karsch, a German poetess, speaking in a tongue unknown to both Yeats and Miss Radcliffe, appeared to contradict Flournoy's assertion that languages which a medium uses in a seance, but of which she is ignorant in everyday life, are the result of telepathic communication with someone present in the room. When he came to write the "Preliminary Examination" it was this question of communication which occupied him most. Not merely had Anna Louise Karsch spoken in German, but a number of other messages had come in Greek, Latin, and Hebrew. Much of the Greek was clearly drawn from the New Testament but some had a fragmentary and tag-like quality that was perplexing. Moreover, words were sometimes transcribed incorrectly, and it appeared that the mistakes were due to mishearing rather than to incompetence. After a number of experiments Yeats arrived at a curious conclusion: he postulated that the long dead, having forgotten how to use language, are obliged to communicate by means of the residual memories of the more recently dead, the later either remaining passive the while, or having already abandoned the shell of such memories. In one of the more striking images in the essay he likens this process to robbers stealing the clothes of bathers.

In working towards these conclusions Yeats was animated by an intense excitement. On the day he found Sister Aloysius he was so "overwhelmed with the wonder of this discovery"[11] that he was obliged to pack up his work and go home. Mention of the town of Winchelsea in one of the scripts sent him rushing down to the South Coast, while a few days later he has made an expedition to the West Country, to seek further information from a medium near Bath. After getting the facts about Thomas Emerson he looked forward to giving Miss Radcliffe "a refutation of every form of the theory of the unconscious & in the process to make a discovery as to the means of spirit communication".[12] A little earlier, fitting his imagery to his enterprise, he had told her that he wanted "to lay the ghost of any possible form, however mystical, of the subconscious theory".[13] In writing to his rationalist and sceptical

11. Unpublished letter dated 21 July 1913.
12. Unpublished letter dated 17 August 1913.
13. Unpublished letter postmarked 28 July 1913.

father, he was eager to show that he had thought out all the possible objections to his findings. He knew, he said, "all the rationalist theories, fraud, unconscious fraud, unconscious action of the mind, forgotten memories, and so on and have after long analysis shown that none can account for this case" and that he was "now elaborating a curious theory of spirit action which may I believe make philosophic study of mediums possible".[14] Even more impressive was his announcement at a speech in Dublin shortly after the completion of this essay that for him "the great controversy is ended", that he no longer had any hesitation in accepting the spiritualist account of supernatural phenomena as the correct one.

He did not make such assertions lightly and clearly his conversion had far-reaching consequences for his philosophy and for his poetry and drama. Given his excitement and his confidence, we may perhaps wonder that his findings were not at once given to the world, that the "Preliminary Examination" remained unpublished. It may have been that Elizabeth Radcliffe, who disliked publicity, did not wish her scripts to be made available. On the other hand Yeats is careful to omit her name from his typescript, and since she herself spoke of producing a small anonymous book a little later, it seems unlikely that she would have held out against publication of the essay. Yet the fact was that Yeats had decided not to print his essay even before he had begun to collect the appendices to it (which is why none of them were included with the typescript and why none of them appear here). Of the more probable explanations for this decision, three in particular seem to us to have weight.

In the first place Yeats was moving rapidly at this time from conjecture to conjecture in his psychic investigations, and once he had recovered from his initial excitement this essay must have appeared not as a bridge into the unknown but as one stepping stone in a wide and swirling river. We must remind ourselves that from the first he saw the essay as a *preliminary* investigation and his tentativeness is apparent at every stage. "I am only at the beginning of a hypothesis," he writes when putting forward his theory of a triumvirate of communicating spirits at the end of Chapter IV, and barely more than half way through the essay he informs us that though we (and he) have been able to understand thus far "presently we will understand no more". His hesitancy and doubt grew rather

14. *Letters*, p. 584.

than diminished with time, for although some of the corrections to the typescript, which he made in June 1914, are merely changes of style, a significant number water down his earlier claims or take the edge off his more aggressive assertions. Even the theory of spirit communication mentioned above, which he had obviously laboured over, does not escape intact. He had at best advanced the theory (that the memories of the newly dead are used by the long-dead) "timidly and amid much uncertainty", and in revising the essay many months later he merely adds to our perplexity by offering yet another theory—that of secondary and tertiary personalities.[15]

Such tentativeness could hardly have been satisfying either to author or reader, and he must have felt this all the more acutely during his 1914 rereading since in the interim he had advanced further with his researches. He had, for instance, conducted more experiments with Mrs. Wreidt and had seen Mrs. Chenoweth, the famous medium, on his trip to America earlier in the year. Moreover his interest seems to have moved towards physical phenomena. In May 1914 he visited Mme Bisson in Paris and reported ectoplasmic manifestations, and from Paris he went on to Mirebeau to investigate the bleeding oleograph of the Sacred Heart, an adventure which is documented elsewhere in this volume. On his return to London he reread Swedenborg's *Spiritual Diary* and began a detailed study of Henry More, the Platonist. One consequence of all this was that the "Preliminary Examination" was superseded by his essay "Swedenborg, Mediums, and the Desolate Places" which, although not published until 1920, was in fact finished in October 1914 and may even have been begun while he was revising the "Preliminary Examination". In the later essay he sets out to answer, with Swedenborg's help, some of the questions left open in the earlier one. In turn the Swedenborg essay was to be overtaken, even before its publication, by *Per Amica Silentia Lunae* and this, in its time, to be modified and amplified in *A Vision*. Indeed, the fourth book of *A Vision* (1925), "The Gates of Pluto", "The Soul in Judgment", contains Yeats's fullest statement on the process of spirit communication and the structure of the spirit world, and in composing it he made use of evidence taken from the Radcliffe scripts. Yet this book is, Yeats confesses, "the most unfinished" section of *A Vision*, and this, as well as his "Introduction" to *The*

15. See below, note 99.

Words upon the Window-Pane, perhaps indicates that he was never able to answer satisfactorily the questions that the 1913 scripts had raised.

The fact that the "Preliminary Examination" is so exploratory leads us to the second possible reason why Yeats decided not to publish it. His customary method in his essays, especially essays treating the supernatural, is affirmation of belief backed up with beautiful or striking illustrations. Thus in "Swedenborg, Mediums, and the Desolate Places" we find such illustrations drawn, among others, from Irish country lore, Japanese Noh plays, Sir Thomas Browne, Porphyry, the *Odyssey*, and Dante's *Paradiso*. Compared with this richness, the "Preliminary Examination" appears thin in style and content. The authentic Yeatsian note sounds from time to time but is broken by the need for continual questions and tentative speculation. It might be argued that he would surely have polished the essay further before publication, but if this was his aim he must soon have realized how intractable his material was. The scripts were important to him in the first instance because of the private counsel they offered and, later, because their existence and the manner of their coming seemed to render rationalist theories of the supernatural inadequate. Yeats is unwilling to divulge the biographical significance of the messages, but we may recall that in May 1913 his mistress had deeply disturbed him by telegraphing that she was pregnant and that he had visited mediums to find out if she could be mistaken (which indeed she was). One of the Latin sentences quoted in the essay could be interpreted as the reassurance he was seeking.[16] This is, of course, surmise: to all intents and purposes we are left with the other, non-personal scripts. Some of these, the ones dealing with Emerson and Sister Ellis for example, are intriguing but very fragmentary. Others, especially the ones in dead languages, reveal themselves on translation to be trivial or banal. In using these languages Yeats supposed the spirits to be purposely demonstrating that they were not to be explained away by telepathy or unconscious memory. What counted, then, was not what was expressed but how it was expressed: the medium not the message. Compared with the structures provided by Swedenborg, the possibilities opened up by Leo Africanus, and the geometric coherence of *A Vision*, the content (as opposed to the nature) of

16. The sentence is "nemini a nobis nascitur recte". See below, note 83.

these scripts vouchsafes little in the way of illumination. Moreover, although Yeats says, in a passage already cited from the Swedenborg essay, that he was not concerned in his investigations with "evidence of the kind the Society for Psychical Research would value", here he has produced a document which seems designed to provide just such evidence, and one which he has obviously been at some pains to set out in as scientific a manner as possible. But the scientific manner was not one that came naturally to him, and he did not continue with it to the point of publication.

Yet supposing the essay had been presented to an investigator from the Society for Psychical Research, what would he have made of it? In postulating this question (and in this context it is a pity that we have been unable to find Professor Hartley's comments), we may perhaps discover a third reason why Yeats was unwilling to publish, for it perhaps struck him during his later readings of the essay that the evidence refuting the rationalist arguments is not quite so unimpeachable as he had at one time proclaimed. It turned out that there had been no need to trouble Scotland Yard over Thomas Emerson, engrossing though that Holmes-like quest had been, since his death certificate had been publicly available all the time. Again, although he checked that there was no report of the suicide in the *Times*, he does not (apart from discovering that there was no local Richmond paper) appear to have searched in any other journal. An account of Sister Ellis's death was also publicly available—in a book written by the very friend she was trying to find.[17] This, of course, is the *Catch-22* of all psychic research. If the sources cannot be traced then nothing is proved: if they can be traced then the phenomena are susceptible to normal or paranormal as well as super-normal explanation. No one who has read Miss Radcliffe's unpublished letters to Yeats would suggest that there was any question of her having deceived him—it is simply that the possibility of subliminal memory has not been so thoroughly excluded as Yeats at one stage believed.

Nor is the case of Anna Louise Karsch quite so impressive when we are reminded (by Yeats himself, let it be said) that Goethe's "Wandrers Nachlied" is sung to a very popular Schumann air, that

17. Mary Aloysius Doyle, *Memories of the Crimea* with a preface by J. Fahy (London: Burns and Oates, 1904). There were, presumably, a number of reviews of the book in 1904, some of which Miss Radcliffe might conceivably have seen.

the lines Yeats murmured from the second part of *Faust* are so familiar that he describes them as "hackneyed", and that the other lines from *Faust*, given by Karsch, "are often, I am told, quoted in sermons". Now Yeats was no great frequenter of sermons, and we may wonder who apprised him of this last fact. It might easily have been Elizabeth Radcliffe herself, for she seems to have been a devout Anglican and Yeats describes her as very pious in a letter to his father.[18] There is a further and curious inconsistency over Yeats's treatment of this German script. He is unwilling to countenance the idea that the lines could have come into the medium's mind by telepathic contact with Mrs. Fowler, an apparently knowledgeable German speaker, who was in the next room. A little later, however, he suggests that certain fragments of a Provençal *alba* were transmitted through the mind of Ezra Pound—yet Pound knew Miss Radcliffe only slightly, if at all, and was, as far as we know, many miles removed from her on the day that these fragments appeared.

There is no reason to suspect that Yeats doubted the authenticity of the messages he received. On reflection he might have decided that they would not be so compelling to others as he had hoped, but he himself remained convinced. And this is the importance of the essay to his development. Hereafter he was to take automatic writing seriously, and he was to be troubled no more by doubts about the claims of spiritualism (although he might question the genuineness of individual spiritualists). In frequenting mediums he was looking for positive proof of his own intuitions and also, after the inability of the Celtic Mysteries and the Golden Dawn to sustain his imagination, for a philosophic structure to underpin his work and, indeed, his life. Elizabeth Radcliffe's scripts provided to his own satisfaction the proof that he wanted, but they are too fragmentary and too oblique to supply any sort of coherent system. This was to come later through the automatic writing of his wife.

And this is another crucial outcome of the Radcliffe scripts: they prepared Yeats for his wife's more systematic writings. In this sense the whole episode has a fascinating biographical twist. In August 1913, when his enthusiasm about the scripts was at its height, Yeats spent two long weekends as a guest of Georgie Hyde-Lees and her mother and step-father in Ashdown Forest. Naturally he spoke to Miss Hyde-Lees of his experiments (in fact so excited was he by

18. *Letters*, p. 583.

them it is probable that he spoke of little else), and as a result of their conversations she checked the information about Anna Louise Karsch for him.[19] Thus we may conclude that when in the late autumn of 1917 she too tried for automatic writing, the writing that was to be the foundation of *A Vision* and much of the later poetry, she almost certainly had the example of Elizabeth Radcliffe in her mind.

19. See below, note 43.

Yeats's Essay

CHAPTER I

I have now in my hands copies of nearly all Miss R.'s[1] automatic script except of that great mass almost the greater portion which deals with private matters and that I have not seen.[2] I understand it is full of evidence of great value. What I have contains script in English, Greek, Latin, Hebrew and of these—after English—Greek and Latin are most abundant, and besides these writings there are a few passages of German, Welsh, Italian and French, one passage in Provençal, one passage in Irish, a few words of Chinese, a Turko-Arabic word, and some Coptic letters, and some Egyptian hiero-glyphics.[3] The medium besides English knows only French, and enough Italian to ask her way. I have asked certain testimonies of this subject to be given in the Appendix to this Essay.[4] It is notice-

1. That is, Elizabeth Radcliffe. Throughout the typescript Yeats crossed out her initial and replaced it with x.
2. We have not discovered the material referred to. It is clear from Miss Radcliffe's correspondence with Yeats that he was more eager than she to record her experiences. In a letter to Lady Gregory dated May 20, 1913 Yeats described his experiments at some length, then observed: "Unfortunately, the controls themselves forbid publication.... It is what I have been waiting for before finishing the essay" (in *Seventy Years*, ed. Colin Smythe [Gerrards Cross: Colin Smythe, 1974], p. 495).
3. Since the manuscript, which is a clean copy in Yeats's best hand, does not contain "and some Egyptian hieroglyphics" and numerous similar additions and deletions, it is clear that Yeats supervised the typing carefully. We have made occasional silent corrections in punctuation, usually in accordance with the manuscript; have called attention in the notes to significant changes in phraseology; and have inserted in brackets several, but by no means all, of the words and phrases from the manuscript which were omitted or changed in the typescript.
4. This sentence is not in the manuscript. We have been unable to locate the Appendix, which was to be an important part of Yeats's proof.

able that French is little used and Italian, I think, only twice. This suggests that these languages are left out deliberately as of less value as evidence than languages unknown to the medium. At first I watched, with Professor Hyslop's[5] discoveries in mind, for unconscious or chance[6] cheating. If a girl in trance can simulate, during a dark seance as he believes, a tambourine floating in the air by throwing it up with her teeth with such exact calculation of time that the camera and its flashlight discover it near the ceiling; and still more if this juggling trance is, as it seems, only partial sometimes (if trance is the right word for something which does not affect the mind) setting free an arm or a foot for actions of which the mind knows nothing[7]; the cheating of an automotist, whose personal honesty is beyond question, is possible and might be of an incredible subtlety. When a question was asked one day and answered the next the reference during momentary trance[8] to a book, a Greek-English version of the New Testament let us say, was a natural [first] hypothesis. I [soon] gave up this hypothesis when I compared examples that occurred in my own presence with similar examples in my copy of the Script and saw that questions sometimes asked only mentally were constantly answered in Greek and in Latin when there had been no time to consult books. There

5. Professor James Henry Hyslop (1854-1920), Professor of Logic and Ethics at Columbia University, whose work is referred to frequently in the publications of the Society for Psychical Research (hereafter cited as SPR). Having been brought "in touch with the supernormal" through the agency of Mrs. Leonore E. Piper, noted American medium, Hyslop reorganized the American SPR in 1906 and wrote extensively about the survival of the spirit. Among his books are *Borderland of Psychical Research* (1906), *Science and a Future Life* (1906), *Life after Death* (1918), and *Contact with the Other World* (1919). The most readily available source of information about him and numerous others conducting experiments concerned with survival after death is the *Encyclopaedia of Psychic Science*, ed. Nandor Fodor (London: Arthurs Press, 1933), hereafter cited as EPS.

   We are greatly indebted to Mrs. R. Tickell, Editor of Publications, and Mrs. I. Barry, Librarian, of the SPR for permission to work in the Library and for assistance and advice.

6. In the manuscript Yeats wrote: "unconscious, or trance cheating in the case of American mediums". He is probably referring to Hyslop's investigation of Mrs. Piper (see note 47, and compare Goldman herein).

7. The manuscript reads: "...is as it seems sometimes only partial effecting an arm or foot unknown to the mind."

8. "During momentary trance" is not in the manuscript.

remained the theory of unconscious memory, of the emerging of forgotten knowledge.[9] If this theory, which is considered by Flournoy and Maxwell[10] to cover so many [all] of the facts of spiritism, applies to the facts of Miss R.'s mediumship it can only do so in its most elaborate [complete] form. She must have access not only [merely] to her [own] most remote memories and to chance sights of books and tongues unknown to her, but to the memories of scholars of many languages. No emergence of her own memories could enable "the control", which is but a dissociated fragment of her own mind according to this theory,[11] to use with knowledge of their meaning passages in many tongues which could very rarely have come to her eyes or ears[12] with the English meaning and the foreign or classical words together. Telepathy from scholars' memories might [does] at a first glance account for many of the facts. The Greek and Latin are, when coherent and grammatical—as they always are in the longer passages,—quotations from texts which any student studying for holy orders would study, or quotations

9. At this point the manuscript contains a sentence which Yeats marked through: "This theory is of knowledge telepathically acquired from others."

10. That is, Professor Theodor Flournoy and Dr. Joseph Maxwell. Yeats's friend Everard Feilding reviewed Maxwell's *Les Phénomènes Psychiques: Recherches, Observations, Méthodes* (Paris, 1904), in the *Proceedings of the* SPR, 18 (1904): 490-501. One of Feilding's distinctions is important to Yeats's experiments: "The phenomena open to research may be divided into two classes, material and intellectual." Under material, according to Feilding, are "phenomena leaving some permanent trace, such as imprints or 'direct' writings or drawings, etc." Under intellectual phenomena are "such occurrences as automatic writing, table tilting, i.e. messages produced by the tilting of a table *with* contact, telepathy, clairvoyance of past, distant, or future events, etc." (p. 492). After ten years or more of experimenting Maxwell explained psychical phenomena as an "unknown force" and concluded that "a kind of collective consciousness produces the intellectual results" [EPS, p. 232].

Flournoy, Professor of Psychology at the University of Geneva, was the author of *Des Indes à la Planète Mars* (Paris, 1900), a very influential book about the mediumship of Mlle. Helen Smith. Flournoy "throws great doubt on the ascertainability of the extra-mundane existence of the entities which communicate through mediums," but "he does not doubt realities of telekinesis, telepathy, and clairvoyance" [EPS, pp. 141-2]. The prime object of Yeats's experiments was to prove that sceptics and doubters like Maxwell and Flournoy were wrong or only partially right.

11. "According to this theory" is not in the manuscript.

12. "Come to her eyes or ears" replaces "passed before her eyes".

from Greek and Latin grammars. It is well known that the manifestations of the unconscious mind continually recall [go back] memories of early life.[13] We dream again and again of being back at school and the manifestations need not lose this characteristic because they take place through another mind. When "the control" replies in Greek or Latin it does not as a rule reply in words that have a detailed correspondence to the circumstances, but in words [sentences] that have an oracular quality, a vague and general application to the matter of our question. They may be very appropriate and they are generally much too appropriate to be the result of chance,[14] but they are as a rule appropriate only as a quotation can be and their appeal is generally to the emotions. The English on the other hand is often[15] exceedingly precise, though here too, when "the control" speaks of religion there is a tendency to fall back upon current phrases. We ask ourselves, are we in the presence of a dream. Is there a world-wide conspiracy of the unconscious mind, of what Maxwell calls "the impersonal mind" that speaks through dreams, to create a false appearance of spiritual intercourse, a seeming proof of the soul's survival after death; a renewed fabrication by nature of an old falsehood necessary perhaps to the order of the world; perhaps, in the end, necessary even to the continuance of human life. The mere formulation of the thought gives to what we call "the unconscious mind", despite its resemblance to our own minds when most conscious, a subtlety which justifies us in personifying Nature and endowing her with all the deceptions of a scheming woman. And yet "the control", a portion of the medium's mind—though it may[16] have access to minds that know Greek and Latin—will not itself know either, and I do not think we will discover that pretended spirits, who claim to report themselves after death, will gather up factitious biographies from exceedingly scat-

---

13. At this point in the manuscript Yeats marked through five lines continuing and expanding the preceding sentence: " . . . & can [?] imagine the unconscious memories delivered up to some ransacking power, those that are oldest, most unconscious having the most definite & independent force [?] perhaps."

14. "And they are generally much too appropriate to be the result of chance" is a significant addition to the manuscript.

15. "As a rule" and "often" are late insertions probably made in June 1914 when Yeats added several notes to the manuscript.

16. At this point in the manuscript Yeats marked through "gather thought from many memories".

tered and recondite sources.[17] The control will not carry its power of selection so far as to compel us to postulate an independent being. It may be cunning, but not profound, for it is only a dissociated fragment of a living mind.

CHAPTER II

I will confine myself for the moment mainly to the evidence of script written in my own presence. It is easiest to examine evidence of the spirits who report the dates of their deaths, their names and certain facts of their lives.

I met the medium first in the Spring of 1912 and some time in the Spring of that year—the script is not dated (for I was still unobservant because incredulous)—two spirits reported themselves. The first claimed to be Bishop Moberly[18] who died in 1885, he had been waiting twenty-six years to communicate. I did not believe in him for I had seen no genuine automatic script [writing] though much that was not genuine and I was impatient for another form of experiment. I interrupted him and he went. A little later on the same day and in a disordered writing, a spirit gave his name as Thomas Creech.[19] He gave the dates of his birth and death, spoke of the positions in life he had held and prefaced it all with the words, "Died by rope, those who die by violence cannot rest, can you not help me". The statements of both spirits—except for a slight error in one of Thomas Creech's dates, were correct. Creech is in the Dictionary of National Biography, and it was perhaps there[20] that

17. Following the period in the manuscript, "I do not think" is marked through.
18. George Moberly (1803-1885) was headmaster at Winchester for thirty years before becoming Bishop of Salisbury. After moving to Oxford in 1918, Yeats wrote to C. Anne E. Moberly, the Bishop's daughter, to ask her opinion of her father's spiritual communication with Miss Radcliffe. Well known herself as the co-author (with Eleanor Jourdain) of *An Adventure* (1911), a book about amazing visionary experiences at Versailles, Miss Moberly warned Yeats gently that her father "considered 'communications' after death through a professional medium misleading". Obviously still planning (in 1918) to publish the "Preliminary Examination", Yeats had expressed his "great anxiety to unravel all the truth" (unpublished letter from Miss Moberly dated March 20, 1918).
19. Thomas Creech (1659-1700) was headmaster of Sherborne School, Fellow of All Souls College, and translator of Lucretius and Manilius.
20. The manuscript contains a parenthetical insertion at this point: "I am writing away from any library where I can consult it." Mr. Jones may be Lawrence J. Jones, President of the SPR in 1928-29.

Mr. Jones—who was present during the writing—verified the facts about the bishop. Nobody present had in either case any conscious association with the names. I was not impressed, for the Dictionary of National Biography is not a difficult source, and I thought the evidence, like that of a message I received about the same time with Mrs. Wreidt—the American medium—at Wimbledon[21] from the spirit of a Spanish moor[22], whose life is in Chambers' Biographical Dictionary, supported the theory of some unconscious action of the mind. The facts mentioned were precisely those in the books, whereas I should have expected from a man long dead and drawing upon his memory alone a more personal selection. In both the case of Creech and the Moor, "the control" spoke of the dictionaries, the Wimbledon spirit to give me evidence of his existence and Creech to contradict the cause given there for his suicide.

On May 17, 1913, came Samuel Gottlieb Gamelin (or Goneline as he first mis-wrote his name)[23] and the medium remembered he had come before when I was not present. I found him in an earlier

21. The manuscript names the place as Cambridge House, the home of William T. Stead (1849-1912), the popular writer, editor, and spiritualist who went down on the *Titanic*. Especially interesting to Yeats because of his gift for receiving communication in automatic writing, Stead was widely known among spiritualists as the editor of *Borderland* (1893-1897), a quarterly psychic magazine in which first appeared *Letters from Julia* (called *After Death* as a book in 1897). These letters were received automatically from his dead friend Miss Julia Ames [see EPS, pp. 367-9]. Mrs. Etta Wreidt (1860-1942), a well-known American medium, made five visits to England, the first at Stead's invitation in 1911 (see Goldman herein). Like Miss Radcliffe, Mrs. Wreidt received messages in languages and dialects unknown to her. See Miss Edith K. Harper's article about the sittings of 1911: "The Mediumship of Mrs. Etta Wreidt", *Light*, 31, Sept. 16, 1911, pp. 439-40.

22. According to a note Yeats made on a report of a seance at Cambridge House, the "First appearance of Leo" occurred on May 9, 1912.

23. The manuscript reads: "as the hand mis wrote his name". We have been unable to find additional information about Gamelin. Yeats preserved the page of script with the details summarized herein about both Gamelin and Noverre. According to a stray sheet of the automatic script, "Gonelin" said: "I wrote a book called Historica Fueorum. It is an account of my travels." Yeats spoke of Gamelin in the letter to Lady Gregory about his experiments with Miss Radcliffe: "While I was with her last week the script was interrupted by a spirit who wanted to find out if a book which he wrote was still read. He gave us facts to identify him by and the name of the book" (*Seventy Years*, p. 494).

script, which no one had verified and by the help of both, put together a series of facts; his birth at Tübingen, the date of his death, his imprisonment, his travels near the Caspian Sea, the Latin name of his chief book. He was anxious to know if his book was still read, and if so how many editions there were. I verified all the facts from the big French biographical dictionary, except that he had been imprisoned in his thirtieth not his twentieth year, and that he had made an error of ten years in the date of his birth. On the same page of the script, with the first mention of this man, I found particulars of the life of Jean George Noverre[24] who claimed to be present. All these I verified except that he described his letters on the history of Dancing as a Dictionary of the Art of Dancing and that I do not know if he knew—as he said—Marie Antoinette and Mons. Garrick.[25] He probably did know Marie Antoinette as he was connected with the Court; and I have little doubt the other was Garrick who visited France when Noverre was in charge of one of the chief Palace [Paris] theatres. He wrote at the end of his message:

Μή αμελει τοῦ ενδοι χαρισμα τειας εδσθη σοι

"Do not neglect the grace which is within you." [26] He did not come in my presence, but as I verified his statements they made a strong impression upon me. Later on, I will give reasons for believing that there is always a control, who guides the medium's hand or gives the words to the medium in some way, and another who speaks. The errors several times imply [show] difficulty in hearing[:] "by sea" in one case for instance seems a mistake for "Winchelsea". In this case I believe a spirit pronounced "Garrick" like a Frenchman, and that the spirit who was in immediate control of the hand did not know whom he referred to. On July 15th last, the control confirmed this conclusion, which I had already arrived at, by saying after writing the word "Myrh" (for myrrh): "the word is being

24. Jean George Noverre (1727-1810), a distinguished French choreographer, studied mime under David Garrick and staged spectacular ballets in London. His *Letters on Dancing* (Stuttgart, 1760) were revolutionary for the time. For further details see *Seventy Years*, p. 495.

25. At this point Yeats made an asterisk with a pen and wrote at the bottom of the page: "Yes he did know both. See *Encyclopaedia Britannica*." This is the first of several such notes which were added in June 1914.

26. From 1 Timothy, IV:14, and should read μή ἀμέλει τοῦ ἐν σοί χαρίσματος, ὅ ἐνόθη σοί—that is, "Neglect not the gift that is in thee, which was given thee...."

spoken for me but I do not know if I have written correctly".[27] In July came John Moorhouse of Miresike in the county of Westmoreland "who departed 1850 from toil and pain" and who gave a motto and the name of his wife. I found in Burke's Landed Gentry that he was John Mirehouse of Miresyke in Cumberland, Common Sergeant, and that he had given the name of his wife and his family motto correctly. I had however to go to *The Times* of February 1850 to find a possible[28] confirmation of "pain and toil". He had been taken ill at the Old Bailey a few days before his death. On July 15th came the words, "Mary Ellen Ellis tell her, tell her sister Mary Aloysius[29] I have lost her. We were together with Florence Nightingale", and when I asked the date of her death the hand wrote, "1897". And a little later the name was corrected to Sister Mary Ellis, and that afternoon the spirit in charge, "The Keeper of the Gate" as they called him, said he knew nothing except that a spirit had come that morning dressed in black and wearing a deep bonnet and that she was in much distress and believed that I could

27. Yeats preserved two long and important scripts for July 15, 1913. The afternoon script contains the sentence about "myrh" with one difference: he changed "repeated" to "being spoken".

   The morning script contains a passage (in Miss Radcliffe's hand) about the feigning of mediums who "allow their minds to be used". At this point Yeats inserted a significant note about his own hopes and attitudes:

   I most wish to know what will help to interpret the script, I would like to ask about symbol after symbol but if that is not your meaning I ask what is the cause of the deception—'a spirit' who seems to have given every proof of goodness will deceive (I think of the cases given by Maxwell). I am looking for some theory that will recover our belief in spirits, in whom I believe, with evidence as to deception.

   The afternoon script contains what appears to be Miss Radcliffe's reply: "I cannot however tell you more about symbols."

28. Yeats changed "any" to "a possible" in 1914.

29. Sister Mary Aloysius Doyle and Sister Mary Helen Ellis served in the Crimea. After their return Sister Mary Aloysius settled in the west of Ireland, ultimately becoming Mother Superior of a convent in Gort; and Sister Mary Helen was assigned to a convent in Bermondsey. Both were awarded the Order of Red Cross during Queen Victoria's Diamond Jubilee in 1897. The Convent of the Sisters of Mercy in Blackrock, Dublin, has a copy of Sister Mary Aloysius's account of her experiences in the Crimea. We are indebted to Sister Nathy, a member of this convent, for our information about both Sisters.

help her to find Sister Mary Aloysius.[30] I have not yet found Sister Mary Ellis but I have found that Sister Mary Aloysius was one of a group of Irish Sisters of Mercy who went with Florence Nightingale to the Crimea and that she died some three years ago in a Galway convent which I pass a few times in every year. On the same day came "Henry Larkin[31] aged seventy-eight, Walter Savage Landor here friends" or perhaps it should read "Here Walter Savage Landor friends". The arrangement of the words on the page leaves it uncertain. Later in the day I was told by "The Keeper of the Gate" that Larkin was a friend of Carlyle's. I find that he was a young man of a hero-worshiping disposition [sort] who had introduced himself to Carlyle and helped him with the index to Frederick. He had once said to Carlyle that Spiritualism turned "the awful stillness of eternity into a penny peep show" and made Carlyle angry by adding, that there was so much about it in the Scriptures it might be true. He is not in the biographical dictionaries but his death certificate, the date for which was got by an advertisement in which a querie [sic] confirms the statement that he was 78 when he died.[32] So far the theory of the unconscious selection of facts from the medium's buried memory or from those of others by telepathic action, though growing more and more difficult as the selective power grew more and more remarkable, could be stretched somehow to cover the facts. I do not remember any evidence given by Flournoy and Maxwell to justify such stretching but one cannot prove it to be impossible. There is nothing here to resemble their mixture of true and false, for the facts are given by the controls with precision and no more error than one finds in all dictation. Then on——[33] we received this message, "Died by self appointment

30. Yeats made an asterisk and wrote an unfinished note at the bottom of the page: "I have since found her. She died a few years ago—I do not yet know the date. She was Mother Superior in her latter years of the convent at...."

31. The anonymous author of *Extra Physics and the Mystery of Creation* (1878), Larkin (1811-1889) not only indexed all Carlyle's works but also wrote a book about *Carlyle and the Open Secret of His Life* (1886).

32. Yeats revised the typescript in ink, changing "and I have not yet been able to find the dates of his birth and death" to read "but his death certificate", etc. Between the completion of the manuscript on October 8, 1913 and the addition of the notes and slight changes in the typescript on June 7, 1914, Yeats had discovered the Registry at Somerset House.

33. Yeats left a blank for a date which he apparently did not find.

Richmond Bridge, Thomas Emerson policeman April 1850". There
is no record in *The Times* of that month and the newspaper room
at the British Museum knows nothing of any Richmond paper for
1850. Mrs. McKenna was so kind as to have enquiries made for me
at Scotland Yard (see letters in Appendix) and discovered that
Thomas Emerson was dismissed from the police force in March
1850.[34] Unless there is somewhere a tombstone with a very unusual
form of inscription (I have not yet had time to search Richmond
Cemetery) nothing will account for this but spirit action.[35] The
papers of Scotland Yard for the period have been destroyed and an
entry in the Scotland Yard Registrar is probably the only record of
Thomas Emerson's existence.[36]

I was in Wiltshire to study a medium[37] in August of this year and
spoke of Emerson and that night—this was before I heard from
Scotland Yard—she was controlled by a certain Thomas who could
not remember his surname but spoke of Richmond Bridge and of
having been wrongly accused. He showed excitement when I spoke
of the Home Office but it was almost the only thing he could remember. He knew all, he said when not in control of the medium,
but this was rather a reply to a leading question of mine.[38]

34. Yeats preserved a letter from Pamela McKenna dated August 13, 1913
"containing all the information that can be traced concerning Thomas
Emerson". She informed him that no public use was to be made of the
records.
35. Yeats made an asterisk and explained in a note the reason for not making
the search for Emerson's tombstone: "I did not know of the death regis-
ters at Somerset house when I wrote this. I have now got the register of
Emerson's death. The body was found at Twickenham, but I believe
there was then no weir & the tide went up. The date is correct."
36. Yeats received this information about the papers and Register of Scotland
Yard through a letter (dated December 12, 1913) from George T. Edwards
to a Mr. Harris.
37. That is, 1913. We cannot identify the Wiltshire medium.
38. "But this was rather", etc. is not in the manuscript. At the bottom of the
page Yeats added a note: "Last night I had a meeting with 'a spirit' at
Mrs. Wreidt's who called herself 'Sister Mary'. I said to encourage the
control, as she was speaking with great difficulty 'Ellis' & asked for the
name of 'the spirit' she had been looking for. She said that her own name
was 'Mary Ellen Ellis' but failed to 'get through' the other name, but said
that [the] other had lived in a convent, & 'John King' said later on [she]
had been 'a Mother Superior' & that three names (correct—May Aloysius
Doyle) & that one was 'Mary' Mary Ellis would give me all later on.
June 7, 1914". (According to Miss Harper [see note 21], 'John King' was

CHAPTER III

My theories changed continually [constantly] until I got what I believe to be clear evidence that "the controls" know languages unknown to any person present. Flournoy accounts for the speaking with tongues which he considers proved, by thought transference from some person present. In questioning the medium we carry on a conversation with ourselves without knowing it. The Moorish Spirit who came to me at Wimbledon professed to have lived twenty years at Rome in the 16th Century and finding that the woman next me knew Italian, I asked her to question it. They carried on a conversation in Italian of which I have a signed record. This case would be accounted for by Flournoy[39] by thought transference, but I do not think anybody has suggested that you can account for answers in a tongue unknown to all present by thought transference from a distant [absent] person. On July 14, 1913, I met Miss R. at Daisy Meadow—Mrs. F.'s country cottage.[40] I spoke of my wish to obtain answers to a question asked by me and in a tongue unknown to all present and to obtain these answers too quickly to allow of any consulting of authorities in trance,[41] or ransacking of distant minds during sleep. After breakfast in the morning of July 15, I was alone with Miss R., and interpreted a passage in an old script about Ister of Arbella.[42] I spoke of the Ister

---

the "presiding genius of all forms of materialisation" during Mrs. Wreidt's seances. In earth-life he was Henry Owen Morgan, the buccaneer, knighted by Charles II and appointed Governor of Jamaica [EPS, p. 190].)

39. Yeats twice changed "Maxwell" to "Flournoy" in this account.

40. How and when Yeats became acquainted with Mrs. Alfred (Eva) Fowler we have not been able to discover. Since she was a friend of Olivia Shakespear, who attended several of the seances at Daisy Meadow (in Kent, near Brasted) devoted to automatic writing, Olivia may have introduced Yeats to Mrs. Fowler, who in turn may have introduced him to Elizabeth Radcliffe. Although Mrs. Fowler corresponded with Yeats over a period of at least four or five years, few of her letters are dated. With a "country cottage" and a fashionable address in London (at Gilbert and Brook Streets) she was apparently a well-to-do if not wealthy woman who spent much of her time at occult pursuits. Yeats's letters to her have not been located.

41. "Consulting of authorities in trance" is a handwritten addition to the typescript.

42. Yeats made an asterisk and noted: "A certain 'Arabula' who seems to be a form of Istar occurs in the writing of Jackson Davis. I quote this because

myth and explained that the controls probably meant that Ister's descent into Hades to rescue her husband was like the soul's descent to redeem the fallen half of the mind. I quoted the hackneyed last words of the second part of Faust, "The eternal womanly leads us on". Mrs. F. came back into the room and Miss R. tried for automatic writing. It came very slowly and presently the hand wrote, "Go and write alone a little upstairs". She came back in twenty minutes. She had written, "A spirit wishes to speak who has not courage to speak before three". "Wer immer strebend sich bemüht Den können wir erlösen", "Warte nur balde", "Ruhest auch du", "Anna Louise Kirsch", "Christ ist erstanden", "Gelegenheitsgedichte",[43] and three quotations from the Greek testament (see

---

it is important to find out if there is a common symbolism among seers."
    Andrew Jackson Davis (1826-1910), "the Poughkeepsie seer", was very popular in America. Yeats refers to *Arabula, or the Divine Guest* (1867), but he probably knew others of Davis's widely circulated books such as *Lectures on Clairmativeness* (1845), *The Principles of Nature* ... (1847), *The Philosophy of Spiritual Intercourse* (1850), and *The Genesis and Ethics of Conjugal Love* (1874). All his early works were composed as "trance utterance" while he was under the influence of a mesmerizer. In 1913 Yeats and his fellow experimenters must have agreed with Davis's basic assumption: "It is a truth that spirits commune with one another while one is in the body and the other in the higher spheres—and this, too, when the person in the body is unconscious of the influx and hence cannot be convinced of the fact; and this truth will ere long present itself in the form of a living demonstration" [quoted in EPS, p. 78]. Section v of "Swedenborg, Mediums, and the Desolate Places" is about Davis.

43. The manuscript also included the date of Anna Louise Karsch's death—1791. Yeats spent considerable time and effort over a period of several months trying to trace the life and career of Miss Karsch (the usual spelling), and he asked several people for assistance. According to an undated letter to Miss Radcliffe, he consulted "an elderly doctor ... associated with the secret mystical societies of Germany" who assured Yeats that Miss Karsch not only influenced Goethe's poetry greatly but also was responsible for initiating him into the "Rosy Cross Society". Yeats concluded that he "may have been the centre of a group of affinities which brought Anna Louisa Karsch". Among the others whose assistance Yeats sought was Georgie Hyde-Lees, who may have observed several experiments with automatic writing at Daisy Meadow and who certainly was informed about the results. She reported to Yeats in a handwritten note signed "G. Hyde Lees" what she had found "Concerning Anna Luise Karschin [*sic*]." Yeats was surely disappointed to hear that "there is no evidence in any biography, biographical sketch or other source, of Karschin's having belonged to any mysticall [*sic*] society. She seems to

Appendix) and a Latin sentence. The first German words are from the second part of Faust and from the same scene I had quoted. They occur a page earlier. They say that the spirits help those who strive. The second quotation is from a lyric of Goethe's from a different book and is a promise of peace—peace coming with death. Both books were in the room but not in the medium's bedroom where she went to write and the second quotation contains an error. The poem as printed ends "du Auch". "Auch du" which ignores the rhyme is as the poem is sung to Schumann's music. The words "Christ ist erstanden" "Christ is risen" are the burden of the song of the angels at the end of the first scene of the first part, where Faust holds in his despair a poisoned cup to his lips but hears the chorus of angels. I had quoted from the Angel chorus at the end

---

have had no inner mysticall [*sic*] life, but to have been religious and a good churchwoman." Although Miss Karsch corresponded briefly with Goethe and wrote "him a poem" when they met in 1778, Miss Hyde-Lees is obviously of the opinion that any influence must have been slight. She concluded her report, however, with an offer of further assistance: "If details of G's [Goethe's] letters or other matters are of any use to you, or you want anything else looked up, send me a post card." Although this note is undated, it was most likely written in the summer of 1913. Yeats also preserved a letter (dated July 6, 1915) from a student named Eva Focke (Mrs. Fowler's niece), who had been asked to help. "A couple of years ago," she wrote, "Mrs. Fowler asked me if I had heard of Anna Louisa Karsch." Although Miss Focke had not, she inquired upon her return to Germany. An old woman, who was reading *Faust* with Miss Focke, remembered seeing some unpublished letters "which showed that Goethe and Anna Louisa Karsch had been very intimate friends for a time, ... that her influence in 'Faust' is very marked and that there are several quotations from her work in the second part of 'Faust'." Miss Focke had not told her tutor why she "wanted to know or anything about automatic writing." "When I went to see the hunting lodge near Burgan," Miss Focke added, "somebody pointed out to me that Goethe had corrected the little poem scratched on the wall 'Über allen Tipfeln ist Ruh' with his own hand; the first version which is in the automatic script is the way it goes in the song."

Miss Focke misquotes two lines from Goethe's "Wandrers Nachlied," which begins "Über allen Gipfeln / Ist Ruh" and ends "Warte nur balde / Ruhest du auch." Set to music by Robert Schumann and entitled "Nachlied von Goethe", the lyric follows Goethe's word order, not "auch du" as Yeats suggests. The quotation beginning "Wer immer" is from *Faust*, Part II, lines 11936-7; the "hackneyed last lines" ("Das Ewig-Weibliche/ Zieht uns hinan") are from Part II, lines 12110-11; "Christ ist erstanden" is from Part I, line 737.

of Faust and after quoting from that, the spirit quotes the corresponding chorus at the beginning of the story.

I found Anna Louise Kirsch and the date of her death 1791 in the French Biographical Dictionary and also that she wrote as the German words say, many occasional poems. She had of course died before the second part of Faust was written so if the German knowledge was here, it was acquired after death. The words "Christ has arisen" link the German and the Greek which echoes the thought of the first chorus. The singers are women disciples and angels. The women lament over Christ laid in the grave and the angels reply that he has arisen. Then the disciples take up the song he has indeed arisen but (I have only Anster's translation to quote):

"We as children deserted, disconsolate languish
   Thou art gone and to glory, hast left us to anguish".

The first Greek sentence is a combination of a few words of Acts 14, verse 17, with a part of Acts 20, verse 19, a combination which of course implies a knowledge of Greek by "the control". The sentence thus made runs as follows:— "He left himself not without witness serving the Lord with all humility". The second passage is Luke, chap. 8, verse 40, and is as follows:— "And it came to pass when Jesus was returned the people gladly received him for they were all waiting for him". It is possible that these sentences which were put into their order by a man knowing both Greek and German allude also to what I had spoken of Ister who was, they would have me know, but a witness superseded by the mission of Christ. They are always very ardent Christians, their Christ being always the mystical Christ who comes to the soul in solitude. The Latin sentence in the end tells us to rejoice because the soul is immortal.

Mrs. F. knows German but her mind could not have helped by any intelligible telepathic theory as she did not know I had quoted from Faust and no one present could have read a sentence of Greek or Latin. If I were to assume that the medium left the room to consult books, I must assume also that she had brought a copy of Faust and of another book by Goethe and learnt the meaning of the German on the chance that I might quote from Faust or in some other way make the books relevant. I might naturally conclude that she carried a Testament in Greek and English about with her for the New Testament is the usual [continual] source of her Greek.

But if I were to accept such a coincidence, why should the Goethe lyric be quoted as it is sung, not as it is printed? Believing as I do, that Miss R. knows neither Greek nor German nor Latin [French], I cannot escape from the conviction that there was a mind present, not the medium's nor mine, nor Mrs. F.'s whose memories were drawn upon. These memories were deliberately chosen and were themselves old memories, such as suddenly become conscious[44] on the spur of the moment. The Schumann song is very well known and the lines from the second part of Faust are often, I am told, quoted in sermons, but the mind that used them arranged them so as to prove that it knew both parts of Faust as well as Greek and Latin.[45]

CHAPTER IV

From this I shall accept the spiritistic hypothesis [theory] as mine and I believe that it will become more and more certain as I go on that no other can explain the work of this [astonishing] automatist. I have left it uncertain whether the spirit guides the medium's

44. The manuscript first read: "naturally rush up into the consciousness".
45. At the end of Chapter III Yeats wrote the following:

"Note: There is much more to find out about Anna Louise Kersch. A friend of Mrs F told her that she had met a German Prof whose name she had forgot who said 'she was very much more important in Goethe's life than scholars have recognized. Some of her verses are in second part of Faust. A few of her poems are very fine though most are popular & bad!' I asked a certain doctor, who is I believe connected with German mystical societies, if he knew anything of Anna Louise Kersch and he said 'she belonged to the Rosy Cross. They did not like the Masons act politically but on individuals. She was told off to look after Goethe. He met her first when he was 16. She had much influence on him when he was 20 or 21 & then they drifted apart. Her influence was renewed when he was 26 & he was then initiated at —— I believe'. I said 'are you sure of this'. He said 'I only know that I was told it in Germany'. A week ago I said to Mademoiselle Du Prats in Paris without giving any clue to my reason for it 'who was Anna Louise Kersch' & she said 'Goethe's initiator'. She thought she had read this in the Figaro, but was not sure. I have failed to find it in the Figaro.

WBY.
June, 1914"

Since this note was almost certainly written after Yeats received the report from Miss Hyde-Lees, he obviously did not believe that she had found all the facts.

hand[46] or only speaks words which are automatically recorded without any other action on the spirit's part. Mrs. Piper's[47] controls state that they merely speak to the hand and this appears to have happened on one occasion at any rate, with Miss R. On the morning of July —— 1913, the hand wrote in my presence what seems to have been a conversation between two troops of spirits who were quarrelling in precisely such words as we might use when angry. One troop we were told afterwards had proposed an experiment which the others thought dangerous.[48] It was only upon reading through the whole that we saw what it was, for sentences ran into one another. (See Appendix) A day later I asked the control about it and the answer was that the "covering" between them and us had got too thin. "She was too near the border, it was only a conversation, had she been further back she would only have caught the words intended . . . . what she got was visualized mentally by her ears. . . . . . . that is the nearest word I can find for a rare physical action performed in a rare state . . . . those actual words were spoken and caught by a highly sensitive physical hand as waves of sound take shape—think of wireless". I had already made the experiment of getting Miss R. to draw an object with her eyes open and then a complex mathematical form with her eyes closed. She drew badly with her eyes open but the complicated [complex] mental image was well drawn, the bounding line returning into itself exactly. I tried to draw a form with closed eyes for comparison, a simpler form than hers and got the proportions wrong. I did not join the line. So far as I was concerned, it was the old game of drawing a pig with the eyes shut and trying to put in the eye and doing no better than usual.[49] It is plain that the muscles of her hand can record what her mind's eye sees without the conscious control of the intellect, and that a conscious control would

46. The manuscript first read: ". . . the spirit writes through the medium".
47. Mrs. Leonore E. Piper (1859-1950) was perhaps the best known trance-medium in Yeats's time. She was credited with the conversion of Sir Oliver Lodge, Dr. Richard Hodgson, Professor Hyslop, and many other well-educated and sceptical observers to a belief in survival after death and the possibility of communication with the dead. She came to England first in 1890 for a series of sittings in Cambridge (at the home of F. W. H. Myers). In 1892 she achieved a "notable evolution" in the development of automatic writing. She returned to England at least twice more, her last sitting occurring on July 3, 1911 [see EPS, pp. 283-7, and Goldman herein].
48. The preceding sentence is not in the manuscript.
49. The preceding sentence is not in the manuscript.

make the record less perfect and it seems that she can record words in the same way without knowing what she does. She is really automatic in certain states; often I think, always perhaps when the Greek or Hebrew alphabets are used, the control guides the hand. The words "rare physical action" imply that it does not want us to consider [think] this automatic state usual, and once at any rate the control claimed in express words to guide the hand with its own hand. I had tried to get both hands to write at the same time and the control tried to explain its failure by the statement that there was not room enough to stand and gave an unintelligible explanation of the impossibility of one spirit controlling one hand and another the other hand. There are certain errors which imply, as I think, a spirit writing and a spirit speaking. I was examining a curious symbolical drawing made in August last to find some proof that it was copied from some image before the mind's eye by either the conscious [superliminal] or the unconscious will, when I noticed under it the word προαεΜΑ.[50] This can only be προιμέ. It seems to me the word was spoken and that the writing spirit did not recognise it and assumed after the second or third letter that it was Latin. One finds also such errors as φορετον instead it seems of φορητον [i.e., "bearable"] and κατά λιβα, two words, instead apparently of the word καταλειβω, "I pour", "I make libation", and so on. I am inclined to assume as an hypothesis that one control who has no very profound knowledge of Greek and Latin acts as amanuensis and that this amanuensis, when the writing is Greek, is seldom or never changed. I judge that he is not changed because the Greek π is continually written as if it were an English W, a way of forming the letter that went out at the beginning of the 18th Century. The spirit either learnt its Greek before the change in the letter or adopted this form of letter as a personal habit while living. I am inclined for the first explanation because in some Greek which came in combination with Latin and Hebrew, a usual combination [mixture] of the present case also, by direct writing through the mediumship of Dugaid in——.[51] Eta is made like an Upsilon, a form

50. Yeats here seems to be thinking of a form of προοίμιον meaning "proem" or "prelude". We are grateful to Professor Fitton Brown for advice on the Greek in this essay.
51. David Dugaid (1832-1907) of Glasgow was a non-professional medium known chiefly for his automatic and direct drawings [see EPS, pp. 110-11], a psychical art practised by both Miss Radcliffe and Mrs. Fowler. Yeats left a blank space intending to fill in the factual details later.

that went out of use in the first century when the control claimed to have lived. The use of an archaic letter, by a spirit whose interests resemble those of Miss R.'s control, slightly increases the unlikelihood of either being an affectation of some modern scholar.[52] Besides the communicator and the amanuensis, I suspect a third mind if it is not the sub-consciousness of either communicator or amanuensis, which is the source of the Greek and Latin and probably of the Hebrew.[53] Just as the amanuensis cannot often be changed because the archaic Pi is constantly though not always there, so this active or passive source of knowledge is not often changed. The communicator, the spirit whose story is being told,[54] changes but certain classical tags, often memories of examples in grammars remain the same. Bishop Moberly who died in 1885 and Thomas Creech are different persons and of very different mood and yet both use the tag παλαι προσδοκω [i.e., "I have been long waiting"], and this tag occurs again in other places with the addition of εκελευσαν μενή[55] ἐλθειν [i.e., "they ordered me not to come"], another grammar example. The Greek sentence which I have quoted, as used by Noverre, is used in a different context and so on. Then again, there are constant quotations from certain books of

52. The manuscript contains a very suggestive sentence Yeats apparently chose to omit at this point: "I have not yet had an opportunity to search for similar archaisms in Stainton Moses note books, whose controls were so like Miss R's—that they may have been the same." William Stainton Moses (1839-1892) was a remarkable medium and religious teacher known primarily for his extensive experiments with automatic writing upon which is based *Spirit Teachings* (1883), *Spirit Identity* (1879), and a series of accounts in the spiritualist magazine *Light* (in 1892). Moses was a member of the Societas Rosicruciana in Anglia, a founding member of the SPR (in 1882), President of the London Spiritualist Alliance (from 1884 to 1892), and Editor of *Light*. Among the papers Yeats left at his death is an extensive typescript (some 260 pages) recording Moses' conversations with spirits. In the envelope which is identified as "Note-Book of Stainton Moses" Yeats deposited records of three sessions at Daisy Meadow on July 15 and 16, 1913.

53. "And probably of the Hebrew" is not in the manuscript.

54. The explanation that the communicator is "the spirit whose story is being told" is not in the manuscript. Its inclusion suggests that Yeats was directing the essay at an audience not fully informed about such matters.

55. The correct form of this would be ἐκέλευσάν με μή ἐλθεῖν. It is possible that Yeats has misread ἐκέλευσάν for ἐκώλυσαν ("they prevented") which would give a meaning closer to the tag he mentions later in the essay.

the New Testament in Greek and a constant association together of Greek, Hebrew and Latin, which suggests one personality, a man who had taken holy orders. It may be even possible to get at his nationality in time. If I were sure that he [his personality] has never changed, I would say he learnt his Hebrew in Germany, for in transliterating Hebrew into English, the hand has written not "ben", as I am told an English student of Hebrew would, but "beyn"[56] as if he pronounced his Hebrew as Jews pronounced it in Germany. Nor do I think this personality, this active or passive[57] source of knowledge, was educated in modern times for I shall show presently that Onkelos is equated with Aquila, an error a modern scholar or a student using a modern reference book would not make.[58] I am only at the beginning of an hypothesis, but if I succeed in persuading friends who are good classical scholars to work with me on the parts of the script that await sufficient examination, I may find other evidence. After I had come to the conclusion that there are perhaps three spirits almost always; an amanuensis, a communicator often changed, and a source of classical knowledge, seldom or never changed, I noticed these words dated in the spring of 1912, "You are guarded by three". So far, all is very simple. It is the description of an office, and we can understand but presently we will understand no more. Death would never have been invented if we were to have the same minds and the same faculties after it as before.

CHAPTER V

In a case recorded by Professor Hyslop in the Transactions of the American Psychical Research Society,[59] the controls claimed an

56. Yeats's note at the bottom of the page is interesting. He began with "Feilding says", then marked through it and wrote: "A friend tells me that this is the way an Englishman would represent the German Hebrew sound. If so it is some evidence of the nationality of the amanuensis." Yeats refers to Everard Feilding, a member of the Council of the SPR, with whom he corresponded sporadically for years. In May 1914, a month before Yeats added the notes to his essay, he, Feilding, and Maud Gonne had gone to Mirebeau to investigate a bleeding oleograph (see Yeats's essay in this volume).
57. "Active or passive" is not in the manuscript.
58. See Note 74 for the evidence Yeats discovered.
59. Yeats left a parenthetical blank in the manuscript for "in the Transactions of the American Psychical Research Society".

elaborate system of communication, one to guide the hand, one to make mental pictures of the facts to be told, one to put these pictures into words. The controls also stated to him that the confusion in his script was caused (1) by the impossibility—the selective powers of the body being removed[60]—of preventing marginal thoughts from reaching the medium as well as the thoughts they wished.

Our marginal thoughts are excluded because we communicate only by what we put into words. If we communicated with one another by telepathy, we would find the same difficulties that the spirits find in speaking to us through a medium.[61] The controls claimed [evidently meant] to have invented the method I have described to get over this difficulty. One selected by putting into speech instead of allowing the whole mind of the communicator to reach the medium. The process seemed to have been a sort of double mediumship, a spirit medium and a human medium. Sometimes the speaker would say, "I turn to the left" or "I pick up an apple" or some such words, showing that the communicator's thoughts had become his thoughts, and his thoughts his world.[62]

(2) Confusion arose also from the action of the spirits upon one another, the thoughts of spirits near or perhaps even far off suddenly interpolating themselves.[63] "I feel," said one control, "a desire to say 'red pepper'." The words were being thrust upon him by some chance rapport.[64] It is as though they obsessed each other. There is a case in Admiral Moore's book (———)[65] where a control explains statements by saying he had been compelled to make them by the influence of a stronger spirit near. Spirits appear

60. At this point Yeats omitted a phrase: "of our hearing and speaking".
61. The preceding sentence is not in the manuscript.
62. The two sentences beginning "The process seemed" are not in the manuscript; the phrase "and his thoughts his world" is a handwritten addition to the typescript.
63. Yeats clarified an incomplete and puzzling sentence by saying "Confusion arose also from the action", etc. rather than "by the action", etc.
64. The manuscript reads "by some mind in chance report".
65. Yeats left a parenthetical blank for the title. He is probably referring to Admiral W. Usborne Moore's second book, *The Voices*, which was published in 1913, the year Yeats's manuscript was written. He most likely would have known the title of Moore's first book, *Glimpses of the Next State* (1911). As an aggressive sceptic, Moore apparently found considerable pleasure in exposing fraudulent mediums.

to be mediums to one another and indeed spiritists often claim that they are. As one turns over the pages of the script, one is continually reminded of this. In the middle of one subject another will be interpolated; solemn sentences, in the midst of matter of fact statement, sometimes a meaningless sentence where all the rest is plain, such as "There are no lambs" and the allusion to radium on page—. The mood shifts, the surface seems to melt away and then another surface and another—a perpetual change of consciousness—allegory or vague religious sentences (as from some spirit who cannot come nearer to our life and thought than broken poetic reverie) interrupting some practical advice [or information] often so definite and simple that we seem talking merely to some particularly businesslike and well-informed acquaintance. The most coherent and simple scripts are where there has been question, question and answer seeming to hold the communicator. I am reminded of Mrs. Wreidt's seances, where the phantoms speaking with a direct voice fade out [vanish] if we cease to question and seldom [only] speak but in answer to questions. One remembers also the shades before they drank the blood-offering of Odysseus. They are not of us and it is but natural that[66] they come to us with difficulty.

CHAPTER VI[67]

This mass of fragments, of interrupted sentences, of unfinished thoughts falls into a few [distinct] divisions. There are (1) the spirits who give the dates of their deaths and certain facts of their lives, or at any rate their names.[68] Almost all have been verified, I believe. One script is signed by thirty-two names, all I think members of the medium's family or friends of the family, and I am reminded of Irish folk belief where often a troup of ancestors seem to attend upon the soul. At another time I find the signature "Joshua Reynolds". Sir Joshua Reynolds was a connection of the medium's, but though it is an 18th Century hand-writing, it does not resemble his signature to certain letters in the British Museum. One name is that of a nun, Marie de la Barre,[69] who was proved to have died in 1743, a few doors from where the medium now lives.[70]

66. The manuscript does not have "it is but natural that".
67. There is no chapter division at this point in the manuscript.
68. The manuscript does not have "or at any rate their names".
69. We have been unable to find anything about Marie de la Barre.
70. Miss Radcliffe lived at 45, Kensington Square, W.

The medium did not remember ever having heard her name. Another spirit, a sister of Mrs. F.'s, to prove her identity, wrote words often used by her in childhood and certainly unknown to the medium, "Marrons, marrons bien glacés et puis pouf—". Mrs. F. was, however, present. Another message from this spirit which I have not seen, as it was private, was signed by initials which Mr. F. tells me are so exactly those of the dead woman that a bank would recognise them. (2) There is much symbolism centreing about the cross, or elaborating some analogy. Three symbols recur, the sun, Christ; the moon in its various phases, the soul; and the star, faith. The sun and moon are used almost exactly as in Plutarch's essay "On the apparent face of the Moon's Orb".[71] At other times the symbolism of bullrushes might have been taken from Swedenborg. (3) There are scripts arranged often with great ingenuity by the spirits so as to prove the possession of knowledge not that of the medium, or of any person present. (4) Questions, often mental questions, are answered in tongues unknown to the medium. For the moment I am most concerned with these two last divisions.[72]

The most curious of the scripts arranged by the controls themselves is probably that dated July 23, 1910 (see Appendix). It begins with a quotation from the Psalms in Hebrew, "More beautiful than the daughters of men", probably a vague compliment to the medium, or commendation of her piety.[73] After that is written "Aquila", then "proselyte" in Hebrew, then "proselyte" in Greek, then "Aquila" transliterated into Hebrew and equated with Onkelos. (An examination of the transliterated words in the script, and there are several, may give a Greek or Hebrew scholar further

71. See "Introduction," note 1. Yeats is possibly thinking of the passage in Chapter 28, concerning the three factors in the composition of man: "earth furnishes the body, the moon the soul, and the sun furnishes the mind...."

72. At this point in the manuscript Yeats made a note important to our understanding of his reason for writing the essay: "It is desirable that in every case where a script contains evidence of a knowledge not that of the medium, the sitter or sitters should sign an account of the circumstances. I have asked Miss R. to get these signed accounts in the case of all scripts mentioned by me, and to add them in the Appendix to this study." This concern for factual detail is characteristic of the methods of the SPR, of which Yeats was an Associate Member from February 1913 through 1928, according to the rolls published in the *Proceedings of the* SPR.

73. The manuscript does not have "or commendation of her piety".

evidence of the nationality of the control.) Thus אֲקִילַס =
אונקלוס.

Aquila was a Greek who became a proselyte to the religion of
the Jews and translated the Pentateuch into Greek. He is here confused with Onkelos who lived in the second Century and put the
Pentateuch into Aramaic.[74] I need not give the whole page which
is in the Appendix; it goes on to say in Latin that they had got this,
presumably the message, through the same as the others, and then
there comes in modern Welsh, "You will be surprised to get a
letter from this distant country, but glad to know that I am alive
and happy"; and in Chinese characters [letters] "Mountain-root" or
"Root-mountain, my fancy name", and at the end are three rather
badly drawn Egyptian symbols which seem to be symbols of Tum,
the god of the setting sun, and that of Horus, the god of the rising
sun,[75] with the symbol of the god of the dead between. The spirit
was, I believe, anxious to show that he was using five languages with
knowledge of their meaning, and some historical learning. He
knows something both of Aquila and of Onkelos, neither of whom
would have been known to the medium or to any ordinary sitter,
and he knows what proselyte is in Greek and in Hebrew, and how
to write Aquila in transliterated Hebrew, and Onkelos in Hebrew,
which no chance memory of some book of reference would be
likely to teach him.

The Chinese (which is written upside down, is divided by the
end of the page and by the Welsh sentence) contains four Chinese
characters [letters] written quite correctly, and in the case of one

74. Having found proof through a scholarly acquaintance, Yeats made
another of his handwritten notes at this point: "I find that the identification of Onkelos & Aquila has continued longest in Germany where a book
to prove it was published in the last decade of the last century. June 8,
1914." He had inquired of Professor Montague R. Emanuel, who informed
Yeats (in an unpublished letter dated December 31, 1913) that the battles
over whether Onkelos and Aquila "were one or two" had been "fought
with all the fury of scholars" throughout the latter half of the nineteenth
century. "As late as 1896" a long pamphlet on the matter had been published in Germany. "The ghostly contributor to your book," Emanuel
concluded wryly, "may therefore well have been a quarrelsome scholar
restating his earthly (& possibly corroborated) convictions. . . ." Since
Yeats did not incorporate this information in the typescript, it must have
been completed before he received Emanuel's letter.
75. The manuscript identifies Tum with the rising sun and Horus with the
setting sun.

character a line is left out which, a British Museum authority tells me, it is a Chinese elegance to leave out. It is a pseudonym and the script contains many. This I think is partial evidence of selection.[76] The Welsh is no casual sentence but sounds like an extract from a letter and is almost witty in its appropriateness. The Latin and the Egyptian symbols also prove selection as well as knowledge. The Egyptian symbols are not, however, a form of writing an ancient Egyptian would have used: they look like scarabs from some museum. Another remarkable page (see Appendix) is also dated July 23, but the year is not given. At the top of the page are the seven Coptic letters, which Coptic does not share with Greek, and after that is a Hebrew word transliterated into Greek; then three Greek words are correctly equated with three different Greek words which resemble them in meaning; then comes in Greek 1 Cor. 2-9; and 1 Cor. 15, 54; 1 Cor. 15, 55; followed by Is. 28, 11-12 from the Septuagint. Quotations are woven into a coherent whole, words being chosen for this purpose from longer phrases, and two words from the Septuagint version το συντριμμα [i.e., "the calamity"] are left out and dots put in their place. After that comes a quotation in Provençal [or is it in Catalon] from a poem:

> "Fair sweet friend let us make a new game
> Within the garden where the — [77] are singing".

Then come a few Latin words:——[78] The phrases seem natural memories, there has been no haphazard research. One, for instance, begins "Eye hath not seen", and not "But as it is written, eye hath not seen". It is, as I believe, a memory of the ear, regulated by habit and attention [natural memory] and not a casual visual memory, the result of some clairvoyant faculty, or unconscious reminiscence of the medium's. As always, the quotations suggest a personality, a personal habit. The Provençal lines are taken from one of the best

76. The preceding sentence was substituted (on June 8, 1914) for a much stronger reference to the methods and beliefs of Yeats's ideological opponents: "There has been selection and no casual emergence from the unconscious, of letters seen on the paper of a tea-box or some paper fan." He had decided apparently that ridicule was an unscholarly weapon.

77. Yeats left a blank, made an asterisk, and started a note which he later marked out: "I have left it blank because the word . . . ." The manuscript does not include the lines of verse.

78. Yeats left a long blank after "Latin words". In the manuscript the reference to these words comes several lines later.

known *albas* [cansones], one known to every student of Provençal, and here I am inclined to suspect that the controls have rifled the mind of a living man, a student of Provençal who is known to friends of the medium, who may have met the medium though he does not remember it. He has published a translation known to Mrs. F., but the Provençal does not accompany the translation. He may have read it in Provençal to her.[79]

After the Provençal and the Latin come two Greek sentences which are common grammatical examples, "I have been long waiting, they prevented me from coming[80]. You cannot escape without giving me satisfaction".

Two of these sentences have been used elsewhere and one both by Thomas Creech and Bishop Moberly. Then comes in Greek, "If they thought of us before death", and this and the sentence before it are run together as if to make one sentence, but the "you" is in the singular, and cannot make one sentence with "they"; after that comes παυω "I stop", but this is bad Greek for παυω is active not transitive. The communicator does not seem to think in Greek though he can recall phrases with perfect accuracy. There are many examples of the kind.

It is as though the controls seize every moment, when the conditions are favourable and no one there to question them and when there is no need [not occasion] for any special advice, to multiply proofs of knowledge not the medium's.

The scripts where questions are asked, sometimes mentally, and answered at once in Greek or Latin are still more remarkable. On page 24 of MS. copybook A, is a script with no date and no questioner's name but with a note that the questions are asked mentally (see Appendix). I think it right to say, before considering this and like scripts, that I myself have in a certain private matter received the most precise and circumstantial answers to mental questions through this medium. They contained some Greek and

---

79. Yeats may be referring to *Provença* (1910), *Canzoni* (1911), or translations of Arnaut Daniel by Ezra Pound, who was closely associated with Yeats in 1913-14 and who, as the unpublished letters of W. T. Horton make clear, observed many of Yeats's experiments. The manuscript reads: "who is slightly known to the medium". Some changes (e.g., "cansones" to "albas") suggest that Pound read this portion of the essay in manuscript.

80. See note 55.

Latin but were mainly in English. I cannot give this case, but taken together with the capping of my quotation from Faust, it justifies me in accepting these pages of question and answer without waiting for the corroboration of sitters now perhaps difficult to communicate with, as in some cases two or three years have passed.[81] The sitter asks first mentally if there is anyone there, and is answered [ὁρᾷς] ἡμᾶς ὅσοι ἐσμεν "You see how many we are", a tag from grammar used to illustrate the anticipatory accusative. The next mental question is, "Can you tell me why those spirits who communicate through writing are thought evil?" The answer is in Greek, "It would be more surprising if they had been honoured"; another tag it seems, to illustrate conditional clauses. Then comes, "Tell me what you think about it". And the answer is another Greek tag which translates, "Take care and do nothing unworthy of the honour".[82] After this the sitter asks, still mentally, about a friend for whose fate, Miss R. tells me, both were ignorant: "Do you remember———? if so, tell me of his end." Now the answer is in Latin "Quum in portum venisset vita excessit, fiat quod futurum est". "He died as the ship came into the harbour. Let what is to be, be", and this was afterwards proved to be true. I do not know if these words are a quotation. The next question is, "Did you know that my brother hated you? What effect does this have on you?" The answer is another tag from a Latin grammar, in which the spirit says that does not trouble him but he is vexed at his own stupidity.

There are many more examples of the kind. I give two or three in the Appendix, and in one of these, words are written backward so that they can only be read in a mirror: "nemini a nobis nascitur recte".[83] There are many like sentences and all tags from grammars

---

81. That is, since 1910 or 1911, as the manuscript was completed on October 8, 1913.

82. The manuscript includes the Greek words. Yeats noted in the manuscript at the time it was written: "The friend who has traced and translated these sentences and many others for me, writes, 'The most reasonable hypothesis appears to me that these passages are unconsciously telepathed to the medium by some person who had in his youth prepared for some elementary Greek examination'.

"I cannot see how a mind that did not see or hear the question can telepath the answer." "Or hear" was added in typescript.

83. That is, freely translated, "to nobody is there a birth emanating from me". See "Introduction," note 16.

or extracts from books and all in answer to questions. A few occur several times. There is no certain evidence of a new sentence in any tongue unknown to the medium. Some simple Latin sentences may be, but the constant quotation suggests that all are quotation.

When the spirit finds no whole sentence that will give his meaning and tries to construct one, except in the possible instance of those few Latin sentences, there is a jumble of unrelated words and phrases. He seems unable to modify even the gender of a word. The word Φιλος [i.e., "friend"] in the script of October 20, 1910, is masculine though it can only refer to the medium, and at other times one gets such a broken mosaic as ὅιτινες ἐκ δεξιῶν διαταγεις δι' ἀγγέλων[84] which seems to mean, "Whoever from the right (or perhaps the lucky side) you bring back into place through angels against a stream to save", but does not even mean this, grammatically. On the other hand we have in contrast those long Greek quotations often with every accent right.

We find in other cases also this necessity to quote, or to use images drawn from some mind dead or alive, to build up the message. The medium Dugaid produced by direct drawing pictures which incorporated pictures from Cassell's Family Bible, the pages of which he had once turned over,[85] and "Madame X" (Mrs. Finch) whose automatic script in Greek was investigated by Professor Richet,[86] answered questions with Greek sentences, which were

84. We have corrected Yeats's Greek to agree with what seems to be in part its source, Galatians III: 19. The sentence might then be translated as "those who on the right hand it was ordained by the angels". It appears to be another example of two texts spliced ungrammatically together. Since the additional phrase ("against a stream to save") in Yeats's somewhat freer translation are not suggested in the Greek, he may have accidentally omitted several words from Miss Radcliffe's script. Originally he had διαναχεις for διαταγείς.

85. The manuscript does not contain "the pages of which he had once turned over". Yeats has, in fact, failed to tell the whole story. Advertised as "the Direct Work of the Spirits", the pictures appeared in Dugaid's romance, *Hafed, Prince of Persia* (1876), which was dictated (in 46 sittings) while he was in trance. Upon protest from Cassell, the pictures were suppressed in the second edition.

86. The manuscript does not identify Madame X. She was Mrs. Laura L. Finch, editor of the *Annals of Psychic Science* (1905-10), bound copies of which are in Yeats's library. In a paper entitled "Quelques Observations de Clairvoyance" presented at a general meeting of the SPR, Professor

without exception taken from the examples in a modern Greek dictionary, which Professor Richet believes her never to have seen. The answers, often given in his presence, were copied by the medium, as she claimed, from writing which appeared before her as if in the air and the occurrence of visual errors confirmed the statement.[87]

CHAPTER VII

Some twenty years ago one heard much among students of these subjects of what were called shells. It was thought that when a man died, his personality, a group of faculties or, at any rate, of memories peculiar to this life remained, at first conscious and afterwards, when the soul had passed to some higher state, unconscious. If we accept M. Bergson's description of the brain as a "pantomimic organ", "a means to impress upon the body the movements and attitudes which act what the mind thinks",[88] the mind itself remains unaffected by the good or evil fortunes of the brain; and we must admit that a group of memories might remain. This group may have its own hour of dissolution, but that hour, we have no reason to believe is that of bodily dissolution. These shells were, it was thought, possessed by souls who wished to communicate and often with the result of a confusion of identities. It was as though

---

Richet reported his investigations of "the writing of phrases, sentences, even of pages of Greek by a person who had written these Greek phrases in a state of somnambulism or of half-consciousness was a lady 34 years of age who was not a professional medium. He would call her Madam X" (*Journal of the* SPR, 12 [1905-6], 91-92). One of Yeats's notes to "Swedenborg, Mediums, and the Desolate Places" mentions both French and English *Annals* together with the names of numerous prominent scholars engaged in psychical research (see Raine herein, note 30).

Dr. Charles Richet (1850-1935) was President of the SPR (1895) and the author of numerous books and articles. *Traité de Métapsychique* (1923) sums up a lifetime of spiritualistic experimentation. After investigating many mediums and reflecting about his experiences, he was "persuaded that we know absolutely nothing of the universe which surrounds us" (EPS, pp. 329-31).

87. See also "Writing in Tongues" (EPS, p. 414).

88. Henri Bergson (1859-1941) was President of the SPR in 1913. These phrases are from his presidential address (delivered on May 28, 1913), a translated copy of which, in some hand other than Yeats's, is preserved in his papers. The "authorized translation" by H. W. Carr is published in the *Proceedings of the* SPR. 27 (1914-15): 157-75.

the descending souls laid hold upon all the shells contained,[89] like robbers emptying the pockets of the dead upon a battle-field, or perhaps like robbers stealing the clothes of bathers.[90] But with the statements of Mrs. Piper's controls[91] or those of other mediums in mind, there is no need to suppose that this takes place only when consciousness [the soul] has been separated from these groups, traces, eddies—one knows not what word to use—of personal memories. It is merely necessary for that consciousness [soul] to be passive to permit its mind to be at the service of another will, to become automatic as the hands of the medium are automatic. If we assume this passivity I think we can begin, though timidly, and amid much uncertainty, to understand [explain].

The possessing spirit has come perhaps, being one of those who have long left the world, from a state of being,—and this Miss R.'s controls affirm—where a different relation to time and space has made language, as it is known to us, impossible.

When it cannot find what it wants in the memory of the medium or in the memory of some sitter it controls the mind of a shade not yet "thrown"—to quote one of Miss R.'s spirits—"far away by the revolutions of Time". But this possession [control] is not perfect or the shade has already begun to forget and the less vivid, the more delicate and complex memories, those needed for composition in Greek or Latin, are not at its disposal. Like a living mind drawing from another by telepathy it acquires words but no new faculty, and it acquires most easily memories made vivid by early association.[92] We continually dream of being at school and we can repeat the alphabet in its right order though we have not read it through since the nursery. The spirit finds most ready to its purpose

89. The manuscript reads "all they remember".
90. "Or perhaps like robbers stealing the clothes of bathers" was added to the typescript in June 1914.
91. See note 47.
92. Yeats had great difficulty with the composition of this paragraph, especially the passage from "But this possession" through "by early association", which he crossed out and rewrote on a separate page. On another page he began and rejected the following: "I am not psychologist enough to make such speculative intuition [?], but though we have many examples of one consciousness drawing on the memories of another, of what we call thought transference, we have no examples of it acquiring anothers faculties, it may acquire a Latin sentence but not knowledge of Latin. The spirits have perhaps the same difficulty."

examples from grammars read at school, passages in the Greek testament of the Septuagint, studied for some college examination. The memory of these, the senses with their continual creation of new impressions away, is perhaps more vivid than any memory we are conscious of [can deliberately employ], like a memory in trance. I can only suggest a study of the effect of passivity upon the memory of a language. It is a difficult study for the subject of it is in another world.[93] I hope for evidence that will show whether the spirits that use still spoken tongues have a more active faculty.[94] The Moor who came to see me at Mrs. Wreidt's claimed to have lived twenty years in Rome in the 16th Century.[95] Thinking to confound him, I got the woman next me, who knew Italian, to speak to him. He replied in what seemed copious Italian, but when I looked through the notes she gave me I found monosyllables "Si, signora", several times and one half-remembered, half-understood sentence which sounds like a quotation, as does the fragment of Italian in Miss R.'s script. My neighbour was not, however, very facile in her Italian and says there was much she could not follow but which she is certain was good Italian.[96]

Perhaps I shall be able to find out from ——, the late Servian Minister,[97] whether those spirits who talked to him at Mrs. Wreidt's [seances] in Croatian and in Servian, did more than quote. I think if they had but quoted he would have noticed it.[98] But he believed himself to be speaking to the shades of those but recently dead and

93. This sentence was substituted for a more positive affirmation in the manuscript: "But this mind, which has become mediumistic, is passive; only its memory, & not its faculties not even perhaps those that have become automatic are at the disposal of the possessing spirit, which must always keep its separate [?] identity certainly I can only suggest. . . . "

94. The manuscript reads: " . . . still spoken tongues converse in those tongues, or depend also upon memory".

95. See note 22.

96. The preceding sentence is not in the manuscript; the part beginning "says there" was added to the typescript in June 1914.

97. Count Chedomille Miyatovitch, Serbian Minister at Court of St. James, lectured at the London Spiritualist Alliance and other societies. In "Ghosts and Dreams" (Light, 24, May 2, 1914, pp. 211-3) Yeats described the Count's "speaking in tongues" as "extraordinary and thoroughly authenticated". He had received communication in his own language through three mediums. Yeats "had himself had experience of mediums speaking in languages unknown to them in their normal state" (p. 211).

98. The preceding sentence is not in the manuscript.

one does not assume that such communicators need more than their own memories. Always when we seem to speak with the long dead, I have noticed what Coleridge calls, in speaking of Sancho Panza's stream of but half-appropriate proverbs, "a twilight of the mind", a vague loftiness which yet serves its purpose of fixing the thoughts upon spiritual life, the speech of spirits to whom it is no longer possible to offer the sacrificial blood.[99]

99. At the end of the manuscript Yeats wrote: "W B Yeats Oct. 8, 1913". Some months after the completion of the typescript, Yeats added the following handwritten note on a separate page:

Another hypothesis is possible. Secondary, & tertiary personalities once formed may act independently of the medium, have ideoplastic power & pick the minds of distant people & so speak in tongues unknown to all present. If we imagine these artificial beings surviving the medium we can account for haunted houses & most of the facts of spiritism. There would be two interdependent races. But then are we also just such artificial personalities? & why should we end & not those others. Yet there may be [is some] interdependence of the two worlds. June 7, 1914

"A Subject of Investigation": Miracle at Mirebeau[1]

George Mills Harper

INTRODUCTION

In 1914, "on Monday, May 11th", as Yeats noted precisely, he, Maud Gonne, and Everard Feilding arrived at Mirebeau, France, "to investigate a miracle": bleeding oleographs of the sacred heart. Almost immediately, certainly before May 17, Yeats dictated an essay to Maud Gonne to record the details of their investigation and his own rather guarded evaluation. Maud's manuscript and a clean typescript which follows it carefully, even to occasional eccentricities of punctuation, are preserved in Yeats's papers. Although he clearly intended to publish the essay, he did not supervise the typing nor revise it, as he surely would have, if he had prepared it for publication.

Maud, who consistently misspelled Feilding's name, did not apparently know him until Yeats brought them together in Paris. Although I have not discovered when Yeats met Feilding, they were good friends by May 1914. An unpublished letter (dated September 15, 1917) from Feilding to Mrs. Eleanor M. Sidgwick

---

1. Yeats did not give his essay a title. I am indebted to Senator Michael Yeats for an opportunity to read Feilding's unpublished letters to Yeats and for permission to print the essay herein. I am also indebted to Mrs. I. Barry and Mrs. R. Tickell, of the Society for Psychical Research, for access to the Library and for generous assistance with information about the work of the Society (hereafter cited as SPR).

makes clear that Yeats and Feilding were well acquainted and had in fact planned together the expedition to Mirebeau. It is likely that they had met at one of the many seances being conducted in and around London.[2] Yeats was especially active in spiritualistic experiments of various kinds during the years of 1912-14. Among the most significant of his experiences besides the visit to Mirebeau were the meeting with Elizabeth Radcliffe in 1912 and the composition of the essay on her automatic writing in 1913, the extended discourse with Leo Africanus (first appearance on May 9, 1912), and the composition of "Swedenborg, Mediums, and the Desolate Places" in 1914.

Yeats probably failed to revise and publish his essay on the bleeding oleograph because he concluded that he and his fellow investigators had been deceived by the Abbé Vachère. But they were greatly excited when they left Mirebeau to return to Paris. On the following day, in a letter to Lady Gregory dated May 13, 1914, Yeats described his experience in some detail, concluding: "The whole thing puzzled Feilding and myself greatly for of course the orthodox explanation is impossible, and a sceptical explanation difficult." Maud, he added, "fell on her knees early in the day and remained on them as far as possible".

Lady Gregory must have answered at once, suggesting apparently that "the miracle working priest" and the Church were in collusion. Yeats responded in a letter of May 17 that he doubted her explanation because the Abbé "is on bad terms with his bishop". By this time, five days after the return to Paris, Yeats had completed his essay. "When you see my account," he said to Lady

---

2. Like Yeats, Feilding was at this time much concerned with establishing the validity of the claims of several well-known mediums. They may have met at some of the widely publicized seances, the most likely being those conducted by Mrs. Etta Wreidt, the American medium, at the home of William T. Stead in Wimbledon. Mrs. Wreidt began a series of more than 200 sittings, recorded by Stead's secretary in 1911 and continuing, with interruptions, through 1914. Yeats attended several, perhaps many, of these and other seances as late as June 1914 (see "Preliminary Examination of the Script of ER," note 38, herein). Yeats also preserved the records of several seances conducted by the well-known medium Mrs. Peters in October 1912. Almost certainly Yeats read Feilding's paper on "Some Sittings with Eusapia Paladino" and the full "Report" in the *Journal of* SPR, 33 (1909): 305-569. Although they were acquainted by May 1914, only one letter from Feilding before that time has survived.

Gregory, "you will find some strange light on our folk-lore."[3] He is, of course, thinking of the materials, including his two essays, that were to become *Visions and Beliefs in the West of Ireland*.

On May 14, the day after his letter to Lady Gregory, Yeats wrote to John Quinn about his visit to Mirebeau. In an effort to anticipate the reservations and perhaps to restrain the ridicule of his unbelieving friend, Yeats emphasized (1) that Feilding was Secretary of the SPR, who had been authorized by the Vatican to investigate the miracle, and (2) that the Abbé might be a somnambulist who had put the blood on the picture during the night. Since Yeats informed Quinn that he was writing an account of his "strange experience" which was not for "present publication"; he was apparently waiting for the result of the analysis of the blood which Feilding had promised to have made.

Eight days later—his last before returning to London, I think— Yeats described his investigation to Elizabeth Radcliffe, informing her that he had written an elaborate account that would interest her. As a medium, she might indeed have been expected to express an interest in his experience, but she made no reference to his "Catholic miracle" in the letters from her preserved in his papers. She probably had little faith in the methods of the SPR.

The cynical Quinn had even less faith, and Yeats was surely not surprised at his response in a letter dated June 3, 1914:

> I enjoyed that part of your letter in which you tell about the Catholic miracle. If Fielding [*sic*], the man you write about, knows his business and knows how to take blood slides or good specimens of the blood, an examination by a competent chemist will be able to give him the blood count and will show whether it is human blood or fake blood, and if it is [a] real saint's blood a real discovery will have been made in the anatomy of the saints, for science will then for the first time be able to tell the relative number of red and white blood corpuscles in the saints' blood. The examination of the blood is of course the key to the whole thing. If you hear from Fielding what the result of the blood examination is, I shall be glad to have you let me know how it came out.[4]

3. Both these letters are quoted in Lady Gregory's *Seventy Years*, ed. Colin Smythe (Gerrards Cross: Colin Smythe, 1974), p. 494. See also Yeats's "Notes," in *Visions and Beliefs in the West of Ireland* (Gerrards Cross: Colin Smythe, 1970) for a reference to the "excommunicated miracle-working priest" (p. 352).

4. I am indebted to Dr. Thomas F. Conroy for permission to quote from Quinn's unpublished letter.

In fact the blood-stained handkerchiefs were not sent to Cambridge for analysis but to the Lister Institute in London. Feilding received what he described as a "somewhat discouraging communication" written by Mr. E. E. Atkin of the Institute on July 8. Two days later Feilding, quoting the report, informed Yeats that "An extract from the handkerchief gave no precipitate with anti-human serum which therefore excluded the possibility of its being human blood". Although Atkin offered to "make the test again" if he were supplied with another sample, he was indeed discouraging: "Perhaps the fact that it is not human blood is sufficient."[5] Despite Yeats's insistence that he "...was born a natural believer",[6] he was obviously convinced by the Lister report that the bleeding picture was a hoax. Receiving Feilding's letter the day after it was written most likely, Yeats noted immediately at the end of Maud's manuscript of his essay: "Analysis says not human blood. July 11. 1914."

For Yeats, I think, "the controversy was closed"; and he no longer considered publishing the account he had written two months before. Though a natural sceptic, as most members of the SPR were, Feilding was more eager than Yeats to find proof that a miracle had occurred: "I have written to Madame Gonne," he wrote in the letter of July 10, "in hopes that she may be able to pay another visit to Mirebeau and to get further samples of the blood. If you have any influence over her do try and persuade her." He had written other letters, including one to Rome asking for "further investigations".

Also, apparently, he wrote again to the Lister Institute. Atkin

5. I am indebted to the Hon. Mrs. Basil Feilding for permission to quote from Feilding's unpublished letters cited in this essay. I am grateful also to Miss Barbara Prideaux, Assistant Secretary of the Lister Institute, for searching its files for further information about this report and two subsequent ones referred to in this essay. Although she informed me that the case had been cited by Dr. Schütze of the Institute, she has been unable to locate his essay.
6. *Light*, 33, Nov. 15, 1913, p. 549. This brief article reprints a "report of an address by Mr. W. B. Yeats on 'Psychic Phenomena' ". Yeats's address, delivered on November 1, was primarily about Miss Radcliffe's experiments with automatic writing. According to a reporter for the Dublin *Daily Express*, Yeats said that "he personally approached the subject as a believer. A man was born a natural believer or unbeliever. He (Mr. Yeats) was born a believer, and he never seriously doubted the existence of the soul or of God."

replied even more firmly on July 15, 1914: "I can say from the test I performed ... that it is definitely not human blood—there is no doubt about this result."[7] This and a further report from one of Atkin's associates were, in Feilding's words, "something of a damper". But he persisted. At Easter 1915 he received a week's leave from his position as a "Political Officer" in the Navy to return to Mirebeau. Much had happened. Having been denounced by the Bishop of Poitiers, the Abbé had been excommunicated and termed "Vitandus" (that is, "to be avoided") by Rome. Feilding asked and received permission to lock the door and carry the key of the room containing the picture. Although he "found the picture again wet", he thought the room had been unlocked by a duplicate key, and he conveyed his suspicions to the Abbé, who was furious.[8] After three days of investigation, including numerous discussions with local people, Feilding returned to duty. Having been transferred to Egypt in 1916, he made an arrangement with a French friend, Mademoiselle J. Lichnerowicz, to investigate further. She made two visits, the first a few days after Christmas in 1916, the other in May 1917. Although she was not positive after several days of careful observation, she informed Feilding that she did not "see how any kind of trick could have been performed before my eyes like this".[9]

As a result of this additional information Feilding decided to ask the SPR to investigate further. On September 15, 1917, he wrote from Cairo to Mrs. Eleanor M. Sidgwick[10] that he was sending her "a budget of queer stuff about ... the bleeding picture of Mirebeau". After summarizing the details of the case which he had observed and learned from others, Feilding expressed his uncertainty: "Stated baldly like this, it sounds like a vulgar and silly fraud. But no explanation that I can think of fits the facts, not even that the Abbé is a case of alternating consciousness, a Sally B. who

7. Quoted by Feilding, "The Case of the Abbé Vachère," in *Transactions of the Fourth International Congress for Psychical Research*, ed. Theodore Besterman (London: The Society for Psychical Research, 1930), p. 132. I am indebted to the SPR and to the Hon. Mrs. Basil Feilding for permission to quote from this essay, hereafter cited as "Case".

8. *Ibid.*, p. 134.

9. *Ibid.*, p. 136. Feilding is translating from her reports in French.

10. The wife of Henry Sidgwick, first President (1882-84) of the SPR, Mrs. Sidgwick was herself later president. Also prominent was Feilding, a member of the Council and the Honorary Secretary from 1903 to 1919.

plays tricks on himself."[11] Unfortunately, Feilding makes no mention of the reactions and attitudes of Maud or Yeats, though he was an Associate Member of the SPR at this time.[12]

Feilding also informed Mrs. Sidgwick of his futile efforts "to stimulate Rome to have a proper inquiry made". He had even considered "setting some sensational newspaper on the case" in order to "force the hands of the Vatican".[13] Clearly still intrigued with the case, Feilding was "most anxious to get someone else to go down & investigate it really seriously". "It is of importance," he wrote to Mrs. Sidgwick, "whichever way you take it, as a spiritistic phenomenon, a miracle, a fraud, a case of double consciousness, or lunacy. Here we have a religious miraculous legend in the making. It is like being in at the start of St. Januarius, or the Holy House of Loretto, or the Walls of Jericho, or Aaron's rod, or Pharaoh in the Red Sea." In Feilding's opinion, the SPR was making a mistake to "let all these golden opportunities go by. We ought to make a push to catch this one." "There at all events is the picture," he warned resignedly, "still bleeding, not daily, but very frequently."

Despite the urgency of his plea, the SPR did not, perhaps felt that it could not, send anyone to investigate, and Mrs. Sidgwick must have written to explain. Feilding replied on January 12, 1918, that he was sorry "nothing can be done about the picture from England", but suggested that "Mr. Arthur Balfour,[14] if nicely worked", could probably give someone in the SPR a permit to go to Mirebeau for a fortnight. "As the Abbé believes the thing to be a direct sign from Heaven regarding the war," Feilding added, "it might reasonably be pleaded that the visit was of direct military importance." Nevertheless, he was resigned: "I shall now try Maeterlinck. If not investigation, let us at least have reclame!" Enclosing a letter to Maeterlinck, who was an Associate and Corresponding Member of the SPR, Feilding asked Mrs. Sidgwick to forward it along with his letter of September 15, 1917, to her and his "annotated copy" of

11. He refers to Sally Beauchamp, a well-known case of divided consciousness. "Sally", who never slept, knew what her alter-ego "Miss B." dreamed, and Miss B. sometimes dreamed about what Sally was thinking (see *Proceedings of the* SPR, 27 [1914-15]: 505, for details).

12. He remained on the rolls as an Associate from February 1913 through 1928.

13. "Case", p. 139. He made this half-playful threat to an old family friend, Cardinal del Val, who "was rather amused".

14. Prime Minister Balfour (1849-1930) was President of the SPR in 1893.

Mlle. Lichnerowicz's report. Since Feilding's letter and the typed copy of the report are in the Library of the SPR,[15] I assume that Maeterlinck never received the "budget of queer stuff".

Although Feilding was "beginning to despair of getting any of our Council to take a haporth of intelligent interest in physical phenomena", he remained curious about the bleeding oleograph. Released from the service in 1919, he married Stanislawa Tomczyk. After a honeymoon in South France, the Feildings visited Mirebeau on the way home and "found things as before". The picture was "almost entirely covered by blood streams", and a "statue of the Infant Jesus . . . had also taken to bleeding".[16] But the Feildings were suspicious, and Mrs. Feilding discovered a pot of water behind some plants which they thought the Abbé had used to dissolve the congealed blood. Despite an "entirely negative" conclusion based upon "personal observation", they took "abundant specimens" of the blood for further analysis by the Lister Institute. Mr. Atkin reported and Dr. Schütze confirmed "that there was little doubt that the substance was, or contained, human blood."[17] Whether or not Feilding's faith was now revived, he continued to write to the Abbé until he died suddenly on June (or July) 17, 1921, after which his property was ultimately divided and scattered.[18]

There the case of the bleeding picture would have rested if Feilding had not discovered a German book which aroused all his investigative instincts and curiosity: Dr. Henri Birven's *Abbé Vachère: Ein Thaumaturg Unserer Zeit* (Brandenburg: Verlag J. Wiesike, 1928). As a result of a careful reading of this book, which includes several striking photographs and extended explanations of the bleeding phenomena, Feilding presented his own version of "The Case of the Abbé Vachère" to the Congress for Psychical Research at Athens. Although he borrowed many factual details from Birven's book, Feilding concluded that its basic argument "involves an excursion into regions so transcendental that I must confess myself unable to reach them". As a confirmed occultist who claimed that "the Abbé was, unknown to himself, a magician", Birven began with assumptions which were untenable to Feilding: "Having proclaimed his conviction of the authenticity of the

15. According to "Case", p. 135. Mrs. Barry has been unable to locate the report or the letter to Maeterlinck, which might also be expected to be in the Library.

16. "Case", pp. 137-38.   17. *Ibid.*, pp. 138-39.   18. *Ibid.*, p. 141.

phenomena, Dr. Birven finds himself, I suppose, before the necessity of offering some kind of explanation of them. As a mere reviewer I am glad to feel myself able to evade this necessity."[19] At this stage in his quest for knowledge of the supernatural, Yeats would surely have been in essential agreement with that conclusion. Although a "natural believer", he required proof—of physical phenomena, in particular.

His own investigations had taken a different direction. He had little interest in the kind of "mixture of Anstey & Haggard & the Arabian Nights" which Feilding described (on 22 January 1914) in reply to a letter Yeats had written, probably about his experiments with automatic writing: "I shd. very much like to see the papers you speak of, if I am allowed," Feilding wrote. "I don't guarantee much intellect (after my recent adventures) but I will certainly have loads of sympathy for even the most flagrantly impossible phenomena."

Nineteen years later, in a letter which suggests warm continued friendship, Feilding replied to Yeats's inquiry about a series of experiments by Dr. Julien Ochorowicz in which he described his experiments in "psychic photography"—in particular, photographs of "an etheric hand on a film rolled together and enclosed in a bottle, and objects suspended in the air without contact."[20] Feilding replied on March 15, 1933, that the "articles have not been collected in book form; & the Annales themselves are dead long ago,"[21] then commented on Yeats's recent activities: "I saw in 'Light' that you had been having some sittings with Margery,[22] & it would greatly interest me to hear or see an account of them." At the end of his letter Feilding added a note which suggests how enduring his interest in the bleeding oleograph had been: "Did you see my paper on the Abbé Vachère & his end in the Report of the Psychical Congress at Athens of 2 or 3 years ago published by the London S.P.R.?"

19. *Ibid.*, pp. 143-44.
20. *Encyclopaedia of Psychic Science*, ed. Nandor Fodor (London: Arthurs Press, 1933), p. 268. Hereafter cited as EPS. Ochorowicz (1850-1918) was co-director of the Institut General Psychologique of Paris. Yeats's letter was dated March 2, 1933.
21. He refers to *Annales des Sciences Physiques* (1891-1919).
22. He refers to Mrs. Margery Crandon, famous American medium. Many issues of *Light* from Vol. 49 (1929) through Vol. 53 (1933) contain accounts and evaluations of her sittings. Yeats was present at several sittings in December 1932 and January 1933.

Yeats must have answered at once. Feilding apologized in a letter of April 1 "to have been so long answering yr. letter". Responding to questions Yeats had asked, Feilding wrote that he had "no recollection of the photograph incident you refer to, & it is useless asking my wife. She has never read the articles in the Annales, & quite apart from the fact that, like yr. wife, she hates spiritualism & won't talk about it, she practically remembers nothing of the phenomena reported by Ochorowicz whom anyhow she absolutely mistrusts as an observer."[23]

In the remainder of this rather long and interesting letter Feilding is disagreeing with observations Yeats had made about the reliability and psychological motivation of mediums. "I can't follow you," Feilding wrote, "when you say that in the unconscious there is a will to cheat *and to be found cheating*. There is a will, according to my experience, to produce phenomena *à tout pris*, whether by cheating or otherwise, but not to be caught." To prove the point, he related his experiences with several mediums, including the famous Eusapia Palladino. "I think all mediums cheat," he concluded, "if they have any opening left to them." Finally, he reminded Yeats again that "My essay on Abbé Vachère, which I shd. like you to read, is obtainable price 7/6 (I think) from the s.p.r. 31 Tavistock Sq. w.c. 1 by anybody."

Whether or not Yeats read Feilding's essay I do not know. Since he was no longer an Associate Member of the spr and was in fact not often in London, Feilding's essay in the *Transactions of the International Congress* was not readily available. Although Feilding obviously wanted Yeats's opinion, there is no suggestion in the surviving letters that Yeats responded. After recording at the end of Maud's manuscript that the "Analysis says not human blood", he apparently made no further comment about the Abbé Vachère and his internationally famous bleeding pictures. Barring some observation in a yet undiscovered letter to Feilding or Maud, we can only wonder, I suppose, whether Yeats could believe after July 11, 1914, that "the image of Adonis in Alexandria may have dripped with blood". Nevertheless, despite his seeming scepticism at this most crucial period in his life and art, he "never seriously

23. Ochorowicz brought the remarkable mediumship of Mrs. Feilding (then Mlle. Stanislawa Tomczyk) to the attention of psychical scientists by a series of experiments at Wisla, Poland, in 1908-09 [see eps, p. 386]. His accounts were published in the *Annales des Sciences Psychiques*.

doubted the existence of the soul or of God",[24] and he continued
to search for "that truth" which came "Out of a medium's mouth".[25]

24. See note 6.   25. *Variorum Poems*, p. 439.

Yeats's Essay[1]

On Monday, May 11th, Madame Gonne, Mr. Everard Feilding and
myself arrived at Mirebeau near Poitiers. Feilding with proper
ecclesiastical authority was to investigate a miracle. Certain oleographs of the Sacred Heart had begun to bleed and spiritual voices
to speak to a certain Abbé Vachère.

Feilding went to find this priest, leaving Madame Gonne and
myself at the Hôtel de France, a little country inn—clean and
ancient, with a great courtyard behind it, one end of it over-
shadowed by a great tree. In front of the inn is the town market-
place, bordered by houses, one or two of which look very old and
all clean and unpretentious. Accustomed to the English towns with
their obscene yellow brick round their railway stations, forcing its
way among the few old buildings which remain, and everywhere
the staring porters and the shop fronts reminding one of a mechanical life and of the struggle of tradesman against tradesman, I had an
impression of peace and of leisure. With the exception of one or
two streets opening from the market-place, all the streets are very
narrow and keep their medieval twists, though the houses along
them keeping here and there their old walls, took perhaps their
present shape in the 18th Century. At some places the town walls
still remained. The town, however, was evidently anticlerical for it
had given certain of its streets such names as Rue Emile Zola, Rue
Gambetta.

Madame Gonne had, however, noticed a shop with white dresses
young girls wear at their first communion hanging in the window.
While waiting for Feilding, who was evidently having a long conversation, Madame Gonne and I went to this shop, but I did not
go in. She bought some pins from the owner of the shop, but when
she spoke to him about the miracle he looked superior and said he
had seen nothing, but that there was a beautiful 15th Century Virgin

1. The manuscript is in the hand of Maud Gonne, to whom Yeats dictated
   the essay. He preserved both the manuscript and a clean typescript, which
   follows it closely. I have silently corrected obvious errors in spelling and
   punctuation.

in the Church of St. Audin whom many people visited. His attitude is no doubt the official attitude of the Church which never encourages a miracle till it has won the people over to it. The parish priest may even be a little indignant at this mystery which is so disturbing and uncontrollable. The landlady of the Hôtel de France was, however, a believer. She had seen the picture and said no one who had seen it could help believing; and she could not understand why so many people should be against the Abbé Vachère for wasn't it a fine thing for the town and he was building a big Calvary[2] on a hill and wouldn't that bring a lot of people. Her husband, a stout man of fifty, who had been a chef in Paris, joined in and said he thought the other priests were jealous of Abbé Vachère who was a much better stamp of man than they were (essence supérieur). He had travelled and had been a professeur and had cured a great many people by his knowledge of herbs, and had been a long time in the country and had everybody's respect.

A moment later, Mr. Feilding returned and said he might have brought us with him, there had been no need for diplomacy, the Abbé had been very glad to see him and had put off a journey to Belgium when he heard we were coming.

He brought us through narrow streets to the Abbé's house on the edge of the village. One wall borders the street. Inside there was a long passage running along this wall, and this passage was covered with religious pictures, hard to see in the dim light. But I noticed amongst them a series of prints representing a religious conversion. He had opened the door himself and said "Welcome to the house of God." He brought us into his study—the room was full of religious pictures, here and there amongst them some secular picture, one landscape by van D— among the rest. A religious design covered the ceiling, painted by himself and showing skill. On an easel stood a copy of an Italian painting given him by a nun in gratitude for a miraculous cure. There was a finely painted portrait of a pope which he attributed to David, and was given him by a lady of the Court of Napoleon the Third. Opposite to where we came in, a glass door opened into his garden which was full of flowers and of box trees clipped into strange shapes, and among the bushes were religious statues. There were hen-coops against the

2. According to Feilding, the Abbé was "building a series of large Stations of the Cross on a hill at Gâtine, about three-quarters of a mile from his house" ("Case", p. 131).

porch wall, pigeons flew about, a little stream murmured in the middle. He was a priest out of a book, a clever, cordial face suggesting neither saint nor medium, but a man wise in the world, a good companion, a charitable friend—the priest dined every Sunday evening with the Marquise de Cuy Cygnes. With this man I could neither associate a true miracle nor one of those strange frauds, the work of the somnambulist that hides within us all;[3] but presently the impression changed. Evening was coming on, and he said we must not delay if we would see the miraculous picture, "and you have come a long way to see it," he added. "It is worth going a long way to see such a thing," Madame Gonne said. "It is indeed," he answered.

We went along a muddy road for about half a mile, and it was now that I got a new impression. Whenever Abbé Vachère became interested in what he was saying, he would stand still. We would stand four or five minutes on the road, and then he would start off again walking very rapidly. He was very full of his subject. Though I read French, I can follow very little when it is spoken, but Madame Gonne interpreted from time to time. He told me where he went to in 1906 he was given by a grave, charitable person, eleven oleographs of the Sacred Heart; he put one of them over the altar in his private chapel. On September 8th, 1911, at 6:30 in the morning, as he was about to say Mass, he noticed three dark stains on the forehead; later on in the day they became drops of blood. The picture continued to bleed until the 15th October, wounds opening in the heart and on the hands, a crown of thorns showing itself in blood upon the head. "The first of my friends to see it was a priest from Lourdes. It was my servant, a boy of fourteen, who saw the coming of the crown of thorns and told me of it when I came in from a walk. Gradually the rumour of it spread, and presently my house was not my own so many came to see it. One day before the Mass—the chapel being already full—so many people gathered in the street that we had to carry the picture into the open air—they had threatened to break in the door if they were not allowed to see it.

3. Like many members of the SPR, Yeats was preoccupied at this time with the cheating of mediums. If so, was the cheating unconscious and therefore uncontrollable: according to Feilding, for example, Eusapia Palladino insisted that "if she cheated she couldn't help it"; and Mrs. Thompson, who was caught by her husband, had "no memory of it whatever".

"A few days after I first saw the blood, I had written to two priests (vicaire capitulaire) of the Cathedral of Poitiers, but there had been no answer. But now I wrote to the newly appointed Bishop, who told me to bring the picture to the ecclesiastical college (Grand Seminaire) at Poitiers to be examined. In a couple of months it was returned to me, but I was told to show it to no one. I hung it in my own room: the blood still flowed. Parting from it had been parting from a great friend, it was the dearest thing on earth. They sent for it again—it is now at Poitiers."[4] Feilding told him it was not there, it had been taken to Rome.

Meanwhile he had been told by a voice out of the tabernacle to build a Calvary upon a hill near, and he had hung another oleograph in a little house where the masons kept their tools. One day some of the masons came and told him this oleograph had also begun to bleed. This was the picture we were about to see.

I had already noticed the three crosses outlined against the sky and had been puzzled by the picturesque pose of what I had imagined to be a group of peasants standing amongst them. We had now come close enough to find that they were life-sized cast-iron figures of the Virgin and St. John and St. Veronica and of the Roman soldiers under the crosses, and two angels a little further off, one on either side. We climbed the low hill through a ploughed field which made our boots very muddy. I had given up trying to follow the conversation and noticed that I could see a long way over the flat country which had a kind of ethereal beauty from the poplars mixed with trees of lighter green and from the absence of woods. The branches were everywhere thin, there were no masses of foliage, one could always see the green ground between the trees or through the branches. It gave one the same impression of peace one finds in the background of a 14th Century Italian painting, though the landscape was of a different type. The voice[5] had told Abbé Vachère that this hill was a symbol of the world and that the principal cross was to be exactly where an old mill had stood. A millstone still lay near, because Christ was the wheat ground for

<hr>

4. The quotation marks enclosing the passage beginning with "The first of my friends" and ending at this point are mine. If the words are the Abbé's, as they purport to be, Maud must have taken notes.

5. The Abbé reported seeing the lips of the picture open and hearing a voice (*la Voix du Bon Maître*) from which he received instructions and lamentable prophecies ("Case", p. 130).

the Salvation of the World. Later on, he was to build there a Basilica with thirty-three domes for the thirty-three years of Christ's life: it would cost millions of francs, but faith would find the millions. He had begun building the Stations of the Cross, and after making the Calvary with the entombment near it he was now making, some two hundred yards away, the Fourth Station—a city gate which still lacked its figures, the voice deciding the order of their construction.

In the tomb there is a cast-iron figure of the dead Christ, and of the Virgin leaning above it. There are red marks on the face of Christ—and on the face of the Virgin miraculous tears of blood. During the last manoeuvres, he told us, 3000 soldiers had come there and had threatened that if he would not open the gate of the little iron railing they would break it down. The officer in charge promised that there would be no irreverence if he opened the gate, and one after another the soldiers had kissed the dead Christ, and some of them had drunk the blood.

Near the Calvary at one side of the level top of the hill were a load of large stones squared for building. They had been intended for use in the making of the Fourth Station, but the carters had become blasphemous, and the Abbé, who was in the little house where the picture is, heard a voice say, "If they go on, I will strike them." He hurried to the cart and found they had not been struck, but they could go no further; six[6] horses had dragged the load up the hill, but now upon the level ground eight could not move it an inch. A little way beyond the heap of stones we came to a long low cottage and on the white-washed wall of a room where there were buckets used by the labourers, an oleograph of the Sacred Heart hung, fastened by six rusty drawing pins. In front of it were some artificial flowers and a branch of fresh hawthorne. The face in the picture had streamed with blood and some of the blood drops were still fresh. The Abbé took our handkerchiefs and touched them with the blood. (Feilding has taken mine away for analysis.)[7] The Abbé, stopping twice to kill a centipede upon the wall, told us how a doctor from the Pasteur Institute had been there, now another doctor had analysed the blood and now only that morning he had given a piece of linen that hung below the picture to a priest

6. The manuscript originally read "four".
7. See note 5 in "Introduction".

from Belgium. Generally where the handkerchief had touched the picture there remained a light-coloured spot where one could see the shiny surface of the oleograph. We waited several minutes but in no case did a new drop form where the old one had been.

We dined that night in a long bare room, opening into the inn courtyard. We were all very puzzled. We all felt that we had seen nothing on which it was possible to form a conclusion. Feilding thought that the only convincing thing would be the formation of drops before our eyes or that the picture should be sealed up under glass by the Bishop and the miracle still continue. Feilding and I discussed sceptical theories—it was hard to believe that a man who had held the respect of his neighbours for twenty years, and who had the simplicity and patience to embroider with little minute stitches, who had been satisfied with his garden and his prayers for many years, should suddenly make a false miracle, putting blood upon an oleograph with a paint-brush, perhaps with his eyes upon the door. I spoke of the somnambulistic cheating of mediums, of juggling that deceived the waking man. Feilding had personally investigated such cases. We went on to cases in which a dream of the unconscious being seems to have had under its control powers of moving objects without contact, and of the materialisation of the images of the mind.

Madame Gonne, however, though doubtful as we were of the fact and as anxious for further proof, upon the chance that things were as they seemed was becoming more and more devout.

Next morning at seven we attended Mass in Abbé Vachère's private chapel. Round the chapel hung twenty-three rather elaborate brass lamps, the work, we heard afterwards, of the Abbé's servant and his brother. They were designed by the Abbé and will be three and thirty for the years of Christ's life. The walls and ceiling had been painted by the Abbé with religious imagery, and upon the walls hung many cases of reliques—he must have been collecting them all his life. Under the main altar was a life-size wax image of a martyr, whose whole head was somewhere in a relique case. This altar had its own tremendous miracle, for here many times the roof had dripped with blood at the elevation, making a pool upon the altar.

Because upon this altar rest always three blood stained wafers, which he has been directed to keep, the Abbé performed Mass at a little altar close to the door. There were already there three devout women, two related to the Abbé, and Mass had begun. We knelt upon the prie-Dieu, very hard under our knees. Up to this I had not found myself moved. The miracle was to me a subject of investigation, but now I realized its place in spiritual drama. Already in the little house upon the hill I had felt the reverence one always feels in contemplation of the reverence of others, but now I tested my own beliefs by the intensity of those about me. I too had my conception of the Divine Man, and a few days before had schemed out a poem, praying that somewhere upon some seashore or upon some mountain I should meet face to face with that divine image of myself.[8] I tried to understand what it would be if the heart of that image lived completely within my heart, and the poetry full of instinct full of tenderness for all life it would enable me to write, and then I wondered what it would be if the head awoke within my head, and here my understanding was less clear and my attention strayed to the Latin words of the Mass, returning presently to the hands, and trying vainly to discover their spiritual meaning. Thoughts out of the Kabbala and out of Swedenborg[9] who has arranged the heavens as a vast man, the angels and the souls making the members of his body. I know[10] that I prayed in my fashion though perhaps Abbé Vachère and the three pious women would not have called it prayer.

When Mass was over, he showed us the white cloths which had covered the altar where the blood had fallen. One blood spot seemed to him to have been miraculously shaped into a heart, another into the image of Christ overcoming Satan, but it seemed to us that this was Fancy putting on a special ornament.[11] He then brought us to the altar and showed us with profound reverence three wafers saturated with blood, two of them now enclosed in their limular (?). The third, the last one, had bled so abundantly that it had dripped on to the altar steps, and had continued to bleed after he had laid it on the pala where it had dried and stuck to the pala (?) as the pala had stuck to the altar cloth.

8. Probably a reference to "The Fisherman". It was completed on June 4, 1914, according to A. Norman Jeffares, who cites an entry "in the Maud Gonne Manuscript Book" (*A Commentary on the Collected Poems of W. B. Yeats* [Stanford: Stanford University Press, 1968], p. 179).
9. Yeats worked on "Swedenborg, Mediums, and the Desolate Places" during the summer of 1914. See Raine herein.
10. The manuscript originally read "think".
11. The manuscript originally read "Fancy discovered these shapes".

After taking off his vestments he brought us into his study and showed us a series of photographs of the picture that is now in Rome, in all its states from the first few drops until the face was almost hidden by blood. He may have some regret that miracle did not choose a picture of more artistic merit, for he was convinced that the expression of the face had been miraculously improved: he repeated several times how much thinner the face had grown, but this seemed to us an illusion, the dark blood making the face look paler and hiding the mechanical smoothness of the modelling. He then said the voice from the tabernacle had told him that the Germans would come first, then the English, then the other Northern nations. Some Germans had already come, and now we had come. "But Mr. Yeats and I are Irish," Maud Gonne said. He replied, "But Mr. Feilding has brought you," and added, "I should not seem a stranger to your country, for there is a legend in my family that we are descended from Mary Stuart by the Dukes of Loraine."

Mr. Feilding spoke of——,[12] a Belgian holy woman, paralysed and having the stigmata, who he had tried to see but had failed. The Abbé said he had been to see her, and that she came in spirit to his chapel, and saw all there as vividly as if she had been in the body. He had seen her in ecstasy in his little room—"Every Friday she rises from her bed, goes through the agony of the Passion, finally falling on the floor of her room, the stigmata bleeding." He added, "she is the Victim for Mirebeau as Benedetta of Viterbo who died last year was the Victim for France." He then told us how Christ came to Benedetta, a Benedictine nun, a teacher of music, and asked her if she was willing to become the Victim. He told her that it would mean being willing to become the Victim. She refused. Christ said, "I will find some other," and then she consented. She became all over paralysed, living only in her head and one hand and remained so for 47 years. He had been to see her with a certain Bishop and when he was going away she gave him the crucifix she had held for so many years in her hand to kiss, and when he would have returned it, told him to keep it. The Bishop says, "You know I have asked you for that crucifix many times and why have you given it to this strange priest?" She replied, "because he also is to become a Victim."

12. Yeats left a blank for the name. Most likely he refers to "the stigmatised German religious seeress Rosalie Putt". The Abbé corresponded with her and "treated her as a kind of oracle" ("Case", p. 142).

We had decided to ask him to let us see the picture again, and now he gave us the key and let us go alone. There was no fresh blood, the spots where he had touched our handkerchiefs were still colourless. When we returned he brought us to see another copy of the same oleograph which hung over the mantlepiece of one of the three women we had seen at Mass. There were several drops of blood. The picture had hung in her house at Le Mans and the blood drops had come while Abbé Vachère who was staying with her was reading his breviary in the room, but other drops had formed after he had gone away.

As we were going away, he said, "I had a message for Mr. Yeats at four this morning when I was at prayer—I pray every morning at four, for at that hour Christ received the worst insult in the Court of the High Priest. The voice said, 'He is to become an apostle: he must use his intelligence for the service of the Sacred Heart. If he does not, our Lord will take his intelligence away and leave him at the mercy of his heart' "—and turning to Maud Gonne he said, "I have a message for you too. You will return here. You will stay in this house."[13] There was more; he spoke of the meaning of the hand, but this is the essential part—and just at the moment of parting he said to me, "Learn some French and come again, for I am too old to learn English and I wish to talk to you."

When we had left him, it suddenly struck me that he must have believed me a Catholic all through and I was ashamed of an accidental deception—my friends had forgotten to explain.

As we drove away, Feilding said, "I feel myself repelled by the orthodox explanation," and I replied, "The image of Adonis in Alexandria may have dripped with blood."

13. Feilding urged Maud to return, but there is no record that she did, though she told Yeats in two unpublished letters (dated July 9 and July 25, 1914) that she hoped to.

"He loved strange thought":
W. B. Yeats and William Thomas Horton

Richard J. Finneran &
George Mills Harper

HORTON AS ARTIST

William Thomas Horton began to study oil-painting and chalk-drawing on October 3, 1893.[1] He was twenty-nine years old and

1. Most of the biographical details in this essay are taken from *William Thomas Horton (1864-1919): A Selection of His Work with a Biographical Sketch by Roger Ingpen* (London: Ingpen and Grant, [1929]). There are comments on Horton in various studies of Yeats, including Joseph Hone, *W. B. Yeats, 1865-1939*, 2nd ed. (London: Macmillan, 1962), esp. pp. 281-82; Virginia Moore, *The Unicorn: William Butler Yeats' Search for Reality* (New York: Macmillan, 1954), esp. pp. 234-35; Earl Miner, *The Japanese Tradition in British and American Literature* (Princeton: Princeton University Press, 1958), pp. 236-37; and Giorgio Melchiori, *The Whole Mystery of Art: Pattern into Poetry in the Work of W. B. Yeats* (London: Routledge and Kegan Paul, 1960), esp. pp. 21-22. By far the most significant account is the lucid commentary on Horton's art by D. G. Gordon and Ian Fletcher in *W. B. Yeats: Images of a Poet* (Manchester University Press, 1961), pp. 101-03.

The following collections of Horton materials were examined in preparing this essay. At the Bodleian: the original drawings and proofs for *A Book of Images*, *The Grig's Book*, and *The Way of the Soul*; most of the original drawings in Ingpen's *Selection*; and a few scattered drawings. At the University of Reading: a large number of published and unpublished drawings; some completed but unpublished works; assorted clippings; and transcriptions of Horton's letters to H. Rider Haggard and of letters to Horton from Thomas Hardy and W. B. Yeats. In the collection of Senator Michael B. Yeats: original letters from Horton to Yeats.

had already tried his hand in several fields. Horton was born in Brussels on June 27, 1864 and spent most of his childhood there; his family later moved to Brighton, where he attended the Brighton Grammar School. He then worked for a Brighton architect and studied building-construction at a local art school.

In 1887 Horton entered the Royal Academy Architectural School, progressing to the point where he exhibited a design for a theatre façade in 1890. About this time, however, he became disenchanted with architecture and decided to become a writer. He submitted a story for evaluation to Thomas Hardy, who advised him to restrict his writing to articles on architecture. Doubtless somewhat discouraged by this advice, Horton next joined with Henry Libby (a printer) to found and edit *Whispers: A Magazine for Surrey Folk.*

As explained in the first issue (March 1893), "*Whispers* will be an up-to-date written journal, giving articles on art, literature, and the drama. It will give a review of Surrey doings month by month." This prospectus is well-evidenced by the contents, which range from a review of *Salomé* to a section on "County Cricket for 1893". Of greater interest is the opening section of a novel by Horton, entitled "The Mystic Will"; this instalment is a detailed description in the naturalistic mode of a boarding house and its inhabitants.

The first issue of the magazine had stated that "*Whispers* comes to see if it is wanted." Apparently the folk of Surrey were not slow in responding to that query, as the journal ceased publication after only four numbers.[2] With the failure of *Whispers* Horton decided to direct his energies towards art.

It was Yeats who was instrumental in finding an audience for Horton's art. Early in 1896 Yeats brought his drawings to the attention of Arthur Symons, with the result that five of them were published in the second issue of *The Savoy* (April 1896). This publication seems to have given Horton an entrance into the artistic circles of London, and in the next few years his work appeared with some regularity in such journals as *The Stationer, Printer and Fancy*

We are grateful to Ian Fletcher for his comments and suggestions and for his gracious hospitality at Reading.

2. The British Museum has a copy of only the first issue, and we have been unable to locate any others. Ingpen, however, states that there were four issues.

Trades' Register (1896), *The Dome* (1897, 1899-1900), *The Pick-Me-Up* (1897-99), *The Artist* (1899), and *The Academy* (1899).[3] In 1896 he designed the poster for Samuel Rutherford Crockett's *The Grey Man* and the cover-frontispiece for Augustus Jessop's *Simon Ryan the Peterite*, both published by T. Fisher Unwin. Horton's *A Book of Images*, with Yeats's introduction, appeared in 1898. The next year he was engaged by Leonard Smithers to illustrate an edition of Poe's *The Raven* and *The Pit and the Pendulum* (with a sketch of Poe by Vincent O'Sullivan) and design the cover for the George Egerton translation of Knut Hamsun's *Hunger*. In 1900 he supplied the coloured illustrations for *The Grig's Book* (Moffatt and Paige), a collection of nursery rhymes.

After the turn of the century Horton's productivity began to decline. In 1901, however, he designed the cover for the T. Fisher Unwin "Popular Edition" of George Moore's *Evelyn Innes*; ironically, although this drawing probably received the widest circulation of any of Horton's work, it was unsigned. Horton also contributed to a number of issues of Pamela Coleman Smith's *The Green Sheaf* in 1903-04 and to a single issue of *The Studio* in October 1905. This appearance in *The Studio* seems to be his last publication until 1909; the primary reason for this hiatus concerns Yeats and will be discussed shortly.

Relatively little is known of Horton's other activities during these years. Ingpen records brief trips to South Africa in the spring of 1904 and to Moscow in August 1908, as well as a trip of several months to America in 1911. In addition, Horton served as editor of the *Brighton and Hove Society* for the first few months of 1905, signing many of his articles "Will O'The Sun".

In 1909 Horton began another flurry of publication, contributing to both *The Pick-Me-Up* and *The Pepper-box*. His major work, *The Way of the Soul: A Legend in Line and Verse*, was published by William Rider & Son in London in 1910. In 1911 he contributed the frontispiece-cover and five illustrations to *The Mahatma and*

3. This list is not intended to be complete. The dates are the years in which Horton's work appears. The unsigned note to the Horton materials in the Bodleian states that he also contributed to *The Evergreen*, but we have been unable to locate any of Horton's work in either *The New Evergreen: The Christmas Book of University Hall* (1894) or *The Evergreen: A Northern Seasonal* (1895-97).

the Hare (Longmans, Green) by H. Rider Haggard, with whom he had corresponded since 1899; later he assisted Haggard with the research for *Moon of Israel: A Tale of the Exodus* (John Murray, 1918). Although Horton lived until February 19, 1919, the final publication we have traced was an article in *The Occult Review* for November 1912, "Was Blake Ever in Bedlam?: A Strange Discovery", appropriately enough on one of his and Yeats's masters.

Horton's oeuvre is divided into an almost bewildering variety of genres. Allowing for the fact that Horton himself would doubtless not recognize any division and would argue that all of his work is fundamentally "visionary", most of his drawings might be classified into the following six types. A relatively small portion of his work is designed for children. In addition to *The Grig's Book*, he also produced the unpublished *Tiny Tim's Flyship* (now at Reading), with words by A. Audrey Locke and coloured drawings by Horton. Children's literature is the only genre in which Horton published in colour; the results often border on the grotesque and seem singularly inappropriate for the intended audience.

Another fairly minor segment of his work consists of landscape drawings, of which "August Noons" in *The Dome* (August 1899) is representative. These drawings, pastoral in mood and symmetrical in design, are lighter in tone than the rest of Horton's work and usually exhibit a great deal of open space. Horton also occasionally attempted satire and caricature through his art. A typical example of a satiric drawing is "Over the Tea-Cups" in *The Pick-Me-Up* (October 30, 1897); the most interesting of the infrequent caricatures is that of Yeats in *The Academy* (July 8, 1899), in which the poet is represented as an effete magus.

A sizeable number of Horton's works fit into a fourth category of illustrations to particular works or of particular writers. The range here is quite extensive: *The Savoy* for April 1896, for example, contains illustrations to both the Bible and Leila MacDonald's "The Love of the Poor". Among the writers whom Horton portrayed are Keats and Blake, each of whom he attempted twice (Keats in *The Savoy* for November 1896 and *The Green Sheaf* in 1903, Blake in two other issues of the latter journal in 1903).

A fifth genre in which Horton worked with great frequency is architectural drawings. "From the Parapet" in the fifth number of *The Dome* (1897) is illustrative of his work in this category, as are many of the drawings in *A Book of Images*. These usually show the building in silhouette, employing large masses of black; they do not attempt the presentation of detail.

The final and most important portion of Horton's drawings are those which are purely visionary, in the sense that they attempt a direct representation of his intuition of some spiritual truth. *The Way of the Soul*, of course, is exclusively in this genre. As Ralph Shirley explained in the Foreword to that work, "the aim of the symbolical pictures of which this book consists, is to portray the upward struggle of the soul of man through conflict and effort on the material plane to the realization of his higher Self." In addition to the visionary drawings in *A Book of Images* and *The Way of the Soul*, Horton published numerous others—such as "Audax in Recto" in *The Green Sheaf* (1903)—and left a large mass unpublished.

It is fair to say that Horton never achieved significant success in any of the varied genres in which he worked. His artistic career consists of short periods of minor fame, preceded, separated, and followed by a life of almost total obscurity. Many of his particular defects will be discussed shortly. But in retrospect, Aubrey Beardsley's very early opinion of Horton's artistic abilities seems prescient indeed: "he has a sort of a kind of talent."[4] But it is of course Yeats's views which are more to our purpose, to which we now turn.

YEATS ON HORTON'S ART

Although, as we have noted, Yeats tried to assist Horton in gaining some public attention in the beginning of his career, it is certain that he always held severe reservations about the quality of Horton's achievement. Yeats's most detailed evaluation of Horton's art is found in the third section of the introduction to *A Book of Images* (reprinted in the appendix to this essay). Although Yeats gives some rather mild praise to parts of Horton's work, especially the relatively conventional drawing of the Magi, and to his "lonely and profound temperament", he does not fail to point out two of the major flaws in his oeuvre: a "monotony" in the subject mater and a lack of technical skill. These two defects are in fact closely related,

---

4. From a letter to Leonard Smithers, dated February-March 1896 in *The Letters of Aubrey Beardsley*, ed. Henry Maas, J. L. Duncan, and W. G. Good (Rutherford, Madison, and Teaneck: Fairleigh Dickinson University Press, 1970), p. 115.

in that Horton is much more concerned with the direct presentation of his "waking dreams" than with the transformation of them through the "magical mirror of his art". Although Yeats admits that Horton's flaws are endemic to the work of any Symbolist—"who can only make symbols out of the things he loves" and who is interested not in "things" but "the meaning of things"—it is clear that he believes Horton to be particularly subject to them. Yeats's conclusion is thus that Horton's art is "immature". The next twenty years were to see little development.

In fairness to Horton, it must be said that he always looked upon his art as a means to spiritual truth and not as an end in itself. He wrote Yeats on 30 July 1896, for instance, that

> My Art is & will continue to be as it were my receptive, peaceful, strengthening work—my Tonic. But my Active Work—I mean work that will affect people, principalities, & powers–is not yet. For this my Art is preparing me. What the Work will be I cannot say now but that the Work will come by & bye I feel sure & think it will be work connected with Leadership in Spiritual Warfare.[5]

With equal consistency, however, Yeats refused to accept Horton's emphasis on content to the detriment of form. On July 15, 1900, for example, Yeats sent Horton a lengthy and rather critical evaluation of a set of drawings he had received. Among the things Yeats objected to were the "monotony and aridity of the ornament" (caused by a lack of technical knowledge of traditional art) and the obsession with "talismans of evil, signatures of the flying lusts and wandering melancholies of the subconscious life". Even in the single drawing he admired, Yeats noted another of Horton's constant problems—"a too decided Beardsley influence". A year later, writing to Horton on July 20, 1901, Yeats most cogently stated his conviction of the interdependence of content and form in the artist's struggle towards higher knowledge:

5. This and other Horton letters referred to in this article are now in the library of Senator Michael B. Yeats, to whom we are indebted for permission to reproduce them. Unfortunately, we have been unable to locate Horton's literary executors, presumably the descendants of his sister, Mrs. Thomas E. Clifton. But Frank R. Horton, the son of a second cousin, has been most helpful in supplying limited details and in "trying to trace any further information or descendants of W. T. Horton" (letter to G. M. Harper, dated May 3, 1974).

In art as in the spiritual life the will is all but all in all and if you cannot force yourself to get over the mechanical and technical difficulties of art you will in all likelihood fail in the spiritual life as well.[6]

Horton was not convinced. Thus when early in 1902 Yeats was selecting the texts for *Ideas of Good and Evil*,[7] he not only eliminated the third section of his introduction to *A Book of Images*, which would have been out of place in the volume, but also removed Horton's name from a list of modern Symbolists in the retained text (re-titled "Symbolism in Painting"). Likewise, he excised a reference to Horton in "The Symbolism of Poetry".[8]

Horton took the lack of any reference to his work in *Ideas of Good and Evil* as a direct affront. As we have noted, after the publication of Yeats's volume in May 1903, the appearance of Horton's work in periodicals came to an almost complete halt, the exceptions being a few drawings in *The Green Sheaf* and a single publication in *The Studio* (some of these may have been accepted before May 1903). What is almost incomprehensible, though, is that Horton did not mention his feelings to Yeats until fourteen years later—and this despite the fact that in the interval he continued to visit and correspond with Yeats. Finally, however, Horton sent Yeats a long letter on March 30, 1917, writing, as he put it, "through my Persona":

The other evening I was at Sturge Moore's shewing some of my drawings & he asked me how it was I was not publishing my drawings. I answered that somehow I lost all initiative after finishing a drawing—suddenly I realized what had originally caused this strange apathy & I told him—that it was ever since you dealt me that blow with reference to the introduction, in my "Book of Images," reprinted with no mention of me in your "Ideas of Good & Evil." I have never really got over that for it led many to think

6. We are indebted to Senator Yeats and A. P. Watt and Son for permission to quote from this unpublished letter.
7. This date is established by a letter to Bullen on June 27, 1902, in *The Letters of W. B. Yeats*, ed. Allan Wade (London: Rupert Hart-Davis, 1954), pp. 398-99.
8. In *The Dome*, New Series, 6 (February-April 1900), 250, the second part of the essay begins "In my introduction to Mr. Horton's drawings I tried...." In *Ideas of Good and Evil* (London: A. H. Bullen, 1903), p. 241, it becomes "In 'Symbolism in Painting' I tried...." Again, the reference to Horton would have been out of place in the volume.

my work was of no further account in your eyes, or that I'd done something that made me no longer fit to be mentioned by you, or that I no longer drew, or was dead.

Although he was obviously depressed over being "laughed at, derided, made fun of in my work", Horton insisted bravely that he was "not in the least" affected personally, then added that "a poison has been working" "silently but ceaselessly" ever since the publication of *Ideas of Good and Evil*. He insisted also, as he frequently did in the correspondence with Yeats, that he wanted to clear the poison "all away once & for all" in order to help Yeats "in matters of *real* importance". He accused Yeats of trying "to fit what I tell you to your Procrustean bed". In fact, he added, you do that "with most of what you hear, read & see". His reference here is primarily to Yeats's occult experiments, especially in automatic writing, which Horton opposed and sometimes derided after his decision to leave the Golden Dawn on April 29, 1896. From that time forward he consistently tried to convince Yeats that "it would be better for you to have nothing to do with the G.D., but to rely on the Inner Christ alone."[9] In part at least the debate between the two friends, which continued for the remainder of Horton's life, focused upon the way to salvation and the means by which the Golden Dawn sought for religious truth. It is important to note that Yeats tried to make a careful distinction which Horton could not understand or refused to accept: "Our Order is not, as you seem to think," Yeats wrote on April 30, " 'spiritist' in any sense but wholly opposed to spiritism."[10]

Since this strong but friendly opposition had continued throughout their friendship, Yeats may not have been totally unprepared

9. From a letter dated May 1, 1896. Only the day before Yeats had written that he was "very sorry" to hear of Horton's decision. "If I thought it were any use," he continued, "I would urge you to get permission from the G.D. to delay for a time and so be sure of not acting upon a sudden impulse.... People with your ascendant are almost always dangerously impulsive and should guard themselves against their own defects" (*Letters*, p. 261).

10. *Ibid.* Wade includes four letters related to the issues. Unfortunately, he is misleading, having identified A.P.S. as Alfred Percy Sinnett (p. 260n). In fact, A.P.S. was Dr. Henry Pullen Burry (Anima Pura Sit), who was Sub-Cancellarius of the Isis-Urania Temple in April 1896. We are preparing an extended study which will trace the record of the Yeats-Horton friendship and discuss the issues raised in their continued religious debate.

for the attack in the letter of March 30, 1917, though he must have been shocked by its intensity. Yeats replied on the very next day, explaining that "I never thought my detachment of the statement of general principles from the critical part of the essay could have seemed [treacherous?] to you..." and asking Horton to call. Apparently he did not; and after several unsuccessful attempts to contact Horton in June 1917, Yeats finally sent him a detailed response in a letter from Coole Park on July 17, 1917. After again stating that he originally wrote the introduction to *A Book of Images* with the idea of being able to detach the third section in some future reprinting, Yeats came to terms with the more significant omission:

> I did not include your name in a short general list of symbolists because interesting and beautiful as your work often is, I could not name it with mature and elaborate talents like Mr. Whistler's and Mr. Ricketts', except in an actual introduction to your pictures. I think you are always upon the edge of some memorable expression of yourself and I am always hoping that some chance, the illustration let us say of some book perfectly suited to your temperament, may enable you to find that expression.

Back in London a few days later, Yeats saw Horton on the night of July 26 but failed to resolve their differences. Horton called at Woburn Buildings the following morning and left a note (not preserved) which must have been inflammatory. Yeats replied that afternoon, telling Horton sternly that if he had taken a little time he surely would not have written as he did. Again, Horton's answer—very bitter, apparently—is lost. Yeats's undated reply, probably written as early as July 29, reminded Horton of "what Blake has said of the accuser of sin" and suggested obliquely that he should avoid "moral self-indulgence".[11]

Although Yeats relented as usual, he left for France on August 6[12] without having appeased the injured Horton. But time may have reduced the friction. At any rate, Horton accepted an invitation from Yeats to come to lunch with Maud Gonne and Iseult on September 20, three days after their arrival from France. Horton left London on October 1 for an extended visit "else-

---

11. *Letters*, p. 263. Not knowing details of the controversy, Wade misplaces this brief but important letter in the correspondence of May 1896.
12. He arrived in France to visit Maud on Tuesday, August 7 (*Letters*, p. 628).

where" and may not have seen Yeats again until he and his bride returned from their honeymoon on November 13. On that evening Horton attended what must have been a sizeable party at which Yeats told of the exciting experiments in automatic writing they had been making. On the following day, in a letter addressed "Dear both of you", Horton warned the newly-weds that "Automatism etc. lead to obsession, depletion, hallucination, utter lack of self reliance & self control, weakness & moral disintegration." By this time, obviously, the differences between the two friends were great. After Yeats moved from London sometime in December,[13] they saw little of each other, though Yeats made an effort to stay in communication. After a partial recovery from a nervous break-down in October 1918,[14] Horton moved to the home of his sister, Mrs. Thomas E. Clifton, who was a Roman Catholic. A few days before his death on February 19, 1919, Horton too joined the Church, hoping to find in it, as he wrote in his last existing letter to Yeats, "peace & rest & ample freedom & repose".

Guilt-ridden to the end over the unintended insult to Horton's work, Yeats offered an apology and paid a tribute to his sensitive friend in both "Dedication" and "Epilogue" of *A Vision*. Despite their ideological differences, Yeats's "Way of the Soul between the Sun and the Moon" was surely indebted to Horton's *Way of the Soul*.[15] In the last letter to Yeats (December 22, 1918), Horton wrote of his pleasure with *Per Amica Silentia Lunae* and expressed the "hope to see your *big* Book someday". He was pleased also that Yeats had been reading Catholic writers who "submitted everything to the Pope" and rested their faith in "Mother France and Mother Church".[16] If he had lived to see Yeats's *"big* Book" (i.e., *A Vision*), Horton surely would have been bewildered and disappointed. He would no doubt have been flattered, if indeed Yeats had "asked him to accept the dedication of a book I could not expect him to

13. He and George were at Ashdown Cottage by December 23, and they were settled in Oxford by 4 January 1918 (*Letters*, p. 643).
14. Ingpen, p. 21.
15. *A Vision* (1925), p. xix. In an essay about "Yeats's Arabic Interests", S. B. Bushrui maintains that *"The Way of the Soul* not only provided Yeats with half of his title, but also influenced his working out of some of the ideas expressed in *A Vision"* (A. Norman Jeffares and K. G. W. Cross, eds., *In Excited Reverie* [New York: Macmillan, 1965], p. 302).
16. *Per Amica Silentia Lunae* (London: Macmillan, 1918), p. 94. Yeats had read these Catholic writers with Iseult.

approve," but the latent poison in his mind would surely have "come to a head" once more at Yeats's failure to identify him in the "Epilogue" as the friend who

> . . . loved strange thought
> And knew that sweet extremity of pride
> That's called Platonic love.[17]

APPENDIX

Part Three of Yeats's Introduction to
A Book of Images

Given below is the third and final section of the Introduction to W. T. Horton's *A Book of Images*, Unicorn Quartos No. 2 (London: Unicorn Press, 1898), pp. 14-16. Yeats omitted this section when he published the first two parts as "Symbolism in Painting" in *Ideas of Good and Evil* (London: A. H. Bullen, 1903) and never reprinted it.

As was his usual practice, Yeats made some relatively minor revisions in the text retained in 1903. For our purposes, the most important of these was the elimination from the list of modern Symbolists of two names, Horton and "M. Herrmann". The latter,

---

17. "All Souls' Night", lines 21-23, *ibid.*, p. 253. Yeats referred to Horton at least once more. In 1925, after reading The Rose poems "for the first time for several years", he observed that

> ...*the quality symbolised as The Rose differs from The Intellectual Beauty of Shelley and of Spencer in that I have imagined it as suffering with man and not as something pursued and seen from afar. It must have been a thought of my generation, for I remember the mystical painter Horton, whose work had little of his personal charm and real strangeness, writing me these words, "I met your beloved in Russell Square, and she was weeping", by which he meant that he had seen a vision of my neglected soul.*

(*Early Poems and Stories* [New York: Macmillan, 1925], p. 527.) Yeats was apparently recalling one of Horton's visions recorded in a letter dated June 24, 1899. Having warned Yeats about pursuing "the occultism brought about by earthly means", Horton urged him to seek "the occultism that develops spiritually in orderly ways":

> *Still do I see the Symbol of the Naked Youth [i.e., Yeats] following after Will o' the wisps the Ideal in tears following him, while within his heart the True Light is ever knocking, knocking & a Voice is saying "Open, open & I will give thee Light".*

apparently the "German Symbolist" of the opening paragraph, is identified by Giorgio Melchiori in *The Whole Mystery of Art* (London: Routledge & Kegan Paul, 1960), p. 17n, as "probably Paul Herrmann, born in Munich in 1864, established in Paris from 1895, and a friend of Oscar Wilde, E. Munch and A. Strindberg...." There are also minor revisions in the later printings of "Symbolism in Painting", including the correction of the title of a Rossetti painting and the addition of a footnote to the text of *Essays* (London: Macmillan, 1924).

---

3. Mr. Horton, who is a disciple of "The Brotherhood of the New Life,"[1] which finds the way to God in waking dreams, has his

1. The Brotherhood of the New Life was founded by Thomas Lake Harris (1823-1906), whose writing and teaching attracted a following in England. His many religious books, articles, and poems were well known to many members of the Golden Dawn, including Yeats, who got the books through Horton. In a note to him dated March 3, 1896, Yeats asked to borrow *God's Breath in Man and in Humane Society* (1891) and added that he would be finished with *The Arcana of Christianity* (3 vols., 1858-1867). Beginning his remarkable career as a Universalist minister, Harris was for varying periods of time a follower of Andrew Jackson Davis the spiritualist, a practising medium, and a Swedenborgian minister before he organized his own society, The Brotherhood of the New Life. After the death of his first wife, he was united in "counterpartal love" to an angelic spirit he called Queen Lily. Harris's Platonic union with his second wife probably inspired Horton's Platonic liaison (referred to in the Dedication to *A Vision*) with Miss Audrey Locke. (See Herbert W. Schneider and George Lawton, *A Prophet and a Pilgrim* [New York: Columbia University Press, 1942], for a detailed account of Harris's "incredible history".) Horton corresponded with Dr. C. M. Berridge (Respiro), an Edinburgh physician who was an ardent follower of Harris and who proposed to publish *The Brotherhood of the New Life; an Epitome of the Works and Teachings of Thomas Lake Harris*, 16 vols. (only 12 were published). (See the bibliography in Schneider and Lawton, p. 566, for titles of the volumes as they were "projected and announced".) Horton probably did not read Yeats's Introduction before it was submitted. He insisted apparently that the following italicized note about "Page 14, Line 4" should be inserted loose in the book:

The Publishers are asked to state that "The Brotherhood of the New Life" claims to be practical rather than visionary, and that the "waking dreams" referred to in the above passage are a purely personal matter.

It is clear that Horton thought there was some onus attached to Yeats's reference to "waking dreams" more vivid than his own.

waking dreams, but more detailed and vivid than mine; and copies them in his drawings as if they were models posed for him by some unearthly master. A disciple of perhaps the most mediaeval movement in modern mysticism, he has delighted in picturing the streets of mediaeval German towns, and the castles of mediaeval romances; and, at moments, as in *All Thy waves are gone over me*, the images of a kind of humorous piety like that of the mediaeval miracle-plays and moralities. Always interesting when he pictures the principal symbols of his faith, the woman of *Rosa Mystica* and *Ascending into Heaven*, who is the Divine womanhood, the man-at-arms of *St. George* and *Be Strong*, who is the Divine manhood, he is at his best in picturing the Magi, who are the wisdom of the world, uplifting their thuribles before the Christ, who is the union of the Divine manhood and the Divine womanhood. The rays of the halo, the great beams of the manger, the rich ornament of the thuribles and of the cloaks, make up a pattern where the homeliness come of his pity mixes with an elaborateness come of his adoration. Even the phantastic landscapes, the entangled chimneys against a white sky, the dark valley with its little points of light, the cloudy and fragile towns and churches, are part of the history of a soul; for Mr. Horton tells me that he has made them spectral, to make himself feel all things but a waking dream; and whenever spiritual purpose mixes with artistic purpose, and not to its injury, it gives it a new sincerity, a new simplicity. He tried at first to copy his models in colour, and with little mastery over colour when even great mastery would not have helped him, and very literally: but soon found that you could only represent a world where nothing is still for a moment, and where colours have odours and odours musical notes, by formal and conventional images, midway between the scenery and persons of common life, and the geometrical emblems on mediaeval talismans. His images are still few, though they are becoming more plentiful, and will probably be always but few; for he who is content to copy common life need never repeat an image, because his eyes show him always changing scenes, and none that cannot be copied; but there must always be a certain monotony in the work of the Symbolist, who can only make symbols out of the things that he loves. Rossetti and Botticelli have put the same face into a number of pictures; M. Maeterlinck has put a mysterious comer, and a lighthouse, and a well in a wood into several plays; and Mr. Horton has repeated again and again the woman of *Rosa Mys-*

tica, and the man-at-arms of *Be Strong*; and has put the crooked way of *The Path to the Moon*, "the straight and narrow way" into *St. George*, and an old drawing in *The Savoy*[2]; the abyss of *The Gap*, the abyss which is always under all things, into drawings that are not in this book; and the wave of *The Wave*, which is God's overshadowing love, into *All Thy waves are gone over me.*

These formal and conventional images were at first but parts of his waking dreams, taken away from the parts that could not be drawn; for he forgot, as Blake often forgot, that you should no more draw the things the mind has seen than the things the eye has seen, without considering what your scheme of colour and line, or your shape and kind of paper can best say: but his later drawings, *Sancta Dei Genitrix* and *Ascending into Heaven* for instance, show that he is beginning to see his waking dreams over again in the magical mirror of his art. He is beginning, too, to draw more accurately, and will doubtless draw as accurately as the greater number of the more visionary Symbolists, who have never, from the days when visionary Symbolists carved formal and conventional images of stone in Assyria and Egypt, drawn as accurately as men who are interested in things and not in the meaning of things. His art is immature, but it is more interesting than the mature art of our magazines, for it is the reverie of a lonely and profound temperament.   W. B. YEATS

2. An illustration to Matthew 7.14 in *The Savoy*, No. 2 (April 1896): 77.

Michael Robartes:
Two Occult Manuscripts

Walter Kelly Hood

Few scholars will appreciate the considerable efforts Yeats put into the composition of his two editions of *A Vision*. While it is proper that emphasis should be placed on the poems and plays, it is also proper that there should be investigation of the origins of *A Vision*, for it is possible not merely to demonstrate the conscious artistry that went into the making of this philosophical work but also to clarify the gradual development of the occult and philosophical thought which occupied many of Yeats's most interesting years and which can usefully gloss the poems and plays written during those years.

A modest contribution to this large endeavour may be made by the publication of two discarded works, "Appendix by Michael Robartes" and "Michael Robartes Foretells".[1] Neither was ever published by Yeats, and the former never reached the usual second stage of a typescript.[2] Both were evidently written for inclusion in *A Vision* (though for two different editions), and both have to do with the symbolic figure of Michael Robartes, who is central to the fictional framework of *A Vision*. At least as important as the simi-

1. I should like to thank Senator Michael Yeats for allowing publication of these two items, and I should also like to thank Professor George Harper, who brought them to my attention.
2. For information on Yeats's habits of composition, see Curtis Bradford, *Yeats at Work* (Carbondale: Southern Illinois University Press, 1965), pp. xi-xiv.

larities, however, are the differences: these point up the development from Yeats's earlier immersion in the arcane technique and detail of his occult system to his later refinement of the cycles into a heroic but deeply human engagement with history. Richard Ellmann has shown that Yeats maintained a consistent identity throughout the development of his works, so the "Appendix" and "Michael Robartes Foretells" demonstrate both change and continuity: Michael Robartes is one of Yeats's most interesting masks precisely because of his evolution over several decades of Yeats's life.

The most convenient method of approach will be to present a commentary on the "Appendix by Michael Robartes", remarks on editorial procedures, and then the work itself: this process will be repeated for "Michael Robartes Foretells". While exact dating of the "Appendix" is impossible, indirect evidence serves to establish its general period of composition. It cannot have been written earlier than 1918, since it refers to *Per Amica Silentia Lunae* as if that work were already available in published form to the reader, and since it is obviously a product of the trance material which Mrs. Yeats began to provide after their marriage on October 21, 1917.[3] The manuscript, too, is replete with the Arabic terms which Robartes is represented as learning from the Judwalis but which Yeats gleaned from Sir Edward Denison Ross, apparently in 1918.[4] The terminal date, though less certain, should probably be placed fairly early in the period of composition of *A Vision*. A small piece of evidence for an earlier date is the use in the manuscript of the genitive singular "hominis" in the title "Speculum Angelorum et hominis"; in later works, Yeats used either the correct genitive plural "hominum" or the incorrect "hominorum".[5] Furthermore,

3. All publication data are from Allan Wade, *A Bibliography of the Writings of W. B. Yeats*, 3rd. ed., rev. and ed. Russell K. Alspach (London: Rupert Hart-Davis, 1968).

4. *The Letters of W. B. Yeats*, ed. Allan Wade (London: Rupert Hart-Davis, 1954), p. 644 (hereafter cited as *Letters*). See also S. B. Bushrui, "Yeats's Arabic Interests", in *In Excited Reverie: A Centenary Tribute to William Butler Yeats: 1865-1939*, ed. A. Norman Jeffares and K. G. W. Cross (London: Macmillan, 1965), pp. 296-97.

5. Yeats and F. P. Sturm had an exchange over the Latin in 1926; see *Frank Pearce Sturm: His Life, Letters, and Collected Work*, ed. Richard Taylor (Urbana: University of Illinois Press, 1969), pp. 93-95. However, Yeats's Latin was variable, and as early as January 4, 1918, he had used the plural "hominum"; see *Letters*, p. 644.

the manuscript suggests that Yeats was not yet sure of his material; at one point he left space to fill in a word later, and he placed several question marks in the margins of difficult passages. Several of the terms used, including some Latin ones discussed below, were not repeated in Yeats's published work. Finally, the manuscript makes it clear that this work was to form an appendix to a prior conversation between Michael Robartes and Owen Aherne, and it therefore seems to belong to the period during which Yeats intended *A Vision* to take the form of a series of Robartes papers. Richard Ellmann informs us that from 1917 to 1919 Yeats "labored to put the whole of the system into the form of a dialogue between Robartes and Aherne, but dialogue proved too clumsy as the automatic writing grew in detail and complexity."[6] Ellmann's date of 1919 may not provide an absolutely certain final date; in the preface to *Michael Robartes and the Dancer*, published in February 1921, Yeats speaks of his hope of publishing a selection "from the great mass of his [Robartes'] letters and table talk" [vp, 853]. But, since he ends Book 1 of *A Vision* with the phrase "Finished at Thoor Ballylee, 1922, in a time of Civil War", Yeats presumably decided on the new format sometime earlier, because he must have taken some time to rethink and rewrite his materials. Probably, then, the "Appendix by Michael Robartes" was written no earlier than 1918 and no later than about 1921.

The manuscript is certainly incomplete, as it ends in the middle of a sentence in the middle of a page; and Ellmann's proposal that dialogue form proved inadequate to the presentation of a mass of technical material is undoubtedly correct. Indeed, the very fact that Yeats was forced to clarify one dialogue by means of an appendix suggests that he found the form inadequate to his needs. Furthermore, it is a strange appendix which presents the central materials of *A Vision*—the meaning of primary and antithetical, the nature of the cycles, and the like. Finally, the "Appendix" wanders from its initial intentions; starting as a commentary on five diagrams, it comments on only one and then roves away from the one, making a return to the topic difficult or impossible. Hence, it was probably rejected both because of its intrinsic flaws and also as part of the general abandonment of the dialogue form.

6. Richard Ellmann, *Yeats: The Man and the Masks* (New York: Macmillan, 1948), p. 234. The rough draft of this abortive attempt is preserved in the library of Senator Yeats.

While much of the content of the manuscript is so similar to its expanded form in *A Vision* as to preclude extensive commentary here, several significant points should be noted. One is a rather curious contrast between Giraldus and the Arabs. Giraldus is described as "theological", and it is he who insists on using the terms "good" and "evil"; on the other hand we have the statement: "It is no doubt this recognition of sin as the preparation of genius which has given to the Arab tribes with whom I have lived their singular tolerance." Similarly, the descriptions of Giraldus' diagrams as "allegorical" and of his Latin as "italianised" seem less favourable. It is as if Yeats intended at one stage that Giraldus should play Aherne to the Arabs' Robartes. In later, published works, disparaging epithets are less obvious, and emphasis falls rather upon the remarkable similarity of Eastern and Western occultism.[7]

Another noteworthy point is the clear aestheticism of the "Appendix". Beauty and ugliness certainly have their place in *A Vision*; indeed, H. H. Vendler has seen that book as primarily concerned with art and the artistic process.[8] Yet there is surely a more obvious focus on aesthetic terms in the manuscript than in the book, and the terms gain by emphasis. The bold identification of beauty with what the world considers "evil" links the manuscript to Yeats's earlier work: evil, according to the world, consists in flouting the mores of the bourgeoisie but is, for Yeats, the means by which genius achieves its distinguishing individualism.

Three Latin terms appear in the "Appendix" which do not occur in Yeats's published work: *daemon beneficium, Persona Artificans*, and *Mala persona* (the spellings and capitalization are Yeats's own). The origin of the terms is unknown; they might have come from the ghostly Instructors or from the Golden Dawn. In context, the *daemon beneficium* is described by Yeats as a "passion for reality"

7. In Yeats's *A Vision: An Explanation of Life Founded upon the Writings of Giraldus and upon Certain Doctrines Attributed to Kusta ben Luka* (London: T. Werner Laurie, 1925), pictures remain "allegorical" (p. xvii), and the Arabs are "tolerant of human frailty" (p. xix). However, the epithet "theological" is dropped, and the text of Giraldus is simply in Latin (p. xviii).
8. Helen Hennessy Vendler, *Yeats's Vision and the Later Plays* (Cambridge: Harvard University Press, 1963), p. 255, remarks that her aim was to show that Yeats's ideas in *A Vision* are "symbolic statements about normal experience ... and that in any case, they are intelligible statements about the poetic process, the poetic mind, and the poetic product".

within a subjective context; why it should be a "beneficent spirit" is not apparent. *Persona Artificans*—the latter is not a legitimate Latin form—is perhaps Yeats's rough translation of some such English phrase as "the shaping mask", suggesting that it artfully creates or shapes personality like the Mask of *A Vision*, and appropriately enough it makes for unity of being. *Mala persona*, evidently to be translated as "evil mask", serves to separate primary from antithetical or vice versa; it operates strongly at Phases 8 and 22 precisely where, respectively, the antithetical and the primary begin to dominate. Beyond the futile struggle to define the terms from inadequate contextual evidence, two points may be observed about them. One is that Robartes speaks as if he is introducing new terms, not referring to matter already established; yet in *A Vision* Yeats is relatively careful to offer definitions of his terms when he first introduces them. The confusion of the manuscript may imply that Yeats was still attempting to master his materials and was not yet clear how to formulate them. A second point is a vague resemblance between these terms and the Faculties of *A Vision*. For example, the *daemon beneficium* is concerned with transcendent reality, and Creative Mind is the Faculty concerned both with a reality external to the individual and also with transcendent reality.[9] *Persona Artificans* suggests the Mask both by translation and from its context, since like the Mask it produces unity of being. *Mala persona*, though it might be connected by translation with the False Mask of *A Vision*, has least connection with the Faculties.[10] Clearly these three terms will remain puzzling until further pertinent evidence becomes available.

One final comment on the content of the "Appendix" should be made. Yeats offers a theological etymology: "The primary is a derivative of the second person of the Trinity, and the antithetical from the third, & the centre of the circle from the first, understanding as St Thomas Aquinas did, the Father as power, the Son as Truth, the Holy Ghost as Good." By the time he had written the first version of *A Vision*, he had established the differences between Faculties and Principles and had read Plotinus: the Celestial Body is now the One of Plotinus; the Spirit, the Intellectual Principle; the

---

9. In *A Vision* (1925), p. 146, for example, the leading member of the four Principles corresponds not to Will but to Creative Mind.
10. For the False Mask, see *A Vision* (1925), pp. 20-21.

Passionate Body, the Soul of the World; the Husk, Nature.[11] When Yeats revised *A Vision* for its second edition, he had clarified his understanding of his own terms and of Plotinus' philosophy: the Celestial Body suggests Plotinus' First Authentic Existant (Yeats's spelling); the Spirit, the Second Authentic Existant; the Daimon or Ghostly Self, the Third Authentic Existant (or Holy Ghost in Christian terms); the Husk and Passionate Body, the First Authentic Existant reflected as sensation and its object; the Faculties, the First Authentic Existant reflected as discursive reason [v, 193-94]. Throughout, Yeats intended to clarify his own strange system by reference to one more familiar, perhaps more authoritative. In this earliest stage of the "Appendix", he began, perhaps defensively, with a Christian frame of reference; later, having read Stephen MacKenna's translation of Plotinus' *Enneads*, he moved to a Neoplatonic equivalence [v, 20].[12]

The primary aim governing the editorial procedures applied to the "Appendix by Michael Robartes" and to "Michael Robartes Foretells" is the presentation of the last stage of Yeats's intention.[13] The eleven-page "Appendix" is in Mrs. Yeats's handwriting and contains only a few minor alterations; Yeats may not have returned to it after initial composition. "Michael Robartes Foretells", a typescript of nine pages, is fairly heavily corrected in Yeats's hand and is obviously closer to a final draft. With few exceptions (recorded in footnotes), deleted passages have not been transcribed because they are mainly simple stylistic corrections; the most interesting alterations are primarily expansions which were incorporated into the final stage of Yeats's writing. Minor liberties have been taken with the originals for the sake of clarity: (1) common words obviously misspelled or mistyped have been silently corrected, but misspelled proper names and foreign words have been allowed to stand as Yeats wrote them; (2) punctuation has been silently altered only where necessary for clarity; (3) paragraph indention has been supplied in a few cases where Yeats would probably have indicated

11. *A Vision* (1925), p. 176.
12. Yeats says that he "read all MacKenna's incomparable Plotinus, some of it several times" [v, 20]; MacKenna's translation appeared in five volumes between 1918 and 1930.
13. A similar editorial policy is stated in Denis Donoghue, ed., *W. B. Yeats: Memoirs: Autobiography—First Draft; Journal* (London: Macmillan, 1972), p. 15; see also Bradford, *Yeats at Work,* p. xv.

it for printers; (4) in the "Appendix", English words in brackets have been substituted for standard astrological symbols. The alterations, then, are some—but only some—of the ones Yeats himself might have made for publication; both texts remain rough drafts.

Appendix by Michael Robartes

The Great Diagram from the Speculum Angelorum et hominis contains the epitome of the philosophy of human life which has occupied me for the last twenty years, and which will occupy me till I die. It cannot however be fully understood without several simpler diagrams, two from the "Speculum", and two of a somewhat different nature from the "Camel's Back". The photographs from the diagrams of the Speculum have been entitled by me the Great Diagram and a, b, respectively, but to my own copies of two diagrams from the "Camel's back" I have given their arabic names, the first "the holy women and the two Kalendars" because it describes the movements of two symbolic suns and moons; and the second "the dance of the Eunuch with the favourite wife."[14]

In the Great Diagram, which is the frontispiece of the Speculum there are three circles one without the other, and all three represent the circle of the Heavens. The inmost however is merely the Horoscope of Giraldus himself placed as we are taught to place a horoscope for its better understanding. The circle immediately outside that has to do with certain symbolical movements of the [sun] in the present position of the Equinoctial Signs, and from it the whole past and future of mankind may be judged and discovered. It is considered both by Gyraldus and the Arabs who have a similar diagram to be related to the actual positions of the different parts of the Zodiac. The outermost circle which was the first to arouse my interest is however purely symbolical.[15]

14. The supposed Arabic titles—"Camel's back", "the holy women and the two Kalendars", and "the dance of the Eunuch with the favourite wife"— do not appear in *A Vision* (1925), nor are they discussed by Bushrui in "Yeats's Arabic Interests".

15. The Great Diagram described here is presumably an early version of the Great Wheel which appeared in *A Vision* (1925) between pp. xiv and xv, in *Stories of Michael Robartes and His Friends: An Extract from a Record Made by His Pupils: And a Play in Prose by W. B. Yeats* (Dublin: Cuala Press, 1931) between pp. 8 and 9, and in *A Vision* (1937), p. 66. The horoscope of Giraldus does not appear in the Great Wheel. It might be noted that in the last two works Yeats reversed the earlier positions of the astrological signs for Libra and Capricorn.

In the Great Diagram the phases of the [moon] are set round it, and it will be noticed that they are not drawn naturalistically. [Sun] and [moon] are combined into a single symbol, the crescent of the first human phase forming, as it were, upon the face of the [sun]; and the thin crescent after full [moon] representing not a dark section of the [moon] but a symbolical solar crescent. Throughout 28 stages, or phases [sun] and [moon] gain and lose respectively, the [moon] gaining until it is full at the 15th phase and then dwindling till the first phase when the [sun] is full. These 28 phases represent the 28 incarnations of typal man as I have explained in my conversation with Ahearne.[16] In reality owing to no soul being perfect the incarnations are much more numerous, one has sometimes to go through the same phase again and again, especially in the earlier phases. The soul is considered to start at full sun, that is to say at the dark of the [moon] and to end the cycle at the last lunar crescent, after which[17]

When the soul starts its journey at full [sun] it begins a symbolical lunar month, and as the [sun] moves through a single sign during that month, the entire number of incarnations are supposed by Gyraldus & the Arabs alike to make up a symbolical year of 336 lives (28 x 12). This is the symbolical structure so far as it was known to Gyraldus. The [sun] is the primary self or the self as it is shaped by race, tradition and environment, and the [moon] is the antithetical self or the individuality itself. One may express them differently and say that the primary is a derivative of the second person of the Trinity, and the antithetical from the third, & the centre of the circle from the first, understanding as St Thomas Aquinas did, the Father as power, the Son as Truth, the Holy Ghost as Good.

In actual life the Primary is naturalistic man, and the antithetical self the ideal, or dream life, the whole of human existence is the struggle between these two; each to the very least detail living in the other's loss. Every man who comes into one's imagination is incarnated under some one of the 28 phases, but some have come to

---

16. The phrasing here is very close to that in Yeats's 1921 notes to *The Only Jealousy of Emer* [VPL, 566]; indeed, this similarity bears on the dating of the "Appendix".

17. This sentence ends in the middle of a line. Obviously the end of this paragraph and the beginning of the following one overlap; Yeats would probably have dealt with the incompleteness and the overlapping had he returned to the "Appendix".

their phase already in earlier cycles and these are the stronger or the more entirely conscious souls. When one comes to examine in detail the Great diagram one finds that between the 18th and 19th phase is marked the sign [Aries] and the word "Head" is added, and that the sign [Cancer] and the word "Loins" are set between the 25th and 26th and the sign [Libra] and the word "Fall" between 4th & 5th phases, and the sign [Capricorn] and the word "Heart" between the 11th & 12th. Heart is the climax of Emotion, Head the climax of Reason and Loins which is opposite to Heart is Instinct or   ,[18] and the Fall which is opposite Head is the first departure from Innocence and also the first awakening of the Ego. The centre of the whole circle, where in diagram A Saturn is placed, is supposed to be the source of all, and perfect balance. What however marks this system as different to any other known to me is that the full [moon] which occurs midway between Emotion and Reason is described as the state of beauty, while full [sun] which occurs midway between loins and fall is marked state of ugliness.

In the diagram of the theological Gyraldus the word "evil" is written at Beauty and the word "Good" at Ugliness. His reason probably was that Beauty binds the Soul to life when Ugliness sets it free, but there is another reason for the attribution of the terms which occur also in the Arabic text; the antithetical life struggling always to subdue the primary that full [moon] or Beauty may be reached, has an entirely individual ideal; whereas the Primary seeks always to be united to the world outside itself. The Antithetical life is subjective and to that degree anarchic, whereas the Primary life is objective, through the Primary we find our fellows and our duties toward them. The moral struggle is very much as described in Mr. Yeats' "Anima Hominis" except for a vagueness in a description at second hand and without diagrams.[19] Starting at complete objectivity the Antithetical develops in a perpetual struggle, from the first to fifteenth stage it is described by both old writers as violent, whereas from the 16th phase to the 28th the Primary is violent. I can only speak at the moment in general terms and must even when I have given all the detail possible to me, leave the elucidation of the system very largely to those who come to make of these diagrams subjects of meditation.

18. Yeats left space here to insert a word and placed a question mark in the margin.
19. The reference is to Yeats's *Per Amica Silentia Lunae* (1918), [M, 331-32].

The Ego from 1 to 15 develops in richness by the passion for reality, which is even described by my later author in his italianised latin as daemon beneficium. The more intense is his passion for reality, the more does he understand that the objects of his desire do not exist in the physical world, he is driven to seek them in the dream world and having found them there to fashion the primary self into their expression. This understanding is intensified by the action of an influence called Mala Persona which working from within the Antithetical Self and acting with fullest power at phases 8 and 22 where Antithetical and Primary are of equal power withdraws the Antithetical from the Primary; it is the waking of the Primary to seek objective reality and of the antithetical to seek subjective intensity. Mala persona before full [moon] therefore is tending to find this intensity by withdrawing from expression. Left to itself the primary sins, that is to say, refuses to submit [to] the Antithetical. Persona Artificans as it is called by Gyraldus acting also from within the antithetical if the antithetical can gain the victory re-unites what has been shattered giving thereby for the first time the consciousness of the unity of the being which becomes, where the contest has been very violent, subjective genius.

It is no doubt this recognition of sin as the preparation of genius which has given to the Arab tribes with whom I have lived their singular tolerance. But it is not only artistic beauty that is the reward of the submission of primary to antithetical; for this submission which must always be a service and not a form of in-action, creates physical beauty. Before however either physical or Artistic Beauty can come in any great intensity many lives have to be lived in a state of struggle which in the greater souls contains every imaginable terror. This struggle centers about that portion of the [moon's] path where the word Heart is written, it is symbolised in the allegorical diagrams of Gyraldus by such images as the man with his eyes torn out by an eagle, and by the garrotted man, images of a soul dumb or blinded by a power from within itself. Every effort is toward the personal Ideal every sin is against it, and men seek solitude and poets describe mountain and wood.

At the full [moon] we have complete beauty, physical or mental, and as the Primary is now entirely lost in the Antithetical expression is now impossible. In the phase after the full [moon], represented in the diagram by a thin solar crescent, the Primary is re-born, and from this as at each succeeding life the nature is more objective.

The process of development is reversed and the passion for reality shows us that we can no longer find within ourselves the objects of desire. We cease gradually to find subjective intensity endurable, and finding no peace within seek external activity. The passion for reality is still daemon beneficium and the effectiveness of our expression in life corresponds exactly to our sincerity in seeking an objective form which is in every case the opposite of the internal state. Mr. Yeats is wrong when he describes his famous actress creating a faint Maeterlinckian beauty by reaction from her own dominating primary.[20] Judging by his description her incarnation is after Beauty, for the primary is violent and the objectivity enlarging. Before full [moon] the psychology had been as he describes it but after full [moon] she is in flight from that faint delicate beauty once achieved with so much labour. She has begun to shrink from beauty and pursue ugliness; she has fallen under the influence of a new perspective. Before Beauty the soul sees utmost energy in the miniatures of harmonious organization, in a movement inward or upward, in an always heightening subjectivity. But now it sees it in the movement of large masses on a single plane.[21] The whole development from full [moon] to full [sun] is from a desire to rest from subjective intensity in forms of dwindling emotional energy; in ugliness. Beauty is the complete expression of the individuality and it is without desire because it is the goal of desire, and being complete individuality it is the soul's triumph over the self. Complete Ugliness is complete objectivity & is the triumph of the race over the individual. Every form of ugliness which the soul puts on represents a passion or an ambition exhausted and a dismembering of the individual. I find in the allegorical pictures of Gyraldus that two of the last phases are represented, the one by an idiot, the other by a Hunchback. In his commentary he describes the idiot as that form where the soul can rest from Spiritual Pride & the Hunchback as its rest from ambition. In reply to the objection that the Hunchback is malicious and that there should only be good in so much ugliness, as ugliness frees the soul, he points out that Hunchbacks have often beautiful eyes or hands, and adds "Even a bitter beauty will account for much evil".[22] These forms are involuntarily assumed but they

20. Robartes again refers to Per Amica Silentia Lunae, [M, 326-27].
21. For the contrast of antithetical line and primary plane, see A Vision (1925), p. 129, and A Vision (1937), p. 70.

may be assumed voluntarily and from that assumption is sanctity. The soul as it is being set free contemplates the sorrow and evil of the world and contemplating it not as before beauty in relation to its own desire, but in relation to God who is the Spiritual objectivity. At phase 26 that is to say between the Hunchback and the Idiot is the incarnation where the soul frees itself, though that freedom can only be attained through a contemplation of ugliness in the mind prolonged for several lives and always acting after the first life of this contemplation, in some degree upon the body. That freedom once attained the soul will inform what ever body, ugly or beautiful, is suitable for its work. Before this however it passes symbolically into the axis the complete balance and the source of energy,[23]

"Michael Robartes Foretells" can be dated with some accuracy.[24] Even before the first edition of *A Vision* had been published in 1926, Yeats was dissatisfied and almost immediately began to rewrite it.[25] One change was the decision to admit that he was not "sole author" and to drop any pretence that the Judwalis were real [v, 19]. Yet, as he remarked, he was saddled with the dependence of several poems upon this framework, and he published in March 1932 the "amended version" as *Stories of Michael Robartes and His Friends*, which was later included as part of the prefatory materials to the second edition of *A Vision* (1937) [v, 19]. Here, Robartes reveals his philosophy and forecasts the future to a group

---

22. The Idiot of the "Appendix" becomes the Fool of Phase 28 in *A Vision* (1925), pp. 115-16. In the following lines, Yeats places an unnamed figure (perhaps the Saint of *A Vision*) at Phase 26, Hunchback at 25, and Idiot at 27; this is at odds with both editions of *A Vision*, in which Hunchback, Saint, and Fool are at Phases 26, 27, and 28, respectively.

23. The manuscript ends here in the middle of a sentence and of a page.

24. Hazard Adams published "Michael Robartes Foretells" as an appendix to *Blake and Yeats: The Contrary Vision* (Ithaca: Cornell University Press, 1955), pp. 301-05. The present text, to the publication of which Cornell University Press has kindly consented, is based upon an independent reading of the original but has been checked against Adams' transcription. Adams devotes only a few sentences of commentary to "Michael Robartes Foretells".

25. Dated 1925, *A Vision* was issued on January 15, 1926. In February of 1926 Yeats spoke of his intention to "republish in three years" (*Frank Pearce Sturm*, p. 93). Certainly by October 1927 he was busy rewriting *A Vision* (*Letters*, p. 730).

of pupils named Huddon, Duddon, Daniel O'Leary, and Denise de L'Isle Adam; as its subtitle indicates, this printed tale was only "an extract from a record". But Yeats was not yet ready to give up this group of characters.[26]

That "Michael Robartes Foretells" was intended as a sequel to *Stories of Michael Robartes and His Friends* is suggested by the text of the typescript, in which Dudden asks, "Have you that prophecy . . . that Michael Robartes made at Albert Road?" In *Stories*, the setting for the prophecy is "the ground floor of a house in Albert Road, Regent's Park".[27] In the typescript, one of the characters mentions that Robartes disappeared into Arabia some seven years earlier; in *Stories*, Robartes announces his intention to return to the desert.[28] Furthermore, the typescript cannot have been completed earlier than Lady Gregory's death on May 22, 1932, because of its reference to the "empty rooms" of Coole House, which was not vacated until her death. But the most important evidence for dating is a letter of Yeats's dated July 26, 1936: "To-morrow I write a story to be added to the Michael Robartes series, (a prelude to *A Vision* which I am now revising in proof). It is almost an exact transcript from fact. I have for years been creating a group of strange disorderly people on whom Michael Robartes confers the wisdom of the east".[29] Though there is no direct evidence that Yeats wrote such a story, it seems entirely probable that he did so and that "Michael Robartes Foretells" was the result.

Had Yeats decided to include "Michael Robartes Foretells" in the second edition of *A Vision*, he might very well have placed it at the end of the book. Such an arrangement would explain the use of technical terms in the typescript, since the reader would already have met them in the five books of *A Vision*, whereas putting the tale at the beginning (as part of the *Stories*) would have left the reader with unexplained terms. The stories would, therefore, have framed *A Vision* within the fiction, and the intervention of the text of *A Vision* would have suggested the passage of seven years after

26. The names of Robartes' three male pupils are from "Donald and His Neighbors", a folk tale included by Yeats in his *Fairy and Folk Tales of the Irish Peasantry* (London: Walter Scott, 1888). Apart from the names, Yeats borrowed little or nothing from the tale.

27. *Stories of Michael Robartes and His Friends*, p. 1.

28. *Ibid.*, p. 20.   29. *Letters*, p. 859.

Robartes' departure. Most important, "Michael Robartes Foretells" would have suited the prophetic tone and content of the historical section, "Dove or Swan", immediately preceding it. Yeats had great difficulty with Book v, saying in July 1933 that he had just rewritten the section dealing with the future for the seventh time. He finally omitted from Book v the section of the first edition dealing with the future and substituted a coda leaving the future to the "thirteenth gyre".[30] Possibly, then, "Michael Robartes Foretells" was one of Yeats's attempts to deal with the future; it would have had the advantage (which Yeats specified in a letter) of allowing the rather harsh prophecy to come from the persona of Robartes rather than from Yeats himself.[31]

The "Appendix by Michael Robartes" and "Michael Robartes Foretells" differ not only in time but in content as well. The earlier work is essentially one of Yeats's many statements about personality types, while the later is concerned almost entirely with history, with "what is past, or passing, or to come". If Michael Robartes began in the early period as a Rosicrucian wearing Druid robes and speaking like Walter Pater, he could develop first into an occult teacher concerned with the intricacies of a new system and then into an aristocratic social commentator. This last personality had already been established in *Stories of Michael Robartes and His Friends*, where in part he rejected contemporary society and argued that war was a necessary revolutionary prelude to a better society.

Though this harsh social commentary cannot be examined fully, a few of its significant points may be noted. Unlike the earlier manuscript, "Michael Robartes Foretells" shows Yeats in full control of his system; Robartes is able to depend upon his gyres without explaining them all again, and so the prose has the terse, condensed excitement of Yeats's later poems.

Robartes makes two or three separate forecasts. The most important of these considers Western civilization from the present to the end of its cycle. We have now passed the significant turning-

30. For Yeats's rewriting of the "future" section of *A Vision*, see *Letters*, p. 812.
31. On September 13, 1929, Yeats wrote to Olivia Shakespear that he hoped to begin the new version of the Robartes stories; Robartes would "discuss the deductions with an energy and a dogmatism and a cruelty I am not capable of in my own person" (*Letters*, pp. 768-69); Robartes is thus related to other personae such as Crazy Jane and Ribh.

point of the 22nd phase and are moving toward the last, most objective phases of a dominantly objective cycle which is, of course, opposed to the subjective cycle which preceded it. For the subjective Yeats and Robartes, the future as far as the end of this cycle is therefore grimly unpleasant. It is for this reason that one of the main comparisons is to the later days of the Roman Empire which Yeats so despised. The logical outcome of this objective civilization must be "imitative, happy, general"; it is the final phases of "liberal Democracy". Students of Yeats's controversial politics will wish to note that Fascist governments are explicitly included within these abhorrently objective phases: "the old age of our civilisation begins with young men marching in step, with the shirts and songs that give our politics an air of sport".[32] Whether they be Fascist or Marxist, uniforms suggest uniformity and lack of individuality. Whatever his earlier feelings, Yeats by 1936 undoubtedly saw in the Fascist mass meetings indications not of aristocratic control but of conformity, loss of individual will, and rejection of the antithetical.

A second major prophecy, offered with less certainty than the first, extends from the end of the present cycle of Western civilization to the beginning of the next cycle. The cycles always overlap, and the end of one is marked by the beginning of the next. Here, the text ends with the forecast of the coming antithetical influx, with a "turbulence" similar but opposite to that which surrounded Christ at the end of the antithetical classical civilization.[33] Whereas Yeats's long note to "The Second Coming" suggested that subjective salvation was practically at hand, here he sees it coming only after several unpleasant decades [vp, 823-25].

A third possible prophecy deals with "some Asiatic Nation". While Yeats's theories of history await a fully detailed reading (if one is possible), it seems clear that he found a significant set of contraries in East and West, which had a complementary relation-

---

32. For studies of Yeats's supposed admiration of Fascism, see V. K. Narayana Menon, *The Development of William Butler Yeats* (London: Oliver and Boyd, 1942), pp. 90-92; Conor Cruise O'Brien, "Passion and Cunning: An Essay on the Politics of W. B. Yeats", in *In Excited Reverie*, pp. 207-78; John R. Harrison, *The Reactionaries: Yeats, Lewis, Pound, Eliot, Lawrence: A Study of the Anti-Democratic Intelligentsia* (New York: Shocken Books, 1967), pp. 39-73.

33. "Turbulence" in the typescript should be compared to the same word in the song from *Resurrection* (1927) [vpl, 931].

ship to one another as in Spengler. While the West awaits the coming of its antithetical civilization, "some Asiatic Nation" will meanwhile achieve an antithetical civilization currently impossible in the West. This Eastern nation will combine "some Asiatic philosophy" with the "psychical research founded by William Crookes". As in "Under Ben Bulben" and *On the Boiler*, belief will be in the eternal return of the soul to earth, to heaven, and back again. Fulfilling a long dream of Yeats's, aristocratic virtue will descend to the people, and there will be the same union of art and action, of transcendent and immanent, as in Byzantium.

Michael Robartes Foretells

I

Daniel O'Leary was sitting by a window at Thoor Ballylea, watching a yellow flooded river pour past, when Hudden, Dudden and Denice walked in unannounced.

"We heard you were here," said the first, "and have come from London to ask you a question."

"Yeats sent me the key," said O'Leary. "Somebody told him that I wanted to spend a week or two within reach of Coole House that I might look into the empty rooms, walk the woods and grass-grown gardens, where a great Irish social order climaxed and passed away."

"Have you the prophecy," said Dudden, "that Michael Robartes made at Albert Road? You wrote it out at the time. In London there are young men fresh from the Universities who perplex us. It is seven years since Michael Robartes disappeared into Arabia. Perhaps we are growing old."

"Yes, that is it," said Denice, smiling at Dudden. "Even I am faithful to the past."

"One night I brought in some London Journalist," Dudden went on. "You began a Communistic argument; I said that the Proletariat was an abstraction and must disappear before the German and Italian conception of the State as moulded by History yet transparent to reason and at last completely intelligible; then the Journalist derided the State, argued that nothing mattered but internationalism, democracy and disarmament."[34]

34. Originally it was the "Absolute State" that the journalist derided.

"Oh, yes, I remember," said O'Leary. "Robartes talked of the next Cycle, forgetting that the Journalist was ignorant of our terms, of the influx at the second, third and fourth Phases, said that some Asiatic Nation would base its whole civilisation upon War, that its governing class would take care of the common people as our governing class could not or would not, that they might obey in War and be loyal in defeat.[35] That its Schools and Universities would combine some Asiatic philosophy with the latest results of that psychical research founded by William Crookes, preparing all to face death without flinching, perhaps even with joy.[36] As according to their philosophy the dead will not pass to a remote Heaven, but return to the Earth, it will seem as though the soldier's dead body manured the fields he himself would till.[37] Furthermore, that they would subordinate class to class, that certain virtues created in leisure might descend to all; whatever music, dancings, painting, literature best served the perpetuation or perfection of the race or man's ultimate deliverance. Yet the State would be but little in men's minds, for the State as an idea, whatever definition we make of it, is but a degree less abstract than that of the Proletariat. Men's minds will dwell upon some company of governing men whom, though they seem every man's, even every base man's very self, it is natural to call noble."

"You are speaking from memory, I thought you had notes," said Hudden.

"No, not of those words. When you had shown the Journalist out and gone to your beds, I asked Robartes if I might put them down. He said, no, he made them up while talking and didn't know whether they were true or not; he knew nothing of the next cycle except that it would be the reverse of ours. I begged him to say what we who took the gyres and cones as the framework of our thought might safely prophesy, and on that night and the two following, we sat up late. I made notes and a few days later I wrote what I could remember. Here it is."

35. This emphasis on war is very close to that of *A Vision* (1937), pp. 52-53.
36. Sir William Crookes, the famous chemist, was also interested in psychical research, and from one of his books Yeats took the central incident of *Resurrection*; see [VPL, 569, 571, 935].
37. This statement of the importance of belief in reincarnation to a subjective or antithetical society is closely paralleled in "Under Ben Bulben" and *On the Boiler*; see [E, 436].

II

"We know that our own life, or the year, or the civilisation must pass through certain changes, that we, or it, approach the prime, or have passed it, that this or that character must increase or decrease, but we cannot know the particulars.[38] When we speak of the past, we can say that La Divina Comedia, or the Russian Revolution, expressed such and such a phase, but are misled the moment we try to imagine some future work of art or historical event.

"I will re-examine the Wheel. Every triad of phases is a separate Wheel.[39] Whatever existence we think of, a Civilisation's or an individual's, it arises from the general mass, wins its victory & returns. All our morality is heroic. This falling back or falling asleep brings its gains with it though conventionalised, formalised, mechanised. I reject Hegel's all containing, all sustaining, all satisfying final wakefulness. I reject Marxian Socialism, in so far as it is derived from him.

"The general mass, call it Nature, God, the Matrix, the Unconscious, what you will, becomes a unity when interlocked with some separating or subsiding existence; nor is it greater than that existence; the Will and Creative Mind of the one, the Mask and Body of Fate of the other, each dying the other's life, living the other's death.[40]

"The 22nd. phase of our civilisation has just passed, the Russian violence and the art and thought of our time where even logic has compelled the isolation & exaggeration of a single element represent the 23rd. phase, the first phase of the first Primary Triad;[41] the Dictatorships in various parts of the world, including the Russian,

38. The deleted sentence which originally began this paragraph was: "It is only possible to prophesy in abstract; every term has innumerable possible, particular expressions." Yeats made the same disclaimer [v, 302] evidently explaining why he could say no more about the future.
39. Yeats makes the same assertion [v, 93].
40. The last phrases are favourites of Yeats's which he borrowed from Heraclitus; see the text cited by Yeats [v, 67]: John Burnet, Early Greek Philosophy, 4th ed. (London: Adam and Charles Black, 1930), p. 138: "Mortals are immortals and immortals are mortals, the one living the others' death and dying the others' life."
41. [v, 166]: exemplars of the 23rd Phase include Synge and Rembrandt; though both are delighted with external, objective reality, neither "shows it without exaggeration, for both delight in all that is wilful, in all that flouts intellectual coherence...."

are the approach of the 24th. Phase. So much we deduce from our general knowledge and from our Cones and Symbols. But after that we have nothing but our cones and symbols. From Phase 22, the *Creative Mind* and the *Body of Fate* cease to be *enforced*, man more and more accepts, more & more thinks his Fate.[42] The *Creative Mind* from the twelfth century has been like stretched elastic, like a swaying pot; now the elastic is released, the pot recovers equilibrium.

"The antithetical is creative, painful—personal—the Primary imitative, happy, general.[43] It is this imitativeness in which there is always happiness, that makes the Movements of our time attract the young. The art and politics of the antithetical age expressed a long maturing tradition and were best practised by old men. That age has ended in the old political jugglers of liberal Democracy. I insist upon the paradox, that the old age of our civilisation begins with young men marching in step, with the shirts and songs that give our politics an air of sport. Phase 24. will perform the task of Augustus, but the end of our civilisation will differ from that of an antithetical civilisation;[44] the imitation of those who seem to express most completely the mass mind, the discovery of the mass mind in ourselves, will create a political system, more pre-occupied with the common good, more derived from the common people, than that of Rome and later Greece. Yet as Phase 25. draws near, in thirty or sixty years—we have no means of fixing the date, nor will it be the same date everywhere—men will turn from the leadership of men who offer nothing reason cannot understand.[45] They will return to women, horses, dogs, prefer to the political meeting, the football field or whatever thirty or sixty years hence may have taken its place. Some equivalent preference will overtake occupa-

42. [v, 111-12]: Yeats emphasizes, first, that he reserves the term Fate for objective phases and Destiny for subjective ones and, second, that in the most objective phases man does not battle with Fate but accepts it as an abnegation of personality.
43. Originally, "personal" was "heroic" and "general" was "peaceful". See [v, 84, 166], as well as "Ego Dominus Tuus", ll. 41 ff., for Yeats's dichotomy of subjective creation versus objective imitation.
44. Originally this clause ended "from that of an antithetical civilisation, from its primary decline".
45. Originally, this sentence ended: "nor will it be the same all over Europe—men will grow weary of systems, and the leadership of men who offer nothing the intellect cannot understand."

tions that have no part in politics; for all thought, under the pressure of some practical necessity will seek unity but weary of all reasoned expressions of that unity.[46] I do not say reason will die as the pot ceases to sway, the return to the normal requires reason.[47] An Achilles will be no longer possible, but some Virgil at Phase 24. may celebrate whatever popularisation our civilisation permits of the perfect official.[48] Carrying out the plan of an Olympian Board of Works amid many perils, amid much self-conquest; may he not gaze from his boat's deck on Dido's pyre; some Ovid of the films, at Phase 25. surpass even his popularity by celebrating our common casual pleasures. Every event will compel man's free acceptance of the external mask, objective man, life lived in common.[49] Fate is multiple, particular, has as it were personality, but the Mask is always one.

"Merely personal distinction, as past times used the word, will be out of date, will no longer exist except in archaic studious circles, or as a pretention of the vulgar; the ugly will sting man to life because it rids him of the desire and hope he can no longer employ.[50]

"I cannot say these things without hatred, I am an antithetical man, born in a still antithetical age, yet the men of that day, lacking our inequality, lacerations, artificialities, judged by any accepted standard will be happier than we are.

"Phases 24. and 25. must see the completion of a public ideal, its assimilation in the common civilisation, where all, whatever degree of rank and station remain, will live and think in much the same way. But at Phase 26. will come, enforced by some intellectual

46. Originally, "unity" was "system" and "all reasoned" was "its intellectual".
47. Originally "reason" was "intellect".
48. In the often-rephrased original passage, the "perfect official" was clearly named as Aeneas. In *A Vision* (1937), p. 206, Yeats speaks of several cultures and says that they, "having attained some Achilles in the first blossoming, find pious Aeneas in their second...."
49. This sentence originally began: "Man will accept his fate, will his fate, think his fate, he will struggle—Will and Mask have to be enforced—but every event...."
50. Originally "as a pretention" was "as imitation and formula, pretentions". [v, 135-36]: Yeats remarks of the quintessentially subjective Phase 15 that "The being has...grown more and more 'distinguished' in all preference"; "distinction" suggests subjective, aristocratic personality. [v, 107]: Yeats makes ugliness characteristic of the objective phases and beauty of the subjective.

necessity or change of circumstances impossible to foreknow, the knowledge of a form of existence, of a private aim opposite to any our civilisation has pursued. This knowledge affecting minorities, and organising their disgust, will create a turbulence, like that we see about us to-day, but moral and spiritual; the knowledge enforced upon Primary Minds of antithetical civilisation."*

* *Note*: In finding concrete events for the dates given me by my instructors, I considered that the historical chart was that of the Christian Era and what led to it. I considered this Era as a distinct cycle, different from those of Greece and Rome, but have the authority of my instructors for making it arise from that of Greece. We must consider the Roman cycle as two or three centuries later than that of Greece. I accept Schneider's identification of Virgil, Ovid, Nero, Epictetus with certain logical developments of Roman thought and I name those developments Phases 24. 25. 26. 27.[51] The personal exaggeration of Nero and his Court may be described as an antithetical vision of a Primary Ideal. In Epictetus that ideal is clearly seen, a Universal Being present in every particular person. A Primary Vision of an antithetical ideal might at Phase 26. be a moral and spiritual Nationalism, but first antinomean differences, personal in their final form, seen as differing ways of life.[52]

51. Yeats's reference is to Hermann Schneider, *The History of World Civilization: From Prehistoric Times to the Middle Ages*, tr. Margaret M. Green, 2 vols. (New York: Harcourt, Brace, 1931). Evidently this is one of the numerous reference works with which Yeats attempted to master history and philosophy between the two editions of *A Vision*; Schneider is referred to in *A Vision* (1937), pp. 205, 206.

52. At the bottom of the last page of typescript is an isolated handwritten phrase which Yeats deleted; it seems to read "with or contains the Christian or Byzantine cycles".

Mr. Yeats, Michael Robartes and Their Circle

Michael J. Sidnell

In Yeats, vision and belief, more than informing the "content" of the poetry, determine its structural conventions, by which I mean chiefly: the use of *personae* in narrative, dialogue, or dramatic forms; allegory and symbolism; ritual and myth. To suppose that Yeats employed certain (curious) conceptions of reality which "work" in the poetry and which are of interest only insofar as their explication helps to reveal his aesthetic mastery is as mistaken as to suppose that the poetry is the neutral vehicle of occult lore, traditional learning, and metaphysical speculation. Far from being an essentially lyric poet who happened to be interested in holistic philosophies, Yeats strove constantly to overcome the limitations of the lyric in the creation of more expansive and inclusive structures. This is part of his greatness and it is intimately connected with the conflict in the man and his work between a passionate attachment to nature and an insistent quest for transcendent reality. The more expansive structures in which Yeats tried to accommodate lyrical utterances are of three major kinds: a mythology of self based on the romantic conception of the integrity and allegorical significance of all the occasions of the individual life; a systematic metaphysic of the history of humanity and the destiny of the individual soul; and, combining these two, an elaborate fiction in which actuality, metaphysic, and vision and all his artistic products (lyrics, plays, essays, and stories) are loosely bound together as the adumbration of a unity unrealizable in the present. From Yeats's attempt at a vast imaginative construction great work resulted, for the most part lyrics which were conceived in the fictive bed and appear now dissociated from their origins. "Imaginative" is not quite the right word for the great enterprise; nor is "fiction". Yeats did not regard the individual imagination as autonomous or supreme.[1] And "fiction", insofar as the word connotes invention as distinct from retailing or ordonnance, is also the wrong word. For Yeats, the distinctions between stories, histories, philosophies, and religions were not categorical, and it was in stories that he found intimations of reality to be peculiarly accessible in the modern age. Yeats's word for what I have called an "elaborate fiction" and "imaginative construction" is *phantasmagoria*, and his word has the great advantage (for him) of by-passing epistemological considerations.[2] The word insists on the unity and the equal status in reality of a great variety of thought, images, and experience of very various origin.

In 1928, Yeats described "The Gift of Harun Al-Rashid" as "part of an unfinished set of poems, dialogues and stories about John Ahern and Michael Robartes, Kusta ben Luka, a philosopher of Bagdad, and his Bedouin followers" [vp, 830]. This "set" (as I shall call it hereafter) was not only left unfinished but had been, by its very design, an aggregation of fragments, a constructed ruin affirming the unrealizable unity; moreover Yeats partly dismantled and partly repudiated the set. The published relics are a number of poems and plays, some notes, some stories, and *A Vision* and these works are not, as Yeats once envisaged, articulated through a continuous fiction.

The cycle of eight poems which concluded *The Wild Swans at Coole* (1919) was the opening movement of the new set.[3] In his

1. "Our modern poetry is imaginative. It is the poetry of the young. The poetry of the greatest periods is an expression of the appetites and habits. Hence we select where they exhausted." W. B. Yeats, *Memoirs*, transcribed and edited by Denis Donoghue (London: Macmillan, 1972), p. 145. See also E & I, 152 and A, 521, [XXXIII].
2. See especially E & I, 509, and the Preface to *The Wild Swans at Coole* (1919 and 1920) [vp, 852].
3. "Ego Dominus Tuus"; "A Prayer on Going into my House"; "The Phases of the Moon"; "The Cat and the Moon"; "The Saint and the Hunchback"; "Two Songs of a Fool"; "Another Song of a Fool"; "The Double Vision of Michael Robartes." Only the first of these had appeared in *The Wild Swans at Coole* (Dundrum:Cuala Press, 1917) and the lapse of

review of the book, J. Middleton Murry raised a fundamental issue, his point of attack being the phantasmagoric substance of the cycle of eight poems to which Yeats had drawn attention in the Preface. Murry's objections, however mistaken they may have been, disclosed a new departure in Yeats's work:

> [The poet] may take his myth from legend or familiar history, or he may create one for himself anew; but the function it fulfils is always the same. It supplies the elements with which he can build the structure of his parable . . . .
> But between myths and phantasmagoria there is a great gulf. The structural possibilities of the myth depend upon its intelligibility. . . . The lawless and fantastic shapes of his own imagination need, even for their own perfect embodiment, the discipline of the common perception. The phantoms of the individual brain, left to their own waywardness, lose all solidity and become like primary forms of life, instead of the penultimate forms they should be. For the poet himself must move securely among his visions. . . . Nothing less than a supremely great genius can save him if he ventures into the vast without a landmark visible to other eyes than his own. Blake had a supremely great genius and was saved in part. . . . Whether Mr Yeats by some grim fatality, mistook his phantasmagoria for the product of the creative imagination, or whether (as we prefer to believe) he made an effort to discipline them to his poetic purpose and failed, we cannot certainly say. Of this, however, we are certain, that somehow, somewhere, there has been disaster. He is empty, now.[4]

What Murry seized as the evidence of Yeats's poetic inanition, the intercourse with phantasmagoria, was, of course, the opening of a splendid phase in Yeats's work, not the sterile conclusion to it; but Murry was not altogether astray in his criticism of what confronted him. Yeats was to make tremendous efforts to bring his phantasmagoria under "the discipline of the common perception", and it was true that he had not begun to "move securely among" them. At a later stage Yeats was relieved to be able to confess that the Robartes poems were, "to some extent" written "as a text for

---

time between the composition of this poem and the later seven is significant. "Ego Dominus Tuus" was the germinal poem of the cycle and more tentative than those that followed.

4. "Mr. Yeats' Swan Song", *Athenaeum*, 4640 (April 4, 1919) reprinted in *The Permanence of Yeats*, edited James Hall and Martin Steinmann (New York, 1950, rpt. Collier Books, 1961), pp. 9-12.

exposition" [vp, 821]. Consciously or otherwise, Yeats's next collection, *Michael Robartes and the Dancer* (1922), constituted a kind of mocking response to Murry, with its ironical concession to common perception and its parodic validation of the idiosyncratic "myth".

In later accretions to the set, Yeats attempted to develop further the unity of metaphysical speculation and passionate occasions through the Robartes phantasmagoria, by which, fantastically, he was stepping outside his own productions and offering to observe the observer. This quest for the anti-self, as it is most familiarly known, was the attempt to explore the world of unrealized possibility (Eliot's rose-garden) which, axiomatically, remains possibility only as long as it is unactualized; yet for the poet demands concrete, not abstract, expression. The unity envisioned by Yeats, that is to say, included the *might-be* by which the *what-is* is defined; the possible-actual connection being made in the future tense as well as the present, and in the past tense most acutely. Apart from the Robartes poems, the poignant dwelling on what might have been, that middle kingdom between youthful aspiration and present facts and memories, is the emotional centre of *The Wild Swans at Coole* and this retrospection is transformed into quest in the Robartes cycle at the end of the book. The paradoxical quest for the incorruptible soul-stuff of unactualized possibility seeks to translate the necessary failure of the act into the triumph of the soul. Through it, Yeats in his last phase becomes a religious rather than a tragic poet. As the theme developed it led not only to the linking of works in various genres but also to the incorporation of Yeats's earlier work into the new structure; the chief agent of this process being the new (and old) character, or phantasm, Michael Robartes. The process itself has remained rather obscure in commentary on Yeats, mostly because *A Vision* has been seen (with Yeats's warrant) simply as a kind of grammar-book of symbols.

Early in 1922, in response to a query by Allan Wade, Yeats offered an "explanation" of what he was up to with Michael Robartes:

> I have brought him back to life. My new story is that he is very indignant because I used his real name in describing a number of fictitious adventures, and that because I called my fictitious hero

by his name, many people have supposed him to be dead. He lived for years in Mesopotamia, but when the war came there returned to England for a short time. In England he got into communication with a certain John Aherne, and through him got into correspondence with me, and finally conveyed to me, without quite forgiving me, the task of editing and publishing the philosophy which he has discovered among certain Arabian tribes. That philosophy now fills a very large tin box upon which my eyes at this moment are fixed. I am giving it to the world in fragments, poems, notes, and a Cuala volume.[5]

Yeats's summary epitomizes the character of the fictive web he was now spinning: new revelations transcend old stories; the modulations from a resurrection to a philosophy, and from a fictional character to an actual tin box indicate the mysterious relations between nature and the supernatural (as well as the irrepressible Christian analogy) which is at the heart of the set. The letter is clearly designed as much to tease the recipient out of thought as to explain; it should, no doubt, be read as a contributory fragment rather than a commentary on the set. It is in keeping with both Yeats's attitude to letters and the relations between actuality and fiction in the set that his bibliographer's query should become part of the story.

The letter contains a minor puzzle which may be cleared up without fuss. Aherne was, of course, the character in "The Tables of the Law" who, having discovered the law of his own being, found himself separated from God. There is clearly a confusion of two Ahernes, for the man in the earlier story is *Owen* not *John*. To make good what was evidently a slip, Yeats split the one Aherne into a pair of brothers; and so a character got himself born.[6] Elsewhere in the set the accretion of characters in stories told within stories is more deliberate. As necessity arises, expressive agents are supplied, and the reader, encouraged to forget who is a character in whose story, must go more and more by that light of pure intuition which, as Croce observed, makes no distinction between subjective and objective images.

5. *The Letters of W. B. Yeats*, edited Allan Wade (London: Rupert Hart-Davis, 1954), pp. 676-77.
6. Yeats sometimes spelt "Aherne" without the final "e". John Aherne may have been a fused recollection of Owen Aherne (founded on Lionel Johnson) and John Hearne, the father of the protagonist in *The Speckled Bird*.

The Cuala volume referred to in the letter to Wade is *Michael Robartes and the Dancer*, a very different entity in this form from the section so entitled in the *Collected Poems*. In the Cuala volume a collection of poems was accompanied by anecdotal-metaphysical essays, rather in the manner of *The Wind Among the Reeds*. The "notes", as these essays are called, were the first published attempts at what was to become the system of *A Vision* and an integral part of the story of which the poems are part also.

The notes Yeats mentions to Wade include also those by which some plays (*The Dreaming of the Bones, The Only Jealousy of Emer, Calvary*) were annexed to the Robartes set [VPL, 777-79; 566-67; 789-91]. In these notes, Yeats employs the Robartesian philosophy in an explanatory way and, more significantly, elaborates the fiction. As much as inventing a story to convey a philosophy Yeats was using explication to tell a tale.

The letter to Wade makes no specific reference to the publication, which Yeats already had in mind, of a "selection from the great mass of . . . [Robartes'] letters and table-talk", nor to the dialogues of Robartes which were written but not published.[7] These were to be major contributions to the story which would not only link specific works but, more generally and sweepingly, accommodate all the poet's productions through the inclusion of "Mr. Yeats" as one of the characters about whom others write. This logically absurd relation of author and character is fundamental. It is analogous to Robartes' figure for reality: great eggs of the Phoenix which turn inside out perpetually without breaking the shell.[8]

As observed, the set was structurally a "ruin", an evidence but not a realization of the whole. It is both affirmation and denial, adumbrating the unity and mocking the incapacity to achieve it. In *Michael Robartes and the Dancer* the need for intelligible myth and its inaccessibility to moderns are rendered with high mockery.

7. I am grateful for the courtesy of Senator Michael B. Yeats and Professor George Mills Harper in making it possible for me to examine the unpublished dialogues. As I read them, they amplify but do not alter the account of the Robartes works given here.
8. *A Vision: An Explanation of Life Founded upon the Writings of Giraldus and upon certain Doctrines Attributed to Kusta Ben Luka* (London: T. Werner Laurie, 1925), p. xxiii, and *A Vision* (London: Macmillan 1937 reprinted 1962), p. 33.

The parody of scholarly machinery in the "notes" with their supporting evidence (of precisely dated letters and pedantic attributions) for revelation sardonically balances the fictive occultation of the source. Reporting what Aherne has reported, Yeats mediates, as sceptic-won-over, between his authorities and the disbelief of his audience. He goes through the motions of domesticating the absolute, annotating the mysterious; thus the spiritual incoherence of the age is shrouded in its appropriate vesture of learned commentary and annotation.

The spiritual tragi-comedy of *Michael Robartes and the Dancer*, indeed the very structure of the original book has scarcely been acknowledged. The insistence of one critic that the "notes" must be either not very intelligent explications of the poems or a spoof is a radical failure to perceive the peculiar character of the book and its tone.[9] Similarly, po-faced readings of the title poem which identify the poet and "He" (as though Yeats were not responsible for the other contribution to the dialogue) not surprisingly find Yeats (as well as "He") a pompous and pedantic enthusiast. Such readings miss Yeats's humour and the burlesque and, more seriously, the fundamental contestation in the book between the lyric poet and metaphysical philosopher. The book turns neither on intensity of feeling nor depth of understanding but on the tension between the one who suffers and the one who knows. These two personalities may almost be distinguished as Mr. Yeats and Michael Robartes, but in moments of visionary intensity they coalesce, and moreover their relation is made complex by the dubiety as to which is the creative force: at times Mr. Yeats is no more than Robartes' scribe, at others his opponent; Robartes is not merely a character *in* a story but a character *with* a story in search of an author.

When Robartes reappears in Yeats's work he is a different kind of character from the Robartes of "Rosa Alchemica", though his doctrine is similar. That earlier character was founded on Yeats's mystical friend (and antagonist) L. MacGregor Mathers who had, as Yeats reports, a deep and abiding influence on his thought:

. . . it was through him mainly that I began certain studies and

9. Donald Davie, "Michael Robartes and the Dancer", in *An Honoured Guest*, edited Denis Donoghue and J. R. Mulryne (London: Edward Arnold, 1965), pp. 76-80.

experiences, that were to convince me that images well up before the mind's eye from a deeper source than conscious or subconscious memory.

Describing images induced by Mathers, Yeats continued:

> ... there rose before me mental images that I could not control: a desert and a black Titan raising himself up by his two hands from the middle of a heap of ancient ruins.   [A, 183-86]

These two passages, which were written close in time to the publication of *Michael Robartes and the Dancer*, correspond to the two pillars of the Robartesian doctrine in that book. The insistence on the "deeper source" of images is found in the "note" attached to "An Image from a Past Life"; the Titan in the desert is clearly related to "The Second Coming" and to the discourse on the cycles of history which is attached to that poem in the guise of a note. The younger Yeats's conversations with Mathers continue, in transmuted and different forms, in both *Four Years* and *Michael Robartes and the Dancer*, and, as will be seen, the correspondence between occasions and fictions recurs as an important and deliberate aspect of the Robartes set. Eventually, the fictive ground was to be almost abandoned though it was the major connective between the formally diverse (though substantively overlapping) apprehensions of *A Vision* and the scarcely less visionary *Autobiographies*.

Though linked with the old character and with Mathers, the new Robartes is more purely an image, his doctrine of the image accounting for his presence, structure and substance reflecting each other. The old Robartes was an image (heightened and distorted) of Mathers, the new one a further visionary clarification of what had already been disentangled from an actual personality and re-embodied as literature. Thus Mathers, Robartes of the Nineties, and Robartes *redivivus* might be described as a progressive subjectivization, though in the last there is an awareness of the two predecessors and of the complex mental (or visionary) quality of the image. There is a fourth stage, also; the reappearance of Mathers (as we shall observe) to occupy the shape of Robartes as that phantasm begins to fade. Yeats is, of course, exploring the waxing and waning of objective and subjective images in the set; the great discoveries in it include such portions of Yeats's mind as

"Synge" in which objective and subjective experience combine
with more vitality than either history or imagination in isolation.
"Memory" is an inadequate description of this reality insofar as it
emphasises the actual rather than the created and transcendent
aspects of such portions of the mind.[10]

As with Stephen Dedalus, then, or Prufrock, the new Robartes
was inextricably bound up with his author's mind. But Robartes'
role does not rest on an aesthetic assumption about the ebb and flow
between identity and difference in the author-character relation.
Robartes is the agent of a metaphysical exploration which sometimes diverges from and at times interferes with art.

The first public manifestation of the resurrected Robartes was in
the glancing reference of "Ego Dominus Tuus". *Ille* in the poem
has discovered that the works of Dante and Keats reveal not themselves but their opposites—their motives for poetry—and, more significantly, he seems on the verge of the encounter with his own
opposite. The book left by Robartes intimates this impossible
encounter. It does not help understanding to gloss this book as the
Speculum Angelorum et Hominum (which Yeats had not at the
time invented) nor even as the book in "Rosa Alchemica". The
essential aspect of Robartes' book lies not in its content (whatever
that may be) but in that (like the tin trunk mentioned in the letter
to Wade) it is the phenomenal evidence of the reality of an image,
and moreover an image created by Yeats. Images and ideas precede
their material embodiments. The book lies neglected in the tower
and the positively absent reader is strongly evoked:

> A lamp burns on beside an open book
> That Michael Robartes left. . .   [VP, 367]

10. In "A People's Theatre" (1919), Yeats's allusion to "a certain friend"
    seems to imply that Robartes, in addition to his other contributions is
    also a poet: "Are we approaching a supreme moment of self-conscious-
    ness, the two halves of the soul separate and face to face? A certain
    friend of mine has written upon this subject a couple of intricate poems
    called *The Phases of the Moon* and *The Double Vision* respectively,
    which are my continual study, and I must refer the reader to these poems
    for the necessary calculations" [E, 259]. Since the poems had been pub-
    lished a few months earlier as Yeats's work, the alert reader would
    quickly recognize a drama of the "halves of the soul separate and face to
    face"—but not in their usual roles.

and later:

> ... the lamp
> Burning alone beside an open book.   [VP, 370]

Like Keats's unheard music, Robartes' unread book implies the superhuman union of the idea and the manifestation. *Ille* searches outside the tower for the image which is sustained only by his reading of the book inside the tower. That is half the irony; as though the poet in the tower were to seek outside it the figure of Major Robert Gregory who is, to the mind inside, a presence outside; or as though Aherne, in "The Phases of the Moon", were to knock at Yeats's door, as he threatens; or, in *The Resurrection*, the heart of the phantom were to beat—which, of course, it does; just as, completing the irony of "Ego Dominus Tuus", the impossible has happened. The fictional Robartes has actually left a book.

From the germinal allusion to Robartes in "Ego Dominus Tuus", Yeats elaborated the cycle of poems in *The Wild Swans at Coole*. In the third poem the situation of "Ego Dominus Tuus" is reversed. The poet is now inside the tower, but our perspective in "The Phases of the Moon" is not the author's but that of the images outside it:

> We are on the bridge; that shadow is the tower,
> And the light proves that he is reading still.
> He has found, after the manner of his kind,
> Mere images; chosen this place to live in
> Because, it may be, of the candle-light
> From the far tower where Milton's Platonist
> Sat late, Shelley's visionary prince:
> The lonely light that Samuel Palmer engraved,
> And now he seeks in book or manuscript
> What he shall never find.   [VP, 373]

As in the earlier poem, when he is outside the tower, so here when he is inside it, the poet's quest fails. Guided merely by poetic tradition, the poet finds "mere images", and the severe limitation of this kind of understanding is not its vagueness but the doubtful status of such images in reality. He cannot be assured (as the audience from its privileged position can be) of the "actuality" outside the tower. What the poet's images are we know precisely. The three narrative passages in the poem, printed in italics, present Robartes and Aherne, their boots soiled and their clothes shapeless; Aherne's high-pitched laugh, twice-repeated; the bat circling with its squeaky cry, and the extinction of the light in the tower. Their journey is measured by the diurnal cycle (the moon has risen) and by the menstrual cycle (it is dwindling) and it is towards the South—the point of complete subjectivity. This narrative corresponds to the song of the phases sung by Robartes. He and Aherne are themselves figures on a lunar wheel like the one Robartes describes. (They are in fact prototypes of the four "Faculties" which reiterated their roles in the drama of the wheel and later replaced them as *A Vision* developed, the fictive action giving way to the more abstract system.) When at the end of the poem the light in the tower is extinguished, the phenomenal world is not distinguishable from the darkness of Phase 28 as the song describes it; Aherne's laugh merges with the cry of the bat. Because the poet's light goes out, we may say, his creations fade: *his* creations, for the poet in the tower is identified as the author of the early stories about Robartes and Aherne. From the common-sense viewpoint, Yeats is both a character in the poem and its author, and from this viewpoint Robartes and Aherne have been sustained by the imagination of the poet; by a mental activity, we may add, of which the paradigm is the lunar wheel.

From the dramatic point of view, however, the poet is unaware of the actuality of Robartes and Aherne outside his tower. For him they are "mere images", and to imagine these mental creations a-knocking at his door, as Aherne twice maliciously suggests, is to imagine the inconceivable—the inconceivable that the poem intimates. The reader of the poem, insofar as he suspends disbelief and takes it on the dramatic terms offered, has the grasp of the reality of the poet's situation that the poet (within the poem) lacks. Once again, a fiction is swallowed by a new story, and one which will, in its turn be incorporated when, in a later work, Aherne is made to tell us that the "words were spoken between us slightly resembling those in 'The Phases of the Moon'."[11]

Yeats placed "A Prayer on Going into my House" between "Ego Dominus Tuus" and "The Phases of the Moon", and the poem is transitional not only in taking the poet inside the tower. More significantly it unifies material images with ideal ones. The simplest furnishings have their origins in ideal forms despite the material

11. *A Vision* (1925), p. xxi.

normality with which the usage of centuries endows them. Analogously, the poet's dream image, however fantastic, may be "normalised" by usage:

> ... yet should I dream
> Sinbad the sailor's brought a painted chest,
> Or image, from beyond the Loadstone Mountain,
> That dream is a norm. ...   [VP, 371-72]

The supreme story of the miraculous realization of the transcendent image is delicately implied in the allusion to "shepherd lads in Galilee"; what was miracle for them became orthodoxy for a later age, just as the idea of table, stool, or anything else may be conventional. The anything else, in this context most obviously includes Yeats's phantasmagoria. What Murry does not allow is here asserted: that Yeats's idiosyncratic dream-image may be made a norm as well as traditional ones. To put it bluntly, the image of Robartes may, like the Incarnation, be a vision of reality.

The incarnation of the absolute is most brilliantly rendered in the fourth poem in the sequence, "The Cat and the Moon". Here Robartes' phasal paradigm is transposed to Yeats's natural image in a way exemplary of the distinction between the lyric poet and the metaphysical philosopher. The animal blood of Minnaloushe is subject to necessity—the tidal pull of the moon—and the first and last parts of the lyric brilliantly evoke the movement of the cat under this lunar influence. In the middle of the song, however, freedom incarnate abolishes necessity; the cat teaches the moon to bring her motions up to date; to learn, as we hear in the rhythm, the syncopated measures of the jazz age:

> Do you dance, Minnaloushe, do you dance?
> When two close kindred meet,
> What better than call a dance?
> Maybe the moon may learn,
> Tired of that courtly fashion,
> A new dance turn.   [VP, 378]

This apt image of historical and individual transcendence at Phase 15 is the confirmation, through minute observation, of Robartes' doctrine. The major events of the poet's experience also confirm Robartes' paradigm.

In "The Phases of the Moon" Yeats's self-presentation is the veritable image of a late phase, "the learned man". Aherne, in his malice, would leave the poet with a cryptic prophecy:

I'd stand and mutter there until he caught
'Hunchback and Saint and Fool', and that they came
Under the last three crescents of the moon,
And then I'd stagger out. He'd crack his wits
Day after day, yet never find the meaning.

He would never find the meaning of the Hunchback, Saint, and Fool in the context of the lunar wheel but also, perfected irony, the meaning of the phases he has yet to live through. But the poet is a little more aware than Aherne supposes. By testing against life the song of the phases (for him inside the head, for us rendered by Robartes outside the tower) its validity becomes apparent. The poems following "The Cat and the Moon" are "The Saint and the Hunchback", "Two Songs of a Fool", and "Another Song of a Fool", and of these the most significant contribution to the amplitude of the sequence comes with "Two Songs of a Fool". From "Ego Dominus Tuus" to "The Double Vision of Michael Robartes" is a progression from a divided to a unified self. In "Two Songs of a Fool" that unity is brought nearer achievement as the poet sees in his life and its occasions the embodiment of the phasal abstractions.

In the first song, the poet as Fool prays for relief from the impossible burden of supplying the wants of his two dependents. In the second song, the burden has been partly lifted, and there is a longer perspective of the Fool's attempt to keep a hare in tame safety. Seen as an objective figure, the Fool is a pathetic portrait of incapacity, sexual jealousy, and deprivation. The little animal fable is a transparency through which we see an actual occasion and the young woman:

Who knows how she drank the wind
Stretched up on two legs from the mat,
Before she had settled her mind
To drum with her heel and to leap? [VP, 381]

The Fool is, however, more than the sufferer merely. As Lear's Fool sees his master's folly ("He's mad that trusts in the tameness of a wolf") so Yeats's Fool perceives his own. The choric line conveys in equal measure nostalgia for the sexual world beyond the hearthstone and a horror of it: "The horn's sweet note and the tooth of the hound." Beyond both nostalgia and horror, the poise of the line expresses the detachment of the Fool as seer. When, as we can hardly fail to do, we associate the Fool, the cat, and the hare with Yeats, George Yeats, and Iseult Gonne, the way in which the poem mediates between actual and emblematic figures becomes the more energetic, the occasion not less felt but seen and known in its phasal character.

With "Two Songs of a Fool" in mind, the preceding poem in the sequence becomes more passionate and personal than in isolation it might appear. The Hunchback is prevented from self-realization by his physical defect. The Saint, on the other hand, resists the visitations of unseasonable passions by mortifying the flesh. Thus the dialectic of the earlier part of *The Wild Swans at Coole* emerges in its emblematic form. The alternate (but not equal) views of aging as the loss of, or the release from, the passionate delusions of youth are now seen against the allegorical paradigm. In the Hunchback the desire for the self-realization of Phase 15 (now impossible since he has been whirled past that phase) still lingers; the Saint, though he is vexed by irruptions of self-hood, is drawn to the perfect self-abnegation of Phase 1. In the poem the contrary attitudes to aging are still very active but so also is a progression of which there is no suggestion in such poems as "Men Improve with the Years".

Since the purpose of these remarks is to elicit the structure of the cycle and a constructive, not lyrical, aspect of Yeats's art, I have passed over "Another Song of a Fool" (in which without intellective understanding, the Fool, literally, holds knowledge in his hands) and will abstain from explicative remarks on "The Double Vision of Michael Robartes".

Whether, in this final (or, as will be seen, *first*) poem in the sequence, the narrator is Robartes himself in the almost inconceivable role of poet, or Yeats, recording—but in the first person—Robartes' vision is a nice ambiguity. It resolves itself insofar as the structure of the whole cycle is perceived. Crucially, the long-sought encounter has occurred; the objective-subjective perplexity has been resolved; the dialogue of *Hic* and *Ille* is now seen as the shadow of real antinomies. The divided self reflects the forces of determinism and freedom in human life. Having passed through Phases 26, 27, and 28 in the preceding poems, the cycle moves into Phase 1 in "The Double Vision of Michael Robartes". The human is an object two removes from autonomous being:

> When had I my own will?
> O not since life began.

> Constrained, arraigned, baffled, bent and unbent
> By these wire-jointed jaws and limbs of wood,
> Themselves obedient. . . .   [VP, 382]

In the context of the paradigm of the phases, the apprehension of Phase 1 must be visionary since the phase is discarnate. And, in the poem, the vision of Phase 1 is not followed (as it had been preceded) by the phases in their order. Instead of such a mechanical presentment, the poem moves, in its second section to the opposite discarnate phase. It is as though, in the inspired moment, the vision of Phase 1 had evoked that of Phase 15, to complete the supernatural part of the paradigm.[12]

In "The Double Vision of Michael Robartes", it is important to note, vision recedes. The first section of the poem is given in the continuous present:

> On the grey rock of Cashel the mind's eye
> Has called up the cold spirits. . . .   [VP, 382]

The second section of the poem is the vision of the apotheosis of the human soul imaged as the dancer who brings to their perfection the minute particulars of mankind (a vision of Phase 15), and it is introduced in the past tense:

> On the grey rock of Cashel I suddenly saw. . . .   [VP, 383]

The third section of the poem, which is not visionary but explanatory, is set further in the past:

> I knew that I had seen, had seen at last
> That girl . . . .   [VP, 383]

It is only in this third section (although I have referred, for convenience, to Phases 1 and 15) that Yeats introduces the metaphor of which the paradigm of the mansions of the moon is an expansion:

---

12. In the title of Yeats's poem, the word "Double" couples Phase 1 and Phase 15. It also couples common and visionary sight. Cp. Blake's:

> *What to others a trifle appears*
> *Fills me full of smiles or tears;*
> *For double the vision my Eyes do see,*
> *And a double vision is always with me.*
> *With my inward Eye 'tis an old Man grey;*
> *With my outward, a Thistle across my way.*

[Letter to Butts, November 22, 1802.]

> ... caught between the pull
> Of the dark moon and the full,
>
> The commonness of thought and images,
> That have the frenzy of our western seas. [VP, 384]

It is structurally quite deliberate that, in the cycle of poems, the paradigm of the phases should precede the vision from which is drawn the metaphor on which the paradigm is based. "Cycle" is, in fact, the right word.

In the third section of the poem the voice is clearly Yeats's, the matter not visionary. The allusions and situation are those met elsewhere and have clear autobiographical reference. The final emphasis of the poem is not on the revelation in itself but the experience of it:

> Thereon I made my moan,
> And after kissed a stone,
> And after that arranged it in a song
>
> Seeing that I, ignorant for so long,
> Had been rewarded thus
> In Cormac's ruined house. [VP, 384]

The song that the poet made has been given already, in "The Phases of the Moon", by Robartes and at Aherne's urging:

> Sing me the changes of the moon once more;
> True song, though speech: 'mine author sung it me.' [VP, 373]

The visions of the final poem are not only the culmination of the poems that precede "The Double Vision of Michael Robartes" but (with the exception of the groping "Ego Dominus Tuus"[13]) their antecedents. As observed, the visions recede, like fading coals, leaving the poet with metaphor and "mere images". He and Robartes are separate until in the visionary state of the final poem "All thought becomes an image and the soul/ Becomes a body". In that state Robartes incorporates Yeats. When, as the vision recedes, image and poet slip apart, Yeats does not return to the state of ignorance and confusion expressed in "Ego Dominus Tuus" but to the dubious intimations and metaphors of "The Phases of the Moon".

In the cycle of poems, the intellectual comedy of the quest itself tends to dominate the structure, but in *Michael Robartes and the*

---

13. See note 3 above.

Dancer, the Robartes fiction pervades the whole as a given, and the tragic implications of the gulf between abstract determinism and natural freedom are made manifest, particularly in the poems concerned with the Easter Rising and its aftermath. After *Michael Robartes and the Dancer*, discoveries made through the intercourse with the phantasmagoria endow the poetry with certitude and power.

"I am full of uncertainty," Yeats wrote, "not knowing when I am the finger, when the clay" [M, 366]. Through the Robartes set this doubt becomes a creative and unifying force in the relation between the author and his characters. Such presences as Cuchulain, Maud Gonne, Lear, and Jonathan Swift though ontologically diverse have the same double status in Yeats's poetry and, indeed, his world. He is both their vehicle and their creator. It is from the basis of the image and discoveries of Robartes that Yeats can assert that Swift has climbed the stair, Cuchulain stalked the Post Office. In "The Tower", the intercourse of mind and nature is superbly rendered by Yeats's summons to his youthful creation Hanrahan. As with the two Hamlets, the meeting of Yeats and Hanrahan on the battlements of the tower envisions a præternatural communication of body and spirit in which (as Dedalus says of the Shakespearian encounter) "to a son he speaks, the son of his soul".[14] Hanrahan being not merely dead, but in death as in life, a fiction, is "shade more than man, more image than a shade", but momentarily he is endowed with more vigorous life than his author. Behind the antinomies of fiction and experience lie those of "memory" in both orders. Yeats's need for Hanrahan's "mighty memories" is a secondary encounter of present and possible worlds. As a figment of mind, Hanrahan has, axiomatically, enacted what his author could only imagine. He has been "there" and may remember (or be the agent of recollection of) the realm of perpetual possibility which he entered. The finely balanced antithesis of the lively character and the aging poet points to the synthesis, so magnificently suggested in this poem, that encompasses mental and material reality. "The Tower", though not part of the Robartes set, was in some fundamental respects its product.

One way of describing the achievement of the Robartes works is as the synthesis of the transcendentalism which came to its fullest

14. James Joyce, *Ulysses* (New York: Random House, 1961), p. 188.

poetic expression in *The Wind Among the Reeds* and the objectivity which, in 1903, had opened a new phase in Yeats's career. In "The Autumn of the Body" Yeats had ranged himself on the side of the artists seeking "an almost disembodied ecstasy" against those whose work was less pure [E&I, 194]. In 1903, he repudiated that mood. His view of reality, he said, had been only one half of the orange, and he now felt in himself and in the world the impulse to "create form, to carry the realization of beauty as far as possible".[15] At about the same time Stephen Dedalus is supposed to have adopted the same attitude to the earlier Yeatsian mood:

> *6 April, later:* Michael Robartes remembers forgotten beauty and, when his arms wrap her round, he presses in his arms the loveliness which has long faded from the world. Not this. Not at all. I desire to press in my arms the loveliness which has not yet come into the world.[16]

Just before Robartes was resurrected, Yeats saw this reflection of his early work in Joyce's self-image (as Yeats firmly characterised Dedalus[17]). Aherne was reflected there as well as Robartes, and whether or not *A Portrait of the Artist as a Young Man* stimulated Yeats's new work, Yeats, in effect if not intention, began to finesse the Dedalian critique: to reconcile the notion of art as the revelation of transcendent reality with that of art as creation from chaos.

"There are so many rooms and corridors I am still building on foundations laid long ago,"[18] said Yeats in 1916, and the Robartes set was most obviously such new construction. In 1917, Robartes is still an "uncompromising Pre-Raphaelite"[19] and through him Yeats's work is re-imbued with the preoccupations, doctrines, and visions that had engrossed him before the turn of the century. And this is much less a matter of continuity than of a deliberate revival of the past. There are some reasonable causes (if we want them) for the re-infusion.

From the Great War ("the great war beyond the sea" [VP, 339]) Yeats remained emotionally detached but it was the fulfilment at

---

15. Wade, *Letters*, p. 402.
16. James Joyce, *A Portrait of the Artist as a Young Man* (New York: Viking Press, 1968), p. 251.
17. Wade, *Letters*, p. 599.   18. *Ibid.*, p. 605.
19. *A Vision* (1925), p. xv.

last of those prophecies of "immense wars" with which Mathers had impressed him [A, 336-37]. The Easter Rising and its aftermath affirmed more directly and feelingly the reality of those abstract forces which human life expresses and demanded an emotionally and intellectually complex response. The only poem in *Michael Robartes and the Dancer* in which vision of the abstract overwhelms the poet is "The Second Coming". In this poem orthodoxy (as indicated by the title and the exclamation) only feebly resists vision; elsewhere, however, the poet pits a passionate attachment to the "minute by minute" of natural good against the inexorable principles adduced by Robartes and historically demonstrated. "On a Political Prisoner" presents the simplest antithesis of natural freedom and the terrible abstract force which drains it of vitality. In "A Prayer for My Daughter" the poet most dramatically presents the opposition of revealed truth and created beauty. On his tower he affirms human freedom against abstract indifference. Prayer is the freedom he opposes to the storm of necessity, and the substance of the prayer is elicited, by contraries, from the recollections of experience with which it is lyrically interwoven. From experience derives the ceremony which momentarily preserves innocence and establishes a petty kingdom of human order. So efficacious is the lyrical ceremony of prayer, that through it, in the poet's mind and the reader's—though not dramatically—the storm is stilled. Ceremony prevails: Yeatsian poetry against Robartesian knowledge, creation against revelation.

Balancing the doctrine of the historical cycles in the "notes" is that of the "image" which concerns the eternity of the soul. The revival of this doctrine may have its biographical matrix in the years 1914-17 when the perplexities of Yeats's sexual life brought him to a state of nervous exhaustion. The doctrine of the source and reality of the image itself goes back, as observed, to Mathers, and Robartes' discourse on the image makes intelligible the life-problems of which the successive proposals of marriage to Maud Gonne, her daughter, and Miss Hyde-Lees are the superficial evidence. "The Double Vision of Michael Robartes" had put the reality of the image most succinctly:

> I knew that I had seen, had seen at last
> That girl my unremembering nights hold fast
> Or else my dreams that fly
> If I should rub an eye,

And yet in flying fling into my meat
A crazy juice that makes the pulses beat. . . .   [vp, 384]

Between the ephemeral dream image and the "meat" (or incarnate world) there is such a mysterious relation as exists between Robartes and his book or, for that matter, Robartes and Yeats. The real reality of Niamh, Maud Gonne, and all the other *dramatis personae* is revealed. The vision of the dancer as the apotheosis of the soul and Robartes' doctrine of the image are redolent of the sexual-apocalyptic theme of *The Wind Among the Reeds*. In *Michael Robartes and the Dancer* the "note" on the image is attached to "An Image from a Past Life", and in the poem, too, the past life might almost be that of Yeats in the nineteenth century so clearly does he echo himself in theme, language and image:

> A sweetheart from another life floats there
> As though she had been forced to linger
> From vague distress
> Or arrogant loveliness,
> Merely to loosen out a tress
> Among the starry eddies of her hair
> Upon the paleness of a finger.   [vp, 390]

In this poem and others in the book, however, Yeats reconciles (as he does not in *The Wind Among the Reeds*) the image and the actual woman. In the doubled perspective, the man's love for the woman is heightened, not devalued, by his awareness that this love is the reflection of a metaphysical action in which the soul is attempting to complete itself. The man in "An Image from a Past Life" does not, of course, define the poet (self-image though it may be); the woman's part is the poet's too, and she speaks fearfully of the overshadowing image, conveying the sense of loss. Their love is not authentic in the way she had assumed if it is the expressive mode of intercourse between the living and the dead. The woman's part in the dialogue here and elsewhere is that of body speaking for the sensual world, though she too is allowed a soul and an over-shadowing image. Whereas in *The Wind Among the Reeds* the poet spoke with one voice of the desolate knowledge of the discrepancy between the image and the woman, the later collection adds new dimensions; in the He/She dialogues most obviously. In "Solomon and the Witch", Solomon puts the apocalyptic view:

> Maybe the bride-bed brings despair,
> For each an imagined image brings

And finds a real image there;
Yet the world ends when these two things,
Though several, are a single light,
When oil and wick are burned in one . . . .   [VP, 388]

Solomon's view is significantly different from those iterated by a
variety of *personae* in *The Wind Among the Reeds*: for one thing
the sexual apocalypse is envisaged without taint of the horror once
heard in such lines as "And lay in the darkness, grunting, and turning to his rest" [VP, 153]. Again, love's equation is reversible: the
woman, too, may be conscious of the discrepancy between lover
and image! (A most significant development, this, in Yeats's love
poetry.) And, connected with the development of the voice, that
of the "independently" perceiving woman, there is a new, comic
element compounded in the tragedy of love. Solomon and Sheba
fail—just—to achieve that consuming ecstasy which would signify
that "this foul world were dead at last", and the end of what "the
brigand apple brought". But as the Fall was in some ways fortunate,
there is some felicity in the failure of sexual love to achieve its
apotheosis. With great verve, "the witch" conveys the tremendous
consolation of their inability to transcend nature: "O! Solomon!
let us try again" [VP, 388-89].

In the introductory story to the first *A Vision*, the distinction
between Robartes and Mr. Yeats, the sage and the poet, is made by
Aherne:

> Now it was my turn to get angry, for I had spent much toil upon
> his [Robartes'] often confused and rambling notes. "You will give
> them to a man," I said, "who has thought more of the love of
> woman than of the love of God." "Yes," he replied, "I want a
> lyric poet, and if he cares for nothing but expression, so much the
> better, my desert geometry will take care of the truth." I replied—
> I think it better to set my words down without disguise—"Mr
> Yeats has intellectual belief but he is entirely without moral faith,
> without that sense, which should come to a man with terror and
> joy, of a Divine Presence, and though he may seek, and may have
> always sought it, I am certain that he will not find it in this life."[20]

This drama and these roles were pre-figured in *Michael Robartes
and the Dancer* but with the emphasis there on the lyric poet's productions and the energy in them stemming from that "love of
woman" and of life. To be a poet at all, to have the means of ex-

20. *A Vision* (1925), pp. xxi-xxii.

pression, it has been necessary for "Mr Yeats" partly to resist and partly to clothe with corruptible flesh the abstractions of "desert geometry". As indicated, "A Prayer for my Daughter" resists the "murderous innocence" of necessity and has tragic implications. On the other hand, the title poem of the book presents the comedy of double vision. For his daughter Yeats prays:

> May she be granted beauty and yet not
> Beauty to make a stranger's eye distraught,
> Or hers before a looking-glass.... [VP, 403]

By contrast, in the poem "Michael Robartes and the Dancer", *He* urges *She* to accept completely the discipline of the looking-glass. The essential difference in attitude is not between father and lover (though this is dramatically important) but between the single and lyrical voice of "A Prayer for my Daughter" and the dialogue of "Michael Robartes and the Dancer". *She* in the poem is the poet's other voice, bringing vision back to nature and placing the action of the poem in a natural setting. This poem concerns the discrepancy between the metaphysical relation of Robartes to his dancer (as *He* perceives it) and the human comedy involving Yeats and Iseult Gonne, or some such couple. *She*, as well she might, resists the visionary relation and conceives of herself as other (or more) than a "lover's wage", the vehicle by which his soul travels to its fulfilment. If *She* in the poem is a very natural girl, *He* is not an unnatural man. *He* speaks dismissively of the impurities of opinion, mixed and unembodied thought, but he argues like a pedagogue. *He* scorns mere book knowledge but has a *latin text* to prove him right! In attempting to lead *She* by the way of instruction to visionary wisdom, *He* is necessarily frustrated. Vision has no arguments and cannot be proved by texts; even painterly images must work through slow-toiling nature. The self-mocking comedy of "Michael Robartes and the Dancer" has been obscured by ingenuous identifications of *He* and Yeats, just as the parodic tragi-comedy of the book overall has been ignored. It is only rarely that abstract wisdom and concrete expression fuse as vision, and even the poet who has seen visions must continue to find in nature the means of expression in his life and his art. Robartes' wisdom needs Yeats's passionate attachment to life for its embodiment and, if the poetry is to be more than a lyrical representation of the accidents of life, then some such abstractions as those of Robartes are needful to it. *Michael Robartes and the Dancer* intimates the union of inarticulate revelation and passionate ignorance while in structure and theme it acknowledges the impossibility of such unity.

Yeats did not give the world the kind of "edition" of Robartes' "letters and table talk" that he had promised in the Preface to *Michael Robartes and the Dancer*. Instead he published the first version of *A Vision*, a work of a different character, in which the fictive paraphernalia, though significant, is not pervasive. The situation of the story told by Aherne by way of introduction to *A Vision* recalls that of "The Phases of the Moon". Once again, and much more circumstantially, the entrance to the story is a visitation made by Robartes and Aherne to Mr. Yeats. The new story gobbles up the previous ones, embracing all the earlier occasions on which the three names have been associated and discriminating fictional exaggeration from "actuality" at the new level. Aherne's Dublin residence (from "The Tables of the Law") and Yeats's Bloomsbury (from the life) are in the same order of reality, but the new conjunction of fiction and nature is rather more contrived. It has less about it of the conviction of phantasmagoria, more of parable.

The middle of Aherne's "Introduction" is a sketch of Robartes' career which, with its vacillating pursuit of arcane knowledge and sensual excitement, embodies his later discoveries. But Robartes is apparently unaware that he has lived his thought before formulating it. As with a number of characters in the Robartes set (including the Caliph and Kusta ben Luka), sexual disturbance leads to intellectual discovery. The quarrel with the ballet dancer sends Robartes first to the bottle then to Cracow. In Cracow the discovery of Giraldus' book is made under circumstances that farcically illustrate its significance. When Robartes' "fiery handsome girl of the poorer classes"[21] props up their bed with the book and lights fires with some of its pages, she symbolizes its meaning as ignorantly and profoundly as she does in the bed. And Robartes, gyring from women, to drink, to philosophy, traces the movement abstractly represented in the book under the bed. In it also may be found the pattern of his subsequent career. The revelation on the road to Damascus brings him to a people "known among the Arabs

21. *Ibid.,* p. xvii.

for the violent contrasts of character amongst them, for their licentiousness and their sanctity".[22] Both Mecca and Jerusalem have been destinations, sensuality and asceticism his ways.

Robartes' arrival among the Judwalis pushes the discoveries further back in time, and Kusta ben Luka begins to assume the major role as their source. I say further back in time because Kusta "historically" is, but in another way we are approaching the immediate present. The essence of the stories about Kusta is that they are intermediate stages between truth and the acts by which it is revealed. When Aherne questions the authenticity of the story of "The Dance of the Four Royal Persons" his orthodox, objective and scholarly approach to the tale is a failure of understanding. The story is not subject to historical nor, of course, aesthetic criticism. It is a parable of artistic and intellectual sincerity. Kusta's pupils make their master's geometry interesting and intelligible in the only possible way, by dancing their lives away to embody it. Reality cannot be made intelligible at no life-cost. That life-cost is in the present we are approaching.

The first *A Vision* is a highly symmetrical structure: the whole is framed by the "Dedication to Vestigia" and "All Souls' Night", two versions of the same aspect of Yeats's experience; after the introductory stories, each of the four books contains exposition of Robartes' systematic philosophy and a prefatory poem by Yeats. These four poems, "The Wheel and the Phases of the Moon", "Leda", "Desert Geometry or the Gift of Harun Al-Raschid", and "The Fool by the Roadside", serve to remind us of the distinction between the lyric poet and the systematic philosopher; Yeats as poet is running a parallel course through the work with Yeats as editor of Robartes' papers. The poems are concrete representations of the abstract philosophy of each book, but the relation of poet to philosopher is rather different in each case. "The Fool by the Roadside" presents one of the emblematic figures of the wheel in the manner of "Two Songs of a Fool". It is an illustrative poem. "Leda" is a symbolic, perhaps visionary, poem apprehending in a single figure the essence of cyclical history as flowing from a series of conjunctions of human and superhuman. The narrative of "The Phases of the Moon" is incorporated into the new fictive structure by Aherne's reference to it in the "Introduction". By

22. *Ibid.*, pp. xviii-xix.

contrast with this poem, the new narrative poem, "The Gift of Harun Al-Raschid", tends to short-circuit both the system and the Robartes fiction to bring us back (where the revised *A Vision* of 1937 is so firmly placed) into the realm of the facts and occasions of Yeats's own life. When "The Gift of Harun Al-Raschid" was published in *The Tower* Yeats announced the abandonment of the "unfinished set of poems, dialogues and stories" of which it was part and which had been further developed in earlier "notes" to the poem [vp, 830]. The poem was, in fact, almost the final stage of the attempt to combine lyric poetry, vision, and systematic philosophy into one vast fictive structure. The Robartes stories which came afterwards were in ironical juxtaposition to a system embedded not in stories but in spiritualism.

With "Desert Geometry or the Gift of Harun Al-Raschid" fiction begins to merge with autobiography, and only the oldest of new critics could conceal from himself the transparency of the autobiographical allegory, and its approximation to the account of the origin of *A Vision* given in the revised edition of the work. Stallworthy has described Kusta and his bride in the poem as "too clearly Mr. and Mrs. Yeats in fancy dress" and the Caliph as a figure of Providence or God.[23] The last attribution is ridiculous and insupportable. The dialogue of the Caliph and Kusta is yet another dialogue of body and soul. For Kusta, "the best that life can give" is:

> Companionship in those mysterious things
> That make a man's soul or a woman's soul
> Itself and not some other soul.

To which, the Caliph, not all like a divinity, replies:

> ... it is right
> Every philosopher should praise that love.
> But I being none can praise its opposite.
> It makes my passion stronger but to think
> Like passion stirs the peacock and his mate,
> The wild stag and the doe; that mouth to mouth
> Is a man's mockery of the changeless soul. [vp, 465]

If Yeats is in fancy dress, he is wearing the costumes of Caliph as well as Kusta. The bride is, allegorically, the body's gift to the soul.

23. Jon Stalworthy, *Between the Lines* (Oxford: Clarendon Press, 1963), pp. 85-86.

(There is also, I believe, a third costume, that of the shadowy Vizir Jaffir, murdered by the Caliph as, in the dialogue poem "Owen Aherne and his Dancers", the conscience murders the lover in the man because the girl is too young. The frustrated lover, the sensual bridegroom, and the married man in whom soul as well as body is appeased make a series of roles in an autobiographical allegory.) Kusta's bride brings to him all the wisdom he has sought in the wrong place, and his story is a radically new one for Yeats. The girl's devotion to Kusta is Desdemona-like and foreboding ill:

> A girl
> Perched in some window of her mother's house
> Had watched my daily passage to and fro;
> Had heard impossible history of my past;
> Imagined some impossible history
> Lived at my side; thought time's disfiguring touch
> Gave but more reason for a woman's care.

Immediately, the bride immerses herself in books:

> ... old dry faggots that could never please
> The extravagance of spring .... [VP, 466]

Were it not fabulous, the story would take the downward plunge. But it departs from the pattern firmly established in Yeats's earlier work; instead of the descent back into nature from some transcendent state (as with Oisin, Hanrahan, or even Solomon) the miracle occurs. Both the woman and wisdom are won. The antinomies are revealed by the young bride in terms reminiscent of "The Double Vision of Michael Robartes". It is "a moonless night" on which she expounds determinism in human life: "Those terrible implacable straight lines" that "Must drive the Arabian host" [VP, 467]. Then, "When the full moon swam to its greatest height" she "marked out those emblems on the sand" [VP, 468]. Unconscious both of her knowledge and the bodily expression of her soul, she has achieved the synthesis long-sought by Kusta:

> The signs and shapes;
> All those abstractions that you fancied were
> From the great Treatise of Parmenides;
> All, all those gyres and cubes and midnight things
> Are but a new expression of her body.... [VP, 469]

Unlike the dancer, the bride is not beheld in dreams, not a supernatural image, but a naturally existent being. She herself is in that state between sleeping and waking which Kusta's forerunners in Yeats have themselves entered in the apprehension of vision and reality. So placed, Kusta can now "read" the embroidered black banners which, while they are "an act of mourning for those ... fallen in battle", also "wait war's music". He is not blinded by the splendour of natural life ("dazzled by the embroidery"), nor, on the other hand, is the price of wisdom to be ("lost/ In the confusion of its night-dark folds") withdrawn from the sensual world. The banner is the emblem of a new synthesis, much more concentrated than the phasal paradigm, linking lives already lived with those still to be spent. Woman's beauty is the symbol of what drives the generations onward and what expresses the individual. Wisdom is not passive. It is actively expressed through sexuality and conflict:

> And now my utmost mystery is out.
> A woman's beauty is a storm-tossed banner;
> Under it wisdom stands, and I alone—
> Of all Arabia's lovers I alone—
> Nor dazzled by the embroidery, nor lost
> In the confusion of its night-dark folds,
> Can hear the armed man speak.   [vp, 469-70]

In relation to this poem, Robartes would appear to be still in the maze in which Kusta, before the marvellous abridgement of his quest, has spent his life. In "The Dance of the Four Royal Persons", Aherne is made to "doubt the authenticity of this story, which Mr. Yeats has expanded into the poem 'Desert Geometry or The Gift of Harun Al-Raschid'."[24] The poet, it appears, is going beyond his licence. He has gone, indeed, almost as far as Crazy Jane's unsystematic grasp of an immanent reality.

It is a basic article of Robartes' philosophy that "the human soul is always moving outward into the objective world or inward into itself", [vp, 824] and the Robartes set necessarily (given the expressiveness of the structure) embodies such a movement. In "The Gift of Harun Al-Raschid" the outward movement is pronounced, and its approximation to immediate experience, contrasting with the density and introversion of the earlier Robartes fiction, leads towards the extreme objectivity of the revised *A Vision*. It is something of a paradox that the system bolstering the idea of subjective

24. *A Vision* (1925), p. 11.

fulfilment should have eventually such an objective basis, the phenomena of spiritualism making materially evident a supernatural world. Already in the first *A Vision*, the outward movement is proceeding in the first and last "framing" sections of the work. The "Dedication to Vestigia" (Mrs. Mathers) begins:

> It is a constant thought of mine that what we write is often a commendation of, or expostulation with the friends of our youth, and that even if we survive all our friends we continue to prolong or to amend conversations that took place before our five-and-twentieth year. Perhaps this book has been written because a number of young men and women, you and I among the number, met nearly forty years ago in London and in Paris to discuss mystical philosophy.[25]

In this long perspective (which contrasts with the "incredible experience", which replaced it in the revised work) [v, 8] the chief expostulant is MacGregor Mathers. The "Dedication" and "All Souls' Night" enclose fiction and system within the more objective story of Yeats and his mystical friends. One step further and the image of Robartes would be re-incorporated with that of Mathers. This did not, of course, occur. Robartes was displaced neither by Kusta ben Luka nor MacGregor Mathers but by Mrs. Yeats. She, like Kusta's bride, becomes the agent of revelation. To her are attributed some of the spiritualist experiences which, at the last stage of Robartes' development as a character, Yeats had discordantly foisted upon him, when Robartes lost the vitality of an image and became a mere disguise.

But the Robartes image was not quite extinguished. In 1932 Yeats wrote, as an antidote and corrective to the earlier fiction, the compound narrative of *Stories of Michael Robartes and His Friends: an Extract from a Record Made by One of His Pupils*. In the revised *A Vision*, the *Stories*, a meditative essay, and an autobiographical introduction offer distinct and partly ironical perspectives of the systematic books which follow. (It is too often forgotten that *A Vision* consists of more than the systematic books.) Briefly, and finally, let us look at the perspective of *A Vision* opened up by the *Stories*.

In them, the earlier mysteries of Robartes and Aherne have been reduced to absurdity. The two characters are now a couple of spiritual detectives better informed and a move ahead of the official keepers of the conscience of mankind. The narrative point of the chronicle is Robartes' search for a proper guardian for Leda's third egg. "Aherne and I will dig a shallow hole," says Robartes, "where she must lay it and leave it to be hatched by the sun's heat" [v, 51]. There are two candidates in the story for the high office of laying the egg, and their qualifications are elicited by the telling of their stories. The loser, as her name suggests, is a somewhat tarnished aesthete. Denise de L'Isle Adam and her lover (like Axel and Sarah) had found no satisfactory bodily expression for the love of souls. Through her lover's physical reserve, however, she has made a modest discovery: "Oh, my dear, how delightful; now I know all about Axel. He was just shy" [v, 43]. She values Duddon's soulful shyness and, moreover, overcomes its major deficiency. As for loving, his patron can do that for him; so Huddon becomes the willing instrument of bodily expression. Huddon and Duddon are allegorically, of course, like the Caliph and Kusta, halves of the one man; in them and Denise we have some such compromise between body and soul as marriage, illustrating Robartes' doctrine given in the story that "The marriage bed is the symbol of the solved antinomy, and were more than symbol could a man there lose and keep his identity, but he falls asleep" [v, 52]. The masks are not opaque, but the farce is not mere disguise for autobiography. It is a stylization through which the allegorical character of experience and the continuum of life and art is made manifest. Through the burlesque of the decadent style also, Yeats makes an amusing criticism of the notion of the autonomy of art, its separateness from nature.

Denise has made her choice and has come to terms with life. She is not chosen to lay the egg. That honour falls to Mary Bell, a more profound character whose name is taken from Blake, a profounder author than Villiers de L'Isle Adam. On her husband's deathbed, Mary Bell has brought him great contentment, making him believe that he has achieved the ambition of his life. He dies supposing that he has corrected the defect in nature whereby cuckoos refuse to build their own nests. In practising this amiable deception, Mary Bell has enjoined the assistance of her former lover, John Bond, an ornithologist. In the collaboration of this couple there may be some echo of the author and of Olivia Shakespear, she supplying nesting materials for Yeats's canaries. Yeats observing innate knowledge in his birds and moralising on them in letters to Mrs. Shakespear and in *Autobiographies*.[26]

The literal nest-building of John Bond and Mary Bell reflects an earlier discipline in their lives. They had allowed passion only a momentary victory and coming back to common-sense had separated, he turning to ornithological studies, she to building, metaphorically, a cuckoo's nest for their son. Because the lovers preserve the secret and the conventions, the illegitimate child is endowed with a house, an ancestry and a tradition which comes to him as though by natural succession from the providence of his suppositious father. In the son's inheritance we have a figure of the natural world (an Eden as Mary's husband sees his estates) [v, 48]; in her conformity to social usage Mary enacts the ceremony by which innocence is preserved; the boy himself is the incarnate issue of pure passion: this story, in short, transposes the conjunction of Zeus and Leda into the comic mode and domesticates the archetype. Mary Bell, the possessor of two secrets, whose discipline has been to keep them, is the fitting actress of Robartes' mystery. The literal cuckoo's nest has brought her husband a sense of fulfilment in life, the metaphorical one (her son's home) has enriched Mr. Bell's life with the tangible myth of a son—happy irony—as well as providing a world of possibility for that son. At the allegorical level, the cuckoo's nest is history, in which the soul may find its seemingly authentic habitation if, as with cuckolded Mr. Bell and his cuckoo-son, the secret be kept from it. Spiritually, the cuckoo's nest does not signify (as it does at the literal, metaphorical, and allegorical levels) deception at all, but revelation. Old Mr. Bell's quest for nests built by cuckoos for cuckoos to live in is no less than a quest for the perfection of nature, for the realization of spirit. When the soul wakes from deception it will no longer need the borrowed nest of history.

As amiable deceptions, ceremonies to preserve innocence, and spiritual quests, Yeats's metaphysical and occult preoccupations, from the early interest in magic to the late belief in spiritualism, and including *A Vision*, are elaborately burlesqued and justified in *Stories of Michael Robartes and His Friends: An Extract from a Record Made by One of His Pupils*. And with *Stories*, too, the fictive elaboration came to an end. A particular set of phantasmagoria faded in a harsh and gay presentation of the necessity and absurdity of the mortal quest for reality.

26. Wade, *Letters*, pp. 669-72, and [A, 270-71].

"Lionel Johnson Comes the First to Mind": Sources for Owen Aherne

Warwick Gould

Studies of the sources for Yeats's characters Michael Robartes and Owen Aherne have been few: critics have, perhaps understandably, been more interested in what Yeats did with these two masks in his works. Another reason for this neglect is the seeming obviousness of sources close to hand; Michael Robartes surely contains aspects of MacGregor Mathers[1], and Lionel Johnson has been suggested, at least as long ago as 1959, by Michael Fixler[2], as a source for

---

1. Maclagan, in *The Speckled Bird*, is more obviously drawn from Mathers, but Mathers clearly is also reflected in Robartes, and is also the likeliest source for much of Robartes' learning. Lady Gregory in her reminiscences writes of Yeats bringing AE to stay at Coole on his first visit, in 1897, and says that Yeats "had told me he had described him [AE] as 'Michael Robartes' in *Rosa Alchemica*, and when one Monday morning I had a letter saying that they would be with me by lunchtime I looked at the passage and read 'with his wild red hair, fierce eyes and sensitive lips and rough clothing, Michael Robartes looks something between a peasant, a saint and a debauchee', so I was rather apprehensive and went down to meet them feeling quite shy, but to my relief found a quiet gentleman, perfectly simple and composed" (*Seventy Years: Being the Autobiography of Lady Gregory*, ed. Colin Smythe [Gerrards Cross: Colin Smythe, 1974], p. 311). Lady Gregory is clearly quoting the *Savoy* text of *Rosa Alchemica* from memory, and the words must have made quite an impression on her, for the only detail missing is that Robartes' lips are also described as being "tremulous".

   I am deeply indebted to the Universities of Queensland and London for financial assistance which made possible the research for this article.
2. Michael Fixler, "The Affinities between J. K. Huysmans and the 'Rosicrucian' Stories of W. B. Yeats," *PMLA*, 74 (1959): 464-69.

Owen Aherne. Lionel Johnson by no means exhausts the subject, though many critics have echoed Fixler's suggestion in later works.

The most accessible and best short account of Johnson's life is the introduction to Iain Fletcher's edition of Johnson's *Complete Poems*.[3] Johnson deserves to be better known, not only for introducing Lord Alfred Douglas to Oscar Wilde, but also for introducing his cousin, Olivia Shakespear, to Yeats. His lecturing work for the Irish Literary Movement is still being uncovered, while his association with the London factions of the I.R.B. and the '98 Centennial Association, as alcoholic as it was illuminist and conspiratorial, is better known.[4] A child prodigy and undergraduate extraordinary, a retired Buddhist received into the Catholic Church, he lives for us in the myth Yeats wrapped about him in *Autobiographies*. Yeats's selection of *Twenty One Poems* for the Dun Emer Press reinforces this myth, and shows it to be largely of Johnson's own creation. The selection opens with "Mystic and Cavalier":

> Go from me: I am one of those, who fall.
> What! hath no cold wind swept your heart at all,
> In my sad company? Before the end,
>
> . . .
>
> Go from me, dear my friend!
> O rich and sounding voices of the air!
> Interpreters and prophets of despair:
> Priests of a fearful sacrament! I come
> To make with you mine home.

"Much falling", Johnson was a secret drinker who "did not want to be cured". "Mystic and Cavalier" contains in its title the "double name" of the "single nature" of Johnson. This duality is evident in the hero of his story about a Carolean soldier-priest, *Mors Janua Vitae*.[5] The story provided Yeats with a singularly effective model for the shape of his *Tables of the Law* and is, like many of Johnson's poems, an "imaginary portrait" of himself. Owen Aherne,

3. *The Complete Poems of Lionel Johnson*, ed. Iain Fletcher (London: Unicorn Press, 1953), hereafter cited as Fletcher.

4. Fletcher, pp. xxviii, xxx.

5. *The Albermarle*, London, Sept. 1892, pp. 99-106. In "Certain Noble Plays of Japan" Yeats wrote of Japanese soldiers, whose education had included the drama, that their natures "had as much of Walter Pater as of Achilles" —another development of the "half monk, half soldier of fortune" double nature he so much admired. [E&I, 235].

"half monk, half soldier of fortune", is similarly divided and, like the Mystic and Cavalier, feels that he "must be hidden away":

> "No, no," he said, "I am not among those for whom Christ died.... I have a leprosy that even eternity cannot cure. I have seen the whole, and how can I come again to believe that a part is the whole? I have lost my soul because I have looked out of the eyes of the angels." [M, 305-06]

When Johnson told Yeats that he did not want to be cured he was hinting at a malaise deeper than alcoholism. It is this spiritual malaise which is at the heart of Owen Aherne's dilemma. Yeats writes of him that "Catholicism had seized him in the midst of the vertigo he called philosophy . . . she had failed to do more than hold him on the margin" [M, 305].

Fletcher writes of the failure of Catholicism in Johnson's life to "do more than hold him on the margin" in "dissipation and despair", singling out his overwhelming problem in the following terms: "To continue after the illumination has passed is the great problem of the religious life . . . ."[6]

The Trembling of the Veil offers the best ground for comparison of Yeats's mythologized portrait of the long-dead Johnson with his earlier counterpart, Owen Aherne. Yeats writes of Johnson that "his doctrine, after a certain number of glasses, would become more ascetic, more contemptuous of all that we call human life" [A, 223]. Aherne in *The Tables of the Law*, though "more orthodox in most of his beliefs than Michael Robartes, . . . had surpassed him in a fanciful hatred of all life" [M, 294]. And Aherne at the end of the story with his "leprosy that even eternity cannot cure" would surely agree with Lionel Johnson that to deny "the eternity of punishment" is "an unspeakable vulgarity" [A, 223].

Johnson's favourite phrase according to Yeats was "life is ritual" [A, 302], and this as well as his penchant for arising "for dinner at seven" [A, 304] must have made him seem, as Fixler suggests, an English Des Esseintes. The unnamed narrator of all three stories, who describes his own life most fully in *Rosa Alchemica*, more strictly fits into Huysmans' mould, and the close congruence between Aherne and his narrator has led some commentators to con-

---

6. Fletcher, p. xvi.

fuse them.[7] Although they share many characteristics—the narrator like Aherne is a divided soul, "the one [self] watching with heavy eyes the other's moment of content" [M, 269]—a careful reading of the stories as they were revised to appear together in *The Secret Rose* quickly dispels any confusion.

There the matter might be thought to rest: Aherne and Johnson, recluses and Catholics, each exercising his exquisite sensibility upon the contemplation of his own downfall, with a penchant for "turning action into dreaming, and dreaming into action" [M, 294]. Except that Aherne's fate had been described in 1896 and Johnson's in 1917-21 in *Per Amica Silentia Lunae* and *The Trembling of the Veil*, Yeats might well have been describing the same person. This impression is confirmed if we look at what Yeats wrote of Johnson before he died:

> ... Mr. Lionel Johnson has in his poetry completed the trinity of the spiritual virtues by adding Stoicism to Ecstasy and Asceticism. He has renounced the world and built up a twilight world instead, where all the colours are like the colours in the rainbow that is cast by the moon, and all the people as far from modern tumults as the people upon fading and dropping tapestries. He has so little interest in our pains and pleasures, and is so wrapped up in his own world, that one comes from his books wearied and exalted, as though one had posed for some noble action in a strange *tableau vivant* that cast its painful stillness upon the mind instead of the body. He might have cried with Axel, "As for living, our servants will do that for us." As Axel chose to die, he has chosen to live among his books and between two memories—the religious tradition of the Church of Rome and the political tradition of Ireland. From these he gazes upon the future, and whether he writes of Sertorius or of Lucretius, or of Parnell or of "Ireland's dead," or of '98, or of St. Columba or of Leo xiii., it is always with the same cold or scornful ecstasy. He has made a world full of altar lights and golden vesture, and murmured Latin and incense clouds, and autumn winds and dead leaves, where one wanders remembering martyrdoms and courtesies that the world has forgotten.
>
> His ecstasy is the ecstasy of combat, not of submission to the Divine will; and even when he remembers that "the old Saints

---

7. See Fixler, pp. 466-67. Richard Ellmann, in *Yeats: the Man and the Masks* (London: Macmillan, 1949), p. 86, conflates these two figures as that "mask" of Yeats which is the counterpart to the Robartes "side of a penny". See also Robert M. Schuler, "W. B. Yeats: Artist or Alchemist?" *R. E. S. New Series*, 22, No. 85, (1971): 37-53.

prevail," he sees "the one ancient Priest" who alone offers the Sacrifice, and remembers the loneliness of the Saints. Had he not this ecstasy of combat, he would be the poet of those peaceful and happy souls, who, in the symbolism of a living Irish visionary, are compelled to inhabit when they die a shadowy island Paradise in the West, where the moon always shines, and a mist is always on the face of the moon, and a music of many sighs is always in the air, because they renounced the joy of the world without accepting the joy of God.[8]

"The ecstasy of combat" for Johnson must have been very painful by 1898, and that last sentence seems to betray Yeats's special pleading. What we have, I suggest, is an account of the two Johnsons. Fletcher has shown the ease with which Johnson could offer contradictory accounts of himself,[9] and "the ecstasy of combat" was probably as genuine as the "dissipation and despair" resulting from the double rejection Yeats mentions. What also is interesting in this passage is that in it Johnson moves from life into myth: "wrapped in his eternal moment"[10] he becomes a key figure in the "phantas-

8. *Dublin Daily Express*, 27 Aug. 1898. Also in *A Treasury of Irish Poetry*, ed. T. W. Rolleston and Stopford A. Brooke (London, 1900), pp. 465-67. Yeats's emphasis upon the "trinity of the spiritual virtues" of stoicism, ecstasy, and asceticism is particularly interesting in the light of his statement in *The Trembling of the Veil* that "Two men are always at my side, Lionel Johnson and John Synge whom I was to meet a little later" [A, 312]. The meeting was, according to Yeats, in the autumn of 1896. In *The Death of Synge* he later wrote "In Paris Synge once said to me 'We should unite stoicism, asceticism and ecstasy. Two of them have often come together, but the three never'" [A, 509]. Here one can see Yeats's mind at work, idealizing and unifying impressions into phantasmagoria; for Synge's comment must have helped him come to his assessment of Johnson and to associate the two men henceforth in his mind until "In memory of Major Robert Gregory".

9. Fletcher, p. xxix.

10. M, 277. The "companies of beings" which appear to the narrator of *Rosa Alchemica* during his temptation at the hands of Robartes have a simpleness and perfection which is the principal expression of their divinity. Maude Gonne's beauty is similarly felt to be "simple as a fire" in "No second Troy". Owen Aherne's hope for the times following the influx of the Holy Spirit is that he will be then able to "create a world where the whole lives of men shall be articulated and simplified as if seventy years were but one moment, or as they were the leaping of a fish or the opening of a flower" (*The Tables of the Law & The Adoration of the Magi* [Stratford: Shakespeare Head Press, 1914], p. 13). The imagination, or reverie, brings "its object to mind with great clearness, yet, as

magoria through which I can alone express my convictions about the world" [VP, 852]—that meeting place in the writer's mind for experiences of men and books, of fantasy and reality, where the synthesis of the real and the remembered and the imagined takes place in reverie. Yeats had said of Johnson's "imaginary portraits" of famous men he pretended to have met, which were repeated "without variation", that they were "the phantasmagoria through which his philosophy of life found its expression" [A, 306], and there is every reason to suggest that Yeats's account of Johnson occupied a similar place in his own *"tableau vivant"*.[11]

Rosa Alchemica appeared first in the second issue of Symons's *Savoy* in 1896. *The Tables of the Law* appeared in the penultimate issue, in November. Discerning readers of *The Savoy*, puzzled by the singular fervour of the heresies in *The Tables of the Law*, might profitably have turned back to earlier issues for some explanation. Yeats's poems, such as "The Travail of Passion", "The Shadowy Horses", and "The Valley of the Black Pig", would have further suggested the animus of that extraordinary story (which Bullen was to judge too controversial to print in *The Secret Rose* but too good to let slip); but Johnson's three superb sonnets in the fourth issue would have provided further examples of its doctrine.

The first of these, "Hawker of Morwenstow", concerns the eccentric Cornish vicar whose poems, under the Biblical and even ninetyish title *Reeds Shaken with the Wind*, were published in 1843.[12] Johnson's poem is a surprisingly neglected example of

---

sometimes happens in dreams, raised a little above its self and above ordinary retrospect." This mythologizing process of the imagination involves a Last Judgement passed upon experience, a Paterian substitution of the "typical" for the "actual". Fletcher mentions this substitution in his essay "Rhythm and Pattern in Yeats's Autobiographies", in *An Honoured Guest*, ed. Denis Donoghue and J. R. Mulryne (London: Edward Arnold, 1965), p. 173.

11. Again, Yeats's description of the experience of reading Johnson's poems is a good description of the phantasmagoria itself. The word did not come into common usage until 1802, and was at that time used as the title of an exhibition of optical illusions in imitation of the "Eidophusikon"—the theatrical extravaganza that De Loutherbourg designed for the amusement of William Beckford at Fonthill Abbey.

12. See Fletcher, pp. 216-17, for all three poems. R. S. Hawker's *Reeds Shaken with the Wind* (London, 1843) could not be said to be apocalyptic

pan-Celtic sentiment, an expression of solidarity in "Catholic faith and Celtic joy". Hawker, "Far on the Western marge, thy passionate Cornish land!" is joined by Johnson in lament: "thine ancient race in twilight lies!" The piece is a skilful evocation of Celtic sanctity and anarchy, while the second poem is addressed to "Mother Ann", the foundress of the Shakers, and establishes not only Johnson's sympathy for members of heretical sects, but by its urgency expresses that very Christian fervour which, striving against God-given bounds of time, courts heresy through excess of apocalyptic desire.

But for readers of *The Tables of the Law* the third sonnet proves the most interesting. "Munster 1534" is dedicated to a fellow member of the Irish Literary Society, Richard Ashe King, to whom Yeats later dedicated *Early Poems and Stories*, and it expresses, as Fixler suggests, "the antinomian animus of the frenzied millenarian Anabaptists who with swords in their hands sought to usher in the age of the Holy Spirit":[18]

> We are the golden men, who shall the people save:
> For only ours are visions, perfect and divine;
> And we alone have drunken of the last, best wine;
> And very Truth our souls hath flooded, wave on wave.
> Come, wretched death's inheritors who dread the grave!
> Come! for upon our brows is set the starry sign
> Of prophet, priest, and king: star of the lion line:
> Leave Abana, leave Pharpar, and in Jordan lave!
>
> It thundered, and we heard: it lightened, and we saw:
> Our hands have torn in twain the Tables of the Law:
> Sons of the Spirit, we know nothing now of sin.
> Come! from the Tree of Eden take the mystic fruit:
> Come! pluck up God's own knowledge by the abysmal root:
> Come! you, who would the reign of Paradise begin.

---

in tone. A later vicar of Morwenstow, H. Hugh Breton, notes that the Church, suspecting Hawker of too great a sympathy with the Wreckers on the coast, "decided he was a dangerous anarchist, and that the safest place for such a dangerous member of society was Morwenstow, and there he stayed to the end of his life" (*Hawker of Morwenstow*, The Morwenstow Series No. 3, n.d.: 38). His deathbed conversion ended thirty years on "the margin" of Catholicism. F. G. Lee (*Memorials of the late Rev. R. S. Hawker* [London, 1876], p. 191) quotes a letter from Hawker's wife to this effect. Lee also prints Hawker's essay "Time and Space", which is based upon a Joachite view of history [pp. 90-95].

13. Fixler, p. 465n.

I suggest these lines are not, as Fixler notes, the "source" of *The Tables of the Law*, any more than their author is simply the "source" for Owen Aherne. What we have here, apart from the textual echoes such as the fruit of the Tree of Eden (also mentioned in *Rosa Alchemica*), is an area of mutual concern. Although this is not one of the poems Yeats chose for his selection of Johnson's work, its lines stayed with him. The first of his "Discoveries" tells how his experiences with the Abbey Theatre in a west of Ireland town convinced him in "a single thought" of the need to "reintegrate the human spirit in our imagination. The English have driven away the kings, and turned the prophets into demagogues, and you cannot have health among a people if you have not prophet, priest and king" [E&I, 264]. Just such a reintegration of the imagination was not only part of the nationalist movement, but also a central element in Yeats's version of the Joachite triumph of the Holy Spirit, where "the beautiful arts were sent into the world to overthrow nations, and finally life herself, by sowing everywhere unlimited desires, like torches thrown into a burning city" [M, 294]. Aherne in this heresy is clearly the mask of both Yeats and Johnson, indeed of all whose personal involvement in the Irish movement was as spiritual as it was political.

The "last, best wine" of the "golden men" or Anabaptist elect recalls the "unmixed wine" of "A Thought from Propertius" [VP, 355]. The centaur's "fit spoil", Maud Gonne, is seen here and in other poems, such as "Beautiful Lofty Things" [VP, 577], as a goddess, one of the "Olympians", the coming race, the elect born not to "live, but to reveal the hidden substance of God", for "the world only exists to be a tale in the ears of coming generations" [M, 300].

Another of the "Olympians", John O'Leary, inevitably comes to mind in a consideration of sources for Owen Aherne. Yeats wrote the three stories when he had "left Dublin in despondency"[14] after he had been staying with O'Leary. O'Leary seemed to Yeats both disappointed and disappointing: he belonged to that generation of revolutionaries who thought that they "above all men, must appeal to the highest motive, be guided by some ideal principle", and he would "split every practical project into its constituent elements, like a clerical casuist, to find if it might not lead into some

14. *Early Poems and Stories* (London: Macmillan, 1925), p. vi.

moral error" [A, 209-10]. Like Aherne in the latter part of *The Tables of the Law*, the old O'Leary must have seemed a shadow of his former self, but such casuistry and moral fastidiousness deeply impressed and deeply vexed Yeats. O'Leary's nobleness is constantly stressed in Yeats's works. When Yeats writes in the following terms of Aherne, he might almost be speaking of O'Leary.

> He was to me, at that moment, the supreme type of our race, which, when it has risen above, or is sunken below, the formalisms of half-education and the rationalisms of conventional affirmation and denial, turns away, ... from practicable desires and intuitions towards desires so unbounded that no human vessel can contain them, intuitions so immaterial that their sudden and far-off fire leaves heavy darkness about hand and foot. He had the nature which is half monk, half soldier of fortune, and must needs turn action into dreaming, and dreaming into action; and for such there is no order, no finality, no contentment in this world.
>
> [M, 293-94]

When Yeats reviewed O'Leary's *Recollections of Fenians and Fenianism* in the London *Bookman* (Feb. 1897, p. 147), he wrote of O'Leary's "passion for abstract right" which he saw as the "Celtic passion for ideas, intensified by that mistrust of the expedient which comes to men who have seen the failure of many hopes ... O'Leary's detachment from his own enthusiasm has not come to him with old age, but has given his whole life a curious and solitary distinction. . . . He is of *that supreme type*, [my italics] almost unknown in our heady generation, the type that lives like the enthusiasts, and yet has no other light but a little cold intellect." Yeats later wrote of O'Leary that "his long imprisonment, his longer banishment, his magnificent head, his scholarship, his pride, his integrity, all that aristocratic dream" [E&I, 510] had been the basis of the attraction his followers felt. O'Leary is recalled searching "the second-hand bookstalls", making "his tranquil way to the Dublin quays" (familiar to readers of *The Tables of the Law* as the scene where the narrator meets Aherne near the bookstalls, ten years after confronting him fired by "the delirium of the brave", and now "a lifeless mask with dim eyes" instead of a "resolute and delicate face" [M, 303]). It is interesting that when Yeats recalls O'Leary in this context [A, 212] he also says that he was writing *The Secret Rose* and O'Leary was writing his *Recollections of Fenians and Fenianism* (1896), the book which disappointed Yeats as being so much less inspiring than its author. At the time, says Yeats, the two men spent their mornings in "casuistry": the writings of Owen Aherne, which contain all his secret law learned in the East as a doctrine for the coming times of the Holy Spirit, are described as an "elaborate casuistry" [M, 304].

Johnson too was a casuist. A deep student of the Church Fathers (Yeats called him the theologian of the movement), his desires for a "measureless consummation" were not channelled into practical revolution. Indeed, like O'Leary, who said "there are things a man must not do to save a nation" [A, 213], the courteous and scholarly Johnson would have agreed that "no gentleman can be a Socialist", though "he might be an Anarchist".[15] The poet who could write "Ways of War" (dedicated to John O'Leary) and say

> A terrible and splendid trust
> Heartens the host of Inisfail:
> Their dream is of the swift sword-thrust,
> A lightning glory of the Gael.
> . . .
> A dream! a dream! an ancient dream!
> Yet, ere peace come to Inisfail,
> Some weapons on some field must gleam,
> Some burning glory fire the Gael[16]

urgently condemned acts of revolution in Ireland, and offered to "find . . . [Yeats] passages in the Fathers condemning every kind of political crime, that of the dynamiter and the incendiary especially". Yeats "asked how could the Fathers have condemned weapons they had never heard of, but those weapons, . . . [the casuist Johnson] contended, were merely developments of old methods and weapons; they had decided all in principle" [A, 309].

This tension between scruple and desire, between orthodoxy and anarchy, lies at the heart of any consideration of O'Leary and of Johnson. It is the common feature of Yeats's estimation of them, and it is the central characteristic of the hero of *The Tables of the*

15. A, 211. See also *The Letters of W. B. Yeats*, ed. Allen Wade (New York: Macmillan, 1955), p. 869.
16. Fletcher, p. 47. Other poems of Celtic fervour and Fenian illuminist sentiment include "Parnell", "Ninety Eight" (dedicated to R. Barry O'Brien), "The Day of Coming Days", "The Red Wind", "The Church of a Dream", "Dawn of Revolution", and "Celtic Speech". "Ways of War" was later published in *Poems of the I.R.B.*, ed. Edward J. O'Brien and Padraic Colum (Boston, 1916).

Law. Ellmann's view[17] that Aherne is "conventional man", who has " 'never looked out of the eye of a saint / Or out of a drunkard's eye' " is puzzling. It is particularly odd that he should choose to (mis)appropriate this quotation, which gives us a picture of the absolute reverse of the Aherne of *The Tables of the Law*, the man who "has looked out of the eyes of the angels" [M, 306]. For each of these three divided characters, Aherne, O'Leary, and Johnson, the "soldier of fortune" is restrained by the moral or religious scruple of the monk, whose dreams of sanctity and the consummation of time have fired the soldier in the first place. The tension is the difference between young and old O'Leary, drunk and sober Johnson, Aherne caught "in that vertigo he called philosophy" and later, "protected by his great piety, ... sunk again into dejection and listlessness", held "on the margin" by the Church,[18] and warning the narrator of the dangerous errors of emulating his Faustian career.

All these men are victims of the dilemma of Wilde's parable which Yeats could not forget: " 'Lord, I was dead, and You raised me into life, what else can I do but weep?' " [A, 287] It was a problem that Yeats himself explored in many ways in the 1890s; ecstasies of vision, of occult experience, awakened nationalism, of hashish even, were there: perhaps accepting Dante's compromise with Olivia Shakespear taught him how to live. The problem has been

17. Ellmann, p. 86. When Yeats felt in 1908 that *The Tables of the Law* needed revision, it was because the hero "must not seem for a moment a shadow of the hero of 'Rosa Alchemica'." Though a case can be made for saying that Yeats is here referring to the narrator of *Rosa Alchemica*, and not to Robartes, and so to the possibility of confusion between the narrator and Aherne, it seems likely that he wished to indicate the difference between Aherne and Robartes more clearly. Aherne then "is not the mask but the face. He realizes himself. He cannot obtain vision in the ordinary sense. He is himself the centre. Perhaps he dreams that he is speaking. He is not spoken to. He puts himself in the place of Christ. He is not the revolt of the multitude" (*Memoirs*, ed. Denis Donoghue [London: Macmillan, 1972], p. 138).

18. M, 306. Yeats's memory of the despairing Johnson, only rising early to go to Mass at Farm St. [A, 319], suggests the assistance the narrator offers to Aherne in the *Savoy* version, when he returns to the silent house with a "Jesuit Father from the College of St. Francis Xavier". The narrator, on the verge of taking the habit of "Saint Dominic" in *Rosa Alchemica*, is not to be confused with the casuist, aesthete and scholar Aherne. His Jesuit education and "priestly ambition" convey a subtly different character.

stated in a more sober reflection upon the Anabaptists than Johnson's:

> We cannot know what John of Leyden felt
> Under the Bishop's tongs—we can only
> Walk in temperate London, our educated city,
> Wishing to cry as freely as they did who died
> In the Age of Faith. We have our loneliness
> And our regret with which to build an eschatology.[19]

II

Another related, but quite separate aspect of the link between Lionel Johnson and Yeats is of interest in any consideration of Owen Aherne. Johnson must have been Yeats's authority upon Joachim of Flora. Yeats saw him as the "theologian" of the movement [A, 221], and he must have been no mean theologian to have been familiar with a subject which at the time was only beginning to be closely examined. Far more is known now about millenarian movements, but the Joachite concept of the Eternal Evangel and the question of who wrote the *Liber Introductorius* were at issue for historians of the religion of the thirteenth century in the 1880s and 1890s.[20]

19. Peter Porter, "The Historians call up Pain", in *Penguin Modern Poets* (Harmondsworth: Penguin, 1962), II: 100. In *The Savoy* (1896), Symons's skilful editing is evidenced by his placing of Dowson's "Epilogue" immediately under the last paragraph of *The Tables of the Law* (p. 87). It has an appropriately similar mood:

> Let us go hence: the night is now at hand;
> The day is overworn, the birds have flown,
> And we have reaped the crops the gods have sown,
> Despair and death; deep darkness o'er the land

> Broods like an owl: we cannot understand
> Laughter or tears, for we have only known
> Surpassing vanity: vain things alone
> Have driven our perverse and aimless band.

20. For example, see H. Denifle, "Das Evangelium æternum und die Commission zu Anagni", *Archiv für Litteratur- und Kirchengeschichte*, I (1885): 49-142. This seminal article contains the surviving extracts from the *Liber Introductorius in Evangelium Æternum* of Gerardo de Borgo San Donnino, the Joachite book which Yeats uses as the basis of Aherne's *Liber inducens in Evangelium æternum*. Yeats would have needed the

Even now, the *Expositio in Apocalypsim* of Joachim de Fiore is unedited, and not available in any but a black letter Latin edition. It does not really support the apocalyptic fervour of the passages which, prefiguring the more elaborate farrago of *Stories of Michael Robartes and His Friends*, Yeats concocted as quotations from Joachim's sacred doctrine. In 1901 Yeats wrote in Quinn's copy of *The Tables of the Law* "The portrait which is by my father & the Latin which is by Lionel Johnson are the only things which are worth anything in this little book".[21] The Latin passages are splendid; Johnson was an accomplished Latinist poet. What I suggest happened was that Yeats and Johnson brooded over the prophecies of Joachim together, then Yeats, fired by Johnson's enthusiasm for such a compelling and saintly heresy, wrote out the story, passages of which Johnson translated into Latin. The process parallels that of Dulac's commission for the portrait of Giraldus in *A Vision*. Doubtless, as with *Axël*, which Yeats found as intractable and as irresistible as a "Babylonian cylinder",[22] the sheer difficulty of uncovering Joachim's prophecies and their novel appropriateness to the "consuming thirst for destruction" which was so predominant in the *fin de siècle*, in the nationalist movement, in the private lives of the members of the Rhymers' Club and elsewhere, added to his sense of wonder at the "unimaginable fanaticism" of Joachim's followers. Here was another version of the Sacred Book of the Arts and another scenario for apocalypse. The I.R.B., the Celtic Mystical Order, the Order of the Golden Dawn, his interests in alchemy and prophecy—all such activities pleaded for the destruction of the present order and the creation of a new one.

Central to the concepts of Yeats's *fin de siècle* Joachitism is that of *Straminis Deflagratio*, the burning of straw. It is this notion of

assistance of Johnson to translate the Latin excerpts from Gerard's heresies. Joachim's doctrines were of profound importance for Yeats in his developing private myth of the nature of history and the nature of apocalypse.

21. Allen Wade, *Bibliography of the Writings of W. B. Yeats*, 3rd ed., rev. and ed. Russell K. Alspach (London: Hart-Davis, 1968), p. 43, Item 24. Subsequent citations from the *Bibliography*, indicated as B, will be inserted in the text.

22. See Yeats's preface to H. P. R. Finberg's translation of *Axël* (London: Jarrolds, 1925), p. 7. Yeats says the play seemed "all the more profound, all the more beautiful, because I was never quite certain that I had read a page correctly."

the attempt to light the "fires of the Last Day", which later informs *Where There is Nothing* and *The Unicorn from the Stars*, that Yeats and Johnson took from genuine Joachimist sources.[23] It is the "curious paradox" which haunts Aherne "half borrowed from some fanatical monk, half invented by himself—that the beautiful arts were sent into the world to overthrow nations, and finally life herself, by sowing everywhere unlimited desires, like torches thrown into a burning city" [M, 294, 299]. *Straminis Deflagratio* is an oddly overlooked aspect of all Yeats's Troy imagery, and is the central notion in "In Memory of Eva Gore-Booth and Con Markiewicz":

> Arise and bid me strike a match
> And strike another till time catch[24].

Yeats later came to see that a "fire of straw" is "useless in the arts", and he uses the image to describe the failure of John Davidson [A, 318]. "Our fire must burn slowly", Yeats realized, but he preserved his admiration for those who could not be content to burn "damp faggots":

> Lionel Johnson comes the first to mind,
> That loved his learning better than mankind,
> Though courteous to the worst; much falling he
> Brooded upon sanctity
> Till all his Greek and Latin learning seemed
> A long blast upon the horn that brought
> A little nearer to his thought
> A measureless consummation that he dreamed.
>
> . . .
>
> Some burn damp faggots, others may consume
> The entire combustible world in one small room
> As though dried straw, and if we turn about
> The bare chimney is gone black out

23. Joachimist prophecy is full of such figurative usages. J. H. Todd (*Discourses on the Prophecies relating to Antichrist in the Writings of Daniel and St. Paul* [Dublin, 1840], p. 454) comments in similar vein: "The Abbé Joachim had conceived, and the pontiffs Lucius, Urban, and Clement, his patrons, had cautiously promoted the idea of setting fire to the church, and leaving to the emperors, their rivals, nothing but its ruins and ashes to triumph over, whilst they raised in its stead a new edifice of priest-craft."

24. VP, 476. A. N. Jeffares (*A Commentary on the Collected Poems of W. B. Yeats* [Stanford: Stanford University Press, 1968], p. 321) has a compendium of cognate images in Yeats's poems.

Because the work is finished in that flare.
Soldier, scholar, horseman, he,[25]
As 'twere all life's epitome.
What made us dream that he could comb grey hair?

[vp, 323-28]

Not only should the images of "In Memory of Major Robert Gregory" be compared to those of "Mystic and Cavalier" but also to "The fire, that wants the whole vast world for room" of Johnson's "Gwynedd", as Fletcher has suggested.[26] *Straminis Deflagratio* was always associated in Yeats's mind with the man who put him in touch with the doctrine, and whose life was such a stunning example of it.

III

Thus far I have concentrated upon the psychological and doctrinal interest of Owen Aherne. In *The Tables of the Law* he is left aware of God's "arbitrary law" that "we may sin and repent". He, like Lionel Johnson, "unrepenting" faces his end; he is no longer among those for whom Christ died, for he has discovered his "secret law". This is the Johnson of "Nihilism", of "The Dark Angel", who has "awakened from the common dream". Aherne Redivivus lies beyond our consideration, but it is interesting to note that he is resurrected, and in a quite different form, at the time when Yeats is writing *The Trembling of the Veil*, when he can tell the full story of the "Tragic Generation" including that of Johnson, long dead, without the need of the mask of Aherne. Johnson assumes his own place, gathered "into the artifice" of the phantasmagoria, under his own name, and the name Aherne acquires an independent significance.[27] I propose not to follow life imitating art and art

25. Aherne is described as "half monk, half soldier of fortune". These characteristics and those of Robert Gregory form two familiar nineties versions of "life's epitome", an Axël or a Faust, Bram Stoker's Dracula is likewise praised as "soldier, statesman and alchemist" in 1897.

26. Fletcher, p. 334.

27. See Yeats's note to *The Wild Swans at Coole*, later rephrased to account for both John and Owen Aherne [vp, 852, 821]. When Yeats writes "I have the fancy that I read the name John Aherne among those of men prosecuted for making a disturbance at the first production of 'The Play Boy' ", he is being less than candid about his character and about his own involvement in the Abbey Riots. Specious vagueness does not disguise the highly significant association of a "Herne" character with an occasion of violence and insurrection, albeit a popular one.

imitating life any further here: that path leads into consideration not only of Johnson and Yeats, but of two readers profoundly influenced by Owen Aherne's heresies, James Joyce and P. S. O'Hegarty. Yeats said of *The Adoration of the Magi* that it was "half prophecy of a very veiled kind"[28]; this is also true of *The Tables of the Law*. I propose now, by a consideration of Aherne's name, to rend the veil that the interest of Lionel Johnson puts over the more occult nature of the Joachite prophecy, which is closely identified with the activities of the i.r.b. and those striving to found the Celtic Mystical Order. A. H. Bullen's "distaste"[29] for the two stories just mentioned may well have been merely the caution of a publisher apprehensive of publishing heterodox opinions, but perhaps he wished not to utter the prophecies for the future of Ireland which Yeats had written to bring his *Légende des Siècles* of *The Secret Rose* up to the present day.[30] The orthodoxy of the narrator's faith serves only to increase the impact each of the three stories makes as prophecy. Yeats finds "safety in derision", but Bullen may have felt the success of this tactic was strictly qualified.

Yeats's commentators have often remarked upon the affinity between his frequent Hearne, Herne, Aherne characters.[31] Seemingly so obvious as to require no further comment, this affinity is worth investigation given that for Yeats the act of naming, and names in general, have a significance which is occult and a force which is deeply impressive. He writes of a meeting of the Irish Literary Society:

> One day, some old Irish member of Parliament made perhaps his only appearance at a gathering of members. He recited with great emotion a ballad of his own composition in the manner of Young

28. *The Letters of W. B. Yeats*, ed. Allen Wade (New York: Macmillan, 1955), p. 280. Subsequent citations from the *Letters*, indicated as *L*, will be inserted in the text.

29. m, 1. But in a ms. version of this note (National Library of Ireland ms. 13583) Yeats says Bullen "made me leave them out". Bullen's "dislike" (as it is phrased in the ms.) was evidently quite strong.

30. Phillip L. Marcus, in *Yeats and the Beginning of the Irish Renaissance* (Ithaca: Cornell University Press, 1970), p. 49, comments upon the historical ordering of the *Secret Rose* stories.

31. For example, see Virginia Moore, in *The Unicorn: William Butler Yeats' Search for Reality* (New York: Macmillan, 1954), p. 402, and Giorgio Melchiori, in *The Whole Mystery of Art* (London: Routledge & Kegan Paul, 1960), p. 51.

Ireland, repeating over his sacred names, Wolfe Tone, Emmet, and Owen Roe, and mourning that new poets and new movements should have taken something of their sacredness away. The ballad had no literary merit, but I went home with a troubled conscience; and for a dozen years perhaps, till I began to see the result of our work in a deepened perception of all those things that strengthen race, that trouble remained. I had in mind that old politician as I wrote but the other day—

> Our part
> To murmur name upon name
> As a mother names her child.   [A, 299-300]

Again, in early versions of *The Adoration of the Magi*, where the annunciation is more assertively Celtic, we read:

> ... a woman lay dying, who would reveal to them the secret names of the gods, which can be perfectly spoken only when the mind is steeped in certain colours and certain sounds and certain odours; but at whose perfect speaking the immortals cease to be cries and shadows, and walk and talk with one like men and women.[32]

One does not have to look beyond Yeats's most frequently consulted books of occult lore to find this doctrine of the power of names. This exposition is that of Cornelius Agrippa:

> That proper names of things are very necessary in Magicall operations, almost all men testifie; For the naturall power of things proceeds first from the objects to the senses, and then from these to the imagination, and from this to the mind in which it is first conceived, and then is expressed by voices and words. The *Platonists* therefore say, that in this very voice or word or name framed, with its Articles, that the power of the thing as it were some kind of life, lies under the form of the signification. First conceived in the mind as it were through certain seeds of things, then by voices or words, as a birth brought forth, and lastly kept in writing. Hence, Magicians say, that proper names of things are certain rayes of things, every where present at all times, keeping the power of things, as the essence of the thing signified ....[33]

32. *The Tables of the Law & The Adoration of the Magi* (Stratford, 1914), p. 28.
33. Henry Cornelius Agrippa, *Three Books of Occult Philosophy* (London, 1650), II: 153-54.

With this in mind, Yeats's names deserve close consideration. The word "herne", Joseph Wright's *Dialect Dictionary* tells us, is an English dialect word for heron, and this is the sense Yeats uses it in, for the most part. However, Edward MacLysaght, in his *Irish Families, Their Names, Arms and Origins* shows how Herne, in all the forms it takes in Irish names, was anglicized from an old Irish word. All the forms, such as O'Aherne, Hearne, Herne, Herrin, Aherne, and others are cognate with Oh Eachtighearn, meaning "horse-lord". The original meaning seems to have dropped out with anglicization, for the family crest (crests are a late import in Irish heraldry) shows three herons argent on vert, surmounted by a pelican in her piety proper, i.e. feeding her young (an alchemical symbol appropriate for the counterpart of Robartes). The motto is "Per Arduo Surgo". As almost all Irish national bibliographies and other authorities are unanimous in their choice of the most famous modern members of the Kerry family of Aherne, which gave an annual burse to the Irish college in Paris, it is to these members, Captain John and Father Maurice Aherne, that I will turn my attention.[34] First, however, it is necessary to make some appraisal of Yeats's use of "Herne" names prior to the appearance of Owen Aherne in *The Tables of the Law*.

Characters with the name "Herne" appear in two oddly overlooked stories: "The Rose of Shadow" from *The Secret Rose*, entitled in its original version in *The Speaker* (21 July 1894) "Those who live in the Storm"; and "The Cradles of Gold" in *The Senate* (Nov. 1896), evidently rejected by Yeats from the

---

34. Joseph Wright, *Dialect Dictionary* (London: Oxford University Press, 1961), III: 147. See also Edward MacLysaght, *Irish Families, Their Names, Arms and Origins* (Dublin: Hodges Figgis, 1957), p. 49. Perhaps a trace of the original Irish meaning of the name is preserved in Yeats's association of it with characteristics mentioned above (note 25). The "horseman" of the epitaph seems similarly related to these images of "life's epitome".

For details of the Aherne family burse to the Irish college in Paris, made on 18 July, 1748, to enable members of the family to train there for the priesthood, I must thank Rev. Michael Manning, St. Brendan's College, Killarney. For details of the Aherne family, see Jeremiah King, *County Kerry Past and Present* (Dublin: Hodges Figgis, 1931), p. 5, where it is stated that the Ahernes were descended from the brother of Brian Boru. See also Robert E. Matheson, whose *Varieties and Synonymes of Surnames and Christian Names in Ireland etc.* (Dublin, 1890) provides a contemporary source.

same collection, as indeed "The Rose of Shadow" was in 1908. Both stories have immediate interest for those who would try to see the essence of Yeats's "Herne" characters. In the first of these, Peter Herne has killed Michael Creed, feared for his "violence and brutality, and . . . many conquests among women, whom he subdued through that love of strength which is deep in the heart of even the subtlest among them."[35] Herne's deed prefigures Owen Aherne's wish to overthrow the Law and usher in the Age of the Spirit which, after the violence of its annunciation, will be an age conspicuous by its freedom from the "dead letter" of the current dispensation. Herne's sister Oona is envelopped in a storm which, depending on the version read,[36] either destroys the house or is "a formless mass of flame which roared but gave no heat"—a far more horrific ending which leaves the Herne brothers on the margin between the real world and the indefinite world to which their sister has been taken. In "The Cradles of Gold" the situation is similar, with the male members of the family (spelt "Hearne") left on the margin of the world of the Sidhe to which Whinny Hearne has been "away" as a nurse to the child of Finivarach, the king of the faeries of Connaught. Afterwards, she

> never saw the children of Dana again; but always, when the moon was at full, a desire to be far away came upon her, and she would stand at the door watching the wild ducks flying in long lines over the water, and would move restlessly hither and thither, and talk excitedly until the moon had begun to crumble a little at one side; but at all other times her voice was low and her touch chill . . . .[37]

The "Herne" characters, then, have the potential for otherworldly experience and illumination, but are condemned by fate to live on the margin between two worlds. Yeats's story "The Old Men of the Twilight" brings out this symbolic association with the heron, the bird of the marshes, more strongly. Here we are immediately aware of the special propensities of the herons seen by old Michael Bruen. He "had never before seen herons flying over

35. John P. Frayne, ed., *The Uncollected Prose of W. B. Yeats* (London: Macmillan, 1970), p. 329.
36. Curtis B. Bradford, *Yeats at Work* (Carbondale: Southern Illinois University Press, 1962), pp. 317-18.
37. Frayne, p. 418.

the sea, for they are shore keeping birds" [M, 191]. These herons long before "were men of learning ... who neither hunted, nor went to battle, nor said prayers, nor sang songs, nor made love." The heron men, who have ignored the spiritual changes wrought by the introduction of Christianity to Ireland, preferring their debate about the merits of the Great and of the Little Metre, are punished by St Patrick.

> O, men who have no part in love, who have no part in song, who have no part in wisdom, but dwell with the shadows of memory where the feet of angels cannot touch you as they pass over your heads, where the hair of demons cannot sweep about you as they pass under your feet, I lay upon you a curse, and change you to an example for ever and ever; you shall become grey herons and stand pondering in grey pools and flit over the world in that hour when it is most full of sighs, having forgotten the flame of the stars and not yet perceived the flame of the sun; and you shall preach to the other herons until they also are like you, and are an example for ever and ever; and your deaths shall come to you by chance and unforeseen that no fire of certainty may visit your hearts.[38]

In this context the Owen Aherne who has lived beyond illumination and now is held "on the margin" of that "vertigo" which has consumed his earlier vitality is eminent. So too, incidentally, are the picture Yeats drew of Lionel Johnson, who "renounced the joy of the world without accepting the joy of God", and Yeats's most personal mask, the Michael Hearne of *The Speckled Bird*, that novel that Yeats could "neither write nor cease to write which had Hodos Chameliontos for its theme". Hearne, as Yeats remarked of Owen Aherne in a note towards the revision of *The Tables of the Law*, is "the centre".[39] He was "to see all the modern visionary sects pass before his bewildered eyes, as Flaubert's Saint Anthony saw the Christian sects, and I was as helpless to create artistic, as my chief person to create philosophic, order" [A, 376]. Allen Grossman[40] has included Owen Aherne in his chapter upon those figures in Yeats's work who are at "the centre", but Yeats's comment is one upon the "artistic" rather than "philosophic" placing of the charac-

38. *The Secret Rose* (London, 1897), p. 215.
39. See note 17.
40. Allen R. Grossman, *Poetic Knowledge in the Early Yeats* (Charlottesville: University Press of Virginia, 1969), pp. 125-39.

ters in the three stories, particularly *The Tables of the Law*. In "philosophic" terms, the Herne characters throughout Yeats are birds of the margin. Michael Hearne, who would sound familiar to readers of *Reveries over Childhood and Youth*, is the "Speckled Bird" of the title, and as his epiphany[41] by the shore on the west coast of Ireland shows, he takes his name, oddly enough, not from the unspeckled heron, but from Jeremiah's owl. He is running along the shore,

> sometimes stopping altogether to look at a sea-gull flying over his head or at a sea-snipe flying over the wet stones by the sea's edge . . . but the sight of a large bird flitting near the water with a number of little birds following it and making a great noise made him stop running. He thought: "It is an owl. That is what the Bible means when it says: 'Mine inheritance shall be as the speckled bird, all the birds of the heavens are against it.'[42] I wonder why the other birds are so angry." He stood watching till the big bird vanished among the shadows of some hawthorn bushes at the edge of the trees.[43]

There is really no contradiction here between Michael's identification of himself with Jeremiah's speckled bird and Yeats's naming him as a heron. If the symbols are seen in their separate contexts, both are meaningful. As so often in Yeats, the locale is of paramount importance here. Hearne's epiphany takes place on the shore, the margin. One recalls that the builders of the Temple of the Alchemical Rose were commanded to build it "between the pure multitude by the waves and the impure multitude of men", and that the narrator, seeing the temple for the first time, is

> possessed with the fantasy that the sea, which kept covering it with showers of white foam, was claiming it as part of some in definite and passionate life, which had begun to war on our orderly and careful days, and was about to plunge the world into

41. Joyce's term is particularly appropriate for describing the method of *The Speckled Bird*. Had it ever been published, it could have made *A Portrait of the Artist as a Young Man* a much harder book for Joyce, who was already obsessed by Yeats's "fantastic romances", to write.

42. Jeremiah 12:9: "Mine heritage is unto me as a speckled bird, the birds round about are against her; come ye, assemble all the beasts of the field, come to devour."

43. William H. O'Donnell, ed. *The Speckled Bird* (Dublin: Cuala Press, 1974), I:2.

a night as obscure as that which followed the downfall of the classical world. One part of my mind mocked this fantastic terror, but the other, the part that still lay half plunged in vision, listened to the clash of unknown armies, and shuddered at unimaginable fanaticisms, that hung in those grey leaping waves.[44]

The owl too, then, is a land bird, being plagued by the birds of the air, just as the narrator at the end of The Adoration of the Magi feels threatened by the "demons of the air" against which he uses an old Gaelic charm. The Sluagh Gaoith, or host of the air, are said by Yeats to be "of a peculiar malignancy" [vp, 803]. Both heron and owl are symbols, in different mythologies, of wisdom, though the owl does not have the holy and Egyptian connotations of the heron.

The heron creatures in Yeats, then, linger on the marshes[45] of a sea as "indefinite and passionate" as Blake's "Sea of Time and

44. M, 278, 280. Arnold's "Dover Beach" seems to lurk in the "clash of unknown armies" as well as the more familiar Yeatsian "music of heaven". For the site of the Temple Yeats probably recalled the frontispiece of Knorr von Rosenroth's Kabbala Denudata (see frontispiece).

45. An interesting possible source for the name Aherne is to be found in Rhys's lectures On the Origin and Growth of Religion as illustrated by Celtic Heathendom (London, 1888), p. 334. Rhys gives, as a possible meaning for the name Aitherne, "procuring knowledge and wisdom from the powers of the nether world by stealth".

Yeats's description of John Sherman should also be noted here: "at that marchland between waking and dreaming where our thoughts begin to have a life of their own—the region where art is nurtured and inspiration born" (Richard J. Finneran, ed., John Sherman and Dhoya [Detroit: Wayne State University Press, 1969], p. 85). Yeats's term "marchland" is almost echoed by Maud Gonne in A Servant of the Queen (London: Gollancz, 1974), p. 88, who writes of "the tearing of the veil which separates those in the flesh from the inhabitants of the borderland". In a review of Finneran's edition, Fletcher suggests that Rev. William Howard "closely resembles Lionel Johnson, whom Yeats probably met at the 'Fitzroy settlement' as early as 1888. The small neat handwriting, Howard's library, Bourget jostling agreeably with Newman and Chrysostom, all are suggestive" (Notes and Queries, July 1971, pp. 275-76). Howard, however, does not seem to draw heavily upon Johnson in any but this external sense. John Sherman himself, while heavily autobiographical, also contains traces of Johnson's deeper divisions.

The heron in Yeats's phantasmagoria is a very stable symbol. Aherne, who has "ceased to be among those for whom Christ died", is recalled in the white heron of Calvary: "God has not died for the white heron" [vpi, 780, 789].

Space". Owen Aherne, the narrator of the three tales of the Order of the Alchemical Rose, and Michael Hearne are three of a kind here, conforming to the psychological type I have examined above in my account of Johnson and O'Leary.

One must ask why Yeats chose to alter the spelling of his heron's name to Aherne. There may be no compelling reason, for the latter form is an anagram of his earlier "Hearne", and yet it seems to me that when he was writing the tales of the Alchemical Rose new characters, which he came across in entirely different contexts, were absorbed into his phantasmagoria. The new contexts are his work for the '98 Centennial Association and the I.R.B.

These activities have received little attention from Yeats's critics; not surprisingly, for little documentary evidence has come to light. Yeats was chairman of the banquet held in London to mark the centenary of '98, and like Johnson, another pan-Celticist, was a member of the Irish Revolutionary Brotherhood. Ellmann[46] tells us that he had introduced Maud Gonne to the Order of the Golden Dawn with the eventual object of carrying "secret spiritual propaganda" for the most profound minds into the nationalist movement. The result was the abortive Celtic Mystical Order project, which seems to have taken its illuminist animus from the example of the Jacobin clubs in pre-Revolutionary France, and the secret organizations of the United Irishmen which copied them, as well as the Masonic organizations of the Northern Unionist movement.

Another and better known part of Yeats's earlier work for the Nationalist Movement is his plan for a series of Irish books to be published by T. Fisher Unwin in 1892-93. A direct result of this plan, though not the one Yeats had intended [L, 199, 201], was the re-editing of Wolfe Tone's memoirs by the associate of Yeats and dedicatee of Johnson's "Ninety Eight", R. Barry O'Brien. As he had hoped to do the editing himself, Yeats must have been a keen reader of O'Brien's work,[47] and possibly of earlier editions of Tone as well. Barry O'Brien, Rolleston, and whoever else helped with the editing of this book (perhaps O'Leary) were deep students of the United Irishmen, and there is no reason to assume that Yeats did not share, or benefit from, their scholarship.

In Wolfe Tone's memoirs, Yeats would have read of Captain

46. Ellmann, pp. 118-37.
47. R. Barry O'Brien, ed., *The Autobiography of Theobald Wolfe Tone 1763-1798* (London, 1893), hereafter cited as Tone.

John Aherne (*c.* 1769-1806). He was a student in Paris in 1789—Yeats mentions the Jesuit education of Owen Aherne and Robartes in Paris—and embraced the cause of the Revolution enthusiastically. In 1794 he was employed in Scotland as a spy, by the French government, and two years later was sent in a similar capacity to Ireland.[48] In a journal entry for April 1796, Tone described Aherne as "a cool man of good republican sentiments".[49] But by June 23 of the same year Tone, sensing that French help really might win the day in Ireland and musing upon the distribution of powers after the revolution there, wrote of Aherne in very different terms:

> N.B.—I do not wish to hurt Aherne, but I had rather he was not employed in Ireland *at first*, for he is *outré*—and extravagant in his notions; he wants a total *bouleversement* of all property, and he has not the talents to see the absurdity and mischief, not to say the impossibility of this system, if system it may be called. I have a mind to stop his promotion, and believe I must do it. It would be a terrible doctrine to commence with in Ireland. I wish all possible justice be done to Aherne, but I do not wish to see him in a station where he might do infinite mischief.[50]

The editor's note here is tantalizing in that it lacks a source, but if it gives a clue to the way Tone's opinion of Aherne was being interpreted in Republican circles in the 1890s, then it is crucial for an understanding of the "very veiled" prophecy of Yeats's story. O'Brien suggests that Aherne had planned agrarian revolution. Not only does this throw new light on the development of the "Hearne" character beyond Owen Aherne into the Martinist-inspired Martin Hearne of *The Unicorn from the Stars*, who seeks, like John of Leyden, to trample Order and usher in the Age of the Holy Spirit by means of his own *Straminis Deflagratio* (to give his incendiarism its Joachite nomenclature); but it also is a stunning parallel to the earlier dreams of Owen Aherne, which concern us here. John Aherne's dreams of *bouleversement* seem to me to be behind the "measureless" reveries of Owen Aherne, who had turned away from "practicable desires and intuitions towards de-

48. Richard F. Hayes, *Biographical Dictionary of Irishmen in France* (Dublin: M. H. Gill, 1949), p. 1. See also Hayes's other works on the same subject: *Ireland and Irishmen in the French Revolution* (London: Benn, 1932), *Irish Swordsmen of France* (Dublin: M. H. Gill, 1934), *Old Irish Links with France* (Dublin: M. H. Gill, 1940).

49. Tone, II: 3, 4.   50. *Ibid.,* p. 53.

sires and intuitions so immaterial that their sudden and far-off fire leaves heavy darkness about hand and foot. He had the nature, which is half monk, half soldier of fortune, and must needs turn action into dreaming, and dreaming into action; and for such there is no order, no finality, no contentment in this world" [M, 294]. Owen Aherne praises kings "that wrought secret murder and so won for their people a peace that was *amore somnoque gravata et vestibus versicoloribus*, 'heavy with love and sleep and many-coloured raiment'." He supports Jonathan Swift who "made a soul for the gentlemen of this city by hating his neighbour as himself," and asks in a series of mocking rhetorical questions " 'why should you, who are no materialist, cherish the continuity and order of this world as those do who have only this world? . . . I shall send out of this chapel saints, lovers, rebels, and prophets: . . . the dust shall fall for many years over this little box; and then I shall open it; and the tumults, which are, perhaps, the flames of the last day, shall come from under the lid' " [M, 299, 301, 302].

What is uniquely Yeatsian about his version of Joachitism in *The Tables of the Law* is its Fenian and Celtic fervour. The interpretation of Joachim in almost any age since the Franciscan extremist Gerard of Borgo San Donnino wrote the *Liber Introductorius* in the mid-thirteenth century has similarly suited the times. Yeats's *Lex Secreta*, which echoes Joachim's genuine "secretis secretorum",[51] is according to Owen Aherne "the true inspiration of action, the only Eternal Evangel" [M, 299]. I suggest, then, that in Aherne and his doctrine we have a mask for the prophecy of coming revolution in Ireland and that the inspiration for this revolution is Yeats's study of the events and personalities of a century before.

Captain John Aherne's career with the secret Irish forces was doomed after Tone wrote of him in the terms we have seen. His reputation was sabotaged by the less than anarchical Tone and the French officials cancelled another trip which had been proposed for him to make to Ireland. Tone wrote of this, "I am not sorry on the whole that Aherne does not go to Ireland."[52] But Aherne did not leave the Irish forces altogether. He went to Bantry Bay with Tone and Hoche on the ill-fated expedition of 1796. He was again active

51. *Expositio in Apocalypsim* (Venice, 1527), ff. 35-36.
52. Tone, II: 61.

in Hamburg in 1798, discussing with Joubert the safest and most suitable places for landings on the Irish coast. After the collapse of the insurrection "he was prominent among the Irish exiles in France who were trying to obtain French aid." He was a captain in Napoleon's Irish Legion, and died suddenly on the march to Berlin after the Battle of Jena, in 1806. Dr. Hayes also quotes that he had " 'the gay manners of a well-bred Irishman'."[53]

Tone was notoriously prejudiced against using priests for any of his secret work, preferring "soldiers of fortune" such as Aherne. But there were many Irish priests in the various colleges in Paris at the time of the Revolution, and their activities would not have escaped the attentions of one such as Yeats, who, in the similarly heady atmosphere of imminent "influx" in the *fin-de-siècle*, studies the events of a century before. Though the priests have not the Freemasonic cloak-and-dagger interest of the United Irishmen, they were nevertheless actors in the "casual comedy" which was "transformed utterly" by the impact of the Revolution on Irish affairs both in France and at home. After the Irish interest in European affairs was made to dwindle by the disarray of post revolutionary France and the defeat of Tone's forces, the British founded Maynooth College, "largely with the idea of extending this severance from the continent to the Ecclesiastical sphere".[54] The British reasoning is not hard to follow. Irish colleges in Paris and elsewhere were faltering, and some had closed due to the "troubles". Home education of Irish priests would seem a magnanimous and pacific gesture, but it was also a very shrewd one, because the priests who were being trained in the colleges which did remain open were returning full of new ideals about the rights of man. Indeed, when Maynooth was founded, something of this spirit penetrated the college before its walls were even raised. Its newly recruited staff had, of course, all been trained abroad, and many, such as Dr. Maurice Aherne, its foundation professor of philosophy, had had long and successful careers in France. He was a "zealous upholder of the Gallican liberties of the Church", and "strongly" condemned "Ultramontane doctrines, especially the temporal power of the Papacy".[55] Educated at Navarre College, where subsequently, as the holder of a Doctorate of Philosophy

53. Hayes, *Biographical Dictionary*, p. 1.
54. Hayes, *Irish Swordsmen*, p. xi.
55. Hayes, *Biographical Dictionary*, p. 2.

from the Sorbonne, he taught philosophy, he was a formidable opponent of the British plan for using the new college as a centre for the conservative training of priests.

It must be added at once that very little of this picture of Maurice Aherne comes through the self congratulatory *Maynooth College: Its Centenary History* (1895), by the most Rev. John Healy;[56] and it must be admitted that if Yeats knew of Maurice Aherne then he went beyond the college history. Dr. Aherne's unorthodox views on the Gallican liberties are cautiously admitted in the history, but some aspects of his career are passed over. Dr. Hayes mentions a letter (dated December 1793) from Francis Drake, Pitt's chief intelligence agent on the continent at the period, to Lord Grenville in which Dr. Aherne is described "as one of a small number of well-conditioned people who could give a perfect account of the secret conspiracies then being hatched in Ireland, and of which only vague knowledge was obtainable".[57] Hayes states that he was one of the priests who remained in Paris after the Irish college had fallen into disrepute, in a college where he would have felt the twin tensions from which Yeats claimed Balzac had saved him, "Jacobin and Jacobite" [E&I, 447], coming from students and priests respectively. No wonder Aherne was in a position to know of plots against the English.

Maurice Aherne, after he left Navarre, became second in command at the Bibliothèque Mazarine, in 1789.[58] By an amazing coincidence, a volume which was considered by Navarre to be so precious that it had been chained to a lectern in the college library, and which went to the Bibliothèque Mazarine at the same time, contains Joachite MSS. Ernest Renan, whom Yeats read upon Joachim of Flora, quotes extensively from it in his essay "Joachim di Flor" in his *Studies in Religious History*,[59] published in the

56. (Dublin, 1895), p. 98 *et passim*. I am deeply indebted to the Librarian of Maynooth College, Father O'Cìosàin, for the opportunity of examining Dr. Aherne's manuscripts.

57. Hayes, *Biographical Dictionary*, p. 2.

58. Alfred Franklin, *Histoire de la Bibliothèque Mazarine* (Paris, 1860), p. 147. See also second (revised) edition, pp. 247, 264. I am deeply indebted to the Conservateur en Chef de la Bibliothèque Mazarine for permission to examine MS. 891 (391 anciens), which contains the Joachite material, and for assistance in tracing the career of Dr. Aherne in the library.

59. Ernest Renan's *Nouvelle Etudes* are published in English as *Studies in Religious History* (London, 1886). A book which would have been

authorized English translation in 1886. It is possibly unnecessary to assume that Yeats connected the MS., which contained extracts from Joachim's genuine doctrine and that of Gerard of Borgo San Donnino, taken from the trial of the latter in 1255, by the commission of Anagni, with Aherne; but Renan lays some considerable stress on the "great preciousness" of the Navarre MS., and on the care it exacted, particularly in the fifteenth century. Yeats's Aherne is deeply concerned with the preciousness of his MS. and the care that has been lavished upon it throughout the ages by artists of all kinds, all custodians of this "Sacred Book of the Arts".

Maurice Aherne fled to Ireland soon after, refusing to take the oath of allegiance to the Republic of France.[60] Disillusioned by democracy in action, he retired to the casuistry of Dogmatic Divinity at Maynooth, perhaps to dream of anarchy. He died in 1801.

In John and Maurice Aherne, then, we have an anarchist soldier of fortune and a philosopher priest of singular distinction of mind. It is too neat an explanation to suggest that together they make up the divided self of Yeats's Owen Aherne who, as we can see, was not immaculately conceived for the story, but a logical outgrowth of a highly complex group of associated images in Yeats's phantasmagoria. But these two men were figures from a period of Irish history being studied intensely for its lessons in the 1890s, a period when, as a century before, the pan-Celtic enthusiasms and unions were strong, when men such as Yeats and Renan were beginning to assert old ties again. Also in these *fin-de-siècle* times old prophecies were being reshaped to fit new political realities, as they had been for the French Revolution. Padraic Colum's poem about the Irish exiles ("We, all bare exiles, soldiers, scholars, priests")[61] expresses these sentiments anew. Yeats, a man as preoccupied with

recommended to Yeats by Johnson, it probably would have been read by him anyway for its Paterian essays on mediæval times. *Poetry of the Celtic Races* was well known to him. Renan translates extracts of Eternal Evangel material, including parts of the Navarre MS. now in the Bibliothèque Mazarine. See also note 20. Denifle's work contains the lengthier and more scholarly edition of Gerard's *Liber Introductorius* extracts.

60. Patrick Boyle, *The Irish College in Paris from 1578-1901 etc.* (London, 1901), pp. 59, 77. See also Hayes, *Biographical Dictionary*, p. 2.

61. Hayes, *Old Irish Links*, p. 12. Hayes also quotes Lady Gregory's translation of an Irish poem by an exiled Franciscan on the hardships of exile. He notes among other comment on "wild geese" in *Irish Swordsmen* (p. 58) one James Rutledge, a journalist and revolutionary of '98 days who

limit and control as he was with their countertruths, anarchy and frenzy, knew that he had to veil his prophecies for the spiritual future of Ireland; violence, though found in nearly every eschatology, could not be revealed in any temporal plans. Studies of Aherne and Robartes which see them as a Janus-like mask for their creator thus tell only half the story, because psychological interest itself masks the real doctrines of violence in the stories themselves.

Owen Aherne is likewise a problem for those who approach Yeats from the Robartesian standpoint of "orthodox" Golden Dawn occultism. He seems perhaps a mere foil in *A Vision* (A & B) to the more Faustian Robartes. Yet his marginal position is an achieved position (see note 17), and he is a fully realized man who can go no further except out of time and into eternity. Both his unveiled message and his tragic stance are paradoxical, and it is a paradox which, I suggest, Yeats himself continued to live.

I have not found any use of the image of the mask in any of Yeats's works prior to *Rosa Alchemica* and *The Tables of the Law*. In those two stories the mask is used as an image rather than as a doctrine, and it is worth examining. The first usage is in *Rosa Alchemica*, when the narrator watches, in the train, the sleeping face of Robartes,

> ... in which there was no sign of all that had shaken me and that now kept me wakeful, ... [and which] was to my excited mind more like a mask than a face. The fancy possessed me that the man behind it had dissolved away like salt in water, and that it laughed and sighed, appealed and denounced at the bidding of beings greater or less than man. "This is not Michael Robartes at all: Michael Robartes is dead; dead for ten, for twenty years perhaps," I kept repeating to myself. [M, 279]

The other usage similar to this is when the narrator, who has last seen Owen Aherne "completely alive" with "Joachim of Flora's multitudinous influx", comes upon him on the Dublin quays—a "lifeless mask with dim eyes" [M, 303]. The implication on the "occult" level is that both characters have sold themselves to the immortals, and that their souls have been consumed "as an ox drinks up a wayside pool" [M, 290]. They have become puppets, in the first case manipulated at will, in the second abandoned by the

---

could be the source for Yeats's name of the ur-version of Martin Hearne, Paul Ruttledge, in *Where there is Nothing*. So far, however, he remains a shadowy figure.

Moods, to put the matter in its Yeatsian doctrinal terms. The use of the mask is really no more and no less than a powerful image of this condition.

But the third usage of this image in the stories is an extension of this idea into something quite new.

> ... the fumes of the incense, helped perhaps by his mysterious glamour, made me fall again into a dream, in which I seemed to be a mask, lying on the counter of a little Eastern shop. Many persons, with eyes so bright and still that I knew them for more than human, came in and tried me on their faces, but at last flung me into a corner laughing; but all this passed in a moment, for when I awoke my hand was still upon the handle.[62]

The neophyte, with his hand on the door of the inner sanctum of the Temple of the Alchemical Rose, has a vision which prefigures his rejection from the order. An element of progression, of destiny, now enters Yeats's notion of the mask, for the failure on the part of the narrator to sustain initiation leads to his escape from the Temple and consequent failure to "die into" immortality with the other adepts, stoned by the peasants of a remote Connemara headland. Already imbued with Blake's doctrine of contraries, Yeats is here moulding his own image of the mask into a doctrine of progression. Perhaps it was Wilde's chance remark that nothing in life interested him but the mask which first made Yeats think about the subject, but from the usage discussed above to the doctrine of *Per Amica Silentia Lunae* is not a long way in terms of ethical thinking. I suggest that this context of the occult stories has been overlooked in discussions of Yeats's doctrine of the mask. Owen Aherne, who like Mongan "becomes a man, a hater of the wind", is a mere husk or shell of his old self, and yet that mask is his destiny, his self-realization. The poetic image, encrusted with the lore of the Moods and bound up in the context of the stories "inseparable from its first expression", was now part of the phantasmagoria, with which we have all along been concerned. The phantasmagoria and its characters not only beget "fresh images" from old ones but fresh doctrines as well.

62. M, 286-87. Aherne and Robartes, as masks assumed and dismissed at will by the immortals, recall the dramatic structure of "The Phases of the Moon" where the same characters are dismissed as mere masks by their creator.

W. B. Yeats and
S. L. MacGregor Mathers

Laurence W. Fennelly

When the young W. B. Yeats joined several mystical orders in the 1880s and 1890s, it is doubtful if many eyebrows were raised. Yeats's initial involvement with the occult was dictated by both the spirit of the age and his own temperament. Many persons of all classes were swept up by the occult revival that occurred during the last years of the nineteenth century; this was part of the inevitable reaction against the rationalism and materialism of the Victorian culture. But, while occultism was for most a passing fad, Yeats's interest did not wane; he was involved with the occult for most of his life.

Most scholars mistakenly wish to dismiss this lifelong preoccupation as a youthful fancy. Like W. H. Auden, many of them find it "embarrassing" that Yeats was not only a persistent student of the occult but a practicing magician as well. But there is no dismissing the fact that for more than thirty years of his mature life Yeats was a member of the Order of the Golden Dawn, or its successors, the Morgenröthe and the Stella Matutina. He has testified repeatedly to the importance of his occult studies, announcing to John O'Leary that, next to poetry, these pursuits were "the most important study" of his life.[1]

1. *The Letters of W. B. Yeats*, ed. Allan Wade (New York: Macmillan, 1955), p. 210. Subsequent citations from the *Letters*, indicated as L, will be inserted in the text. Verification that Yeats's membership in the Golden Dawn lasted for over thirty years is provided by unpublished letters from

Finally, the importance of Yeats's membership in the Golden Dawn is beginning to receive its proper emphasis. This new appreciation is due in large measure to the recent revival of interest in the occult and the consequent publication of considerable hitherto unknown information about the Golden Dawn.[2] Although it has been noted briefly in several studies that S. L. MacGregor Mathers, one of the Chiefs of the Order, played a crucial role in the formation of Yeats's thought, the extent of Mathers' influence has yet to be fully appreciated.[3] To a large extent, it was not so much the Golden Dawn as Mathers that influenced Yeats. As another member of the Order so aptly observed, "the Golden Dawn *was* MacGregor Mathers."[4] Yeats recognized this fact when he said, in speaking of the Order, that "Mathers was its governing mind."[5] Later, referring to the three Chiefs of the Order, he added that ultimately "their authority all devolved on one—our late chief, the

Christina Mary Stoddart which make clear that both Yeats and his wife were still members in 1922.

2. The most significant works published recently on the Golden Dawn are Ellic Howe's *The Magicians of the Golden Dawn* (London: Routledge & Kegan Paul, 1972) and Francis King's *Ritual Magic in England, 1887 to the Present Day* (London: Neville Spearman, 1970). King is also the editor of *Astral Projection, Ritual Magic and Alchemy* (London: Neville Spearman, 1971), a collection of the so-called Flying Rolls of the Golden Dawn; the Flying Rolls consist primarily of lessons to be mastered by the members of the Golden Dawn as they passed upward through the various grades. The rituals which marked the passage through the grades have been brought to the public eye by R. G. Torrens in *The Secret Rituals of the Golden Dawn* (New York: Samuel Weiser, 1973). The most important of the recent Golden Dawn unearthings, however, is the document which, from whatever source, originated the entire business. Edited by Christopher Newton, *The Cipher Mss. of the Golden Dawn* was published in 1973, in mimeograph form, at an unknown location in England by the Jolly Roger Press Gang. This pirated edition, published by a rather aptly named house, is described by the editor as "positively the last word on the Golden Dawn".

3. The most extensive assessments of Mathers' importance are found in Virginia Moore's *The Unicorn* (New York: Macmillan, 1954) and in H. R. Bachchan's *W. B. Yeats and Occultism* (Delhi: Motilal Banarsidass, 1965).

4. Israel Regardie, *My Rosicrucian Adventure* (1936; rpt. St. Paul: Llewellyn, 1971), p. 147.

5. *The Autobiography of William Butler Yeats* (New York: Macmillan, 1953), p. 113. Future citations, indicated as *Auto*, will be contained in the text.

G. H. Frater D.D.C.F. [Mathers]."[6] It was from Mathers that Yeats "learned a practice, a form of meditation" that was "perhaps the intellectual chief influence" on his life up to his fortieth year.[7]

Very little is known about this man who apparently played such a formative role in Yeats's life. Because the Golden Dawn swore its members to secrecy, Yeats's writings on the subject of Mathers and the Golden Dawn are not in proportion to their importance to him. Yeats refers only briefly to Mathers in the *Letters* and in both the draft and final versions of the *Autobiography*. But when these sources are coupled with accounts of Mathers by other contemporary occultists, a reasonably complete picture emerges of Mathers, his relationship with Yeats, and the resultant effect on Yeats's life and art.

Yeats's first meeting with Mathers took place in London sometime prior to 1890. Whatever the date, both men were already students of the occult. Yeats's temperament seems to have inclined him always in the direction of mysticism. Even as a youth he had yearned to be a magician-poet, and by degrees he deliberately embarked on the study of mysticism. At the Metropolitan Art School in Kildare Street he met George Russell, who shared his belief that the source of art is the spiritual world. Finding conventional religion, in its vain attempt to reconcile the physical and the spiritual, to be of no value, they turned to the publications of the Theosophical Society. Their reading of Madame Blavatsky and A. P. Sinnett supplied the impetus to found the Dublin Hermetic Society in 1885. Two years later Yeats moved back to London and formed further occult affiliations. He joined the Theosophical Society, and he may have joined a Hermetic society in London as well.

Yeats has recorded that he was initiated into a society called "The Hermetic Students" at a Charlotte Street studio in May or June of 1887. Until now, scholars have assumed that Yeats was

6. Quoted by Aleister Crowley in "The Rituals of the Order of Rosae Rubeae et Aureae Crucis", *The Equinox*, 1 (1910), 253-54. Members were known within the Order by the initials of their secret mottoes. Mathers was best known as Deo Duce Comite Ferro (God as my leader and the sword as my companion), although he occasionally was known as 'S Rhiogail Mo Dhream (Royal Is My Race), a motto he retained from his membership in the Societas Rosicruciana in Anglia.

7. *Memoirs*, ed. Denis Donoghue (London: Macmillan, 1972), p. 27. Subsequent citations, indicated as *Mem*, will be inserted in the text.

referring to the Golden Dawn, and presumed that he simply had his dates and places confused. This is possible but not likely: Yeats was precise and carefully preserved important documents and letters for future reference. A copy of his initiation announcement, affixed to one of his notebooks, plainly states that his initiation had taken place on 7 March 1890 at Fitzroy Street.[8] Since Yeats took great pains to be precise in the *Autobiography*, it is likely that there was an 1887 initiation, not into the Golden Dawn but into another Hermetic society.

In any event, it is certain that Yeats did join Madame Blavatsky's circle. When she settled in London in May, 1887, she already enjoyed considerable fame. Her arrival soon brought many new adherents to the Theosophical Society, among them Yeats, who was attracted to it because it was a "romantic house" [*Auto*, 111]. Soon, having learned from Blake to hate all abstraction, and irritated by that very quality in so-called "esoteric teachings", Yeats became one of the organizers of an Esoteric Section. This new committee regarded the purely theoretical approach to the unseen world as far too limited and began a series of practical experiments.[9] When complaints arose that the activities of this new section were causing a "disturbance", Yeats realized that he was not in agreement with the Theosophical Society's "methods or their philosophy" [*Auto*, 111].

Eventually Yeats was asked to resign, probably in 1890, but it was a matter of little importance, since he had already met Mathers.[10] From the Theosophists Yeats had learned to value a comprehensive cosmology; now he was ready to enter into more daring undertakings. His meeting with Mathers could not have come at a more opportune time. Interest in the occult, as a consequence of the work of Sinnett and Blavatsky, was high, and Yeats's

8. George M. Harper, "From Zelator to Theoricus, Yeats's 'Link with the Invisible Degrees' ", *Yeats Studies*, 1 (1971), 80. The studio is probably that of Moina Bergson.

9. Yeats's experiments consisted of using symbols to evoke dreams [*Auto*, 111].

10. Yeats undoubtedly had heard of Mathers before their meeting since *The Kabbalah Unveiled* (1887) was known to the Theosophists. Anna Kingsford's group had a series of Hermetic lectures in 1886, and Mathers delivered two of them. See Edward Maitland, *Anna Kingsford: Her Life, Letters, Diary and Work*, 3rd ed. (London: John M. Watkins, 1913), II: 17-18. First published in January 1896.

own temperament was in tune with this new movement of the zeit-geist. Considering the personal and social forces at work, one is justified in suggesting that Yeats's meeting with Mathers constituted a perfect coincidence of the man with the moment. Yeats was, in his own words, "at a most receptive age" [*Auto*, 112].

Less is known about Mathers' occult activities prior to 1890. They must, however, have been extensive since he was already learned in the arcane sciences at the time when Yeats was introduced to him. Some knowledge of Mathers' background can be obtained from a brief biographical memorandum written by William Wynn Westcott.[11] A less reliable source is Mrs. Mathers' Preface to *The Kabbalah Unveiled*.[12] Westcott tells us that S. L. MacGregor Mathers was born in Hackney in 1854, the son of a commercial clerk. His father having died young, Mathers lived with his mother at Bournemouth until her death in 1885. He had become a Mason in 1877, and shortly thereafter was admitted to the Societas Rosicruciana in Anglia. It was here that he became associated with W. R. Woodman and Dr. Westcott, the two men who later collaborated with him in founding the Isis-Urania Temple of the Hermetic Order of the Golden Dawn. Mathers, a full-time occultist, took Rosicrucianism seriously, and in 1887 published a translation of Knorr von Rosenroth's *Kabbala Denudata*. This work, translated as *The Kabbalah Unveiled*, is the basis for many Golden Dawn rituals; it established Mathers' occult reputation and may have been read by Yeats before he met the author. After the death of his mother, Mathers moved to London, where he continued his association with Westcott.

Mrs. Mathers' Preface to the fourth edition of *The Kabbalah Unveiled* (1926) appears to fill in some of the gaps in this story, but since there are other obvious exaggerations in the Preface, her account of her husband must be suspect. According to Mrs. Mathers, her husband was educated in the classics and, even as a young boy, was a student of the Celtic tradition and symbolism. His mystical interests were strengthened by coming into contact with Kenneth Mackenzie, the author of the *Encyclopaedia of Masonry*; after moving to London, he was invited by Madame

11. Quoted in Howe, pp. 37-38.
12. S. L. MacGregor Mathers, *The Kabbalah Unveiled* (1887; rpt. London: Routledge & Kegan Paul, 1954), pp. vii-xiii.

Blavatsky to join her in the formation of the Theosophical Society, but declined for ideological reasons.[13]

Thus, when Yeats met Mathers, sometime between 1887 and 1890, both men were already launched on occult studies. Undoubtedly Yeats, hearing of Mathers' book and his lectures, was anxious to meet the famed authority, especially since the Cabala is in the mainstream of both Hermeticism and Theosophy.[14] Yeats was impressed by Mathers' physical appearance even before the two were introduced. While compiling an anthology of Irish fairy stories at the British Museum, he "often saw a man of thirty-six or thirty-seven, in a brown velveteen coat, with a gaunt and resolute face, and an athletic body", who seemed, before Yeats knew either his name or the nature of his studies, "a figure of romance" [Auto, 112]. After Yeats had become a colleague of Mathers, he was still taken by his mentor's physical presence: "In body and voice at least he was perfect; so might Faust have looked in his changeless aged youth. In the credulity of our youth we secretly wondered if he had not met with, perhaps even been taught by, some old man who had found the elixir" [Auto, 115].[15]

Mathers apparently made a striking impression on even the casual observer. A. E. Waite, best known as the designer of the Rider Pack of Tarot cards, also met Mathers during the 1880s at the Reading Room of the British Museum. Waite's experience was remarkably similar to Yeats's:

> It must be confessed that I grew curious as to the identity of this strange person, with rather fish-like eyes, and more especially as

13. Mrs. Mathers apparently is speaking of the formation of the Blavatsky chapter of the Theosophical Society in 1887, since the original Society had been founded ten years before. Mathers' book was published in 1887, and he was undoubtedly hard at work on his research. The fact that he lectured to Anna Kingsford's splinter group the year before indicates that he was not totally out of sympathy with the Theosophists.

14. According to Bachchan (p. 220), Madame Blavatsky's teachings are not truly Eastern; they consist mainly of Western concerns disguised under Eastern nomenclature.

15. One of Mathers' associates was "an old white-haired Oxfordshire clergyman, the most panic-stricken person" Yeats had ever known. He was the Rev. W. A. Ayton, who kept his alchemical laboratory in his basement so the Bishop would not find it. He believed that he had found the elixir of life, but, being timid, he failed to use it, and it evaporated [Auto, 113]. Ayton presided at Mathers' wedding in June 1890.

to what he was after. Some other melancholy votary of that sanctuary made us known to one another in the end, and he proved to be S. L. Mathers, for the MacGregor prefix had not as yet been adopted. I suppose that we must have spoken of occult books or subjects in one of the corridors, for he said to me in a hushed voice and with a somewhat awful accent: 'I am a Rosicrucian and a Freemason; therefore I can speak of some things, but of others I cannot speak.' ... However, we got slightly acquainted, and the more I saw of him the more eccentric he proved to be. I remember comparing him in my mind to a combination of Don Quixote and Hudibras, but with a vanity all his own. He would accost me suddenly, to deliver the inspiration of the moment. One of them concerned his great military ardour and his intention to join the French Zouaves in Africa, that he might spend 'the rest of his life fighting and that sort of thing' ... I met him one morning wearing a scarlet tie, to which he pointed proudly because it was assumed as a symbol of his fighting instincts, which he had proved unable to gratify in any more practical manner. We encountered on another occasion, he staggering as usual under a load of books, and he said: 'I have clothed myself with hieroglyphics as with a garment,' so I inferred he was then deep in Egyptology.[16]

It is not surprising that Yeats, with his affinity for mysticism, became a follower of such a mysterious personality, especially since the two men met at a most opportune moment. Mathers was in the midst of a project that would have repercussions to the present day, the founding of the Golden Dawn.

Although the various histories of the Order are not entirely in agreement as to its origins, the story which emerges from the conflicting accounts is roughly as follows. In 1884 an apparently ancient cypher manuscript was alleged to have been discovered by either Westcott or W. R. Woodman. One account contends that Westcott, a London coroner with occult interests, found the manuscript on a bookstall.[17] Another version of the story suggests that it was discovered among the papers of the late Fred Hockley (1809-1885) by Woodman, a retired physician and Supreme Magus of the Societas Rosicruciana in Anglia. The proponents of this theory believe that the manuscript was written by Kenneth Mackenzie, and was based on notes he had taken at a German Rosicrucian ceremony.[18]

16. Quoted by Howe, pp. 41-42.
17. Howe, p. 3.
18. King, *Astral Projection, Ritual Magic and Alchemy*, p. 19.

Whatever the origin of the manuscript, it came into the hands of Westcott, who invited his friend Mathers to devise rituals out of the material contained in it. In the manuscript was the name and address of a certain Fräulein Anna Sprengel, a German Rosicrucian. Westcott allegedly corresponded with this continental adept and received authorization to form an English branch of a German occult society called "Die Goldene Dammerung". Thus, on March 1, 1888 Westcott, Woodman, and Mathers became the three Chiefs of the Hermetic Order of the Golden Dawn. At the outset, Westcott apparently exercised the greatest control over the Order, Mathers being preoccupied with his research; soon, however, Mathers' superior knowledge of magic asserted itself, and control of the Order passed into his hands.

By the time Yeats was initiated on March 7, 1890, Mathers had devised the rituals up to the 5-6 grade. The Order was prospering; already there were twenty-two members, half of whom were women.[19] Some of the distinguished people who had already joined were: Moina Bergson, the sister of the philosopher, later to become Mrs. Mathers; Mrs. Violet Tweedale, later a novelist; Mrs. Alexandria Mackenzie, K. R. H. Mackenzie's widow; the Reverend W. A. Ayton, an alchemist, and his wife; Mrs. Constance Mary Wilde, the wife of Oscar Wilde; Annie Horniman, the daughter of Mathers' subsequent employer and the patron for a time of Mathers as well as the Abbey Theatre; and several foreign noblemen.

Many more prominent members followed Yeats in the next few years. Yeats himself is believed to have been the sponsor of Florence Emery, better known as the actress Florence Farr and the mistress of George Bernard Shaw. Others joining within a year or two were: Maud Gonne; Yeats's uncle, George Pollexfen; the writer J. W. Fitzgerald Molloy; A. E. Waite; J. W. Brodie-Innes, an Edinburgh lawyer; and William Peck, the Municipal Astronomer of Edinburgh. By 1893, the Golden Dawn had some one hundred twenty-four active members, including the members of smaller Temples at Weston-super-Mare, Bradford, and Edinburgh.[20] In spite of their esoteric activities, these distinguished initiates appear to have been a rather dull group. Maud Gonne recalls that she was oppressed by their drab appearance; her fellow

19. Howe, p. 49.   20. Ibid.

mystics seemed "the very essence of the middle class".[21] Aleister Crowley had much the same impression, finding with few exceptions the membership to be "utterly undistinguished" and "vulgar and commonplace", for the most part "muddled middle-class mediocrities". One of the persons whom Crowley excepted was Yeats, "a lank disheveled demonologist who might have taken more pains with his personal appearance without incurring the reproach of dandyism".[22]

Since Yeats seemed to stand out in this middle-class assembly, the question must be asked why he remained in the Order for some thirty years while most members resigned after a few years. In part, at least, the answer seems to be Mathers. He was clearly a magnetic personality, but more than this, he was constantly described by his friends and enemies alike as an extraordinarily able and learned magician. Yeats is typical of those who have chronicled Mathers' career. While seeing his virtues, he also sees his failings. Speaking in the *Autobiography* of the effects of his membership in the Golden Dawn, Yeats observes that "Mathers was its governing mind, a born teacher and organizer. One of those who incite—less by spoken word than by what they are—imaginative action" [*Auto*, 113]. Yeats later realized that he had considered Mathers an "idol" [L, 339] and an "idealized figure" [*Auto*, 342]. Even his criticism was tempered with praise: "I believe that his mind in those early days did not belie his face and body—though in later years it became unhinged . . . for he kept a proud head amid great poverty" [*Auto*, 112].

Yeats was not the only member of the Golden Dawn to remark on Mathers' dignity as well as his ability. Aleister Crowley, who joined the Order in 1898 and who later became an accomplished magician himself, saw in Mathers "that habit of authority which inspires confidence because it never doubts itself". Although Mathers' rival, and later even his enemy, Crowley regarded him as "unquestionably a Magician of extraordinary attainments" as well as "a scholar and a gentleman".[23] This is very generous praise, especially from a rival. Crowley surpasses even Yeats, who while

21. *A Servant of the Queen* (London: Victor Gollancz, 1938), p. 257.
22. Aleister Crowley, *The Confessions of Aleister Crowley*, eds. John Symonds and Kenneth Grant (1969; rpt. New York: Bantam 1971), pp. 169-70.
23. Crowley, *Confessions*, p. 188.

finding Mathers to be a man of "much learning" and "much imagination", saw in him "little scholarship" [*Auto*, 115].[24]

Israel Regardie, another member of the Golden Dawn, also admitted Mathers' shortcomings but still praised him highly: "His scholarship at times is alleged to have been faulty. He may have been incompetent and irresponsible as a leader, as still others claim. Nevertheless, it is my firm conviction, and I feel impelled to register it strongly, that there was more magic capacity and spiritual insight within the least part of his frame than has the entire sterile Adept body of the Stella Matutina. Concealed within the Order documents is a vast wisdom, true secrets, indicible, and incapable of being communicated."[25] In Regardie's opinion, "spiritual pride" and "delusions" were Mathers' only vices.[26] Dr. Robert W. Felkin, who became head of the Order after the expulsion of Mathers, suggests that Mathers' pride and love of power grew to a point where he demanded greater loyalty to himself than to the magical operations of the Order.[27]

But for several years before his expulsion, Mathers and the Order prospered. At the time the Order was founded, of course, Mathers was only one of its three Chiefs. During the early years, he was intent on his studies at the British Museum, where he was first seen by both Waite and Yeats, and was content to leave the practical details of the Order to Westcott. But Westcott was no magician, and after the death of Woodman in 1890, the balance of power began to shift to Mathers. Mathers hastened this development by announcing that, while on a visit to Paris, he had been in contact with the Secret Chiefs, who had authorized him to establish a Second, or Inner, Order, the Rosae Rubeae et Aureae Crucis, of which he was to be the sole Chief.[28]

At this time too his personal life was flourishing. By 1890 he had married Mina (later Moina) Bergson, and had met one of her

24. In the original version Yeats said, "without the standards of a scholar" [*Mem*, 74]; in *The Trembling of the Veil* (London: T. Werner Laurie, 1922) he says that Mathers had "no scholarship", but when Mrs. Mathers took exception to this description, he amended it to the form it retains in the *Autobiography*.
25. Regardie, p. 108.   26. *Ibid.*, p. 14.
27. Quoted by Regardie, p. 15.
28. Aleister Crowley subsequently used this same device on Mathers; Crowley claimed that the Secret Chiefs had instructed him to form yet a third order.

friends from the Slade School of Fine Art, Miss Annie Horniman, the daughter of a wealthy tea importer. She also was introduced to Mathers at the British Museum. Eventually she persuaded her father to employ Mathers as curator of his private museum at Forest Hill, thereby enabling Mathers to marry; and she contributed to his support for many years.

It was about this time that Mathers demonstrated to Yeats the power of symbols, saying, "We only give you symbols because we respect your liberty" (*Mem*, p. 27). He taught Yeats the use of symbols to induce *visions*, and these experiences revealed to him that "images well up before the mind's eye from a deeper source than the conscious or subconscious memory" [*Auto*, 112]. Yeats first had heard of Mathers' powers of evocation from Florence Farr, who described how Mathers had given her a piece of cardboard on which was coloured a geometric symbol and told her to hold it to her forehead. Suddenly she had "found herself walking on a cliff above the sea, seagulls shrieking overhead" [*Auto*, 113-4]. Later, Mathers conducted the same experiment with Yeats. For Yeats the images "came slowly, there was not that sudden miracle as if the darkness had been cut with a knife . . . but there rose before me mental images that I could not control: a desert and a black Titan raising himself up by his two hands from the middle of a heap of ancient ruins." Mathers explained that the creature was of the Order of Salamanders, because the symbol he had shown Yeats was theirs. Yeats added that "it was not necessary even to show the symbol, it would have been sufficient that he imagined it" [*Auto*, 114].

It is obvious from many of Yeats's personal writings that this ability of Mathers made a considerable impression on him. Numerous letters, several essays (especially "Magic"), the *Autobiography*, and *Memoirs* all contain descriptions of the visionary power of symbols. In "Magic" Yeats describes a visit to what is obviously Stent Lodge at Forest Hill while Mathers was curator of the Horniman Museum. Yeats's fellow visitor, initially a skeptic, was told of visions which revealed his past life and which corresponded to his recurring dreams. Later, Yeats was shown visions from one of his past lives. For him, the experience was "proof of the supremacy of imagination", not of the inherent power of the symbols, and it was not long before he had "mastered Mathers' symbolic system" [*Auto*, 114].

Shortly after Mathers had introduced Yeats to his visionary method, the Second Order was founded. The Second Order transformed the Golden Dawn into a practical magical Order. Whereas the adepts of the Outer Order studied the Cabala and other works which form the theoretical basis for the practice of magic, the initiates of the Inner Order were required to begin the crafting of the magician's tools. Not long after the establishment of the Second Order, Mathers moved to Paris and there opened the Ahathoor Temple. In the Preface to the fourth edition of *The Kabbalah Unveiled*, Mrs. Mathers explained that her husband was "told by his occult teachers to transfer his centre".[29] Actually, the explanation is more mundane. In 1891 Mathers had been discharged from his post at the Horniman Museum, and sometime that year, probably after he had lost his position, he and his wife twice visited Paris. That same year Mrs. Mathers began to ask Annie Horniman for money. Miss Horniman gave her several loans; the transactions were kept secret, and continued until July 14, 1896. Early in 1892 Miss Horniman gave Mrs. Mathers sufficient money to go to Paris and study painting. MacGregor decided to accompany her, and they departed on May 21, 1892, leaving Florence Emery to head the Order in his absence: this turn of events did not please Miss Horniman, who thought the presence of her husband would deter Mina in her work.

While in Paris Mathers continued the research that he had begun at the British Museum. At the Library of the Arsenal he discovered the manuscript of *The Sacred Magic of Abra-Melin the Mage*. Aleister Crowley suggests that this discovery may have led to Mathers' undoing because, while Mathers was an "expert magician", he was accustomed to dealing with *The Greater Key of Solomon*, a much less potent grimoire than *Abra-Melin*. Crowley recounts that Mathers repeatedly had bicycle accidents while making the long trip from his home to the Arsenal. It was his belief that Mathers had fallen prey to the "malignant forces of the book".[30] An alternate hypothesis, also put forward by Crowley, is that the Matherses had been possessed by Rose and Theo Horos, two American frauds who tried to convince Mathers that Mrs. Horos was Fräulein Sprengel.[31]

29. Preface to *The Kabbalah Unveiled*, p. xiii.
30. Crowley, *Confessions*, p. 169.
31. *Ibid.*, p. 349. See also Howe, pp. 237-40.

Whatever the cause, after 1891 and especially after the move to Paris, Mathers' increasingly eccentric behaviour made him "a necessary extravagance"; but he had been flamboyant and a *poseur* from the beginning. Yeats described him in the *Autobiography* as one who "had carried farther than anyone else, a claim implicit in the Romantic movement from the time of Shelley and of Goethe", a claim the pursuit of which resulted in astonishing behaviour. He loved the past, and even though it is unlikely that Mathers had ever seen the Highlands of Scotland, for him "the eighteenth-century controversy [the Jacobite question] still raged" [*Auto*, 202].

Yeats reports after one of his visits to the Matherses in Paris that "under the impact of the Celtic Movement, as our movement is called in England, they had cast off Mathers and become plain Mac-Gregor" (*Mem*, p. 105). At night Mathers would dress himself "in Highland dress and dance the sword dance, and his mind brooded upon the ramifications of clans and tartans". Yeats believed at this time that Mathers' singular behaviour was due to the fact that he was living under "some great strain" [*Auto*, 202]. It may be that the great strain was the magical forces unleashed by his work with the *Abra-Melin* manuscript. Like other habits, Mathers' drinking of "whiskey" was part of his Scottish pose, but his drinking seems to have gone far beyond the posing stage. He began "drinking too much neat brandy, though not to drunkenness" [*Auto*, 202]. It was Yeats's opinion that Mathers' behaviour was caused by the strain of his evocations.

For whatever reason, Mathers grew more and more unhinged. He almost shot a fellow occultist, Allen Bennett, in a petty quarrel over the powers of the words "Shiva, shiva, shiva".[32] His delusions of grandeur increased. He foresaw great "changes in the world; announcing in 1893 and 1894 the imminence of immense wars.... He imagined a Napoleonic role for himself, a Europe transformed according to his fancy, Egypt restored, a Highland Principality, and even offered subordinate posts to unlikely people" [*Auto*, 202-3].[33] The addition of Egyptology to Mathers' range of interests does not come as a surprise since most of the Western occult

32. *Ibid.*, pp. 234-35.
33. According to a note in the Yeats papers, Mathers considered joining the Russian Secret Police in 1897. He always had harbored military aspirations, and in 1884 had published *Practical Instruction in Infantry Campaigning Exercise*, a translation of a French military manual.

tradition can be traced back to Egypt. By 1899 Mathers was performing his rite of Isis in public theatres and had even converted his house into a temple.

In July 1896 Miss Horniman terminated her subsidy. To compensate for his poverty, Mathers "remembered a title Louis xv had conferred upon a Jacobite ancestor who had fought at Pondicherry and called himself Comte de Glenstrae, and gathered about him Frenchmen and Spaniards whose titles were more shadowy ... the most as poor as he and some less honest." By this time Mathers was living "in a world of phantoms. He would describe himself as meeting, perhaps in some crowded place, a stranger whom he would distinguish from living men by a certain tension in his heart" [*Auto*, 203].

While Mathers roamed the streets, meeting his secret teachers in the crowded boulevards of Paris, he was frequently attired in full Highland garb with knives stuck in his stockings. He remarked to Yeats on one such occasion, "When I am dressed like this I feel like a walking flame" [*Auto*, 204]. Indeed, to Yeats all of Mathers' actions seemed like an effort to become a walking flame. Yeats accounted for Mathers' increasingly eccentric behaviour as the result of his efforts to prolong his youthful dream, to mount to *Hodos Chameliontos*. Yeats spoke from experience when he remarked, "I have known none mount there and come to good that lacked philosophy" [*Auto*, 203]; he once had felt that he was lost there himself.

The fact that Mathers' extravagant behaviour met with disapproval from his fellow occultists is attested to by Scribe QM, whom unfortunately I cannot identify. Through this scribe the Secret Chiefs announced that Mathers "kept not the vows of his obligation, but sought and claimed personal honour and obedience, not to us [the Secret Chiefs] but to himself". Furthermore, the ambitious Mathers "did associate himself with certain lewd persons [the Horos couple], who by black magical processes had attained a certain clairvoyance, in the hope that they could procure for him what we for good reason withheld .... " Mathers is also accused of "attempting to sell our high and holy knowledge for money".[34]

34. I was able to examine a copy of Scribe QM's manuscript through the generosity of Professor George M. Harper. The reference to selling the secret knowledge of the Order probably stems from Mathers' public performances of the Rite of Isis in Paris.

Other members of the Golden Dawn had similar impressions of Mathers after the founding of the Second Order. In his *Confessions*, Crowley speaks of "the most insane pomposities of Mathers, a notorious rascal" [p. 700] who "lived in sodden intoxication" [p. 191]. Crowley suggests that Mathers was reduced to petty thievery from his friends, citing the mysterious disappearance of some expensive luggage which he had left with Mathers. After he and Mathers quarrelled Crowley even suggested that Mathers had attacked him with magical forces. Crowley's own eccentricities always tend to colour his opinions, but he is least reliable as a commentator on Yeats and Mathers in his novel *Moonchild*, written long after he had broken with both of them.[35] Thinly veiled autobiography in fictional form, the novel is a rendering of some of Crowley's occult experiences, and in this sense it is similar to Yeats's *The Speckled Bird*. Many of the allusions are recognizable by even the most casual student of the Golden Dawn. Although the novel serves primarily as a vehicle for unflattering parodies of Crowley's enemies, it does provide some useful information.

The hero, in the traditional sense of the word, is Cyril Grey, an idealized version of Crowley. Grey once belonged to a magical order which he calls the Black Lodge; he left the Lodge because he realized that it worked to attract innocent people under the false pretense of wisdom and virtue. Grey's membership in such an organization is excusable because he merely pretended loyalty to the Lodge in order to destroy it. The head of this Black Lodge is known in occult circles as s.r.m.d.; he is Count Macgregor of Glenstrae, formerly known as Douglas. This description coincides in almost every detail with earlier ones of Mathers.

Mathers receives much harsher treatment in *Moonchild* than in Crowley's other writings. At one time Douglas "had been well educated, became a good scholar, and developed an astounding taste and capacity for magic." But he had fallen; he is accused of using his magical powers to gain control of his Lodge. But because Douglas had "chosen the wrong road", the Lodge deteriorated; it was always "seething with hate. . . . Douglas found his prestige gone and his income with it. Addiction to drink, which had accompanied his magical fall, now became an all-absorbing vice. He was never able to rebuild his Lodge on its former lines; but

35. *Moonchild: A Prologue* (London: Mandrake Press, 1929).

those who thirsted for knowledge and power—and these he still possessed in ever increasing abundance as he himself decayed—clung to him, hating and envying him . . . . "

But "the vilest thing charged against that vile parody of a man" was his "treatment of his wife, a young, beautiful, talented and charming girl, the sister of a famous professor at the Sorbonne". Douglas' wife's earnings as a streetwalker were alleged to be supplemented by blackmail. In spite of these libellous suggestions, Crowley's portrait of Douglas is not without its favourable aspects. Douglas' "knowledge of the minds of others was uncanny", and his abilities as a magician are never denied. Crowley simply believes that Douglas undid himself by "repeated acts whose essence was the denial of the unity of himself with the rest of the universe". This opinion, however, runs contrary to Yeats's belief that the only philosophy known by Mathers was the medicinal phrase, "There is no part of me that is not of the Gods" [*Auto*, 203].

Yeats is not spared either; Crowley had long believed that Yeats was envious of his own superior abilities as a poet, although the truth probably was the opposite. Yeats is transparently disguised as Gates, who "had a pretty amateur talent for painting in water-colours: some people thought it stronger than his verses." Although in league with Douglas, Gates is not so much villain as dupe:

> He had no business in the Black Lodge at all; it was but one of his romantic phantasies to pose as a terribly wicked fellow. Yet he took it seriously enough, and was ready to serve Douglas in any scheme, however atrocious, which would secure his advancement in the Lodge. He was only there through muddle-headedness; so far as he had an object beyond the satisfaction of his own vanity, it was innocent in itself—the acquisition of knowledge and power. He was entirely the dupe of Douglas who found him a useful stalking-horse, for Gates had a considerable reputation in some of the best circles in England [pp. 152-53].

Yeats and Mathers do not share the brunt of Crowley's parody alone. Many of their colleagues in the Golden Dawn also receive attention. Arthur Edward Waite appears in the novel as Arthwait; William Wynn Westcott is Vesquit; the Horos couple are Cremers and Butcher; and Anna Kingsford is probably the model for Annie. Although a fictional account, *Moonchild* does provide useful insights into the personalities of the key members of the Golden Dawn. Crowley's characterization of Gates as lacking "virility" is probably closer to the truth than Yeats would have liked to admit. Also interesting is the charge that Douglas planted the documents which resulted in Vesquit's decision to resign from the Lodge and leave Douglas in sole command.[36]

The picture that emerges from the documentary and fictional accounts of the Golden Dawn in the nineties is that of an organization ridden with internal strife and headed by a gifted but unbalanced leader. Throughout this period Yeats seems to have remained on good terms with his Chief. In the *Autobiography* and *Letters* he frequently mentions staying at Mathers' home in Paris. Between the "many" visits Yeats and the Matherses kept up an amiable correspondence.[37] The most frequent subjects, in the letters which survive, were news of mutual friends, the Matherses' activities in Paris, the possibility of producing a Yeats play there, and the Celtic revival with which Mathers was assisting Yeats.

One gets the impression from this correspondence that Yeats and Mathers were on intimate terms and that the Celtic revival was their most pressing concern. In addition to his concern with the Celtic revival, the letters reveal his interest in Egyptology and his hope to establish a centre for the Egyptian Mysteries in Paris. One of the letters in which Mrs. Mathers speaks of being "plunged in 'Egypt' " contains an interesting insight into Mathers' mode of living. She mentions how delighted she and her husband were to meet William Sharp, with whom they "felt greatly in sympathy". Yeats heard the story from Sharp in somewhat different terms: "William Sharp met Mathers in the Louvre, and said, 'No doubt considering your studies you live on milk and fruit.' And Mathers replied, 'No, not exactly milk and fruit, but very nearly so'; and now Sharp has lunched with Mathers and been given nothing but brandy and radishes" [*Auto*, 209].

In spite of the congenial picture which emerges from this correspondence, it is probable that Yeats and other members of the Second Order in London were losing patience with Mathers' excesses. Yeats has recounted how in earlier days when Mathers "made some absurd statement, some incredible claim, some hackneyed joke, we would half consciously change claim, state-

36. A more factual account of this incident can be found in Howe, pp. 165-68.
37. There are copies of several letters from the Matherses to Yeats in the possession of Professor Harper, who has kindly allowed me to examine them.

ment or joke, as though he were a figure in a play of our composition, . . . a necessary extravagance." Apparently this tolerance was more difficult to maintain as Mathers grew increasingly willful and arrogant. Eventually matters reached a crisis. Although the story of Yeats's break with Mathers has already been told, a few of the essential details will be cited here in order to preserve the continuity of the story of Mathers and Yeats.[38]

On February 16, 1900 Florence Farr Emery received a letter from Mathers alleging that the original letters from Fräulein Sprengel which had authorized the founding of the Isis-Urania Temple were forged by Westcott. Mathers contended that he was in touch with Fräulein Sprengel, she being at that moment in Paris assisting him in his work.[39] Since the validity of the Order, as well as Mathers' position in it, hinged on the letters of authorization, Mrs. Emery appointed an investigation committee. Mathers, resenting being questioned, refused to recognize the committee. Subsequently, he dispatched Crowley as his deputy to London to seize the Order's rooms and to demand that each of the "rebels" sign a pledge of loyalty recognizing Mathers as Visible Head of the Order.

Although Yeats stayed out of the battle of letters between Mathers and Mrs. Emery, he seems to have been the strategist for the rebels. In a letter to Lady Gregory he wrote, "I told you that I was putting MacGregor out of the Kabbala. Well last week he sent a mad person—whom we had refused to initiate—to take possession of the rooms and papers of the Society." At this juncture, Yeats was forced "to take the whole responsibility for everything, to decide on every step" because, in his words, "my Kabbalists are hopelessly unbusiness like" [L, 340].

The "mad person" sent by Mathers was Aleister Crowley, who was later to become the self-styled Great Beast. Crowley found Yeats to possess more "virility" than he had suspected. An absurd melodrama ensued in which Crowley "seized the rooms and on

---

38. The details of Yeats's quarrel with Mathers have been recounted by Professor Harper in " 'Meditations upon Unknown Thought': Yeats's Break with MacGregor Mathers", *Yeats Studies*, 1 (1971), 175-202.

39. A considerable controversy has raged over whether or not Mathers actually believed Mrs. Horos to be Fräulein Sprengel. In a letter to Yeats, Mrs. Mathers denied that her husband was duped; Crowley insists that he was.

being ejected attempted to retake possession wearing a black mask and in full highland costume and with a gilt dagger by his side" [L, 340]. Foiled, Crowley retaliated by taking the matter to court, but the verdict went in favor of Yeats and his colleagues. Crowley withdrew his suit and paid the costs [L, 343-44].

The outcome of the lawsuit, however, was secondary in importance to the suspension of Mathers from the Order several days before, on April 19. This action, for all practical purposes, ended one of the most important relationships of Yeats's life. But not entirely; for, as Yeats remarked of Mathers in "All Souls' Night", "Friendship never ends".

It is a curious fact that, while Yeats frequently was at odds with many of his fellow cabalists, and was utterly furious with Crowley, he seemed to bear no malice toward Mathers. At the close of his letter to Lady Gregory he writes: "I arraigned Mathers on Saturday last before a chapter of the Order. I was carefully polite and I am particularly pleased at the fact that in our correspondence and meetings not one word has been written or said which forgot the past and the honour that one owes even to a fallen idol .... We have barbed our arrows with compliments and regrets and to do him justice he has done little less" [L, 340]. Several weeks later Yeats reiterated these feelings in a letter to George Russell (AE). Admitting that Mathers "behaved in several amazing ways", Yeats is still friendly: "MacGregor apart from certain definite ill doings and absurdities, on which we had to act, has behaved with dignity and even courtesy" [L, 344].

Yeats records in the *Autobiography* that after his quarrel with Mathers he "heard of him from time to time" up to his death in 1918. It is ironic that Mathers died in the midst of the event he had so long prophesied. In anticipation of the war he had made his wife learn ambulance work, and at the outbreak of war turned his house into a recruiting office.

In 1908 some unidentified person, probably a fellow Rosicrucian, made an attempt to reconcile Yeats and Mathers. In a letter addressed to this unknown party Mathers sets forth the conditions under which he would be able to receive Yeats in a "friendly attitude".[40] Briefly, the conditions were that Yeats would side with Mathers on the original question that had resulted in his being

---

40. A copy of this letter is also in the possession of Professor Harper.

ousted from the London Temple eight years before. The conditions apparently were not met, and the two men were still estranged at the time of Mathers' death. The letter, signed "MacGregor de Glenstrae", showed Mathers clinging to this title in the face of ever-declining fortunes. Yeats describes how his old friend "gathered about him Frenchmen and Spaniards whose titles were more shadowy [than his] . . . and in that dreamcourt cracked innumerable mechanical jokes—to hide discouragement—and yet remained to the end courageous in thought and kind in act" [*Auto*, 203]. Although considerably less kind, Crowley's account of Mathers' last years confirms Yeats's.

Even after he was in the grave, the thought of Mathers weighed on Yeats's mind. He figures in both versions of *A Vision*, and the 1925 version is dedicated to his widow. Yeats continued to carry on an intermittent correspondence with Mrs. Mathers. On at least five occasions after 1924, she replied to letters from Yeats. Three of her letters pertain to the "caricature portrait" of her husband in *The Trembling of the Veil* (1922). Mrs. Mathers objected strongly to Yeats's description of her husband's character and activities during the years after their estrangement. Yeats agreed to qualify several of his statements, but the question of the "awful book" was never resolved to her complete satisfaction. Nevertheless, with one exception, their correspondence was cordial. One of the letters indicates that Yeats had proposed sending some of his fellow occultists to study under Mrs. Mathers so that they too might benefit indirectly from the wisdom of her husband.

The last two letters pertain to the Golden Dawn. As late as 1926, the year after *A Vision* (A), Yeats was still trying to determine whether or not Mathers had believed Mrs. Horos to be Fräulein Sprengel. At the time of this inquiry, Yeats was no longer affiliated with any magical order [*Auto*, 342]. Yeats never seems to have been able to put his old friend and mentor out of his mind.

A Vision, the culmination of Yeats's religious quest, was dedicated "To Vestigia". In 1925 only a few would have known that Vestigia Nulla Retrorsum (No Traces Behind) was the motto of Moina Mathers in the Golden Dawn. The explanation for Yeats's decision to honour Mrs. Mathers in this way lies in a rejected draft of the dedication. In the published version Yeats observes, "Perhaps this book has been written because a number of young men and women, you and I among the number, met nearly forty years ago in London and in Paris to discuss mystical philosophy." In the rejected version "you and I" reads "you and one other—with whom I quarreled years ago".[41] Yeats's tribute to Mathers and the other "young men and women" is repeated in poetic form in "All Souls' Night", a poem written in 1920 but used as the Epilogue for *A Vision*. As Yeats calls up the souls of his friends in "strange thought", Mathers is last summoned but most discussed.

There is one further way in which readers of Yeats can see the importance of Mathers to him. He not only influenced Yeats's work and launched him on the course of thought that culminated in *A Vision*, but he also appears in several of Yeats's works as well. Michael Robartes, who in Yeats's poetry and fiction represents half of his divided self, is modelled after Mathers. Much of Yeats's short fiction was published in 1897, when Mathers' influence was at its height. Although many of the stories deal with the timeless legendary past, Mathers is clearly visible in those concerned with contemporary mysticism.[42] In the prefatory matter to *A Vision*, it is even more obvious that Mathers is present in "Stories of Michael Robartes and his Friends". This identification of Michael Robartes with Mathers is especially revealing because Yeats originally intended to attribute his entire system to a source discovered by Robartes. In similar fashion, Maclagan, in Yeats's autobiographical novel *The Speckled Bird*, is modelled after Mathers. A comprehensive treatment of Mathers' role in Yeats's fiction cannot be made until both manuscript and typescript of *The Speckled Bird* are printed.[43]

Scholars should treat Mathers and the Golden Dawn as seriously as Yeats himself did. The Golden Dawn is beginning to receive its share of attention in Yeats studies; perhaps Mathers' contribution to

41. A copy of this discarded version, in Yeats's hand, was examined through the kindness of Professor Harper.
42. The influence of Mathers at this time is visible even in the titles of Yeats's fiction. Several stories in *The Secret Rose* reflect the Rosicrucian antecedents of the Second Order. The tone of this collection also demonstrates the truth of Yeats's belief that his experience with Mathers' symbolic method of evoking visions had caused his writing to become "more sensuous and more vivid" [*Mem*, 28]. Rosicrucianism is more heavily in evidence in the other stories of 1897, especially "Rosa Alchemica", as its title indicates.
43. The typescript of *The Speckled Bird*, edited by William H. O'Donnell, has recently been published in two volumes by The Cuala Press.

Yeats's life and art will, as a result, receive its just recognition. "The Golden Dawn was MacGregor Mathers." Yeats took seriously the man who started him on an exploration of the unseen world that was to last for more than thirty years, and those the years of his greatest productivity. Yeats learned from his occult studies that truth, the object of his lifelong search, is not "something that could be conveyed from one man's mind to another"; rather, it is a "state of mind" [*Auto*, 281]. Surely this is what he meant when he said of Mathers, "Though he did not show me the truth, he did what he professed, and showed me a way to it" [*Auto*, 342].

Yeats and Mr. Watkins' Bookshop

Geoffrey M. Watkins

"I did not know where Mr Yeats lived, but said that we could find out from Mr Watkins the book-seller in Cecil's Court: and having so found out, he said we must call upon Mr Yeats . . . . "[1]

So much has already been written about Yeats and the influence which his magical and occult associations exerted upon his work that little remains to be said. Nevertheless, to know something of the bookshop which he used to frequent and where he found very many of the books which he must have read over a period of some thirty years may serve to add another detail to the picture we have of him.

In the early 1880s my father, John M. Watkins, became a member of the Theosophical Society, having been introduced to Madame Blavatsky's Sunday afternoon tea-parties. He became involved in the setting up of the Society's publishing and book-selling activities, living and working at the headquarters of the Society, where Madame Blavatsky was living. One of his first tasks was to help in the work of seeing the first edition of *The Secret Doctrine* through the press in 1888.

It was a year or so after Madame Blavatsky's death in 1891 that he founded his own business as bookseller and publisher. After one or two moves he finally opened the bookshop at Cecil Court in 1900, where the business still is. At that time his customers were

1. *A Vision* (London: T. Werner Laurie, 1925), p. xvi.

drawn mostly from the ranks of the Theosophical Society, the various spiritualist societies then in existence, and the Order of the Golden Dawn. The business grew slowly and steadily, catering to those interested in Theosophy, Christian and Oriental mystical philosophy, astrology, alchemy, and other esoteric subjects. In 1891 the Adelphi Lodge of the Theosophical Society was founded by Dr. William Wynn Westcott (also one of the founders of the Order of the Golden Dawn), Percy Bullock (a member of the Golden Dawn), and my father. Meetings were held at Cecil Court and continued until about 1907 or 1908. Among the many visitors were W. B. Yeats, G. R. S. Mead, George Russell (AE), A. P. Sinnett, E. T. Sturdy, William Kingsland, and other well known members of the Society.

It was a natural development that the shop should have become a meeting place for all who were interested in the matters in which my father specialised. There was a constant stream of visitors from both home and overseas. The bookshop was a sort of sounding-board for all the gossip and varying activities of the time. More and more books in the field were appearing. Westcott's series "Collectanea Hermetica", A. E. Waite's translations of the works of Eliphas Lévi, MacGregor Mathers' writings and his translations of magical texts, Professor Max Muller's great series on "The Sacred Books of the East", and translations from Sanskrit works issued by the Theosophical Society in India. These were among the works which were being read and studied at the time, and many of them were read by Yeats.

The year 1909 saw a great upheaval in the Theosophical Society. Following a disagreement with the policy of the president some four or five hundred members resigned en bloc. From a number of these former members G.R.S. Mead formed the Quest Society, which continued for twenty-one years. At the same time my father published for the Society a periodical called *The Quest* which numbered among its contributors many distinguished scholars. So far as I know Yeats was never a member of the Quest Society, but he was a frequent visitor to the weekly meetings in Kensington Town Hall and later in a large studio in Clareville Grove, South Kensington. He was also an occasional contributor to *The Quest*.[2]

2. Wade records only one contribution, "The Mountain Tomb", *The Quest* (April 1913). The poem is concerned with the myth that Father Christian

I did not join the business until 1919, when I left the army at the end of the First World War. By that time my father was almost blind, and much of the day-to-day conduct of the business and the ever-increasing correspondence fell upon my shoulders, leaving my father free for talks and discussion. He was rather a quiet and retiring person with great wisdom and understanding, and there are many who must have owed a great deal to his gift for sympathetic listening.

From the time I joined the firm and for many years after I can remember the people who came for *tea*, *talk*, and *theosophy* (Theosophy in its earlier and wider sense). Among the visitors were Yeats, AE, James Stephens, Stephen MacKenna (the translator of Plotinus), Darrell Figgis (the author of a fine book on Blake's paintings), Standish O'Grady (the delightful re-teller of Irish tales and legends), and many others.

When Yeats and Mead would meet by chance at Cecil Court, they would talk at length on Plotinus, the Gnostics, and Indian philosophy. Occasionally, Waite would be there, and he and Yeats would talk on the Kabbalah and the world of Faerie. With C. J. Barker, who was editing a new edition of the works of Jacob Boehme, Yeats would discuss Boehme and his influence on Blake. At nearly all the meetings my father would take part, acting sometimes as peace-maker when discussion grew heated. I almost wrote pace-maker, but there was never any need for that when Yeats was there.

On one morning I can recall Yeats arriving in a state of high dudgeon. An impressive figure, dressed in a slightly theatrical manner, rather like the popular conception of a poet: a broad-brimmed black hat, a flowing tie, a broad ribbon hanging from his horn-rimmed pince-nez, and a voluminous black overcoat. In a high-pitched voice he complained bitterly because someone had taken a pot shot at him while he was breakfasting the previous day in Dublin. AE and James Stephens took great pains to calm down the justifiably exasperated Yeats.

It was my father who was responsible for introducing Yeats, through the Hon. Mrs. Davey, to Shri Purohit Swami. This association led finally to the publication of new English versions of *Ten*

Rosencreuz lies buried in the seven-sided tomb at the heart of the Holy Mountain of Abiegnos (G. M. Harper).

Principal Upanishads and of Patanjali's *Aphorisms of Yoga,* in both of which Yeats collaborated.

It is interesting to note that many of the occult books which Yeats read during these years have stood the test of time and are being reprinted, a number of them in paperbacks, which is a sure indication of the increasing interest in these subjects.

Perhaps I may be allowed to close on a personal note by expressing my own impression of W. B. Yeats. In common with my father's other Irish friends he possessed the engaging characteristic of paying attention to one as a person, which was something very much valued by me as a quite junior member of the firm. His usual opening question was: "Where is your father?" followed by "Let us go and seek him out, we must talk." How could one fail to respond to such an approach? I am grateful to Providence for the opportunity of having known such people in the stimulating circle of "Mr Watkins the book-seller in Cecil's Court".

An Encounter with
the Supernatural in Yeats's
"The Spirit Medium"

Stuart Hirschberg

"The Spirit Medium" (1938) is a strange, powerful, though little known poem that superbly illustrates Yeats's skill in adapting and re-working features of the traditional ballad in order to dramatize his own lifelong search for esoteric, "occult" wisdom [VP, 599-600].

The speaker in the poem describes himself as once having loved poetry and music, before his present obsession with matters beyond life made him lose touch with his everyday world. Contact with the beyond, as he describes it in each of the poem's three stanzas (which resemble the ballad form in their occasional alteration of four and three stresses, and in their steadily more ominous refrains), has seemingly weakened his attachment not only to poetry and music, but to life itself. To the extent that Yeats himself felt that occult wisdom came through him from sources beyond the pale of the conscious mind, the narrator seems to be identifiable with Yeats. When seen in this light, "The Spirit Medium" seems to present Yeats's ambivalent attraction towards the joint pursuit of both occultism and poetry.

The poem opens abruptly with the dramatic revelation that pursuit of matters beyond the grave have vitiated the very things that were to have benefited by such occult investigations:

> Poetry, music, I have loved, and yet
> Because of those new dead
> That come into my soul and escape
> Confusion of the bed . . . .

The change from a life of active enjoyment to a state of passive acquiescence is underscored by the skilful use of rhythm, meter, and rhyme. Thus, the renunciation of the medium's individuality is forecast both by the change from the narrator as subject (in "I have loved") to the narrator as object ("Because of those new dead/ That come into my soul"), and by the shift from the assertive trochaic meter to less emphatic iambic feet for the remaining stanzas of the poem. Yeats makes use of the supernatural in a way that recalls the traditional folk ballad. Certain phrases, for example, seem to be deliberately left unexplained in order to heighten the reader's sense of mystery. Thus, the "confusion" of the dead mentioned in the poem arises from their unwillingness to accept the fact that they are, indeed, dead. As Yeats explained in his essay, "Swedenborg, Mediums, and the Desolate Places", "the dead do not yet know they are dead, but stumble on amid visionary smoke and noise, and . . . angelic spirits seek to awaken them but still in vain" [E, 51]. In reality, the connotations of "bed" (the place of generation, birth, and death) suggest that the dead have escaped from the confusions of identity always present in life, for, as Yeats wrote, "the ghost is simple, the man heterogeneous and confused" [M, 335]. The concluding four lines of the opening stanza suggest that the medium is forced to relinquish his personality in order to be of service to yet unborn souls (the "unbegotten") waiting to enter life:

> Or those begotten or unbegotten
> Perning in a band,
> *I bend my body to the spade*
> *Or grope with a dirty hand.*

The powerful, chant-like effect of the italicized refrain stresses the profound moral and psychological transformation which the spirit medium must undergo by equating his job to that of a grave-digger. In contrast to the pleasant aesthetic pastimes of music and poetry, the medium must now "grope with a dirty hand"; that is, he must attend to the difficult work of dealing with the dead. When viewed as a poem that has biographical application, "The Spirit Medium" acquires additional significance; like the protagonist of the poem, Yeats experienced an ambivalent attraction to both occultism and aesthetic pursuits throughout his life. In an effort to connect these divergent interests Yeats formulated a theory that, in both mysticism and poetry, the evocation of symbols and rhythmic incantations can release the subliminal mind from conscious control. As he explained in the essay "The Symbolism of Poetry", "the mind liberated from the pressure of the will is unfolded in symbols" [E&I, 159]. Furthermore, Yeats believed that "in the making and in the understanding of a work of art, and the more easily if it is full of patterns and symbols and music, we are lured to the threshold of sleep, and it may be far beyond . . . " [E&I, 160]. In the poem's second stanza the domination of the medium's conscious mind by the unconscious is conveyed both by the use of incantation and the rhythmic repetition of the phrase "those begotten or unbegotten". Yeats makes use of alliteration in both the sixth and seventh lines of the first stanza ("Perning in a band, / I bend my body to the spade"), and deliberately echoes the initial consonants of the first line ("Poetry, music, I have loved") in the initial word in the sixth line of each stanza ("Perning"-"Moulding"-"Makes"). In stanza two Yeats explores his belief that the dead move through purgation as a collective entity and the "unbegotten" find their identities through participation in a common activity:

> Or those begotten or unbegotten
> For I would not recall
> Some that being unbegotten
> Are not individual,
> But copy some one action,
> Moulding it of dust or sand,
> *I bend my body to the spade*
> *Or grope with a dirty hand.*

In effect, the souls described in this stanza have no individual personalities but exist only insofar as they are bound together through the same fate. As Yeats wrote in his essay on Swedenborg, "They have bodies as plastic as their minds that flow so readily into the mould . . . and Swedenborg remembers having seen the face of a spirit change continually and yet keep always a certain generic likeness" (E, 41-2]. This same idea was also used by Yeats in a later poem, "Cuchulain Comforted", where a group of Shrouds chant " 'We thread the needles' eyes, and all we do/All must together do' " [CP, 395]. Yeats believed that "moments of common memory" unite the dead into "one mediatorial communion". These moments are constructed by the dead using the shaping power of their collective imagination and Yeats wrote that when this happens "all their thoughts have moulded the vehicle and become event and circumstance" [M, 356]. It is interesting to consider that Yeats's description of the power which the dead possess to mould past events through imagination evolved from a relatively simple physical concept to the highly complex scheme of moral purgation and psychological catharsis in Book III ("The Soul in Judgment") of *A Vision*, where

> ...the *Spirit* is compelled to live over and over again the events that had most moved it; there can be nothing new, but the old events stand forth in a light which is dim or bright according to the intensity of passion that accompanied them.   [v, 226]

This idea of moral purgation is itself a fusion of two earlier, more rudimentary, spiritist conceptions. The first was derived by Yeats from his readings of Henry More, whose idea it was that, "The soul has a plastic power, and can after death, or during life, should the vehicle leave the body for a while, mould it to any shape it will by an act of imagination . . ." [M, 349]. The second idea can be seen in Yeats's essay on Swedenborg where he outlines the process by which the dead use "ethereal" substances (the "dust or sand") to project selected moments of intensity ("copy some one action") in order to purify their intentions before entering a new rebirth, "all the pleasures and pains of sensible life awaken again and again, all our passionate events rush up about us and not as seeming imagination, for imagination is now the world" [E, 35]. The last stanza dramatically shifts from the purgatorial process to the disintegrative effects made by the spirits recalled from death on the medium's personality:

> An old ghost's thoughts are lightning,
> To follow is to die;
> Poetry and music I have banished,
> But the stupidity
> Of root, shoot, blossom or clay
> Makes no demand.
> *I bend my body to the spade*
> *Or grope with a dirty hand.*

The emphasis here is less on the cause than the consequences (expressed in powerfully gnomic images) of what has happened.

The uncanny effect of these lines, and especially the phrase "to follow is to die", arises from the fact that Yeats does not merely mean the literal death of the medium, but, more significantly, the extinction of the medium's personality—his "death", in effect, to the things of this world. Yeats expertly uses the anonymity traditionally associated with the ballad form to stress further our sense of the medium's involuntary surrender of his own personality to the spirit world. This theme is present in Yeats's essay "*Prometheus Unbound*" (1932), where he warns against the danger of becoming "obsessed by images" [E&I, 422] from the beyond, as well as in his essay on Swedenborg where he describes the danger that may arise to the medium who becomes a channel for the spirit world:

> For the most part, though not always, it is this unconscious condition of mediumship, a dangerous condition it may be, that seems to make possible 'psychical phenomena' and that overshadowing of the memory by some spirit memory, which Swedenborg thought an accident and unlawful. [E, 50]

Despite the lack of particularizing details within the poem, the protagonist's emotions come through strongly: the longing to escape, and the sense of powerlessness which involves a fearful surrender to supernatural forces that do not kill, but drain one's sense of life. For the medium, the loss of "poetry and music" brings an acceptance (that is clearly felt to be a self-impairing surrender) of his role as a passive receptacle for impulses originating in the spirit world. It is interesting to note how Yeats uses the four stages of a plant's cycle ("But the stupidity/Of root, shoot, blossom or clay/Makes no demand") to convey the medium's contempt for the essentially mindless processes of existence by which he is now so completely dominated. Gradually, the repetitive nature of the refrain acts as a formal equivalent for the inescapable fate the medium suffers; it assumes a dominance equivalent to the enforced nature of the medium's obsession. This deadening effect (on the medium's will produced by the spirit world) is itself underscored by the monotonic "u" sounds in "stupidity", "root", and "shoot". In effect, the practice of mediumship "makes no demands" on his conscious mind, and the words he speaks in "mesmeric trance" [E&I, 441] come through him from the "beyond". Thus,

"The Spirit Medium" not only is a parable expressing Yeats's life-long ambivalent preoccupation with the occult, but as a poem, it belongs to a category dealing with the intrusion of the spirit world into the human one, which embraces Yeats's poetry from "The Man Who Dreamed of Faeryland" to "All Souls' Night" and its ultimate realization in "Byzantium".

A Preliminary Note on the Text of A Vision (1937)

Richard J. Finneran

〜〜

It is common knowledge that the 1925 version of *A Vision* was extensively revised for the second edition of 1937: as Allan Wade noted, "so much which appeared in the first version ... has been omitted and so much new material added, that this is almost a new book."[1] However, an atypical error in the Wade/Alspach *Bibliography*[2] has heretofore obscured our awareness that the 1937 version exists in three different states and that the 1962 London edition apparently is the best available text. This note, necessarily a combination of fact and conjecture, is intended only as a prolegomenon for the needed definitive edition which will hopefully be undertaken in the near future.

The second version of *A Vision* was published by Macmillan in London on October 7, 1937 and in New York on February 23, 1938. So far as I have been able to discover, the texts of these printings are identical. The only differences between the editions involve such matters as bindings, title pages, the spacing of the lettering under the frontispiece, and the larger page size and lack of signatures in the American edition. Indeed, since the American volume was printed by the "Polygraphic Company of America", some photographic process was almost surely used.

1. Allan Wade, *A Bibliography of the Writings of W. B. Yeats*, 3rd ed., rev. Russell K. Alspach (London: Rupert Hart-Davis, 1968), p. 192.
2. On p. 215 in the *Bibliography*, the last two sentences describing the 1956 *A Vision* (item 211M) should be eliminated.

A Vision was first revised after Yeats's death in 1939 in connection with the "Coole Edition", a project which had been in sporadic existence for several years but which was never published owing to the outbreak of the Second World War.[3] Macmillan began to prepare a proof for *A Vision* on May 11, 1939 and completed it on August 30. Now catalogued as Additional MS. 55893 in the Macmillan Archive of the British Museum,[4] this proof was heavily corrected by both Mrs. W. B. Yeats and Thomas Mark of Macmillan. A corrected proof was then printed; this set, Additional MS. 55886, has no date-stamps but bears the Coole Edition colophon and the date of 1939. I conjecture that both sets of proofs remained with the publisher and were not again used until the preparation of the 1962 edition.

In any event, the first revised edition of *A Vision* to be published was released by the Macmillan Company in New York on April 17, 1956; it is described on the title page as "A Reissue With the Author's Final Revisions". All of the corrections in this printing are also found on Additional MS. 55886; but since the edition ignores many other revisions on the proof, it must have been prepared without reference to the Coole Edition material. What authority the publisher had for the changes which were made is not now

3. Few details are available on the Coole Edition. Yeats seems to have first worked on it in 1931, at which time it consisted of seven volumes. In *Writers at Work* (London: Chatto & Windus, 1931), p. 8, Louise Morgan quotes Yeats as saying "I've just finished the *de luxe* edition of my works that Macmillan is bringing out. I deposited on his floor the other day six of the seven volumes." Although on February 20, 1932 Yeats wrote that Macmillan "is about to publish 'an edition de luxe' of my work" (*The Letters of W. B. Yeats*. ed. Allan Wade [London: Rupert Hart-Davis, 1954], p. 792), his optimism was not fulfilled. By the time of his death the edition had grown to eleven volumes. A prospectus is found in British Museum Add. MS. 55890. This prospectus indicates that the volume containing *A Vision* was to be called "Discoveries" and incidentally confirms that Yeats had approved the contents and title of *Mythologies*. For more on the Coole Edition, see *Letters*, p. 797, n. 2; and the full-page advertisement (p. 4) in the Yeats number of *The Arrow* (Summer 1939), which announces publication "this Autumn". Proofs for the Coole Edition are found in both the British Museum and the collection of Senator Michael B. Yeats.

4. For information on this collection, see William E. Fredeman, "The Bibliographical Significance of a Publisher's Archive: The Macmillan Papers," *SB*, 23 (1970): 183-91, and Philip V. Blake-Hill, "The Macmillan Archive", *BMQ*, 36 (1972): 74-80.

known. Some of the revisions involve obvious errors, as in "Phase 1 and Phase 28 are not human incarnations" to "Phase 1 and Phase 15" (p. 79), "Thomas Luke Harris" to "Thomas Lake Harris" (p. 153), or "Paul Valery in the *Cimetière Marine*" to "Paul Valéry in the *Cimetière Marin*" (p. 219). But there are more important changes which involve the establishment of either partial or total uniformity between the "Table of the Four Faculties" and the information given for the individual phases. For example, the False Creative Mind of Phase 12 is changed from "Enforced law" to "Enforced lure" (p. 97). The Will of Phase 11 is revised from "The Image-Burner" to "The Consumer" (p. 124). The Will of Phase 13 becomes "The Sensuous Man" instead of "Sensuous Ego" (p. 129). Finally, the Body of Fate of Phase 22 is corrected from "The 'breaking of strength'" to "The Temptation through Strength" (p. 157). Of these four changes, only the first and the third result in complete consistency between the Table and the phases; similarly, "The Phases of the Moon" was brought into conformity with the Definitive Edition of the *Poems* (1949), but not "All Souls' Night". In short, the 1956 edition is an improvement on the 1937/8 text but cannot be considered definitive.

The 1956 text was not immediately issued in London. Indeed, when Mrs. Yeats and Thomas Mark were selecting the material for *Explorations* (1962) they considered including the prefatory matter from *A Vision*; thus Additional MS. 55886 has a note stating "1-58 removed to send to Mrs. Yeats. Aug. 1960". This plan was abandoned. Instead, Macmillan in London obtained sheets of the 1961 second issue of the 1956 text and issued their own edition on December 7, 1961.[5] However, it must have quickly become apparent to either Mrs. Yeats or Thomas Mark that this text did not incorporate all the corrections on the Coole Edition proofs. With commendable speed, Macmillan prepared a new edition, based on Additional MS. 55886, and published it on September 27, 1962.[6]

5. The verso of the title page reads "Copyright 1938...Printed in the United States of America". This edition also uses the larger page size of the American editions.
6. In this edition "A Reissue With the Author's Final Revisions" is dropped from the title page. The verso reads "First Edition printed privately 1925 / Second Edition published by Macmillan 1937 / Reissued with corrections 1962", which is more accurate than the statement on p. [306]: "Printed 1937...Reprinted 1962 by Photolithography". This edition returns to the smaller page size of the English editions.

Many of the important changes in this third state of *A Vision* concern the remaining discrepancies between the Table of the Four Faculties and the descriptions of the phases. For instance, the Body of Fate of Phase 22 is changed from "Temptation versus strength" to "Temptation through strength" (p. 99). The Will of Phase 11 is now given as "Consumer, Pyre-builder" (p. 124), the Body of Fate of Phase 17 as "Enforced Loss" rather than simply "Loss" (p. 141). "Thought" is eliminated from the description of the True Creative Mind of Phase 26 as "Beginning of the abstract super-sensual thought" (p. 177). In addition, there are numerous minor revisions in the 1962 edition, such as the correction of a Synge quotation (p. 167)[7], the change from "First A.E." to "First Authentic Existant" (p. 194), or the substitution of "Pope Pius XI" for "the present Pope" (p. 214); and "All Souls' Night" is brought into conformity with the Definitive Edition. An important revision concerns one of the most-quoted sentences from *A Vision*: "The particulars are the work of the *thirteenth sphere* or cycle which is in every man and called by every man his freedom" (p. 302). In 1962 *"Thirteenth Cone"* replaces *"thirteenth sphere"*.

The following diagram may serve as a useful summary of the textual development of *A Vision*:

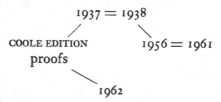

In sum, it seems clear that the 1962 edition of *A Vision* (not available in America at this time) is the best available text. Further research in the archives of Macmillan in both New York and London and in Yeats's library may shed light on the puzzling matter of the authority for the 1956 revisions. Such research will make possible a textual variorum of this central work.

7. The same correction is made in *Explorations*, sel. Mrs. W. B. Yeats (London: Macmillan, 1962), p. 416, as noted by Marion Witt in "Yeats: 1865-1965", *PMLA*, 80 (1965): 315. Witt's essay is an important statement on the textual problems in Yeats's prose.

Contributors

LAURENCE W. FENNELLY   Chairman, Department of Special Studies, Macon Junior College, Georgia. Dissertation on Yeats and Mathers.

RICHARD J. FINNERAN   Associate Professor of English, Newcomb College, Tulane University. Latest publication: *Letters of James Stephens*. Forthcoming publications: *Anglo-Irish Literature: A Review of Research* (editor and contributor); *Letters to W. B. Yeats* (co-editor).

WARWICK GOULD   Lecturer in English literature at Royal Holloway College, University of London. Co-editor of the forthcoming variorum edition of *The Secret Rose*.

ARNOLD GOLDMAN   Professor of American Studies at Keele University. Author of *The Joyce Paradox* and of many essays on Joyce, Yeats, O'Neill, Faulkner, British theatre, et cetera. At present working on a study of the relationship of nineteenth-century American writers to England.

GEORGE MILLS HARPER   Professor of English, Florida State University, and President of the College English Association. Author of *The Neoplatonism of William Blake*, *Yeats's Golden Dawn*, *Yeats's Quest for Eden*, *Yeats's Return from Exile*, and numerous papers on Yeats and the Romantic poets. A contributing editor to the Blake Concordance, he is co-editor (with Kathleen Raine) of *Thomas Taylor the Platonist*.

STUART HIRSCHBERG   Department of English, University of California at Riverside. Has published articles on Yeats, Joyce, Pinter, and others. Has just completed a book on Yeats's poetry.

WALTER KELLY HOOD   Associate Professor, Tennessee Technological University. At present preparing, with George Harper, an edition of Yeats's *A Vision* (1925).

JOHN S. KELLY   Lecturer in English at the University of Kent at Canterbury. He is Director of the Yeats International Summer School, Sligo, and co-editor of the forthcoming *Collected Letters of W. B. Yeats*.

WILLIAM M. MURPHY   Professor of English, Union College, Schenectady, New York. Author of *The Yeats Family and the Pollexfens of Sligo* and of the forthcoming definitive biography of *John Butler Yeats*.

WILLIAM H. O'DONNELL   Assistant Professor of English at Pennsylvania State University. Editor of *The Speckled Bird*.

JAMES OLNEY   Professor of English at North Carolina Central University. Publications include *Metaphors of Self: The Meaning of Autobiography* and *Tell Me Africa: An Approach to African Literature* (both from Princeton University Press). At present working on a book on Yeats and Jung.

MICHAEL SIDNELL   Associate Professor, Trinity College, University of Toronto. Co-author of *Druid Craft: The Writing of The Shadowy Waters*; author of numerous articles on Yeats, Joyce, Synge, Shaw, and the theatre.

KATHLEEN RAINE   Distinguished poet and critic. Publications include *Blake and Tradition*; *Thomas Taylor the Platonist: Selected Writings* (with George Mills Harper), *Defending Ancient Springs*; *Yeats, the Tarot and the Golden Dawn*; *Death-in-Life and Life-in-Death: 'Cuchulain Comforted' and 'News from the Delphic Oracle'*; and several volumes of poetry.

GEOFFREY NIGEL WATKINS   Retired owner of Watkins Bookshop, the most famous of all occult book stores. It was founded by his father, Yeats's friend John M. Watkins, to publish the writings of Madame Blavatsky and her circle in the Theosophical Society. Through his many years in the Bookshop, Geoffrey Watkins was well acquainted with many members of the Golden Dawn.